Reading Asian American Literature

Reading
Asian American Literature

FROM NECESSITY
TO EXTRAVAGANCE

Sau-ling Cynthia Wong

PRINCETON UNIVERSITY PRESS
PRINCETON, NEW JERSEY

Copyright © 1993 by Princeton University Press
Published by Princeton University Press, 41 William Street,
Princeton, New Jersey 08540
In the United Kingdom: Princeton University Press,
Chichester, West Sussex

Library of Congress Cataloging-in-Publication Data

Wong, Sau-ling Cynthia.
Reading Asian American literature : from necessity
to extravagance / Sau-ling Cynthia Wong.
p.   cm.
Includes bibliographical references and index.
1. American literature—Asian American authors—
History and criticism.   2. Asian Americans—
Intellectual life.   3. Ethnic relations in literature.
4. Asian Americans in literature.   I. Title.
PS153.A84W66   1993   810.9'895—dc20
92-42251   CIP

ISBN 0-691-06875-5 (cloth)
ISBN 0-691-01541-4 (paper)

This book has been composed in Adobe Galliard

Princeton University Press books are printed on acid-free paper
and meet the guidelines for permanence and durability of the
Committee on Production Guidelines for Book Longevity of the
Council on Library Resources

Printed in the United States of America

3   5   7   9   10   8   6   4

"Chinese Hot Pot" from *Expounding the Doubtful Points* (Bamboo Ridge Press) by
Wing Tek Lum. Copyright © Wing Tek Lum. Reprinted by permission of the author.

To George, Helen, Lulu, and Huan-Hua

———————————

CONTENTS

ACKNOWLEDGMENTS

MY FIRST and deepest thanks go to my former research assistants (many now respected colleagues and close friends), who have spoiled me with their meticulousness, initiative, knowledge of the field, and intuitive grasp of my research needs, and put up with much mind-numbing work and many last-minute panic calls from me: Giulia Fabi, Cynthia Liu, Kathy Lo, Barry Maxwell, Angela Pao, Shelley Wong, and Stan Yogi. Shelley, Barry, and Giulia, in particular, virtually "copiloted" the project during its most formative (and frustrating) stages. Their wisdom and good humor were lifesavers.

Special thanks, too, to my colleagues in the Asian American Studies Program, Department of Ethnic Studies, University of California, Berkeley: Elaine Kim, for opening up an entire world for me with her pioneering book on Asian American literature, sharing research generously, giving helpful comments on my manuscript, and being my mentor, role model, and friend; Ling-Chi Wang, for first encouraging me to enter a field that has changed my life, for helping create, as program coordinator and department chair, a work environment of relative sanity during my arduous tenure bid, and for daily inspiration; Michael Omi, for reading portions of the manuscript and suggesting useful sources from a social scientist's viewpoint; and Ron Takaki, for taking a strong and early interest in my project and making valuable suggestions, such as including Asian Indian writers and using the terms "Necessity" and "Extravagance" (from my journal article on *The Woman Warrior*) explicitly to unify my chapters. Helen Hong and Barbara Quan went way beyond the call of duty in "the office"—more accurately, the nerve center of the department—to smooth my way; they, Liz Megino, and Wei Chi Poon (head of the Asian American Studies Library), strong women all, have been "mothering" me steadfastly over the years. Finally, although Sucheng Chan left Berkeley some years ago, her commitment to helping junior colleagues and promoting Asian American studies; the example she sets with her brilliance, exacting standards, and formidable productivity; as well as the timely assistance she offered me at critical stages of my career have all made me a better scholar on the whole; she too, has made this book possible.

The care and intelligence with which the following people read part or all of the manuscript and provided comments, as well as the generosity of their esteem, have saved me from embarrassing errors, strengthened my arguments, broadened my vision, and built up my confidence when I needed it most: Bill Andrews, King-Kok Cheung, Maryemma Graham, Paul Lauter, Shirley Lim, Amy Ling, David Palumbo-Liu, Lisa Lowe, LaVonne Ruoff, Gayle Sato, Steve Sumida, Anthony Yu. Others who have suggested sources and revisions, encouraged early incarnations of my project, given access to their work, answered queries, and otherwise made the book possible include Davina Chen, John Eakin, Larry Howe, Caren Kaplan, Frances Loden, Wing Tek Lum, Ruthanne Lum McCunn, Katherine Newman, Jeff Ow, Jim Payne, Harriet Rohmer, Joe Skerrett, Christine So, Cecilia Wang, Shawn Wong, Judy Yung, Henry Yiheng Zhao. The students in my courses at Berkeley, through their avid interest in and tough questioning on Asian American literature, have helped me refine the ideas in this book.

Thanks to *MELUS* for allowing me to reprint portions of my article, "Necessity and Extravagance in Maxine Hong Kingston's *The Woman Warrior*: Art and the Ethnic Experience" (vol. 15, no. 1 [Spring 1988]: 3–26], in chapter 4 of this book.

My deep appreciation to Robert Brown, literature editor at Princeton, for expertly steering this project through and bearing with missed deadlines graciously, and to Roy Thomas for his meticulous copy-editing and patience.

Finally, my gratitude to George, Helen, and Lulu Chye, without whose love and unstinting support I would have had neither book nor career; and my daughter Huan-Hua, for patiently putting up with my frantic schedule, for sustaining me with her sweetness, lively mind, and wonderful sense of humor, and for her profound love. To them I dedicate this book.

Reading Asian American Literature

———————————

CONSTRUCTING AN ASIAN AMERICAN
TEXTUAL COALITION

THIS BOOK is a thematic study of Asian American literature. But perhaps even more important, it is a book about the reading of Asian American literature as a critical project within the academy.

Since its inception in the late 1960s, as part of the ethnic studies agenda established by student activism, Asian American literary studies have been gaining increasing institutional recognition across the nation, particularly on the West Coast, and especially since about 1986[1] A number of book-length studies by Asian American critics have appeared or are forthcoming,[2] and recent publishing projects to broaden the canon of American literature have all, to varying extents, included Asian American authors (e.g., Gilbert and Gubar; Elliott et al.; Lauter et al.; Phillips et al.; Reed et al.). Growing academic interest in the subject, even from quarters previously indifferent to it, coincides with a recent explosion of publishing activity by Asian American authors,[3] a phenomenon that has caught the interest of the "mainstream" media (e.g., Feldman; Simpson; Solovitch). In the half decade preceding the writing of this study,[4] there have appeared a large number of first novels, most of them well received;[5] new novels by established writers;[6] several award-winning short story collections;[7] many other interesting additions to Asian American literature;[8] anthologies of Asian American writing, especially by and/or about women;[9] a Broadway hit;[10] and many volumes of poetry, several of which garnered national honors.[11] The year 1991, in particular, is something of an *annus mirabilis* for Asian American writing; it witnessed the appearance of an extraordinary number of well-received books, some of them debuts for first-timers, others representing new directions for established authors.[12] As this study goes to press in 1992, Asian American literature continues to thrive.[13] In the words of one journalist, the "silence" that once shrouded painful Asian American experiences "has ended in a burst of voices as Asian Americans—long successful in fields such as medicine, engineering and business—are making their mark in the literary world" (Solovitch 1991:18).

The commercial success and general popularity of some Asian American writings, such as Maxine Hong Kingston's *The Woman Warrior*, Amy Tan's *The Joy Luck Club* and *The Kitchen God's Wife*, and David

Henry Hwang's *M. Butterfly*, have raised fundamental questions about how Asian American literature is to be read. Specifically, concern has been voiced about the misreading, appropriation, and co-optation of this literature by white readers and critics.[14] Debate on this matter is part of a larger controversy on the direction of American studies in general and the reading of marginalized literatures in particular. Does the study of a marginalized literature require membership in the given group, participation in appropriately typical historical experience, "insider" cultural knowledge, and a group-specific methodology?

The approach that has come to be known as the "ethnicity school"[15] charges that an affirmative answer to any of the above questions would open the floodgate to a host of ills: exclusivist "biological insiderism" and a " 'good vibes' methodology" (Sollors 1986a:11); an untenable "exceptionalism" (Sollors 1990a:186); as well as further isolation of the marginalized group, fragmentation of American studies as a discipline, a tendency toward "one-sided reading," and perhaps most ominously, undermining of "the possibility of acknowledging an American national culture" (Fox-Genovese 1990:27, 23, 8). Opponents of the "ethnicity school," on the other hand, take issue with its homogenizing invocation of "ethnicity" as a unifying force in American culture, its facile conflation of ethnicity with race, its unwarranted privileging of immigration and assimilation as quintessentially American experiences, its erasure of group-specific historical injuries, and its insensitivity to the distinctive textual features of marginalized literatures. These critics prefer to stress the interacting operations of race, class, and gender in such literatures, attend to their particular sociopolitical contexts, and promote a "text-specific" (Gates 1987:xix) reading methodology which may, however, selectively draw upon universalist literary theories (Wald 1987). A third approach, allied with the "race, class and gender school," advances a "minority discourse" framework that shifts critical focus away from minority-white relations to minority-minority relations. Its premise is that shared historical experiences of oppression have created literary affinities among minorities that cannot be adequately addressed by a model centered on a hegemonic culture (JanMohamed and Lloyd 1990a). This debate on critical methodology, though often couched in terms familiar only to the literature specialist, has far from esoteric implications. The background to its emergence is a rancorous backlash against multiculturalism in education prompted by radical demographic transformations of American society, a backlash that takes forms ranging from attacks on affirmative action to calls for a return to Western classics in college curricula.[16]

To begin to answer the question "How is Asian American literature to be read?" within such a charged context, one must first gain some understanding of the term *Asian American*.

The task is much more difficult than it seems. The term is inherently elastic and of fairly recent currency (the odd title of Lemuel Ignacio's book—see Works Cited—is not a matter of whimsy). It carries within it layers of historical sedimentation. Not merely a denotative label with a fixed, extralinguistic referent, it is a sign, a site of contestation for a multitude of political and cultural forces. It is the semiotic status of the term *Asian American* that shapes our understanding of what kind of discourse Asian American literature is, and in turn, what kind of practice Asian American criticism is.

From a legal perspective, the peoples previously known as Orientals and now designated as Asian Americans have almost all, at one time or another, been excluded from U.S. citizenship. (Recent refugees and immigrants from Southeast Asia in the wake of the Vietnam War constitute an exception.) As Jeff H. Lesser notes in a review of Supreme Court rulings regarding Asians, "Naturalization is the ultimate means whereby a government decides who is acceptable—and who is not" (1985–86: 83): acceptable, that is, as Americans. The Naturalization Act of 1790 passed by Congress employed explicitly racial criteria limiting citizenship to "free white persons"; after this act was successfully challenged on behalf of blacks after the Civil War, "Asian immigrants became the most significant 'other' in terms of citizenship eligibility" (Lesser, 85). In the *Ozawa v. United States* case (1922), the Supreme Court ruled against a Japan-born applicant to naturalization (who had lived most of his life in the United States), arguing that "had these particular races [like the Japanese] been suggested, the language of the act would have been so varied as to include them in its privileges."[17] To circumvent the question of color, the Court defined "white" as "Caucasian." However, when an immigrant from India, Bhagat Singh Thind, attempted to gain citizenship by arguing that he was Caucasian, the Supreme Court changed its definition again, brushing aside anthropological and historical issues and appealing to the popular meaning of the term "white" (S. Chan 1991:94). Furthermore, in its 1923 decision against Thind, the Court invoked the criterion of assimilability to separate the desirable immigrants from the undesirable ones: Asian Indians were distinguished from the swarthy European immigrants, who were deemed "*readily amalgamated*" (italics in original) with the immigrants "already here" (Lesser, 88).

These and other Supreme Court cases prevent Asian Americans from "mov[ing] out of the sphere of 'the other' and into the sphere of 'American' " (Lesser, 94). The legal contortions resorted to in order to maintain exclusion suggest that Asian Americans have historically functioned as a peculiar kind of Other (among other Others) in the symbolic economy of America. Generally speaking, they are, to borrow the subtitle of

James W. Loewen's study of the Mississippi Chinese, "between black and white";[18] however, since Native Americans and Chicanos are also thus placed, the description must be refined. We may say that Asian Americans are put in the niche of the "unassimilable alien": despite being voluntary immigrants like the Europeans (and unlike the enslaved blacks), they are alleged to be self-disqualified from full American membership by materialistic motives, questionable political allegiance, and, above all, outlandish, overripe, "Oriental" cultures. On this last point they are differentiated from the stereotypes of "primitive" or "uncultured" Native Americans, African Americans, and Chicanos. Asian Americans are permanent houseguests in the house of America. When on their best behavior (as defined by the hosts), they are allowed to add the spice of variety to American life and are even held up as a "model minority" to prove the viability of American egalitarian ideals. However, their putative unwillingness or inability to assimilate comes readily to the fore when scapegoating is called for, as recently as in the debate preceding the 1986 Immigration Reform and Control Act (Lesser, 95) and in the English-only movement (Chen and Henderson 1987; Takano 1987).

The Asian American movement of the late 1960s was precipitated by massive demographic changes within Asian American communities caused by the immigration reforms of 1965. Galvanized by anti-Vietnam War activism and modeled upon the Black Power struggle, it represents, among other things, a refusal to acquiesce in the roles and expectations imposed by white society. *Asian American* has since been adopted as the preferred self-designation of the "ethnically conscious" elements in the community, in contradistinction to the exoticizing *Oriental* (P. Wong 1972; Kim 1982:xii). What is more, the new term expresses a political conviction and agenda: it is based on the assumption that regardless of individual origin, background, and desire for self-identification, Asian Americans have been subjected to certain collective experiences that must be acknowledged and resisted. If Asian American subgroups are too small to effect changes in isolation, together they can create a louder voice and greater political leverage vis-à-vis the dominant group (Kim 1982:xiii). Nevertheless, this subsumption of identity as Chinese, Filipino, Korean, Japanese, etc. in a larger pan-Asian identity has to be *voluntarily adopted* and highly *context-sensitive* in order to work; it is not meant to obscure the unique experiences of each subgroup, but merely to provide an instrument for political mobilization under chosen circumstances. Otherwise, the term *Asian American* is in danger of reproducing some of the damage caused by the earlier, stereotypical *Oriental* label (Lyman 1974:173–75).

This double-edged nature of the term *Asian American* is clearly seen when we examine decennial census categories to designate groups of

Asian descent. A glance at the questions pertaining to "Color" or "Race" in *Twenty Censuses: Population and Housing Questions 1790–1980*, compiled by the Bureau of the Census, reveals fluctuations in the official recognition of the Asian American presence. Since the introduction of "Asiatic" in the 1860 census, categories referring to Asian-ancestry Americans have undergone many changes: from "Chinese" in 1870, the categories have proliferated to nine checkoff boxes under the heading of "Asian or Pacific Islander" on the 1990 form (Robey 1989:18). However, the addition and maintenance of new categories have come about primarily as a result of skillful and tenacious lobbying from the Asian American community, which is concerned that inappropriate categories—either overnarrow or overbroad—would jeopardize the Asian Americans' claim in government resource allocation (Lowry 1982:53; Robey 1989:18).[19] The 1990 census is an especially instructive case. Originally, the Bureau of the Census designed a form on which one could write in specific labels under the umbrella category of "Asian or Pacific Islander"; being more cumbersome and open-ended for the respondents, this form would lead to a less accurate picture of the Asian American population. The Asian American community and its advocates in Congress objected vigorously to this lumping, and even after a presidential veto, succeeded in effecting a return to the checkoff format (Robey, 18). In this instance, Asian American subgroups acted in coalition, but the goal of such action is to ensure that interests of diverse subgroups do not get erased: they *united* with each other in order to protect their *separate* interests. In doing so, they illustrate one social science theory that sees ethnic groups as interest groups—political coalitions—rather than anthropological, cultural, linguistic, or religious ones (Petersen 1982:18; Omi and Winant 1986:19).

As even such a brief survey shows, the term *Asian American* is intrinsically complex: it focuses all the contending sociopolitical and cultural forces that affect the daily life of Asian Americans. The uncertainties surrounding everyday usages are part of this picture: though *Asian American* has been gaining increasing acceptance in the public arena, in private most Asian Americans continue to define themselves by reference to the subgroup; in addition, the term may signify "American-born Asians" as well as "persons of mixed Asian and Caucasian parentage." Users of the term, even those within the group itself, cannot count on a consensual usage, but must constantly negotiate its meanings in context.

Transposed to Asian American literary studies, this phenomenon means that critics have not reached any agreement on how their subject matter is to be delimited. Prescriptive usages exist side by side with descriptive ones; some favor a narrow precision, others an expansive catholicity. As Shirley Lim (1990) points out in a conference paper on the intersection of feminist and ethnic literary theories in Asian American

literature, anthologists differ in their criteria for inclusion. In their influential "Introduction" to *Aiiieeeee! An Anthology of Asian-American
Writers* (1974b), Frank Chin and his coeditors operate on the premise
that a true Asian American sensibility is non-Christian, nonfeminine,
and nonimmigrant; they also limit their selections to three subgroups—
Chinese, Japanese, and Filipino—each seen as possessing a distinctive
tradition within the broader definition. While this approach has hardened considerably over the years into a rigid distinction between "real"
and "fake" Asian American literature in *The Big Aiiieeeee!* (J. Chan et al.
1991), with a concomitant narrowing of focus,[20] a number of recent anthologies, notably those by and about women, counter the practice by
broadening the definition of *Asian American* and dispensing with ethnic subgroup designations. For example, Lim and Tsutakawa's *The Forbidden Stitch* and Watanabe and Bruchac's *Home to Stay* both include
Korean and Asian Indian writers, some of them first-generation, while
Asian Women United of California's *Making Waves*, a multigenre collection, contains selections by Vietnamese authors as well. Like the anthologists, the scholars also differ in the way they elect to demarcate
Asian American literature. In her *Asian American Literature: An Introduction to the Writings and Their Social Context*, Elaine Kim limits her
survey to literature written in English by Japanese, Chinese, Korean, and
Filipino Americans, citing both ideological, pragmatic, and personal reasons for her decision, but expressing a hope that immigrant writing in
the Asian languages will some day be incorporated (1982: xi–xiv). In
editing their annotated bibliography of Asian American literature, King-
Kok Cheung and Stan Yogi choose a nonprescriptive approach, listing
"works by writers of Asian descent who have made the United States or
Canada their home, regardless of where they were born, when they settled in North America, and how they interpret their experiences." They
also list authors of mixed descent and nonpermanent residents who have
written specifically about Asian life in America (1988:v).

This multiplicity of opinions is not an embarrassing symptom of con-
fused thinking or mere factionalism on the part of scholars and critics,
but a necessary result of Asian American literature's interdiscursivity in
history and in contemporary life. (A good reminder of this fact is the
title of Lisa Lowe's 1991 theoretical essay on Asian American "differences"—"Heterogeneity, Hybridity, Multiplicity.") An Asian American
work may allude to Asian classics or folklore, draw upon an oral tradition maintained by immigrant forebears, participate in dominant Western genres like the realist novel or movements like postmodernism, serve
class interests, engage in gender politics, and do a host of other things
that multiply-situated texts do. At any point in the interpretive process,
in order to arrive at an articulation of emphasis satisfactory to themselves, careful readers have to balance the centrifugal and centripetal, the

heterogenizing and homogenizing, tendencies inherent in the term *Asian American literature*. Calibration is all.

Still, whatever their disagreements, and however their foci may shift according to the task at hand, students of Asian American literature tend to be united by a desire to ensure that voices of Asian Americans are heard and to make known the richness and complexity of Asian American writing. Just as the Asian American ethnic group is a political coalition, Asian American literature may be thought of as an emergent and evolving textual coalition, whose interests it is the business of a professional coalition of Asian American critics to promote.[21] Apart from being an intellectual challenge, criticism is also praxis. Unlike those whose subject matter has been canonized and protected by an established power structure, Asian American critics have to establish their professional domain; through doing so, and through disseminating the products of their efforts, they play a role in building their community. For although coalitions necessarily retain a certain degree of provisionality, the very process of creating a coalition feeds back into history, to further realize what has hitherto been tentative and unstable.

To return to the earlier question on how to read Asian American literature, given the constructed status of Asian American literature as a textual coalition, reading, too, involves conscious inhabitation of a reading position. As Diana Fuss reminds us, "there is no 'natural' way to read a text: ways of reading are historically specific and culturally variable, and reading positions are always constructed, assigned, or mapped" (1989:35). Asian American critics have always had choices to make: notably between tracing Asian influence in the texts and demonstrating their grounding in American historical experiences; between accentuating their universal accessibility and uncovering their particular preoccupations. My choice in this study, to focus on the latter of each pair, is based on the conviction that the tendency to "de-Americanize" Asian American literature is too rampant to need any inadvertent abetting. The literatures of other major peoples of color in the United States, though also vulnerable to exoticization, are less susceptible in this regard: Native Americans, being the indigenous inhabitants of the North American continent, cannot be regarded as foreign;[22] Chicanos can also draw on a long history of settlement predating the Anglos' arrival, while as a result of slavery, the culture that African Americans have had to develop is indisputably American. In contrast, Asian American writers, however rooted on this land they or their families may have been, tend to be regarded as direct transplants from Asia or as custodians of an esoteric subculture.[23] Thus it is incumbent upon Asian American critics to orient discussions away from exoticization and to ensure that the word *American* is not blithely excised from the term *Asian American*.

Two key terms that will appear frequently in my study, *contexts* and *intertexts*, reflect my priorities in developing a reading strategy tied to the above concept of Asian American literature as a textual coalition. *Contexts* is an allusion to Elaine Kim's book on Asian American literature, whose subtitle, *An Introduction to the Writings and Their Social Context*, stresses the indispensability of historical knowledge to any responsible reading of the corpus. In pluralizing the term *context*, I affirm and extend Kim's project but also seek to underscore my conviction that, given the multiple subject positions of the writers, there is no single, conclusive version of Asian American history to anchor their works and safeguard "correct" readings. Rather, the critic has to select from a number of possible contexts, each serviceable for a different purpose, in which to read a given text. My emphasis on context aligns this study with "new historicist" critical projects in general, which include, in one scholar's handy synopsis, "a return to empirical scholarship, revivals of the critique of ideology, studies of how material conditions determine writing and publication, research on gender, race, and class in the production of literature, and inquiries into the structural affinities of representational and social systems" (Jay 1988:1).[24]

The second term crucial to the establishment of my reading practice, *intertexts*, has a poststructuralist genealogy—Kristeva's concept of intertextuality, which regards "any text" to be "constructed as a mosaic of quotations" and "the absorption and transformation of another" (1980:37)—at first sight incongruent with the new historicist agenda. Nevertheless, my use of the term *intertexts* again highlights choice and praxis. Instead of theorizing about intertextuality at a high level of abstraction, I give a name and habitation to the phrase *any text*: I specifically address the question of which texts, among many possible candidates in many possible discursive traditions, a given Asian American text is to be juxtaposed with and read against. "Quoting," "absorbing," and "transforming" presuppose a relationship, yet relationships between texts are not naturally occurring connections passively awaiting an elaborating intelligence. The perception that two texts are relatable at all, and that the relationship between them is not trivial, is not ideologically innocent. While a dominant literary tradition may be conveniently reified, so that intertextuality within it appears to map the intrinsic or the self-evident, the reading of "minority" texts like Asian American ones demands the much more fundamental (and conscious) operation of determining appropriate intertexts for them. Without such a deliberation, any analysis that aspires beyond the boundaries of the single text would, by default, be governed by monocultural notions of canonicity. The resulting intercourse between the selected texts, then, would simply replicate the asymmetrical sociopolitical relationships in the extratextual realm, and the task of deepening one's understanding of an Asian American literary tradition is brought up short. The spirit in which I explore intertextuality in this study is catholic—I consider a wide range of possible intertexts for the Asian American works under consideration—but what interests me first and foremost is how mutual allusion, qualification, complication, and transmutation can be discovered between texts regarded as Asian American, and how a sense of an internally meaningful literary tradition may emerge from such an investigation.

The manner in which I employ the term *intertextuality* departs considerably from received usages in Euro-American high theory. In the French tradition, intertextuality takes such an extreme deconstructive form that it not only dissolves the autonomous, intentional subject but also precludes the validity of any extratextual reality—indeed contradicts the very notion of context itself. Nonetheless, intertextuality has never been a monolithic concept to begin with,[25] and by now the term *intertextuality* has become sufficiently part of a general critical lexicon to admit of varied applications (O'Donnell and Davis 1989a:xiii). The more flexible definition of intertextuality I subscribe to may be described by Thaïs Morgan's formulation: a rethinking of literature and literary history "in terms of space instead of time, conditions of possibility instead of permanent structures, and 'networks' or 'webs' instead of chronological lines or influence" (1989:274).

O'Donnell and Davis note that intertextuality is an anxiety-provoking concept: it "signals an *anxiety* and an *indeterminacy* regarding authorial, readerly, or textual identity, the relation of present culture to past, or the function of writing within certain historical and political frameworks" (1989a:xiii; italics in original). They go on to ask: "Can the discussion of intertextuality successfully address problems of extra-literary reference, or is its explosive force merely 'interlinear' . . . ? How sound, ideologically, is the investment in the attention to and appraisal of the intertextual process?" (xv).

The issues raised by O'Donnell and Davis are especially relevant to critics of marginalized literatures. For some (e.g., R. B. Miller), anxiety stems from suspicion of the poststructuralist idea of the infinite play of signifiers on which intertextuality is based; allowing that texts are open and derive meaning from each other poses the risk of hermeticizing them, or as Miller puts it, "sever[ing] most ethical ties to the world outside the game itself" (1987:394).[26] However, as Henry Louis Gates, Jr., shows in his intertextual reading of Zora Neale Hurston and Alice Walker, intertextuality need not imply a divorce from the extratextual world of values. It is possible to put intertextuality to use for a minority literature, by investigating models "for a self-defined, or an internally defined, notion of tradition" (1989:166). Along similar lines, I maintain that the concept of intertextuality need not be a source of misgivings for Asian American critics; rather, it could inspire them to attend more closely to the myriad ways in which texts grouped under the Asian American rubric build upon, allude to, refine, controvert, and resonate with each other. In doing so, they contribute to a sense of an Asian American literary tradition. This tradition is not an observer-independent parade of texts canonized by putatively objective standards of excellence; instead, it is a representation constituted by praxis: informed and "interested" (or "motivated") close reading and critical analysis.

The following four chapters essay this kind of reading, which is always a meticulous negotiation of meaning among competing claims for attention. Each chapter focuses on a motif that could, if one so chooses, support homogenizing generalizations and minimize the differences between Asian American texts and European or Anglo-American ones. While acknowledging elements of meaning shared with dominant traditions, I try to demonstrate how Asian American deployments of the motif, when contextualized and read intertextually, form distinctive patterns.

My primary sources are mostly prose narratives—novels, novellas, autobiographies, short stories—because, relative to works in other genres, they are likely to exhibit more readily discernible linkages to the extratextual world and are therefore more amenable to my project. Personal inclination is also a factor: not only have my training and research interests always been in fiction but, given the rapidly increasing size and variety of the Asian American corpus, I feel a multigenre study would simply be beyond my powers. As a result, I have applied myself to mostly fiction and autobiography and, to a lesser extent, drama; poetry will make at most a sporadic appearance in the following chapters. Nevertheless, I trust that the broader issues I address here are generalizable enough that the term *literature* in the title of my book is not a misnomer.

Chapter 1 identifies several ways in which Asian American writers use alimentary images (which derive from bodily functions common to all human beings) to explore issues of economic and cultural survival. Chapter 2, on the double or doppelgänger, argues that while the figure was first identified in European literature, the psychological mechanisms generating it take on different forms under different historical circumstances, and that Asian American manifestations are specifically concerned with assimilation. Chapter 3 contends that "mainstream" myths of unfettered mobility, a key component in American ideology, do not apply to Asian Americans because of historical circumscription of their legal and social freedoms; writers in each Asian subgroup have developed symbolic strategies to engage this issue. Chapter 4, on images of art and artists, maintains that in showing an intense interest in the "playful" and seemingly gratuitous aspect of artistic creation, Asian American authors are not, as a mechanical analogy with universalistic Western ludic discourse would suggest, promoting a rarefied aestheticism. Instead, they are formulating an "interested disinterestedness" appropriate to their condition as minority artists with responsibilities to their community but also a need for room to exercise their creativity. The first two chapters devote more space to the fine points of devising a reading practice appropriate for Asian American literature; in particular, because of the European origin of the double figure, chapter 2 gives more consideration than usual to existing scholarship on the subject. Whenever possible, potential comparisons with uses of the motif in other minority American literatures will be pointed out. (The exception is chapter 1, because of the profusion of semiotic approaches available on the vast subject of food and eating.)

The four chapters are woven together by two terms, *Necessity* and *Extravagance*, derived from two passages in Maxine Hong Kingston's *The Woman Warrior* respectively on Brave Orchid's thrifty habits and the adulterous liaison of the "no name woman."

> My mother has told me once and for all the useful parts [of the no name woman's story]. She will add nothing unless powered by Necessity, a riverbank that guides her life. She plants vegetables rather than lawns; she carries the odd-shaped tomatoes home from the fields and eats food left for the gods. (1977:6)

> Adultery is extravagance. Could people who hatch their own chicks and eat the embryos and the heads for delicacies and boil the feet in vinegar for party food, leaving only the gravel, eating even the gizzard lining, could such people engender a prodigal aunt? (7)

The terms *Necessity* and *Extravagance*[27] signify two contrasting modes of existence and operation, one contained, survival-driven and conservation-minded, the other attracted to freedom, excess, emotional expressiveness, and autotelism. All four motifs studied can be related to these modes. *Necessity* usually appears with words like *force*, *demand*, or *constraint*; *Extravagance* with words like *urge*, *impulse*, or *desire*. This might hint at an outer-inner dichotomy, pitting "objective" or "neutral" conditions against individual vagaries. However, the disposition of the study as a whole is constructionist. The concepts of Necessity and Extravagance, themselves deconstructible, function mainly rhetorically, to tie together related tendencies; the collocations used with the two terms should therefore be taken as descriptions of perception, which is contingent upon concrete social circumstances. Because Necessity and Extravagance operate at a high level of abstraction, there is always a danger that they will reduce historical experiences to schemata and parable; only a scrupulous grappling with textual complexities can counteract this bias.

In addition, my chosen terms of analysis, because of their bias toward "content," do not leave much room for investigating possible tensions between the thematic import and the stylistic inflections of a work. Certainly a lesson in Extravagance might be subverted by an austere manner of presentation, or a plea for Necessity might be couched in such an Extravagant form that its persuasiveness becomes questionable. Hisaye Yamamoto's understated mother-daughter stories about the perils of repressed life come readily to mind as an example of the former. The latter contradiction is a source of disorientation for the narrator/protagonist of *The Woman Warrior*, whose mother mixes inhibiting messages with imaginative wordplay and to that extent embodies the author's own proclivity toward exuberance. These and related cases will be examined in chapter 4, where I undertake a radical unpacking of the Necessity/Extravagance binarism through close readings of selected Asian American ludic discourse. Elsewhere, formalist observations are typically incidental or subordinate to the thematic argument.

As my entire book (and especially chapter 4) will make clear, I do assume a common human psychology at certain levels of analysis, which also implies a belief in the power of literature to communicate across cultural boundaries. (Otherwise I would hardly have been engaged in the teaching and study of Asian American literature.) This does not mean, however, that my faith is unqualified by an acute awareness of social realities, or that I consider demonstrating the common humanity of Asian Americans, as communicated through their writings, to be a particularly worthwhile or useful focus for Asian American critics at this point. Much depends on one's assessment of what kind of work is needed in given situations. The same goes for the question of "Americanness." Disentangling Asian American literature from Orientalist expectations—that is, establishing its American character and presence—is a major mission of this book. Yet given the Asian American past and current interracial relations, the best way for the group to "claim America" (to employ Kingston's term in *China Men*) may well be to *differentiate* Asian American symbolic configurations from those considered "mainstream American." It does not consist, as Sollors proposes in his essay on the direction for American studies, in proving that "mules," "mares," and "even stallions" are all "quadrupeds" (1990a:186). Universalism is not, as he seems to deplore, "passé" (181), but *premature* (see also Wald 1987:30–32). Considering how much more one needs to know about minority literatures in order to establish an adequate understanding of their traditions, the practice of drawing simplistic, ill-informed parallels with the dominant tradition would most likely have a leveling and suppressing effect. In that case, the abstract idea of a national culture might be preserved, but only at the expense of what would make it truly valuable: its richness. In his "Canon Theory and Emergent Practice," Paul Lauter has argued persuasively that "neither separation nor integration provide wholly satisfactory methods for presenting or studying marginalized cultures," and that a "dual process" involving both is needed to do justice to the plural realities of American literature (1991:165). To Lauter's formulation may I add that separation and integration are not, everyday usage notwithstanding, discrete or disjunctive mechanisms. Since separation is always separation *from* something, the two entities must already have borne some integral relationship to each other for the notion of division to make sense; likewise, integration is not thinkable without some prior divergence. Given the close mutual implication of separation and integration, it is not surprising to find that an ostensibly integrationist rhetoric often conceals an exclusionist intent, whereas an ostensibly separatist approach might well express an ultimately unifying cultural vision. In my study, I try to avoid the dangers of both a hermetic ethnic essentialism and a premature foreclosure of differentiation, but especially the latter.

A few concluding clarifications of terminology may be in order. The terms *race* and *ethnicity* (and their adjectival forms) are highly problematic. Both words have accrued highly partisan ideological associations, and conflating them frequently leads to consequences damaging to minorities (Petersen 1982:7; Omi and Winant 1986:23). At the same time, the two words are indeed often used interchangeably. In the post-Nazi era, *ethnicity* has come to serve, to some extent, as a euphemism for *race*; such a usage has been adopted by not only neoconservatives but also advocates of minority rights (as in "ethnic studies departments" or "multiethnic American literature"). Petersen notes that "the separation of the two terms has been inhibited . . . by the confusion in real life between physiological and cultural criteria" (1982:6). Given the looseness of everyday usage, it would be difficult to adhere to a single word choice. In the present study, I have availed myself of some of the advantages of this fuzziness. But on the whole, and especially in chapter 2 on the double figure, I favor an emphasis on race, partly to avoid confusion with the aforementioned "ethnicity school," and partly to take into account Omi and Winant's persuasive demonstration of the continuing importance of race in American life.

The term *mainstream*, as in *mainstream literature*, is problematic to the extent that it encourages what Lauter so aptly calls "the Great River theory of American Letters," which implies noncanonical works to be merely "minor rills and branches" (1990:9). Such a hidden metaphor would undermine, to however subliminal an extent, the very autonomy of the Asian American literary tradition that this book seeks to establish. Nevertheless, as a shorthand label describing the current imbalance of discursive power, *mainstream* continues to be convenient and will appear in the following chapters in quotation marks only when special attention to its disputed status is called for. The same goes for a term like *minority literature*, which again could be argued to be an unconscious replication of hegemonic cultural values.

As for the terms used in thematic analysis, such as *theme, motif, image, symbol*, or *metaphor*, much ambiguity exists, especially in view of the Continental lineage of the method and the differences between German and English usage (Weisstein 1973:124–49). Ziolkowski's distinction between *motif, theme*, and *symbol*, as opposed to the more general *image* (1977:3–17), is to my mind the most convincing clarification available on the subject. Nevertheless, partly because Ziolkowski's scheme is designed to organize a specific set of materials (15), in practice it is difficult to implement it consistently. I have opted for less technically precise usages.

In the majority of cases in this book, the *American* in *Asian American* refers to the United States, but it must be stretched to mean "North American" in reference to Canadian writer Joy Kogawa's *Obasan* (1981). The practice of including Kogawa in the Asian American roster is standard in the field. Perhaps it is because scholars feel that *Obasan*, so exemplary in its integration of political understanding and literary artistry, is simply too good to pass up: it has proven equally effective as an eye-opening course reading, as an indisputably respectable subject of formalist inquiry, and as a powerful weapon to defend minority literatures against uninformed charges of inferiority. Perhaps they prize *Obasan* for its authentication of a pan-Asian sensibility, by so compellingly bringing out parallels between Asian experiences in the United States and Canada. Or perhaps the subsumption of "Asian Canadian" under "Asian American" is a matter of temporary, strategic alliance-forging—a coalition, to use our earlier term again—since the Asian American (U.S.) corpus has so far been more substantial than the Asian Canadian and its critical study more established.[28] Under other circumstances and for other purposes, Asian Canadian literature can and should be differentiated from Asian American; perhaps, as publications become more numerous,[29] a separate Asian Canadian critical tradition will arise. In the meantime, this book will continue to draw on *Obasan* as a key text in Asian American literature.

This question of under what rubric to study *Obasan* uncovers a potential problem with my chosen methodology that must be addressed before we turn to the thematic chapters. As the Kogawa example shows, the classificatory scheme and reading strategy adopted in this study have to maintain an extremely delicate balance between historicity and ahistoricity. In grouping together texts that could be placed in narrower, historically more familiar ethnic categories, and in extracting common imagery to formulate an Asian American tradition, the intertextual investigation I offer in the following pages is in danger of lapsing into what Shelley Wong (1990) calls "literary strip-mining." That is to say, ahistoricity, decontextualization, insufficient respect for the integrity of each work and the complex intents and operations of each author—the very ills the reading strategy has been devised to counter—could result from too steady a gaze on isolated aspects of content. The only way to forestall such an ironic possibility is to be vigilant of the localization and segmentation inherent in the motif-study method and to reinsert the detached imagery into its specific, differentiating history as soon as intertextual affinity is demonstrated. Thus is a constant back-and-forth movement sustained between commonality and uniqueness, generalization and particularization, but the overall emphasis is still on a collectivity of visions derived from shared experiences. This choice of emphasis is determined not only by my training and temperament, with their inevitable idiosyncrasies and blind spots, but also by my conscious assessment of what gaps need to be filled in Asian American literary studies at this juncture in its development. If my book succeeds, however modestly, in establishing a sense of Asian American literature's historical coherence, thereby providing a conceptual basis for the discipline beyond accidents of authorial nativity and the tacit consensus of practitioners, the risk of temporarily evoking a transcendent thematic unity would have been well worth taking.

Chapter One

BIG EATERS, TREAT LOVERS, "FOOD
PROSTITUTES," "FOOD PORNOGRAPHERS,"
AND DOUGHNUT MAKERS

EATING IS one of the most biologically deterministic and, at the same time, socially adaptable human acts: a meal can be a simple prelinguistic *phenomenon* or a multivalent *sign* coded in language, manners, and rites (Brown 1984:11). As a result, alimentary images pose particularly intriguing interpretive challenges for students of nonmainstream literature.

On the one hand, because food is indispensable for human survival, alimentary images share a number of universal meanings, and many semioticians have proposed useful general frameworks for reading them. For example, anthropologist Claude Lévi-Strauss, focusing on the universality of cooking, postulates a "culinary triangle": "the cooked is a cultural transformation of the raw, whereas the rotted is a natural transformation." Hence in the culinary operation there is an underlying double opposition of meaning between "elaborated/unelaborated" and "culture/nature" (1966:587). Literary critic James W. Brown, in an extensive introduction to his *Fictional Meals and Their Function in the French Novel, 1789–1848*, suggests that "appetite attests to, and even comes to symbolize, the space existing between subject and object, between 'me' and the 'world' " (1984:12). Furthermore, precisely because appetite or desire signals distance, it "gives birth to social consciousness," which is the realm of communication. "Eating and speaking share the same motivational structure; language is nothing more than the praxis of eating transposed to the semiosis of speaking: both are fundamentally communicative acts by which man appropriates and incorporates the world" (13). These and other approaches offer cross-culturally valid insights on which any student of alimentary images can draw.

On the other hand, biological universality notwithstanding, eating practices are shaped to an extraordinary extent by culture and can thus serve as elaborate mechanisms for encoding and expressing social relationships. Thus Mary Douglas, in a paper tellingly titled "Deciphering a Meal," analyzes food as a code expressing a "pattern of social relations" (1972:61), reading the contents and sequencing of meals as if they were texts. K. C. Chang, in *Food in Chinese Culture*, speaks of "food semantics" (1977:39–46). The "foodways" scholars' interdisciplinary explorations of culinary semiotics are based not on general theories but empirical research on individual cultures (Brown and Mussell 1984; Humphrey and Humphrey 1988). Alimentary images being so context-sensitive, students of nonmainstream literature must guard against too facile a reliance on axiomatic principles. This is especially so since certain Western representations, like the Last Supper and the Eucharistic communion, have come to assume canonical status. A large number of enlightening studies exist of alimentary images in the Western tradition, such as Bakhtin on feasting (1984:278–302); Barthes on the "Frenchness" of wine and steak in *Mythologies* (1972:58–64); Lindsey Tucker's survey of repasts in James Joyce's *Ulysses*; or David Bevan's anthology on literary gastronomy. Nevertheless, these are of only qualified relevance to those for whom terms like *culture, transformation, appropriation*, or *subject* and *object* inevitably evoke specific relationships of domination. Images of food and eating in Asian American literature provide an especially cogent illustration of this point.

THE CASE OF THE STONE BREAD

At the beginning of *Obasan*, Joy Kogawa's powerful novel about the mass relocation of West Coast Japanese Canadians during the Second World War, the narrator visits her aunt Obasan upon receiving news of Uncle's death. On the kitchen counter Naomi finds a hard, black loaf made by Uncle, perhaps in the last act of his life. This "stone bread" (1981:13) appears several more times throughout subsequent chapters, either as a material object or in figures of speech, and conspicuously calls for explication. The stone bread motif, if seen as a structuring device internal to *Obasan* through which certain themes are realized, poses no unusual problem of reading. Kogawa's tale of trauma and renewal, consisting of a series of chronologically scrambled narrative fragments, is held together—or, as reviewer Katherine Govier suggests, narrated—by recurrent images. Despite the disruptiveness inherent in her subject matter and the often strained syntax of her lyrical prose, Kogawa the craftswoman insists on rich texture, full development, gripping denouement—in short, good form—in the overall narrative. As a result, in this seemingly disorganized but ultimately tidy novel, the intricate network of recurrent images can be relied upon to be meaningful, and each of them can be singled out for profitable study through close reading of a type with which New Critics would feel quite at home.

Yet issues of context and intertextuality are unavoidable even when one reads a novel as apparently self-contained as *Obasan*. The motif of the stone bread, if readily decipherable from internal textual evidence, also reverberates with many images of food and eating in other Asian American literary works. One critic, noting the recurrence of stone bread and other images, describes the novel as built on an "ideographic principle": "Its components [are] arranged not only horizontally, so to speak, to propel the narrative along on its temporal and thematic path, but also vertically, to be added to each other in endless possibilities of sums" (Milton 1982:8). We might borrow this spatial analogy by visualizing various Asian American literary works as transparencies overlaid on each other, each bearing a "picture" of Asian American life, each uniquely structured "horizontally," on the flat surface. But some images, such as those of food and eating, recur from work to work, so that they also form a "vertical" pattern. The play of significance therefore takes place along both axes. Yet the intertextual pattern is no more "given" than the intratextual design (though the latter is more easily argued to be a product of authorial intention). The "vertical," intertextual configuration emerges only through an ideologically motivated act of reading, one that presupposes Asian American literary works to be emanations of certain common historical experiences.

It is my contention that alimentary images, thus juxtaposed and read as a group, symbolize Necessity—all the hardships, deprivations, restrictions, disenfranchisements, and dislocations that Asian Americans have collectively suffered as immigrants and minorities in a white-dominated country. The nature of this thematization can be understood more precisely with the aid of analytical frameworks from anthropology, psychology, or other disciplines. Eventually, however, only historicization of the literary works would allow the gestalten peculiar to Asian American alimentary images to emerge.

Using the stone bread image in *Obasan* as a point of departure, this chapter offers a contextualized and intertextual interpretation of alimentary images in Asian American literature, exploring, in the process, questions of "right" reading in ethnic American literature.

STONE BREAD: AN INTRATEXTUAL READING

What does the stone bread in *Obasan* stand for? On the level of emplotment, the stone bread may be adequately read drawing on internal textual evidence alone. By being associated both metaphorically and metonymically with Aunt Emily's package of relocation documents and family correspondence, the stone bread represents a mystery to be solved, a "hard nut to crack," as the colloquial expression would put it.

Naomi's mother, visiting in Nagasaki at the time of the atomic bomb-
ing, dies after being severely disfigured. Obasan, Uncle, and Aunt Emily
have learned of her fate but have decided to honor her dying wish by
withholding this knowledge from the narrator and her brother Stephen.
The ironical result of this gesture of love is that Naomi has been emotionally paralyzed in a state of death-in-life. The narrative unfolding of
Obasan details her slow approach to the knowledge needed to deliver
her from limbo.

Before Uncle's death, Aunt Emily has tried to interest Naomi in her
collection of documents: " 'Read this, Nomi. . . . Give you something
to chew on,' she said. She was eating a slice of Uncle's stone bread with
a slab of raw onion" (36). Unlike Aunt Emily with her "strong teeth"
and "tough digestion" (36), at first Naomi is not ready to read the papers with attention. (Her typical reaction to the stone bread is, "How
can you eat that stone? . . . It'll break your teeth" [13].) Gradually,
however, as the shock of Uncle's death forces her to reexamine the past,
Aunt Emily's forbidding chronicles of pain prove amenable to understanding: "In Aunt Emily's package, the papers are piled as neatly as the
thin white wafers in Sensei's silver box—symbols of communion, the
materials of communication, white paper bread for the mind's meal"
(182). The thick, hard stone bread, having broken down into paper-thin
wafers, is ready to be absorbed. The mystery that propels *Obasan*'s plot
is finally solved when the letters disclosing the mother's fate are read to
the now middle-aged children.

In a sense, the image of the stone bread also serves as an allegory of
reading: the reader's effort to get through the narrative complexities of
Obasan parallels not only Naomi's quest for knowledge but also the
physical process of ingesting and digesting the stone bread.[1] Naomi's
tragedy is not merely a personal one, for the elders' decision to remain
silent is made in the context of the wholesale destruction of the Japanese
Canadian community: it is because the family has already suffered so
much from the government's repeated betrayals that *kodomo no tame*
("for the sake of the children") becomes such an overriding concern.
The historical events responsible for Naomi's grim childhood and ado-
lescence are chronicled in numerous diary entries, letters, government
notices, and newspaper clippings, which Kogawa drew from Muriel
Kitagawa's papers in the Public Archives of Canada. Inserted, often with
minimal editing, into the account of Naomi's homecoming (which is
itself repeatedly disrupted by long flashbacks triggered by Uncle's
death), these documents frustrate the novel reader's expectations of
total artistic processing, of smooth, uniform narrative flow, of transparent verbal presentation. In other words, as a novel *Obasan* does not "go

down easy."[2] The effect of these documentary inruptions would be comparable to that of encountering the following list of abuses against the Japanese Canadians, in a form of discourse that normally relegates it to footnotes:[3]

- Over 21,000 Canadians of Japanese origin, some 80 percent of them citizens by birth or naturalization, were expelled from the West Coast of British Columbia on no evidence of espionage and sabotage and with no legal recourse.
- The Royal Canadian Mounted Police was given unlimited power to enter homes without warrant. Fishing boats, automobiles, and radios were seized.
- Families were arbitrarily and forcibly separated. The men were interned in remote road camps. (Those refusing to abandon their families were sent to prisoner-of-war camps.) Others were housed in animal pens and later removed to ghost towns in the interior.
- Later, families were allowed to stay together on condition that they work in the beet fields of Alberta and Manitoba. They were inspected and chosen like slaves at public auction and were prohibited from buying or leasing land.
- The Custodian of Enemy Property, in whose trust Japanese Canadian homes, businesses, and property were placed, liquidated them without the owners' consent, at fire sale prices.
- In 1945, even after the war was over, Japanese were subjected to a second uprooting in the form of banishment to Japan; "proof of loyalty consisted of 'volunteering' to remove oneself east of the Rocky Mountains." Over 4,000, half of them Canadian-born, were deported before the measure was stopped by public outcry and United Nations criticism.
- Japanese Canadians were required to carry identification papers until 1947; they were not given the franchise or allowed to return to British Columbia until 1949, five years after the end of the war.

Like Uncle's surprise ingredients—leftover oatmeal and barley, carrots and potatoes (13)—the apparently unconverted nuggets of reality in Naomi's tale force the reader to work hard to extract meaning. *Obasan* not only contains a story to be read but is itself a story about reading.

Obasan is unusual among Asian American literature in that, like the Escher print showing two hands drawing each other, it is constructed to be "self-sufficient." Context here is not conceived of as some extratextual background, to be tucked away in footnotes or supplied by helpful critics. Rather, the sociohistorical information needed by the reader is explicitly integrated into the story:[4] context and story generate and subsume each other. Thus a fruitful reading of the stone bread motif can be achieved even if we were to stay entirely within the covers of the book.

In another way, independent of deconstructivist strategies or the technicalities of emplotment, we can also derive meaningful interpretations of the stone bread motif with no reference to other Asian American literary texts. An excellent case can be made for claiming the Bible as an essential, indeed intended, intertext for *Obasan*, and for distilling a "universal" message from this "ethnic" work. To anyone conversant with the Bible, the pairing of the two words *stone* and *bread* evokes ready associations. Christ's dictum on the grace of God comes immediately to mind: "Or what man is there of you, whom if his son ask bread, will he give him a stone?" (Matt. 7:9).[5] Naomi asks her absent mother for proof of love and seems to be endlessly rebuffed; yet the stone turns out to be bread after all: the mother's love is found to be much greater than Naomi could ever have guessed. A religious reading of the story's thrust—religious in a spiritual, not institutional or doctrinal, sense— would be endorsed by Kogawa herself, who quotes in the epigraph to *Obasan*:

> To him that overcometh
> will I give to eat
> of the hidden manna
> and will give him
> a white stone
> and in the stone
> a new name written.
>
> (Rev. 2:17)[6]

With the mention of bread in a Christian context, one recalls the Eucharist, which reenacts Christ's giving of Himself at the Last Supper (Watts 1953:145–50). The Christlike sacrificial figure is Naomi's mother, who literally loses her flesh and blood, but it can also be the Japanese Canadian community, which has been dismembered and consumed by the white majority. Kogawa is explicit in her Christian allusions: she gives a detailed account of the communion celebrated by the exiled Japanese in Slocan, on the eve of its second forcible dispersal (177). Just as the service is, as a matter of course, conducted in both Japanese and English, Christianity in *Obasan* is never portrayed as "Western," as opposed to "Oriental." In this sense, then, the stone bread may be read as a religious symbol devoid of specifically ethnic connotations; it hints at God's redemptive grace, often disguised in adversity: a transcendent force generous enough to encompass all lesser human allegiances and contentions. At the conclusion of the novel, when one reaches the gruesome descriptions of the atomic holocaust at Nagasaki, one is transported to a realm of pure pain in the face of which ideological issues become, if not irrelevant, at least transformed into spiritual issues of human suffering and compassion, sin and forgiveness.

The stone bread in *Obasan* is not, then, what one would instantly identify as an ethnic sign. After all, originating as Uncle's whimsical variation on a giveaway recipe, it seems idiosyncratic, private, the source of family jokes that need to be explained to outsiders (13). Its symbolic potency can in no small part be credited to the scrupulous care with which Kogawa manages her intricate network of images. Yet once we move beyond *Obasan* as a hermetic text abundant in authorial hints and read it intertextually, focusing on its participation in the larger discourse of Asian American literature, the stone bread image begins to look different. When read alongside the many other images of unpalatable food and strenuous eating found in Asian American literary works, the image loses somewhat in novelty but assumes the ethnic group-specific meaning of Necessity.

STONE BREAD: AN INTERTEXTUAL READING

Members of Naomi's family react to the stone bread quite differently. Uncle, Obasan, and Aunt Emily ingest it readily: Uncle pronounces it "beri good," Obasan likes it broken and soaked in a homemade weed-tea (13), and Aunt Emily puts raw onion on it (37). Stephen has devised a way to eat it: smearing it with margarine (13); but in the climactic scene in which the family tragedy is revealed he balks at the bread, breaking off a corner of the loaf and then sticking it back on (232). Naomi objects to it vehemently, refusing even to classify it as food: "If you can't even break it, it's not bread," Naomi states. "It's all stone" (13). In being such dauntless eaters, the elders in *Obasan* reveal an affinity with the immigrant parents in Maxine Hong Kingston's *The Woman Warrior* (1976), Fae Myenne Ng's "A Red Sweater" (1986),[7] and Ashley Sheun Dunn's "No Man's Land" (1978).

The Woman Warrior contains a lengthy excursus on eating in the "Shaman" chapter (1977:104–108). Maxine grows up with a mother who turns the most unlikely creatures into food and allows absolutely no waste in her household. According to the narrator, Brave Orchid has cooked for them "raccoons, skunks, hawks, city pigeons, wild ducks, wild geese, black-skinned bantams, snakes, garden snails, turtles that crawled about the pantry floor and escaped under refrigerator or stove, catfish that swam in the bathtub" (106). She boils weeds pulled up in the yard, including a kind that has "no taste" (106). Indeed, the concept of "weed" is probably alien to someone who "plants vegetable gardens rather than lawns," "carries the odd-shaped tomatoes home from the fields," and "eats food left for the gods" (6). "Eat! Eat!" (108) is Brave Orchid's earnest daily injunction. Disposing of uneaten food is sacrilege, simply unthinkable: "We'd have to face four- and five-day-old leftovers until we ate it all. The squid eye would keep appearing at breakfast and dinner until eaten. Sometimes brown masses sat on every dish. I have seen revulsion on the faces of visitors who've caught us at meals" (108). Maxine relates her mother's superior eating ability to the story of her triumph over the "sitting ghost" (78–88), thus placing her in the company of fabulous Chinese heroes who overcome ghosts, monsters, and assorted evils by devouring them, or who manage to blackmail gods by threatening to do so (104–106). Revolted by what she perceives as the Chinese people's cult of ruthless and indiscriminate eating, American-born Maxine vows: "I would live on plastic" (108).

Though less vocally tyrannical than Brave Orchid, the narrator's mother in Ng's "A Red Sweater" is also a determined practitioner of thrift and an eater of uninviting food. As a special treat for her family, she cooks pigeons bought live and fattened at home by the daughters. As the young ones feast on the best pieces, she sits alone in the kitchen "sucking out the sweetness of the lesser parts: necks, backs, and the head." "Bones are sweeter than you know," she says. To make the most out of the pigeons, she has her daughters save the bones in brown paper bags, to be used later for soup; as with Brave Orchid, "No waste" (336) is her motto.

The list of Brave Orchid's culinary conquests reappears, in greatly attenuated form, in Dunn's "No Man's Land," a story about the relationship between two Chinese American soldiers in the Vietnam War, one American-born, one a Hong Kong immigrant. Sam, the immigrant, tells of eating "cicadas, worms, snakes and stuff" (117) as a child. After moving to America he has come to be nauseated by the very thought of such food, but his father persists in trying to reproduce it, catching cockroaches in the house or pigeons from the rooftop. Unlike Brave Orchid's well-trained and iron-stomached children though, Sam's family get sick, and the father has to content himself with less ambitious projects (118).

What unites the immigrants in these stories is an ability to eat unpromising substances and to extract sustenance, even a sort of willed enjoyment, from them; to put it symbolically, it is the ability to cope with the constraints and persecutions Asian Americans have had to endure as immigrants and racial minorities. This core connotation of Necessity can hardly be fully appreciated without a detailed rehearsal of Asian American history; a literary study of this nature, organized thematically rather than chronologically, can only adumbrate some of the most egregious injustices perpetrated against the race, as they appear in specific works. Yet even such common English expressions as to "swallow" one's pride or "stomach" an insult, to have a decision "shoved down one's throat," to find a situation "unpalatable" or a character "unsavory," and to "eat one's words" or "eat crow," all at root alimentary metaphors, bespeak the aptness of the trope for a history fraught with involuntariness of all kinds. As Roger Abrahams notes, "It is only human that we regard the major orifices, especially our mouths, as providing an access to our selves that must remain inviolate except in the most privileged moments, when openness is valued more highly than protection" (1984:19). Opening the mouth to eat is essential to keeping alive, but the act also brings with it the threat of unwelcome intrusion (Frazer 1964:207–208).

Ingestion is the physical act that mediates between self and not-self, native essence and foreign matter, the inside and the outside. The mediating relationship is crucial: until eaten and absorbed into one's bodily system, food is no more than a substance "out there." The nature of this transaction, concealed from consciousness when food is properly nutritious and delectable—that is, when life is familiar and easy enough to allow a taking-for-granted of physiological functioning—becomes apparent when the demands of survival necessitate an inventive stretching of one's definition of food. Disagreeable food puts to the test one's capacity to consolidate one's self by appropriating resources from the external environment, to convert the seemingly useless into the useful, refuse into nutrition. Physical survival is incompatible with a finicky palate; psychological survival hinges on the wresting of meaning from arbitrary infliction of humiliation and pain; survival of family and the ethnic group not only presupposes individually successful eating but may demand unusually difficult "swallowing" to ensure a continued supply of nourishment for the next generation. No wonder, then, that big eaters abound in the literature of Asian Americans, who at various points in their history have been kept out of America by discriminatory immigration legislation; exploited as cheap, dispensable labor; ghettoized while being faulted for refusal to Americanize; denied citizenship, land ownership, or a chance to raise families in the United States; scapegoated during hard times; run out of town, lynched, and slain; forcibly interned, relocated, and dispersed on no evidence of disloyalty; deprived of property by confiscation or virtual confiscation; and, even in an era of liberalized immigration, subjected to stereotyping and racial violence.

The stone bread image in *Obasan*, read in this light, is a brilliant exploitation of the multiple symbolic dimensions of eating. The government's summary abridgment of the civil and human rights of Japanese Canadians is inexcusable, especially given its self-proclaimed commitment to democracy; in that sense it sits like a stone in the gullet of the betrayed—hard, harsh, and implacable, impossible to accept without doing major violence to one's political and philosophical beliefs. The relocation orders are "foreign matter" in another, bitterly ironic sense: many of the uprooted are Canadian citizens, as native to Canada as white citizens, yet overnight they have been reclassified as extraneous, to be grouped with "enemy aliens" and treated with equal suspicion. Thus is a newly concocted alienness shoved down their collective throat. Then there is the "pervasive" and "inescapable" "hardship" (194) of working in the beet fields of Alberta, relived in excruciating detail by Naomi twenty-seven years later (190–99). *Hardship* and *hardness*, we may note, share the same root word.

Faced with one tragedy after another, Uncle's and Obasan's response has been to "swallow," to accept their lot silently. Their making do to give Naomi and Stephen some semblance of family life, their managing to feel grateful to Canada just for letting them stay alive (42), are the equivalent of drawing sustenance from stone bread. However, for such mute and stoical eating they have had to pay a steep price: they themselves have taken on the characteristics of stone, have become dry, inert, impassive, no longer capable of crying (12). Aunt Emily, though also an expert eater of stone bread, owes the preservation of her emotional vitality to an act that reverses the direction of eating and thus symbolically neutralizes its potential damage: she speaks out. "How different my two aunts are. One lives in sound, the other in stone. Obasan's language remains deeply underground but Aunt Emily, BA, MA, is a word warrior" (32). Obasan can indeed tolerate "foreign matter" put inside her, but she has no outlet for her pain. Her psyche has become like her scrap-filled refrigerator, with "indescribable items" lurking in its "dark recesses," "too old for mould and past putrefaction" (45). In the final pages of the story, the image of Obasan's face is dominated by a mouth resigned to more intake ("a small accepting 'o' ") but incapable of output: "Obasan rubs her eyes and tries to speak but the thick saliva coats her throat and she does not have the strength to cough" (245). Obasan has indeed attained physical survival for herself and her younger charges, but only at the expense of their psychological well-being. The example of forbearance set by Obasan and Uncle has delayed Naomi's healing. Despite repeated goadings from Aunt Emily, Naomi assimilates the contents of the document package with great reluctance, opening herself up only when her defenses have been weakened by Uncle's death: "We were the unwilling communicants receiving and consuming a less than holy nourishment, our eyes, cups filling with the bitter wine of a loveless communion" (182).

THE IMMIGRANT AS CHAMPION EATER

It is more than a matter of accident that outspoken Aunt Emily is Canadian-born (20), while Uncle and Obasan, the quiet ones, are of the immigrant generation (18), like Brave Orchid in *The Woman Warrior*, the
parents in "A Red Sweater," or Sam's father in "No Man's Land."
Something about the immigrant situation—if not immediate memories
of privation, then the shock of permanent relocation to a white-dominated society and the daily attritions of adjustment—causes the first generation to value efficient eating unquestioningly, almost as a measure of
spiritual stamina.

What might be called the immigrant creed of dietary fortitude is most
fully explored in Kingston's *The Woman Warrior*. Brave Orchid's many
and often conflicting drives and inhibitions reveal the complexities of
Necessity, its rewards as well as perils. Having experienced firsthand the
abject poverty and depredations of war which have, since the mid-nine-
teenth century, driven numerous rural Cantonese emigrants to America
(and other parts of the world), Brave Orchid retains a frugal habit of
mind, perpetually anticipating and safeguarding against future scarcities
not only in food but in other necessities of life (e.g., 139). Along with
thriftiness she has internalized the social values governing the distribution of scant resources in her ancient, overcrowded homeland. The
Confucian concept of the social hierarchy, with its emphasis on obedience and communal responsibility, imposes another kind of Necessity
on Brave Orchid: as a woman, hence relegated by her culture to the
bottom of the pecking order (which is, in fact, a feeding order), she is
expected to acquiesce in her own subordination. Though partly a "new
woman" coming of age during China's turbulent modernization period,
a college-trained itinerant doctor with her own successful practice,
Brave Orchid has learned her gender role well. Her adventures as an
independent individual are short-lived, unobjectionable to herself and
the watchful villagers only because of the social usefulness of the medical
profession. In an act of self-sacrifice that signals commitment not only to
her own family but also to social coherence and cultural continuity,
Brave Orchid cuts short her career as soon as her emigrant husband calls
from America, joins him in a Stockton laundry, and proceeds to bear six
children after age forty-five (124). To ensure her family's survival, the
lady scholar in silk dresses has learned to carry hundred-pound sacks of
Texas rice up and down stairs. "She could work at the laundry from 6:30
a.m. until midnight, shifting a baby from an ironing table to a shelf between packages, to the display window" (away from the germs of the
soiled laundry) (122). Finally, as a person of color in America, she has
had to endure humiliating "No tickee, no washee" jokes from racist cus-

tomers, her only revenge a retort scribbled in Chinese on the clothes package (123).

Brave Orchid's inspiring strength may be attributed to her omnivorousness toward experiences, her willingness to follow the spoken and unspoken dictates of Necessity without protest. These qualities have enabled her to provide for a large family, saving her children—even the "worthless" daughters—from destitution. (She is mortified when Maxine fails to "fatten up," fearing what the Chinese back home would say: "Years in America . . . and they don't eat" [119].) As the narrator concludes, comparing Brave Orchid to the legendary monster eaters of Chinese lore, "my mother could contend against the hairy beasts whether flesh or ghost because she could eat them" (108). Among the most memorable lessons Maxine has learned from her mother are "All heroes are bold toward food" (104) and "Big eaters win" (105).

However, submission to Necessity exacts a psychological price in the form of a dulling of sensitivity, a diminishment of compassion, a fettering of the imagination. If Obasan has turned to stone, so has Brave Orchid, though to a somewhat less tragic extent. ("My mother is not soft" [69], Maxine notes.) As a "Gold Mountain wife" left behind by an emigrant husband, she must have felt her share of unfulfilled desires, but since "the work of preservation demands that the feelings playing about in one's guts not be turned into action" (9), Brave Orchid keeps her emotions in check and allows practicality to prevail. She is known as a sensible woman, not one of those "inappropriate" women "teased for 'longing' after men" (108). She dismisses the adulterous aunt who (Maxine imagines) dares to assert a private life in times of collective deprivation (14). That the "no name woman" is a fellow "Gold Mountain wife," a "widow of the living," evokes in Brave Orchid no conscious pity, no empathetic identification as in Maxine.[8] The lesson to be learned from her downfall is more utilitarian than moral: irresponsible coupling results in an extra mouth to feed and will not be forgiven by the family. "My mother has told me once and for all the useful parts. She will add nothing unless powered by Necessity, a river bank hat guides her life" (6).

THE CHILDREN OF NECESSITY

In her children Brave Orchid expects an uncomplaining suppression of spontaneous sensory response for the sake of nutrient absorption: when she dismembers skunk in the kitchen, the children hold candy over their noses to mask the smell (106–107). She inculcates a sort of secular puritanism about food and, by extension, about experience: "If it tastes good, it's bad for you. . . . If it tastes bad, it's good for you" (108).

Pleasures of the senses—the "melting cones" that the penny-pinching parents bring home from work and the "American movie on New Year's Day" (6)—are invariably accompanied by guilt. "Whenever we did frivolous things, we used up energy" (6). Likewise, squeamishness of any kind is a squandering of emotional energy, a luxury that the serious-minded cannot afford. The Rabelaisian list of animals and birds that end up on Brave Orchid's dinner table (in part a parodic, antiexotic jab at Chinatown tourist types whose understanding of Chinese American life is limited to the bastardized food of chop suey houses) is also a measure, only half-satirical, of the lengths to which Necessity can drive one in the struggle for survival. Maxine remembers hiding with her terrified siblings under the bed, ears plugged up "against the sounds of slaughter in the kitchen, the bird screams and the thud, thud of the turtles swimming in the boiling water" (106). The children are horrified to find their mother throwing scraps of chicken into her constantly simmering pot of chicken feed (143).

To survive in such a household, thrift-obsessed to the point of callousness or even cruelty, Maxine must carefully husband her own emotional resources. Her alternative to Brave Orchid's wholesale insensitivity is to learn to control imaginative identification: its object, timing, and extent. When Brave Orchid recounts the legendary monkey brain feast of China and dislodges a "curtain [flapping] loose" inside her susceptible daughter's mind, Maxine cuts short her empathetic questioning: "Did she say, 'You should have seen the faces the monkey made'? Did she say, 'The people laughed at the monkey screaming'? It was alive? The curtain flaps closed like merciful black wings" (108).

The powers of the imagination are released only when it is safe to do so, as in the lengthy fantasy sequence in the "White Tigers" chapter. The Fa Mu Lan–like heroine is successful precisely because she can control—not deny, not obliterate—her feelings, closing a mental "wooden door" when she realizes that she is not yet ready to save her loved ones from the wicked baron (39). "I had learned on the farm that I could stop loving animals raised for slaughter. And I could start loving them immediately when someone said, 'This one is a pet' " (39). Brave Orchid's problem, as we have seen, is that her psychology of scarcity respects no boundaries, spilling over even into a reasonably comfortable retirement (121–22): potentially, anything can be "for slaughter."

As one of the "useless" daughters unqualified to carry on the family name, Maxine finds her aspirations being frustrated by Brave Orchid's single-minded insistence on utility and her unreflecting championship of traditional Chinese values (including, ironically, the subordination of women). Maxine finds no joy in her achievements; after all, "you can't eat straight A's" (54). She feels compelled even in adulthood to prove that she is "worthy of eating the food" (62), that she is not, as the Chinese term goes, a "maggot" in the rice (*zhumichong*) (222). Guilt overwhelms her when she fights to break loose, first in compensatory flights of the imagination, then in real life, from the daily reminders of her superfluity as a person.

Part of Maxine's struggle, of course, is the "universal" one of growing up and leaving home: detaching oneself from parental pressures to lead a life of one's own. However, the figure in which she expresses her guilt recalls the monkey brain feast and implies that, in a sense, Maxine too has been a victim of "slaughter," a sacrificial offering to the dogma of Necessity: "[Brave Orchid's] eyes are big, inconsolable. A spider headache spreads out in fine branches over my skull. She is etching spider legs into the icy bone. She pries open my head and my fists and crams into them responsibility for time, responsibility for intervening oceans" (126).

Instead of being given free rein in personal development, the narrator is expected to be a custodian for the well-being of the entire family, including starving clan members in Communist China who are virtual strangers to her (59–60). She feels obligated to take on "tyrants who for whatever reason can deny my family food and work" (58). In reaction, Maxine develops an aversion to cooking, especially cooking for others, activities at which her mother so excels: "Even now, unless I am happy, I burn the food when I cook. I do not feed people. I let the dirty dishes rot. I eat at other people's tables but won't invite them to mine, where the dishes are rotting" (56). Such wastefulness, such a foolhardy refusal to cultivate competence and self-sufficiency—one can almost hear Brave Orchid's clucking and scolding here—must seem to any striving immigrant a silliness of which only the spoiled Americans are capable.

QUASI-CANNIBALISM: FAMILY AND SACRIFICE

Chicken scraps going into chicken feed, humans reaching into monkey skulls: these are quasi-cannibalistic images with overtones of sacrifice. "Like devouring like" probably appears to most people as a rather unusual and extreme motif. Interestingly, however, it reappears in several other Asian American works depicting relationships between immigrant parents and American-born children, suggesting that Necessity might have taken a peculiar and acutely distressing form in Asian American immigrant families.

Ng's "A Red Sweater" is a direct descendant of *The Woman Warrior* on the subject of Necessity. Like Maxine's parents, the narrator's are honest working-class immigrants (the mother a piecework seamstress in San Francisco's Chinatown; the sporadically employed father by turns a laundryman, a seaman, a small restaurant owner, and a cannery worker), but they have little to show for their thirty-three years of toil. Their chronically impoverished life results in a hardness of demeanor ("I know the hard color of his eyes and the tightness in his jaw. I can almost hear his teeth grind" [339]) as well as of personality. Husband and wife are constantly exploding at each other, cataloguing each other's failures and insensitivities, their ugliness "alive," "thick and impossible to let go of":

> *What about the first one? You didn't even think to come to the hospital. The first one, I say! Son or daughter, dead or alive, you didn't even come!*
>
> *What about living or dying? Which did you want for me that time you pushed me back to work before my back brace was off?* (339; italics in original)

Like Maxine, the three daughters are victims of the sexism of Chinese tradition; their very birth signals a "failed family" (332). The parents' voluntary privations—the pigeon necks and bones that the mother sucks on, in order that the children may enjoy the meaty parts—only deepen their sense of guilt. Parental self-sacrifice generates expectations of filial self-sacrifice, and the entire family is trapped in endless cycles of pain.

The symbolism of quasi-cannibalistic sacrifice takes several forms in "A Red Sweater." The parents' fury at each other is literally murderous: the need to measure everything by its usefulness has made emotional monsters of them. "How many times did my sister and I have to hold them apart? The flat ting! sound as the blade slapped onto the linoleum floors, the wooden handle of the knife slamming into the corner" (340). The mother yells "Get out and go die! Useless Thing! Stinking Corpse!" The father threatens to jump off the Golden Gate Bridge (337). Toward their daughters the parents apply the same ruthless standard: they have to be "good for something," namely, be able to bring money and "face" to the family, or else they are "rotten, no-good, dead [things]" (333). Fairytales notwithstanding, the magic number "three" means nothing: birth order only shapes one's doom, and none of the daughters is blessed. The middle one breaks under the pressure and jumps off a building, thereby making good the father's "thousand-year-old threat" (337) and taking his place. The eldest daughter Lisa, the "good" one about whom the parents boast, quits college to work and help support the family. Her only prospect for escape seems to be marriage to a rich man; in the meantime she stagnates in a kind of death-in-life. "She can stay at that point of endurance forever" (340). The youngest daughter, the narrator, finds she can survive only by completely removing herself from the gut-wrenching conflicts of the family. To her parents she is as good as dead. After getting pregnant—in retrospect she detects opportunity in the accident—she is roundly cursed by the mortified parents, in terms much like those applied to the no name woman in *The Woman Warrior*. "I would die in a gutter without rice in my belly. My spirit—if I had one—wouldn't be fed" (333). Now the narrator is a flight attendant with Pan Am, flying through time zones like a disembodied spirit, keeping in touch with the parents' doings only through annual dinners with Lisa.

In light of the daughters' destinies, the pigeon feasts recalled so fondly by the two surviving sisters take on an ominous air.

> A stench filled the alley. The crowd squeezed in around the truck. Old ladies reached into the crates, squeezing and tugging for the plumpest pigeons.
>
> My sister and I picked the white ones, those with the most expressive eyes. Dove birds, we called them. We fed them leftover rice in water, and as long as they stayed plump, they were our pets, our baby love birds. And then one day we'd come home from school and find them cooked. (336)

Did the little girls learn to control their tender feelings with a mental trapdoor like Maxine's alter ego, the swordswoman? Or did they, uncomprehending and helpless, simply learn to endure the abrupt swings between love and violence that seem to rule their family? "Baby love birds" to their parents, are they not also a food source, valued only for what they can give, to be slaughtered, cashed in on, when the time for repaying previous feeding comes? The pigeon bones, picked clean and saved in brown paper bags periodically checked by the mother (336), become an emblem of the daughters' possible fate.

The parents' labors are meant to break the cycle of Necessity, to make possible the luxury of choice for the next generation: "Our parents forced themselves to live through the humiliation in this country so that we could have it better" (341). "Mah and Deh both worked too hard; it is as if their marriage was a marriage of toil—of toiling together. The idea is that the next generation can marry for love" (338). In practice, however, the code of Necessity creates its own enslavement: one sacrifice calls for another. Superficial improvements in material conditions alone—the two remaining daughters are now making decent money—cannot, in short order, undo the effects of a lifetime of scraping and scrimping. Expectations of further neediness and hurt are not easily overcome. In a fancy bay-view restaurant, the sisters still practice the eating habits of the poor. "We eat slowly, chewing carefully, like old people. A way to make things last, to fool the stomach" (338). Beautiful Lisa, sought by many suitors and showered with gifts, psychologically still feels no freedom of choice. "She grabs at things out of despair, out of fear. Gifts grow old for her. Emotions never ripen, they sour. Everything slips away from her. Nothing sustains her" (339–40).

In an effort to save her sister from unhappiness, the narrator buys Lisa an expensive red angora sweater, one that would help her find the right man. "I want her beauty to buy her out" (341). The gift carries through the twisted logic of Necessity: images of love and violence are again inextricably mixed. The red sweater of the title, "swollen with good cheer" (332)—note the connotations of physical battery and pathology in *swollen*—epitomizes this ambivalence. The color of rejoicing and good luck in Chinese culture, used on wedding dresses and gift money packets, red is also the color of blood—menstrual blood which marks the daughters' initiation into the adult responsibility of relieving the parents through a "good" marriage; the virgin's blood on the first night, a valuable commodity (squandered by the narrator) that should be guarded to ensure a profitable return; the blood of the sacrificial victim, breast bared for slaughter. The startling concluding paragraphs of the story bring together these complex strands of meaning, belying the statement "We are the lucky generation" (341).

> A red sweater. 100% angora. The skin of fuzz will be a fierce rouge on her naked breasts.
> Red. Lucky. Wear it. Find that man. The new one. Wrap yourself around him. Feel the pulsing between you. Fuck him and think about it. 100%. Hand Wash Only. Worn Once. (341)

The pounding rhythm of mono- and disyllabic words hint at inexorability, at bargains clinched and fates sealed. Yet the immigrant parents probably would never understand the element of drivenness in their children's lives. To the middle daughter's suicide, the family's shrugging response is: "It was her choice" (332).

Like the narrator of "A Red Sweater," the second-generation protagonists in Amy Tan's *The Joy Luck Club* (1989) are cousins of Maxine, fellow children of Necessity. Images of grim eating (32), unsentimental killing for food (e.g., Jing-Mei's birthday crab dinner, 201), and oppressive parental expectations (especially in the chapters "Rules of the Game" and "Two Kinds") recur as in the other two works. These shared representations raise an interesting question about the intertextual approach adopted in this study. Ng and Tan are post–*Woman Warrior* writers, which means that the remarkable parallels between the alimentary images in *The Woman Warrior*, "A Red Sweater," and *The Joy Luck Club* can very plausibly be attributed to direct influence. Given this possibility, how much importance can one justifiably attach to the motif of quasi-cannibalistic familial sacrifice as it has been read here? After all, the mother-daughter conflict (whatever the cultural background), like many other feminist themes, has a long tradition and has been a staple of

American women's writing for decades (e.g., C. N. Davidson and E. M. Broner; M. Hirsch; M. Pearlman). We might further grant, for the sake of argument, that the enormous popularity of *The Woman Warrior* may have somehow induced younger Asian American women writers to favor the mother-daughter relationship—its bittersweetness, its taxing yet inspiring duality—as a subject. However, when all that is said, the question still remains as to why Ng and Tan have found the alimentary images (out of a host of possible figures) potent and attractive enough to echo in their own works. Derivativeness (in the descriptive sense) seems inadequate to explain the recurrences we have identified; some commonality of historical experience must ultimately be invoked. To phrase the issue in another way, if the later works serve as a kind of echo chamber for a motif in *The Woman Warrior*, the resultant sound is not any less worthy of scrutiny for having undergone "exaggeration." The coming into being of the amplifying agents themselves calls for a historical accounting, and this accounting cannot be separated from that given for the articulation of the original sound.

Additional evidence for such a view—namely, that the motif of quasi-cannibalistic sacrifice pertains to the immigrant parent/American-born children configuration—may be found in an unlikely source: Frank Chin's short story, "Food for All His Dead" (1962), anthologized in Hsu and Palubinskas's *Asian-American Authors* (1972). I say unlikely because Chin has openly condemned Kingston and Tan for writing in a Christianized tradition that distorts Chinese American life (F. Chin 1985, 1989, 1991a); his announced credo as a creative writer seems bent on disavowing all affinities with Asian American women's writing (F. Chin et al. 1974b). Yet a thematic thread links "Food for All His Dead" to the three works cited in this section.

Chin's title itself embodies the idea of quasi-cannibalistic sacrifice, describing as it does many American-born Asians' perception of their situation vis-à-vis the immigrant generation. (One Chinese critic, J. Lau, felicitously renders the title as "*xisheng*," the term originally referring to animal offerings in ancestor worship which has come to stand for "sacrifice" in the more general sense.) In Chin's story, the phrase "Food for All His Dead" has at least a twofold meaning. Johnny's ailing father, a prominent Chinatown leader, insists on joining the lion dance parade for the annual "Double Ten" celebration (to commemorate the founding of the Republic of China in 1911); after exerting himself to make a speech to his beloved constituency, he dies of a blood-spitting attack. In this sense he is food for his own dead, a willing sacrifice for traditional loyalties that have become "frozen" in the economic and cultural ghetto of Chinatown. (Ironically, Johnny helps his father to become a martyr by confronting him with his rebellion and hastening his death. The mother accuses Johnny of murder [60].) In addition, the father wants to sacrifice Johnny to his values. By drawing Johnny into the complicity of concealed suffering, the father tries to extort from him a promise to carry on his good name in Chinatown: " 'You know,' the man said, 'I wan' you to be somebody here. Be doctor, mak' moneys and halps da Chinee, or lawyer, or edgenerer, make moneys and halp, and people're respack you. . . . You tall me now you won' leab here when I die, hokay?' " (53). Johnny, having gone to school outside Chinatown and absorbed the scorn of whites, finds himself no longer able to submit to the father's demand for face-enhancing, security-providing success.

Much of the son's bitterness comes from the perception that the father shows no defiance against white racism but is content to stay in a Chinatown that exists for the diversion of tourists, much like an Indian reservation (52, 58). Though the father is not depicted as a "big eater" with a history of overcoming material difficulties, the implication is that he has endured more than a man of true pride should have—he seems oblivious to the fact that he is a "curiosity" to whites. (To Johnny the father's pride in his Chinese heritage doesn't count as valid.) Knowing only what he doesn't want, not what he does want, Johnny wallows in guilt and nostalgia for the simplicity of childhood: " 'I really had it made then, really, and I knew more then than I do now. . . . I didn't have to ask about anything; it was all there; I didn't have questions; I knew who I was responsible to, who I should love, who I was afraid of' " (59).

Johnny's outcry sheds light on the inherent ambiguity of Necessity: being guided in all one does is synonymous with having no choice. Such a state of existence obviously has both a sheltering and an imprisoning aspect. Johnny is simultaneously attracted to and repelled by it; in this he resembles the narrator in "A Red Sweater," who, having cut loose by hurling herself into space (she becomes a flight attendant), enviously projects a reassuring "peace of heart" onto the obedient sister who remains with the family on the ground. Yet she also knows the dichotomy is not as clear-cut as it may seem: "Once a year, I come in, asking questions. She's [Lisa] got the answers, but she hates them. For me, I think she's got the peace of heart, knowing that she's done her share for Mah and Deh. She thinks I have the peace, not caring" (334). Unlike the compassionate though anguished narrator of "A Red Sweater," Johnny seems utterly incapable of imagining an alternative point of view on his own plight. The ambiguity of Necessity produces in him not compassion or even resignation but helpless hatred (61).

The alimentary image in Chin's story, explicitly represented in the title and implicitly informing the plot, suggests that the motif of sacrificial eating cuts across the boundaries of not only gender but also announced politics. If the works of Kingston, Ng, and Tan show a family resemblance, Chin is dedicated to proving the fraudulence of such a "family"—what he sees as an irremediably compromised, white-pleasing "missionary tradition" in Chinese American literature, practiced by women and emasculated men. Yet in spite of vast differences in style and outlook, Chin turns out to share a symbolic code with those he most energetically opposes. In this code alimentary images occur in several permutations, all associated with the immigrant experience. The survival-minded elders are capable eaters who have "swallowed" a great deal, in terms of either physical hardship or humiliation; they also tend to be remorseless slaughterers, blind to the sufferings of their victims and intent only on extracting benefits from them. The American-born children often have reservations about the parents' food choices (and by implication their life choices); they identify with the creatures slaughtered for food; they experience the parents' attempts to pass on the doctrine of usefulness as a kind of force-feeding; and, most distinctively for this body of works, they frequently feel themselves sacrificed—made into a food source—for the parents.

READING QUASI-CANNIBALISM IN CONTEXT

The long-discredited practice of biographical criticism may provide a ready, but hardly compelling or rewarding, explanation for the metaphoric affinities in the works of Kingston, Ng, Tan, and Chin. All these writers are American-born (all but Chin children of immigrant parents), and most of them have apparently been subjected to intense parental pressure to achieve in conventional ways.[9] Such a reading inflates the element of disguised autobiography or self-therapy in imaginative literature and minimizes the shared nature of semiotic systems. Even less useful to the Asian American reader are universalistic anthropological perspectives on the symbolic meaning of cannibalism (e.g., Frazer 1964:301, 385, 541–42), which are too closely tied to actual, specific "exotic" cultural practices to illuminate contemporary Asian American literature.

To me, the motif of quasi-cannibalism is most intriguing when read against the "model minority" thesis,[10] which, while invoking the American immigrant myth, assiduously searches traditional Asian cultures for clues to the Asian American success story. In the journalistic and social science literature on the "model minority," the Asian family, especially the immigrant family in more immediate contact with traditional values, is routinely cited as the ultimate source of strength for Asian Americans (Osajima 1988:170, 172). (Another article suggests that Japanese Americans—today the only predominantly American-born Asian American group—have assimilated themselves out of the model minority and

into mainstream mediocrity [Viviano 1989:9].) The high expectations
of immigrant parents, their willingness to sacrifice for the children's education, the family's tight hierarchical structure of obligations and responsibilities, and the children's obedience and dedication to the goal of
family upward mobility are all extolled as values that white Americans
(not to mention other minorities of color) would do well to emulate
(Viviano 1989). After repeated criticism from the Asian American community for presenting a biased picture, the "model minority" thesis has
begun to assume a somewhat muted form, with most pieces nowadays
devoting some space to negative aspects—the obstacles still facing Asian
Americans, the price one has to pay for success, or the subgroups that
haven't made it (Osajima, 168). Some specifically mention the damaging impact of parental pressure on Asian American students (e.g.,
D. Bell; R. Oxnam). Still, the Asian immigrant family remains a much
analyzed and greatly romanticized institution. At times seen as a formidable import, it is also sometimes held up as the truest realization of
traditional *American* values, which whites have lamentably forsaken.
Laudatory accounts of the Asian immigrant family are at once a re-
affirmation of the "immigrant makes good" myth and a sobering "pep
talk" to embattled whites, who have sensed a slipping away of supremacy
along with numerical majority.

Each in its own way, the four works depicting quasi-cannibalism offer
implicit critiques of the myth of the Asian immigrant family. The pieces
span twenty-seven years, with Chin's story bearing a first copyright date
of 1962 and Tan's novel appearing in 1989. "Food for All His Dead"
predates by only a few years the *New York Times Magazine* article commonly taken to mark the inception of "model minority" discourse in the
mass media (Petersen 1966); since that time numerous variations on the
theme have appeared in the popular press. Without assuming in the four
creative writers any deliberate espousal of a revisionist argument or assumption of a polemical stance, we can still see in their rendering of
parent-child conflicts, especially in their gravitating toward images of
quasi-cannibalism, a counterbalancing perspective to media idealiza-
tions of the Asian immigrant family.

This is not to suggest that the writers possess indisputably "correct,"
because "authentic," insight on the subject. Their status as cultural "in-
siders" obviously does not necessarily entail endorsement of any one
view; indeed, there are many members of the Asian American community with equal claim to "insider's" authority who find the "model minority" notion accurate and complimentary. What is clear, however, is
that as creative writers, Kingston, Ng, Tan, and Chin have observed and
included in their works many more details of immigrant family life than

can be forced into a single discursive statement on either its virtues or its ills. Further, the resources of metaphoric language (traceable eventually to "human" functions like eating) have afforded them a shared means to present complex, ambivalent meanings about the experience. For that reason—and independently of their own stated political beliefs—they are able to expose the ideological motivation of "model minority" discourse.[11] The very presence of as startling a motif as quasi-cannibalistic sacrifice undermines the Norman Rockwell glow that some writers choose to cast over the Asian immigrant family (Viviano 1989:8).

The selection of "model minority" discourse as intertexts for the literary works is, of course, itself ideologically motivated, but unlike in majority discourse there is no pretense to "objectivity," since marginalized groups like Asian Americans have already had their positions marked as specialized. What distinguishes our reading of quasi-cannibalism from similar revisionist efforts by Asian American scholars in social science disciplines (Osajima; Yun) is this: while pertinent factual data can furnish correctives to the "model minority" thesis, they do not elucidate the workings of ideological myths. In particular, social science writing does not illustrate how even those most adversely affected by the myths may mobilize them to give shape to conflicts in their lives, perhaps the better to displace or manage the personal pain. The rich texture of literature (literature is the "thickest description" possible of a people's life, to use cultural anthropologist Clifford Geertz's term) means that the critic can recover the sociohistorical forces that have left traces in the works, however faint these may be due to the individual author's thematic or formal emphasis.

As applied to the four Asian American works under discussion, the reading strategy advanced here would "depersonalize" the motif of quasi-cannibalism—that is, remove the focus from the personalities and idiosyncracies of the characters to a larger arena. While the second-generation characters in the four works may feel themselves being slaughtered and devoured by unsympathetic parents, they are actually contending with more diffuse and potent societal forces, such as the structural enclosure of minorities or stratification of the labor market by race and gender. The very fact that the American-born children identify with the slaughtered animals, not with the parents who have to conduct the slaughter, shows the extent of their obliviousness to the context of the family's life. Furthermore, conditioned by the dominant society's inclination to think the worst of their parents, they may have exaggerated the brutality of the latter's "big eating" and the inhumaneness of the ancestral culture. As will be shown later in this chapter, while the consumption of "unlikely" (to Westerners) foods in Asian cultures had its historical source in poverty, over time the ability to savor them has generated its own momentum, evolving into the mark of a true gourmet. A remark like "Bones are sweeter than you know," made by the mother in "A Red Sweater" (336), thus cuts several ways and is not simply a self-serving investment to leverage the daughters' future sacrifice.[12]

While cultural misunderstanding may occur between parent and child, it cannot be emphasized enough that the contextual forces determining the extent and nature of "sacrificial eating" are not *merely* cultural in nature. Certainly parent and child alike may experience and even describe their generational conflicts as cultural ones. Upon closer inspection, however, certain details of setting or dramatization would reveal a process of "ideologization" at work: both generations are given to deploying terms in the prevailing American ethos to formulate a superficially rational alibi for one's needs. After all, it is easier to seize upon an external, socially sanctioned account of conflict than to examine one's convoluted motives or to work through highly charged emotions in an intimate family relationship. Most importantly, the nature of ideology is such that it is normally not accessible for scrutiny, for its very function is to conceal the most acute contradictions and hardest-to-challenge material structures in society. Intergenerational cultural conflicts are real and often serious, but often they serve as convenient fictions veiling more unruly issues, such as those of economic equity.

Thus it is that we find Mrs. Woo in *The Joy Luck Club* phrasing her unrealistic expectations for Jing-Mei in terms of the American myth of immigrant success: "My mother believed you could be anything you wanted to be in America. You could open a restaurant. You could work for the government and get good retirement. You could buy a house with almost no money down. You could become rich. You could become instantly famous" (132). What she does not seem to realize is that it is precisely because this myth has *not* worked for her that she has to displace her hopes onto her daughter. At the same time, when Jing-Mei proves resistant to her efforts to make a superachiever of her, Mrs. Woo does not accuse her of being insufficiently "American"; instead, she falls back on her most self-righteous position and uses the Chinese cultural precept of filial piety to browbeat Jing-Mei. However, this strategy backfires, because it endows Jing-Mei's rebellion with the emboldening classic form of American modernity versus Asian traditionalism: "I wasn't her slave. This wasn't China" (141). (This very same opposition informs an earlier Chinese American work, Jade Snow Wong's 1945 autobiographical *Fifth Chinese Daughter*, and was responsible in no small part for its great success among white readers [Evans 1950; Wolfe 1950; Wyatt 1950].) The characters' multiple invocations, betraying not only subtle interpersonal dynamics but also the process of "ideologization," are in the text for the reader to take note of.

Similarly, we find Brave Orchid in *The Woman Warrior* labeling any undesirable behavior in her children "American." In "At the Western Palace," when her son refuses to abet her meddling with Moon Orchid's life—meddling that goes far beyond what Chinese culture would endorse—Brave Orchid scolds, "You Americans don't take life seriously" (174). On the other hand, Maxine conflates cultural difference with the effects of poverty when she contemplates her mother's photograph and concludes: "My mother is not smiling; Chinese do not smile for photographs. Their faces command relatives in foreign lands—'Send money'—and posterity forever—'Put food in front of this picture'" (68). While putting food in front of pictures of dead ancestors is indeed a Chinese cultural practice, asking relatives abroad to send money is not a cultural but an economic act, and facial expression in photographs has little to do with either. Posed pictures just tend to look stiff; candid snapshots are a more recent product of affluence and technological advance. It is this tendency to overgeneralize about what Chinese do or don't do, encouraged by the stereotyping by whites, that has made Maxine's growing up so confusing and difficult: "Chinese Americans, when you try to understand what things in you are Chinese, how do you separate what is peculiar to childhood, to poverty, insanities, one family, your mother who marked your growing with stories, with what is Chinese? What is Chinese tradition and what is the movies?" (6).[13]

The notion of cultural conflict between the immigrant and American-born generations—the enlightened, freedom-loving son or daughter struggling to escape the clutches of backward, tyrannical parents—is one of the most powerful "movies" ever created to serve hegemonic American ideology.[14] According to Sollors, the rhetoric surrounding the "persistent conflict between consent and descent" (1986a:15) is what unifies diverse groups and socializes them into a single, quintessentially American "forward-looking culture of consent" (1986a:4). However, the pervasiveness of this rhetoric does not alter its status as a cultural script that certain ethnic groups, as a result of racism, will never be able to enact in full. When we take into account the constructedness of the descent-consent script, we would be able to detect suppressed noncultural forces at work in the Asian American images of quasi-cannibalistic sacrifice.

For example, F. Chin's "Food for All His Dead" is set in 1956, in a period of great isolation and anxiety for the Chinese American community living in the Cold War's shadow (Tsai 1986:133–36; Daniels 1988:299–309). It was a time of post–Korean War finger-pointing, of McCarthyism, of the "Confession Program" for "paper sons," of high suicide rates for the Chinatown elderly (Lyman 1974:152); the community retrenched and turned inward, hoping to avoid the fate of Japanese

Americans during the Second World War (Daniels, 302–303). Johnny's venomous self-hatred is thus in part a function of Chinatown's structural location in American society at a certain juncture in history; behind the sacrifices depicted in the story is the hidden sacrifice of the Chinese American community to the melting pot myth.

Compared to Chin's story, "A Red Sweater" takes place in a decidedly more open period in American history, after the liberalization of immigration laws in 1965.[15] Author Ng eschews the clichés of cultural conflict in portraying parent-child confrontations, but their effects on the second generation are readily discernible. The narrator, in escaping the poverty of the typical post-1965 Chinatown immigrant family (Nee and Nee 1972:253–71; Reimers 1985:107), has also had to abandon Chinese culture. "The only chopsticks I own, I wear in my hair" (334). The implements that once enabled her to participate in a living culture are now reduced to ornaments advertising her exotic origin; an air of unquestionable naturalness accompanies the narrator's account of this change. But there are enough details in the text about the parents' disadvantaged positions in a race- and gender-linked labor market (the mother considers herself lucky to have steady employment as a work-at-home seamstress, while the father belongs to a surplus pool of chronically underemployed immigrant workers upon which the economy draws as needed) to suggest that lack of acculturation is not the root cause of their desperation.

AN EXPANDED VIEW OF NECESSITY

We are now ready to tackle a deferred question that the perspicacious reader may have already raised: if Kingston, Ng, Tan, and Chin are all Chinese American, why should we not take at face value what some of their characters say about the oppressive nature of Chinese traditions? Why resort to a roundabout account of the common motif? Why bring in other Asian groups via the "model minority" thesis? After all, the images of cannibalism and human sacrifice have been applied to feudal, patriarchal Chinese culture by modern Chinese writers themselves.[16] Some social scientists have theorized about the role played by traditional culture in promoting Chinese American achievement: a combination of Confucian respect for education, concern for "face" and family reputation, habituation to hierarchical structures, and belief in filial piety (e.g., Oxnam 1986:73). There may well be a streak of "pushiness" in Chinese culture, one sufficiently pronounced to engage the interest of American-born writers.

As the foregoing discussion implies, the reason a culturalist explanation is inadequate is that it ignores the *American context* for the charac-

ter's behavior and assertions. Culture is not a piece of baggage that immigrants carry with them; it is not static but undergoes constant modification in a new environment. Rather like the tropes of incest and family
violence in African American literature,[17] the motif of quasi-cannibalism
says less about the cultural practices of the minority group than its positioning within the larger society. Incest recurs in African American fictional worlds not because it is condoned or encouraged by black culture
but because it is an apt metaphor: a subjugated group powerless to
change the larger society would turn on itself. Quasi-cannibalism should
be read in a similar way.

Only the most benighted critic would turn to African tribal mores to
account for episodes of incest in, say, *The Bluest Eye*. Yet many are eager
to engage in culturalist readings of Asian American literature, with scant
regard for contextual considerations. Herein, perhaps, lies a unique
curse on Asian American literature, one that distinguishes it from other
literatures of people of color in America: that its "indigenousness" may
never be adequately recognized except by the community itself and its
allies, and that it may remain ever vulnerable to facile culturalist interpretations. This state of affairs is in keeping with what we know of the
place historically occupied by Asian Americans. Being a group that entered American history through immigration, Asian Americans do share
some similarities with the experiences of European ethnics: dislocation,
poverty, prejudice, as well as conflicts between the first and second generations. With European ethnics, however, there is enough cultural congruence with the Anglo mainstream, and enough reality in the promised
rewards of assimilation, to validate the rhetoric of consensual nation-
building and blunt the damage of generational divisions. Asian Americans are socialized into embracing the same expectations but are denied
their full realization on a collective basis. Perceived by whites as perpetual house guests at best and invading vermin at worst, Asian Americans
are especially susceptible to culturalist accounts of their predicament,
which, though debilitating in the long run, at least renders the reality of
their exclusion less transparently unjust.

To the manifold forms of Necessity we have identified so far, then,
should be added one arguably peculiar to Asian Americans: a particular
vulnerability to culturalism. In this light, the motif of sacrificial eating
shared by Kingston, Ng, Tan, and Chin may be attributable to common
Chinese ethnicity after all—though not in the familiar sense of feeling
stifled by the same ancestral culture. Rather, we may say that of all the
Asian American subgroups, Chinese Americans are probably the most
fettered by stereotypes of cultural retentiveness, given the group's long
history in America as well as China's centrality in Orientalizing projec-
tions by the West. The devouring ferocity of the Chinese American situ-

ation consists in the impossible *version* of it with which the second generation is presented: cultural integrity and economic participation seem
mutually exclusive. One must choose between being like one's parents—ghettoized spiritually and/or physically, confined to the survival
mode—and being accepted only on condition of denouncing one's origins. That is not much of a choice at all.

The essence of consent, as conceptualized by Sollors, is the casting
aside of blood ties (which one cannot choose) so that one can enter
freely into new relations and new ways of life; Necessity, the absence of
voluntariness, is the very antithesis of consent. The Asian American images of coerced eating, especially those connoting cannibalism, thus call
into radical question the supposed universal applicability of the descent-
consent paradigm.

TREATS: THE SEDUCTION OF THE AMERICAN-BORN

If the immigrant generation, like Aunt Emily in *Obasan*, is characterized
by "strong teeth" and a "tough digestion," the American-born may be
said to suffer from a collective "sweet tooth"—a taste for treats. Images
of treats, ranging in tenor from comic to somber, occur in a number of
Asian American literary works; at times confined to scattered observations, they may also function as controlling motifs commenting on the
Asian American condition.[18]

Staples are Necessity; candies, snacks, and fancy foods from stores and
restaurants are Extravagance, going beyond what is needed for survival.
Of course, the definition of "survival" can be quite elastic. The criterion
is not starvation or destitution; what is at issue is the frame of mind of
the character in question. When pursuing the interests of survival, members of the immigrant generation are self-absorbed and single-minded,
indifferent to their reception by whites. Such indifference is part of the
overall desensitization to the environment that enables them to be good
providers. Yet it tends to rankle the American-born, who, because of
their somewhat easier life, often find the elders' caution claustrophobic
and white society's promise of acceptance alluring. They want to be able
to enjoy the good life that they see around them. However, treats do not
come cheap: sometimes the American-born find themselves selling their
birthright for a mess of pottage (Kogawa 1982:184).

In *The Joy Luck Club*, Waverly Jong, chess prodigy and rival of the
chief narrator Jing-Mei, tells of a childhood craving for candy that her
mother has taught her to control. Waverly's family is not deprived in the
strict sense of the word; "Like most of the other Chinese children who
played in the back alleys of restaurants and curio shops, I didn't think we
were poor. My bowl was always full, three five-course meals every day"

(89). There is money for main meals, but impulse buying of "forbidden candies" (89) must be curbed, for it diverts both attention and resources from the serious business of helping the family stay ahead.

> I was six when my mother taught me the art of invisible strength. It was a strategy for winning arguments, respect from others, and eventually, though neither of us knew it at the time, chess games.
>
> "Bite back your tongue," scolded my mother when I cried loudly, yanking her hand toward the store that sold bags of salted plums. (89)

Significantly, when Waverly does heed the lesson and bites back her tongue the next time, her mother quietly buys her the coveted salted plums. Partly a gesture of maternal love, Mrs. Jong's withholding of gratification is also an effective lesson in the primacy of the Necessity principle.

In *The Woman Warrior*, Brave Orchid portrays her offspring as foolish creatures who get drawn to store-bought food. When she takes the family to the airport to meet Moon Orchid, she is equipped as for an expedition. "On the floor she had two shopping bags full of canned peaches, real peaches, beans wrapped in taro leaves, cookies, Thermos bottles, enough food for everybody" (132)—a regular "encampment" (133). That one might look odd spreading out a picnic in an airport concourse is of absolutely no concern to her: what matters is being able to fulfill a physiological need while spending the least amount of money possible. In contrast, her American-born children refuse to be seen eating homemade food in public (132). Instead they allow themselves to be "lured away by the magazine racks and the gift shops and the coffee shops," the "pay TV's or the pay toilets" (132): "Her bad boy and bad girl were probably sneaking hamburgers, wasting their money" (133). The children, then, are more interested in the consumerist aspect of food than the substantive. They take for granted a smooth-running social machinery governing the production and distribution of food, an economic structure over which they have no direct control but in which they place complete trust and feel free to participate.

The American-born's lack of interest in self-sufficiency, like their desire for snack food, indicates a greater openness to American society. Nevertheless, as is shown in the "reparation candy" episode in the final chapter of *The Woman Warrior* (197–99), such an openness may also be a spiritual liability.

Sweets are not entirely absent from Brave Orchid's world, but they always serve a function: to mask the smell of cut-up skunk (106–107); to sweeten the beginning of some enterprise, such as Moon Orchid's husband-reclaiming (140); or to accompany Chinese herbal medicine (199). Once again, one must guard against a hasty culturalist conclusion: obviously, given the decadent excesses to which Chinese cuisine is often given, the Chinese do not lack the concept of treats. The parents buy the children ice cream cones when they can afford to (6), so it is Brave Orchid's customary parsimony, not a Chinese cultural injunction, that prevents her from dispensing candy as treats. However, the example concerning Moon Orchid's visit does bring out an interesting phenomenon: that the cultural meaning of food is capable of overshadowing its actual physical attributes. What attracts Brave Orchid's children to candy is less its sweetness per se than its status as a "useless" Extravagance. Having what they perceive as excessive cultural strings attached to the candy (Brave Orchid vows that she would "make them eat it like medicine if necessary") takes all the fun out of eating it. To resist the utilitarian imposition, they would rather pass it up, causing their mother to marvel: "Who would think that children could dislike candy?" (140). As the American-born narrator attempts to navigate between Necessity and Extravagance, her course complicated by real cultural differences and unequal power relationships between whites and Chinese Americans, she finds herself not only constantly misunderstood but also developing responses that compromise her sense of wholeness and pride.

The "reparation candy" incident concerns a wrong delivery that has been made to Maxine's house by the neighborhood pharmacy. Brave Orchid makes Maxine ask the druggist for candy to remove the curse. The girl finds it impossible to get across the concept: "I felt the weight and immensity of things impossible to explain" (198). Making herself "cute and small," she stammers out the request, but the result turns out to be not only unexpected but humiliating: the druggist thinks the impoverished family is begging for treats that it cannot afford and from then on gives the children candy all year round. In this comedy of errors, one party assigns candy a ritual function, the other can only conceive of candy as a luxury, and Maxine is caught in between. It is because Brave Orchid remains well-schooled in Necessity, is self-contained and utterly oblivious to her environment, that she is able to register the incident as a triumph for her beliefs. Maxine, much more attuned and susceptible to white Americans' condescending views of Chinese, suffers silently; her only means of resistance is to refuse to eat the candy. What is worse, she receives reinforcement in a coping strategy that does little for one's dignity: "No one hurts the cute and small" (198). (When she later tries the opposite strategy—open challenge and vocal protest—she is pointedly ignored by her arrogant white employers [57–58].)

The act of making oneself "cute and small," in order to inflate the sense of power and liberality in those who have control over one's life, is thus associated with the ability to obtain treats. In *The Woman Warrior* the association is minor and occurs through a misunderstanding, but in several other Asian American works it takes on a much darker meaning: that of prostitution.

In Milton Murayama's *All I Asking For Is My Body*, a 1959 novel about a Japanese American family in Hawaii before World War II, the narrator Kiyoshi (Kiyo) befriends Makoto (Makot), the son of a Japanese prostitute catering to Filipino plantation workers. Makot, generally ostracized, tries to buy the friendship of younger children with fancy lunches. Whereas Kiyo's family, headed by a fisherman father, eats fish and rice three times a day (1975:2), Makot is able to give his friends corned beef and onions, Campbell soup (which the narrator gets only when he is sick), pie, ice cream, chow fun (panfried Chinese rice noodles), and candies (4–6). Store-bought, nonstaple food is thus the sign of a margin of comfort beyond subsistence and is naturally tempting to the deprived Kiyo.[19]

The only Japanese family able to indulge regularly in treats is also the only one with curtains, ferns, and flowers in the house as well as a Model T, commodities otherwise exclusive to the *haoles* or whites (10). Although Makot's mother does not directly serve *haole* men, prostitution is depicted as only one of two means by which Asian Americans can gain access to the *haole* life (the other, much more uncertain, being to escape to the mainland, as Kiyo's older brother tries to do through a boxing career). This is so due to the plantation's blatantly exploitative economy, visually represented in the pyramidal structure of the company town in Pepelau: the *haole* overseer's residence at the top; then the nice homes of the Portuguese, Spanish, and Nisei *lunas* (foremen); and at the bottom the identical frame houses of Japanese Camp and Filipino Camp (28). The admission of Nisei into the *luna* class suggests that the American-born may be rewarded with relative material success if they are willing to cut themselves off from their community (which parallels, in a way, the alienation of Makot's mother). Unless they compromise some essential part of themselves, then, Asian Americans are barred from partaking of the good life, which has been held out in promise to all but is in truth reserved for only a few. Kiyo, a Nisei, is potentially vulnerable to being "bought." The dilemma he is caught in—on the one hand drawn to the undeniable pleasures of the treats, on the other constrained by a vague sense of loyalty to "his own kind"—grows out of the immigrant generation's frustrating encounters with America. The metaphoric picture of the Asian American situation provided by alimentary images is thus extended and elaborated to include a longitudinal dimension.

In Lonny Kaneko's short story on Japanese American internment camp life, "The Shoyu Kid" (1976), the linking of prostitution with treats, only oblique in *All I Asking For Is My Body*, is spelled out in a blunt, unsparingly graphic allegory. Three Nisei boys, finding their erstwhile hanger-on, the Shoyu Kid, regularly supplied with chocolate bars, decide to torture him into revealing the source. The source turns out to be a red-headed camp guard, who pays with candy for the Kid's sexual services. Although the three gang members are scandalized by the discovery, they also feel oddly complicit. The end of the story finds them unsettled and defeated, their earlier cockiness evaporated and their innocence lost.[20]

In a wartime setting, the image of the chocolate bar recalls numerous propaganda photographs and film clips of friendly American GI's overseas giving out candy to eager, undernourished children. It evokes at once the enviable plenty of America—that which attracts immigrants from all corners of the world—and the concomitant power that makes domination possible abroad or at home. When juxtaposed with the barbed wire of the internment camp, the chocolate bar image makes a powerful comment on the Asian American situation: it seems that, once Asian Americans quietly accept their confinement and subordination, white America can be generous with material rewards, but the giver of candy is also the holder of the gun, and the threat of force is ever present. The Nisei boys, who are contemptuous of their "too-Japanese" elders, psychologically identify with their oppressors, imitating the swagger of white heroes in cowboy and war movies. At the same time, in being so anxious to find out where the chocolate comes from, they share the weakness of the Shoyu Kid. It is precisely because at heart they do not find the act of prostitution so unthinkable, in view of the rare treat to be had in exchange, that they greet the Kid's revelation with a sense of personal shame no less than moral outrage.

Like Makot's mother in Murayama's novel, the Shoyu Kid is a social outcast at the bottom of a hierarchically organized society. Held together by a combination of militaristic supervision and the tightly regulated distribution of rewards, both the Pepelau plantation and the Minidoka Relocation Center may be construed as the respective author's vision of America, a microcosmic reproduction of the racial stratification in the larger society. The prostitute in each case is, ironically, the one with the most direct access to white wealth and white power, which makes a mockery of the creed of hard work and loyalty preached to and followed by the "good" Asian Americans.

Makot's mother is identifiable as a prostitute by her lipstick worn in broad daylight. The visible sign of the Kid's degradation is more complex. The gang members think that his revolting brown snot is caused by eating too much shoyu, or soy sauce, an essential seasoning in Japanese cooking; to avoid being like the despised Kid, they even stop using shoyu. However, the narrator also suggests that the Kid's snot may have turned brown after he has been able to get chocolate bars from the soldier. What the three boys think of as the Kid's most contemptible trait—his Japanese origin—turns out, then, to be rather the selling-out of that origin. The source of shame is not a congenital handicap but an act of betrayal, both of self and of community.

The question of complicity—that one may, at some deep level, be a willing party to one's own degradation—is explored in the Old Man Gower episode in Kogawa's *Obasan*, which also involves candy and child molestation. Naomi recalls the one secret that divides her from her beloved mother: as a four-year-old child she has been repeatedly fondled by Old Man Gower, a white neighbor who is, ironically, later entrusted with the uprooted family's belongings (69). In his person Old Man Gower embodies the Canadian government's Custodian of Enemy Property; an unmasked Santa Claus with a large, soft belly and a moustache "scratchy as a Christmas tree" (61); and the serpent in an already fallen Garden of Eden, described as a hidden backyard with junglelike, sexually suggestive vegetation (62). The complexity that Kogawa injects into the issue is this: although Old Man Gower does attempt to buy off Naomi and forestall Stephen's discovery with candy (62, 64), Naomi keeps quiet not because of the bribe but because of other, more intangible and disturbing, reasons.

When Old Man Gower offers Naomi toffee, the entire transaction is steeped in ambiguity: "I neither wish nor do not wish to have the candy, but it is more polite to refuse. He thrusts it into my hands" (62). Does a polite refusal or a show of indifference imply that her heart in fact wants the candy, much as the young Maxine craves chocolate chip cookies while disclaiming hunger, as required by Chinese etiquette (Kingston 1977:25)? Does having candy thrust into one's hand constitute true acceptance?

Naomi relates her childhood predicament to a nightmare in which seduction is now seen as originating from the victim, not the perpetrator. When all pretense of material reward for good behavior has fallen away (the Japanese Canadians' property is openly appropriated), only the guns remain: the armed guards of the dream do not give out candy. Like Maxine trying to stay out of harm's way by being "cute and small," the Oriental women in the dream act unthreatening and accommodating:

> The only way to be saved from harm was to become seductive. . . . [T]hree beautiful oriental women lay naked in the muddy road, flat on their backs, their faces turned to the sky. . . . The woman closest by made a simpering coy gesture with her hands. She touched her hair and wiggled her body slightly—seductively. . . . She was trying to use the only weapon she had—her desirability. (61–62)

But the soldiers shoot them anyway, crippling them in the feet. Through the compressed logic of dreams, Old Man Gower's pretext for keeping Naomi—to fix a nonexistent scrape on her knee—is thus exposed as its opposite. There is no defect in being Japanese that can justify the white man's "fixing" or the repeated dispersals allegedly beneficial for their assimilation into Canadian society (*Democracy Betrayed*, 18–20). If there is a "Japanese Canadian problem," it is created by those who stand to gain by appointing themselves to solve it (ibid., 16–18).

Yet Naomi cannot shed her sense of personal responsibility. After the initial encounters, Naomi confesses: "I go to seek Old Man Gower in his hideaway. I clamber unbidden onto his lap. His hands are frightening and pleasurable. In the center of my body is a rift" (65). This same combination of contradictory emotions is repeated when an older Naomi, relocated to Slocan, is molested by a white schoolmate, Percy. Candy is no longer mentioned, just the feelings of "terror and exhilaration," "fascination and danger" (61). The self is divided, at once innocent victim and knowing accomplice.

In the absence of tangible payments, why would a victim submit to debasement? (The Shoyu Kid's arrangement seems so much more businesslike and understandable.) Does being attached to the source of power (if only via exploitation) itself create satisfaction? Are pleasure, exhilaration, and fascination by-products of danger and secrecy, mere alternative labels on the adrenalin rush? What keeps Naomi silent when she knows that her mother is not given to laying blame (60)? Is it loss of faith in her ability to protect? Is it some instinctual urge to separate from one's origins (mother), through transgressions if necessary? How explicitly brutal does the oppressor have to be before prostitution turns into rape? How, eventually, is one to understand the native-born Asian's situation vis-à-vis the dominant society—are they free agents, victims, or accomplices? These are some of the searching questions on complicity raised by Kogawa's handling of the prostitution motif. Since the molestation begins before the outbreak of the Second World War, in a time of relative plenty and ostensible social harmony, it cannot be dismissed as a wartime aberration, as the Shoyu Kid's case might be.

One detail, other than the presence or absence of candy, must be taken into account in any answer: Naomi is four years old, towered over by an old man who whispers in her ear, "Don't tell your mother."[21]

ONE MAN'S STAPLE IS ANOTHER MAN'S TREAT: PROSPECTIVE IMMIGRANTS AT AMERICA'S DOOR

The figure of prostitution is not confined to American-born characters. First-generation characters in Asian American literature have also been depicted as exchanging food for performing sexual services, or at least as acquiescing in a marital arrangement. There does, however, appear to be a major difference between these two sets of instances: in the latter, prospective immigrants sell themselves simply to be able to enter and stay in the United States, an exigency reflected in the no-frills food involved in the transaction. The prize is not something as remote and uncertain as the prospect of assimilation, just the opportunity to lead a less grueling life. The simple creature comforts that the American-born tend to take for granted are an Extravagance. To the hungry, even the most modest fare is a treat.

Bienvenido Santos's "Immigration Blues" (first published 1977) presents the prospective immigrant's plight with a comic touch. Monica, a young teacher in the barrio from the Philippines, is sent for by her sister Mrs. Zafra, who notices with alarm that she has been "getting thinner and more sickly" (1979:13). Monica has overstayed on her tourist visa and is now hounded by the Immigration Service. Mrs. Zafra, more aggressive, less scrupulous, and fatter, descends with Monica in tow on an "o.t." ("oldtimer") with U.S. citizenship, Alipio, and tries to talk the stranger into a "green card marriage." (Between the Philippines' independence in 1946 and the immigration reform of 1965, the immigration quota was set at merely one hundred per year—hence Monica's desperation.) Monica is ashamed of the dubious ethics of the proposed arrangement, but, propelled by Necessity (and her sister), she begins to promote her case by signaling her willingness to eat anything Alipio eats. The hilariously devious three-way negotiation takes place disguised as a chat on food preferences. As Alipio prepares a lunch of unheated canned sardines and raw onions on rice, Mrs. Zafra offers Monica's services as cook, the old man defends his preferences, and Mrs. Zafra prods her reluctant sister into an answer:

> "Monica loves raw onions, don't you, Sis?"
> "Yes," Monica said in a low voice.
> "Your sister, she is well?" Alipio said, glancing toward Monica.
> Mrs. Zafra gave her sister an angry look.
> "I'm okay," Monica said, a bit louder this time.
> "She's not sick," Mrs. Zafra said, "But she's shy. Her own shadow frightens her. I tell you, this sister of mine, she got problems."
> "Oh?" Alipio exclaimed. He had been listening quite attentively.
> "I eat onions, raw," Monica said. "Sardines, too, I like uncooked." (8–9)

Monica is favorably impressed by Alipio's well-stocked kitchen. There are cabinets with cans of "corn beef, pork and beans, vienna sausage, tuna, crab meat, shrimp, chow mein, imitation noodles, and, of course, sardines", two drawers of "bags of rice, macaroni, spaghetti sticks, sugar, dried shrimps wrapped in cellophane, bottles of soy sauce and fish sauce, vinegar, ketchup, instant coffee, and more cans of sardines," and

a freezer "cramped full of meats," mostly lamb chops (which Monica
immediately claims to like as well) (9). This inventory, even though superior to the catalog of pressed-into-service foods in *The Woman Warrior*, consists only of basic victuals. Yet it makes up in quantity what it
lacks in elegance, while the preserved nature of the food—canned, dried,
frozen—spells stability of supply. To the aspiring immigrant, then, the
old man's hoard is awe-inspiring enough to symbolize America's plenty.
(Alipio himself is excited by it. "After all, food meant life, continuing
sustenance, source of energy and health" [9].) Finally, if the sardines
and onions cause the sisters some consternation, it is not as idiosyncratic
or outlandish as it might seem to the non-Filipino reader. The combination, I was told, is common in the Philippines.[22] Thus it is possible that
while Monica initially balks at the dish, she is also reassured by its cultural familiarity.

The prospect of being able to enjoy material security—maybe even to
help out relatives in the Philippines by periodic gift packages, as her sister and brother-in-law have been doing (13)—proves irresistible to
Monica. With a little help from the gentle old man, who accepts the
sudden intrusions into his life with an endearing equanimity, Monica
gradually eases herself into the role of Alipio's bride. Soon the line between rationalized acceptance and genuine enthusiasm, between deliberate accommodation and spontaneous caring, becomes so blurred that
it ceases to matter.

> "Look," Monica said, "I finished everything on my plate. I've never
> tasted sardines this good, especially the way you eat them. I'm afraid I've
> eaten up your lunch. This is my first full meal. And I thought I've lost my
> appetite already." (14)

Whether Monica's and Alipio's marriage will be consummated is left
vague: though disabled, Alipio is said to still have "fire" left in him (16).
Despite this ambiguity, however, Santos's story is a study in the psychology of self-persuasion more than the moral perils of what might be
called "food prostitution." He looks good-naturedly on his characters,
rather like Mrs. Zafra's conveniently tolerant Catholic God, Who is willing to suspend moral niceties when His faithful are desperate for a
"green card" and the better life it promises to bring (13).

The overtones of prostitution become salient only when one reads
"Immigration Blues" against reports of a thriving "mail-order bride"
business in Asian women, especially Filipinas (more likely to be English-
speaking because of America's historical ties to the Philippines); of those
who advertise their availability in "catalogs," most hope to immigrate by
marrying a U.S. citizen, some with the express purpose of helping their
poverty-stricken families. Australia and Europe are desired destinations

as well (Villapando 1989). "Immigration Blues" offers an early and a benign version of a "green card marriage," its mercenary aspect softened partly by the author's comic slant on human foibles, partly by the common cultural understanding and mutual caring between the characters. Yet the potential for abuse in exchange relationships is considerable in the more typical case of the Filipina throwing in her lot with a white man, for there simply exists too great a disparity between the two partners' material conditions—one party has extra while the other has less than enough. The "mail order bride" may, as the protagonist Nina does in Villanueva's story "Opportunity" in the *Ginseng* collection (1991:65–72), maneuver herself into a sense of agency and optimism. She may perceive her Necessitous move as pursuit of Extravagance. (The title says "opportunity"; "opportunity to do what?" is left vague.) But as Nina enters the hotel lobby to meet her American fiancé, she notices the bell boys snickering and whispering *puta*, whore (72): an unwelcome reminder that American economic and cultural colonization of the Philippines forms the backdrop to her supposedly individual and measured decision. To the extent that the most typical cases of Asian immigration to the United States stem from an imbalance of resources writ large in the world economy,[23] it holds in itself the seed of exploitation.[24]

This last point is explored with a disturbing starkness in Bharati Mukherjee's *Jasmine* (1989), a nightmarish tale of an Indian woman's odyssey across the seas and her subsequent absorption into America's sick heartland. Jyoti's circuitous illegal passage to America in various "phantom" vessels requires prostitution: "numbed surrender to various men for the reward of an orange, a blanket, a slice of cheese" (121). Half-Face, the trawler captain who takes Jyoti to a run-down motel upon landing in Florida, also expects sexual slavery from her. "Just you keep it coming and I'm your meal ticket outta here. Give me grief and you're dead meat" (115). The water she begs for comes with rape (which is then repaid with murder). The narrator's common-law marriage to Iowa banker Bud Ripplemeyer is depicted with an almost calculating ambiguity: to the reader "Jane" never reveals her true feelings toward his disabled mate, but hints at the nature of the transaction by recalling that the romance begins when she first arrives in Baden looking visibly famished. ("You need a meal as well as a job, dear" is the way old Mrs. Ripplemeyer brings the exotic-looking woman into Bud's life [196–97].) For all we know (at times food appears more metaphorical than real, and the protagonist's definition of Necessity is so slippery that one suspects her of creating an elaborate self-justifying alibi), Jasmine might be a "food prostitute" like her less articulate sisters. Her case is admittedly an extreme one ridden with unusual circumstances (for example, Jyoti's initial intention is to commit ritual suicide in the United

States, not, as with most undocumented entrants, to seek a better life). For this and many other complex reasons, *Jasmine* has been highly controversial, especially among Indian readers. Nevertheless, if nothing else, the suggestions of "food prostitution" cast an ironic shadow over the American myth of the self-improving immigrant perennially reenacting the Pilgrims' noble mission, which elsewhere in the novel seems to excite and inspire.

Mukherjee is perhaps the first Asian American writer to exhibit a full awareness of the global context of contemporary Asian immigration: she deconstructs cultural clichés, looks beyond the push-pull between two nations to acknowledge the reality of the world economic system, and sets her tales against a background of intertwined, transnational economic activities and mass uprootings caused by proxy wars in the Third World. This global perspective deepens the meaning of images of food and eating found in American segments of the novel. Thus Half-Face is not only an embodiment of pure evil in a metaphysical or "universal" sense (116); he also represents the dark side of America's involvement in Asia. A Vietnam vet disfigured in the war, he cautions Jyoti, "Look, just don't fuck with me. I been to Asia and it's the armpit of the universe" (112). When Mukherjee presents him as wielding power over something as indispensable to life as water, she in effect questions the idea of voluntary immigration and voluntary nation-building that supposedly unites the generations of entrants from all over the world. Whereas, in Santos's short story, involuntariness is happily transformed into voluntariness, an opposite process informs *Jasmine*. Not only does prostitution turn into rape, much more explicitly and violently than in the Asian American stories of second-generation seduction, but "legitimate" marriage itself— defined here by romantic love rather than legal status—shades off into prostitution. It is never entirely clear whether Jane's wifely loyalty stems from genuine caring or from appreciation of Bud as a not-too-degrading "meal ticket." Apart from sex, what Jane offers her husband in return seems to be a less guilt-inducing and more heart-warming image of, and relationship with, Asia. (This last function is also performed by their adopted son Du, a Vietnamese war orphan. Jane feels a sense of camaraderie with Du, a fellow survivor and "big eater" who was kept alive in the refugee camp by a sister's gifts of love: "rats, roaches, crabs, snails" [225]. "Like creatures in fairy tales, we've shrunk and we've swollen and we've swallowed the cosmos whole" [240].)

In "Immigration Blues" the economic, political, and social forces that bring Monica into Alipio's life are muted, assumed in the background. Though hardly hospitable to Filipinos, post–World War II United States is still seen as a more or less sheltered realm with a paternalistic government and a material abundance whose sources and continuity are unquestioned. Immigration restrictions are inconveniences to be cleverly circumvented. The immigration officer is understanding and gentle-manly, like "a salesman for a well-known company in the islands that dealt in farm equipment" (12). In contrast, a sinister shadow falls across the post-Vietnam world of *Jasmine*. When Bud Ripplemeyer is paralyzed by a bankrupt farmer's bullet, his disability is no longer a matter of individual misfortune like Alipio's crippling. Rather, it connotes the decay of the American body politic, its fall from a state of confident strength. American agriculture is vulnerable to global market forces. The producers of food are now "eaten." (In a grisly scene, the body of Darrel Lutz, another bankrupt farmer driven to suicide, is chewed up by his hogs [234–35].) Although disparities in resources still bring Asians (and other Third World peoples) to America's door,[25] a note of desperation has crept into their interactions, on *both* sides. In a world where no corner is exempt from upheavals, the Asian immigrant's place is as precarious as ever. Jane's role of the ministering consort does not last: she must ceaselessly reinvent herself, and no resting place is in sight.

"FOOD PORNOGRAPHY"

Thus far we have identified two major sets of alimentary motifs in Asian American literature: "big eating" to the point of quasi-cannibalism, typically associated with the immigrant generation; and "food prostitution": "selling" oneself for treats in the case of the American-born, for basic foodstuffs in the case of prospective immigrants. In each case a survival strategy (survival being defined with some flexibility, ranging from barely keeping alive to ensuring continued well-being for the family or ethnic community) is shown to be warranted by circumstances but also susceptible to excesses. The ability to obtain food (of varying degrees of desirability and availability) is related to the ability to work around the terms set by powerful others. If the powerful control resources, the powerless must devise means to maximize their resources by either overcoming Necessity or submitting to it. But successful eating often occurs at the expense of spiritual integrity.

There is one other survival strategy of note, one equally capable of going awry and perhaps doubly galling to Asian Americans for historical reasons. Frank Chin calls it "food pornography": making a living by exploiting the "exotic" aspects of one's ethnic foodways. In cultural terms it translates to reifying perceived cultural differences and exaggerating one's otherness in order to gain a foothold in a white-dominated social system. Like exchanging sexual services for food, food pornography is also a kind of prostitution, but with an important difference: superficially, food pornography appears to be a promotion, rather than a vitiation or devaluation, of one's ethnic identity. Whereas, in the case of American-born Asians lured by treats, the implication is that they will become more like whites, food pornographers seem to take pride in their apartness from the mainstream. They seem to be acknowledging and proclaiming, not playing down, their difference. Nevertheless, what they in fact do is to wrench cultural practices out of their context and display them for gain to the curious gaze of "outsiders." If immigrants tend to assimilate "foreign matter" into their own systems and the American-born tend to assimilate to mainstream norms, conceding their own "foreignness," food pornographers (of whatever nativity) are the ones who capitalize on their "foreignness." Their nonassimilation is highly selective and staged, ingratiating rather than threatening. They feed their white patrons "foreign matter" that has been domesticated, "detoxed," depoliticized, made safe for recreational consumption. While Chin's impassioned, almost savage, rhetoric on this subject (see below) leaves little room for a nuanced view of cultural presentation and transformation, it thought-provokingly identifies a persistent strain in Asian American cultural politics.

Not merely a metaphor for cultural processes, the concept of food pornography has a basis in Asian American history, especially Chinese American history. Early Chinese immigrants, driven from the mines and scapegoated by white workers, had to create a niche for themselves by working as cooks (as well as laundrymen and houseboys—in short, by serving). In need of food but barred from fair competition for employment, they could only get fed by preparing food for others. Early on, the Chinese learned that the fastest way to a racist's heart might be through his stomach. From doing "women's work" in white establishments early Chinese Americans moved on to opening their own restaurants, which offered one of the few avenues to an independent livelihood free from white competition. The primary clientele changed from fellow Chinese to whites apparently during the early decades of the Exclusion period. Since then the restaurant trade has continued to be the economic mainstay of Chinese immigrants (Lai, Huang, and Wong 1980:77; Lyman 1974:73–74; Tsai 1986:32, 105, 149; Melendy 1972:53–56). Other Asian American groups, because of their different settlement histories, are less dependent on the restaurant trade, but on the whole the presentation of ethnic cuisine, preferably in an "exotic" setting, provides most Asian immigrant groups with a relatively low-cost entry into business ownership, in the process generating a large number of jobs for fellow immigrants with limited English or technical skills. At one time or another, in one way or another, Asian American groups have all been active in food-related occupations: one thinks of Hawaiian sugar cane plantation workers from Japan, Korea, China, and the Philippines; Chinese and Japanese farmers and fishermen, and Asian Indian farmers in California; Filipino migrant farmworkers in California and cannery workers in Alaska; grocery store owners (the latest wave being Koreans in the fruit and vegetable retail business); and more recently, Vietnamese fishermen and Hmong farmers. But the restaurant trade apparently has the greatest staying power, because it can install itself in the interstices of major economic trends.

Although cooking and serving food for a living is extremely common in human societies, for ethnic Americans both European and non-European, the activity does not merely entail a matter-of-fact exchange of food for money. The majority of mainstream patrons would also expect the dining experience to be a cultural excursion that is at once adventurous and tame, leaving their sense of cultural superiority intact at the end. In general, offering ethnic food to someone from an outgroup may be a genuine gesture of sharing, like asking a guest to enjoy grandma's home cooking from treasured family recipes. "At a symbolic level, eating foods across groups suggests crossing or even breaking down social boundaries" (Kalcik 1984:50). But in a commercial context, given the current state of race relations in the United States, the symbolic meaning of inclusiveness cannot operate in ethnic restaurants that cater to an outgroup clientele. What appears to be hospitable acceptance of the outsider is really the ethnic's appeal for acceptance by the mainstream customer, who has the power to decide what is agreeably authentic and what is unthinkably outlandish. As a result, ethnics in the food trade often find themselves forced to play up stereotypes of their own group. Roger Abrahams writes: "Paradoxically, the very act of food preparation and cooking may simultaneously proclaim and undermine ethnicity. . . . The foods being served up to the public are often the very ones focused on in the stereotype of the ethnic in the past ages" (1984:26).

The degree to which the restaurant business may debase one's ethnicity is a function of the group's place in American society, of the projected compatibility of its culture with the mainstream. To the extent that Asian Americans occupy a lower position than European ethnics in the social hierarchy, their exoticism is felt as more intense: more fascinating but also potentially more evil. The sense of lurking danger about Asian cuisines can be titillating to mainstream American patrons: it can heighten their enjoyment, which has to be wrested from initial skepticism if not outright revulsion. The following sketch on chop suey eating, written in 1987 by a white "guide" to Chinatown, reveals the racist mentality that the restaurant trade must learn to play to:

> Take a friend to Chinatown for the first time and watch his face when the savory chop-suey arrives. He looks suspiciously at the mixture. He is certain it has rats in it, for the popular superstition that the Chinese eat rats is inbred. . . .

He quickly puts aside the Chop stickes [*sic*], which are evidently pos-
sessed of the devil, and goes at the stuff with a fork. It is a heroic effort, but
it is not sustained. The novice gets a mouthful or two, turns pale, all the
time declaring that it is "great."

It is a long time before he can be persuaded to go again, but he is sure
to surrender eventually to the enchanting decoction. . . . For a while he
half believes there must be "dope" in the stuff. He is now certain there are
no rats in it. He is a confirmed chop-suey eater. (R. Yu 1987:8)

With the spread of Asian cuisines in recent decades and a corresponding increase in customer sophistication, this account has acquired an air
of quaintness. Yet the attitude toward Asian Americans underlying it has
far from dissipated; it repeatedly resurfaces in periods of national insecurity, as demonstrated by stories of dog-eating Vietnamese refugees,
which have persisted since the group's settlement in the United States
after the Vietnam War (Kalcik 1984:37); or by a *Newsweek* article entitled "Pass a Snake, Hold the Rat," appearing a propos of nothing, in
which "unusual" animal dishes served in China are rated (Liu 1991).
That stories of dog-eating coexist with the growing popularity of Asian
restaurants is no contradiction. Asian restaurant owners make their living on the knife-edge between novelty and familiarity, risk and comfort.
Their battle with reluctant palates is not unlike the collective struggle
that Asian Americans have to undertake in order to maintain a viable
identity. Even in the post-1965 era, when *diversity* and *pluralism* are the
new catchwords, catholicity of taste, whether culinary or cultural, still
has an edge of exploitation to it.

We become equal-opportunity eaters, especially in situations where we can
sample unaccustomed foods while standing and walking around, as at a
festival. This appears, in historical perspective, to be an extension of a capitalist approach to life in which exploitation of subordinated peoples is not
only expressed in terms of labor but also in appropriating their cultural
styles, including their ways of cooking and eating (Abrahams 1984:23).

Asian Americans may be haunted by the phrase "strange people but they
sure can cook" (Kalcik, 37), finding themselves valued only in those
areas of life where they are allowed to tend to the needs of the dominant
group.

THE MAMA FU FU COOKBOOK

As might be expected, the coiner of the term *food pornography* is the
most incisive analyst of the phenomenon. Frank Chin's play *The Year of
the Dragon* (1981; first produced 1974) is a dazzling study of food pornography; in his hands alimentary images become complex metaphors,

commenting on aspects of Chinese American life ranging from family relationships to the art of writing, from cultural transmission to ethnic entrepreneurship.

The protagonist, Fred Eng, is a Chinatown tour guide exemplifying the survival strategy of food pornography (which, it should be clear by now, also stands for cultural pornography). He becomes top guide by pandering to the worst fantasies of gawking tourists, feeding them appropriate doses of "foreignness" in his double capacity as confiding friend and trained professional. His parodic sales pitch on Chinese food is a masterful evocation of contradictory stereotypes about the Chinese—the gracious, solicitous Oriental host and the vice lord promising wicked delights; the healing herbalist and the fiendish brewer of mysterious potions; the harmless cheap laborer and the formidable purveyor of imperial glamour.

> You wanna know where to go eat in Chinatown, I betcha.
>
> . . .
>
> I'm telling you right now. Only ninety-nine restaurants and suey shops in
>   Chinatown. I eating in every one and can telling you, it's TRUE! What
>   you hear about . . .
> Cantonese sweet'n'sour goes straight to your scrotum.
> Pekingese goo makes you dream in 3-D.
> Shanghai hash cures blind drunkenness and raises your I.Q. six points!
> And the universal peanut grease
>   of the Chinatown deepfry lights up
>   every nerve of your body,
>   from your vitals to your fingertips
>   in a glittering interior chandelier
>   glowing you up so nice and so warm,
> Chinatown all you can eat faw two dollar fi'ty cen' is all you can eat. (77)

Fred's practice of food pornography is shown as stemming directly from struggles between the immigrant and his children;[26] it is a stopgap solution devised to satisfy the conflicting demands of Necessity and Extravagance in the short run. The ailing elder Mr. Eng (Pa), a solid citizen of Chinatown like Johnny's father in "Food for All His Dead" (of which the play is an greatly elaborated and expanded version), wants his "number one son" to continue his travel and tour business after his death. An unquestioning believer in Necessity, he sees absolutely no redeeming value in the creative efforts of Fred, a talented aspiring writer whose ambition is to create the "great Chinese American novel" (83). To Pa, Fred's writing is child's play, mere fooling around, irresponsible craziness. "You gimme you story. Torty year ol' you come home, what you show for it? T'ree stupi' page in a cheap book?" (109). "Nobody read dat stuff" (137). Feeling defeated, Fred gives up his dreams to become a Chinatown tour guide. "Blabbing at the tourists is as close to writing I can do without Chinatown hating me" (109). Even so Pa is disappointed: "I gib you travoo agen's meck you some responsiboo what happening? You run aroung like doze tour guys you hire. . . . You never be famous. Wasting time!" (109).

Unable to communicate with his father because of profound differences in outlook as well as language, Fred realizes that "food's our only common language" (85): if there is any love between parent and child, it can only be expressed silently through special dishes, not through words. On the other hand, both Chinese food and English words can reach the white tourist. Fred hits upon an idea: Why not combine the two to make a fortune? He collaborates with his outmarried sister Mattie (who has a barometer of white taste in her Orientalia-loving husband, Ross) to create the "great Chinese American Cookbook" (83). "Your recipes and my smut knocked me out, Sis. You invented a new literary form. Food pornography . . ." (86). Instead of the great Chinese American novel that no one reads, Fred will write "a book of recipes telling the story of a Chinatown family" (86). The print medium promises to fix the ephemeral, local form of the tour guide's spiel and sell it to a national audience. In an appropriate spirit of self-deprecating (but at heart vengeful) shucking, the cookbook is to be named the Mama Fu Fu Cookbook, *mama fufu* being Cantonese for "perfunctory," "sloppy," or "mediocre." The team envisions "a chain of Mama Fu Fu's. Franchises. Mail order . . . A syndicated column . . . Frozen food . . ." (118). Eventually, Sis reminds Fred, he may be able to retire on the income from the Mama Fu Fu project and return to serious writing (81). He may also be able to get Ma and his young brother Johnny out of Chinatown. Fred is excited by the possibility of permanently freeing himself from Necessity by a temporary indenture to it. The plot of the play is propelled by his hesitations about promising Pa to stay in Chinatown after his death.

As the name Mama Fu Fu implies, Fred's scheme is doomed because it is by nature makeshift and phony. At the end of the play Fred is back to hawking "local color" (79) of the most demeaning sort.

> You don't feel comfortable about eating in a neighborhood that shows no
>   cats.
> The dogs here don't look healthy. And you seen garbage climb out of the
>   trash wearing the clothes of old dead men.
> And act like bums.
> Makes you wonder what Chinamans eat, don't it
> I know the feeling . . .
> BAD FEELING. (142)

The references to the stereotype of cat- and dog-eating Asians recall other Chinese American stories we have examined that portray attachment to pets (farm animals, "dove birds," crabs) as an indulgence disdained by the hard-boiled immigrant generation.

Nonprofessional "Food Pornographers"

To the extent that Fred's peddling of bastardized ethnic food is a means of livelihood, one can speak of the Mama Fu Fu enterprise as adaptation and consider *The Year of the Dragon* a reflection of a certain stage in the economic development of the Chinese American community. But to the extent that food pornography represents a stance toward white society characterized by simultaneous dependence and subversion, it also implies a certain limited vision of Chinese American community—one that cannot yet conceive of, or cannot yet take for granted, a robust culture created and maintained by free-acting, self-possessed men and women. Such a vision, though originating with the Chinese with their early involvement in food services, is by no means confined to them. Since white society tends to treat all Asians alike (the derogatory *Chink* is "generic"), the kind of identity conflict embodied by Fred Eng is experienced by many Asian Americans who believe, rightly or wrongly, that they have to choose between being "somebody" in a closed, suffocating ethnic community and being "nobody" in the larger, more hostile white world (116–17). How many Asian Americans actually feel this way, how acutely they feel it, how soon or how thoroughly they give up the search for an alternative, how readily they take on the role of cultural comprador, how closely they allow their means of livelihood to be tied to such a role—all fluctuate with the vicissitudes of Asian American history. It is safe to say, however, that Fred's dilemma represents a widespread phenomenon that is likely to persist for some time to come.

Thus it is that we find versions of the food pornographer in Asian American literature since at least the 1930s and up to at least the mid-1980s. These characters differ from Fred Eng in that they are nonprofessional—that is, they practice food pornography in personal relationships (including relationships with an intended reader) rather than in their occupations. They also differ from each other in their attitude toward the role: some take it on good-naturedly, others shamelessly, still others in desperation. However, their strategies for winning white attention and favor show a fundamental commonality.

Korean American writer Younghill Kang's fictionalized autobiography, *East Goes West* (1937), shows an interesting early example of food pornography. Chungpa Han, the protagonist who has left Japanese-occupied Korea for intellectual adventures in the West, uses his familiarity with New York's Chinatown to woo his Caucasian dream girl, Trip.[27] He takes her to an ornate Chinese restaurant, buys her Chinese teas and preserved fruits in a small shop, and goes down into a cellar to get Chinese wine. (The narrative is set during Prohibition, which lasted from 1919 to 1933.) While Trip is waiting for him outside, she is questioned by a detective who is doing his duty to "protect American girls in Chinatown." The adventure excites her: it confirms her image of Chinatown as a titillating den of iniquity. "Marvellous! detectives! danger! Just what you expect from Chinatown, and never get" (345–46). When Trip gets home, she shows off her gifts to her roommates and flaunts her newfound expertise in things Oriental: "All different kinds of mysterious things, and there is one thing—a little ugly black thing—when you break it between your teeth—you taste a marigold's smell—not at first, but slowly and gradually" (345–46). Though the episode is rendered in a light-hearted, self-mocking tone, as befits the fantasy nature of Han's unsuccessful (in retrospect, impossible) courtship, it is reminiscent of the more blatantly condescending account of the "chop suey eater," whose initial misgivings are transformed into delight under the guidance of a friendly insider.

A piece of advice given to Chungpa Han by Kim, a talented but luckless fellow exile (Kim eventually takes his own life after a frustrated love affair with a highborn New England woman), epitomizes the kind of self-Orientalizing cultural stance of which food pornography is a common manifestation.[28] "You have to eat. And to eat, you must enter into the economic life of Americans. Listen then. . . . In making a living, Oriental scholarship may help you more than your American education. . . . *You must be now like a Western man approaching Asia*" (276–77; italics added). The comparative scholarship that Kim advocates, involving self-alienation and adoption of the foreigner's gaze, may be considered merely a subtler, more elegant version of food pornography.

The variety of nonprofessional food pornography found in *East Goes West* also appears in Chinese American writer Chuang Hua's *Crossings* (1968; rpt. 1986). In this modernist novel about a deracinated upper-class Chinese American woman's "wanderings and homecomings" (187), the narrator (known as Fourth Jane in the family) is shown trying to save a waning affair by a series of home-cooked dinners. Although the setting for this given instance of food pornography is Europe (where Fourth Jane does some of her wandering), the narrator suffers from a recognizably Asian American identity problem (121–22), and her use of ethnic food to win the heart of her white lover is reminiscent of Chungpa Han's attempt to impress Trip. Both protagonists do not feel they can be appreciated for what they are, since their white lovers have

certain preconceptions about their Asian background. That Chungpa
Han can show Trip around Chinatown vastly overshadows the fact that
he is well-versed in Western literature from Shakespeare to T. S. Eliot.
Fourth Jane's lover goes as far as to deplore her "Americanness" (which
she cannot have avoided), preferring to think of anyone of Chinese ancestry as simply "Chinese" and belonging only in China (120).

At the beginning, the alimentary images have no particular ethnic
connotations; after all, the association of eating with sensuality or seduction is not only common in mainstream Western literature from *Tom
Jones* to *Ulysses* but arguably "universal" (Mote 1977:195–257). When
Fourth Jane prepares special dishes (*Crossings*, 24, 61, 67, 97) as "offerings" (117) to her none-too-enthusiastic lover, she joins the ranks of
numerous mistresses, East and West, who have hoped to tie down their
men by creating the illusion of home with gastronomic feats. However,
as it becomes increasingly clear that the journalist has no interest at all
in deeper attachments, and that he has expected her to be more of a
Chinese and less of a drifting exile (120), Fourth Jane abandons West-
ern-style cooking. She resorts to her pièce de résistance: Chinese-style
duck, marinaded in "honey, salt and pepper, crushed ginger and garlic,
chopped scallion, soy sauce, and . . . sherry and bourbon" (116), and
slowly roasted in the oven. The silent message Fourth Jane is sending to
her man is that she is no waif. She is not a "generic" woman interchangeable with other warm bodies but someone who can divert him
with a unique array of culture novelties; cosmopolitan as she appears,
what little she has retained of her ancestral culture should suffice to mark
her as different and therefore more worthy of favor. Her culinary labor
of love is, for God's sake, *ethnic*. (The *Tao Te Ching* in translation that
Jane tries unsuccessfully to read to him serves the same purpose [116,
118].)[29] This mentality, though expressed in the context of a love affair,
is clearly an analog of the professional Chinatown tour guide's and
shares with the latter a wider applicability: an inclination to justify one's
existence as an Asian American by appealing to white taste for exotica.

In addition to literary works showing characters who practice food pornography in romantic relationships, we also find autobiographies in
which the narrator takes the white reader on a verbal gastronomic tour.
Pardee Lowe's *Father and Glorious Descendant* (1943) and Jade Snow
Wong's *Fifth Chinese Daughter* (1945) both contain descriptions of
Chinese meals, taking pains to explain the ritualistic significance of certain meals and folk beliefs about the medicinal properties of certain ingredients. In *Father and Glorious Descendant*, in addition to brief paragraphs on the dishes for seasonal district and family association banquets
(46), Chinese New Year's (69–70), and Father's birthday feast (315),

Lowe devotes a chapter to the family's comic encounter with "wildcat soup," a tonic meant to increase one's strength and vigor (259–66). *Fifth Chinese Daughter* is even more openly solicitous in anticipating the white reader's curiosities. The obligatory disquisition on Chinese New Year delicacies (39–45) is augmented by a lengthy section on Chinese housewifery (which includes tips on how to cook perfect rice and salvage burnt rice) (56–62); an account of a dinner for the narrator's college friends (which details the proper way to cook egg foo yung and tomato beef, accurate to the tablespoonful) (159–62); and a chapter on a "rediscovered" Chinatown herb shop, complete with an elucidation of the Chinese theory of humors (217–25).

A remark that the narrator lets fall reveals the eagerness for acceptance that motivates the food pornographer: "Within half an hour, her comrades had raised Jade Snow high in their estimation. To be worthy of this new trust, Jade Snow racked her brains to decide what dishes she could cook without a Chinese larder" (158). Although Jade Snow's friends are not exclusively Caucasian, it is obvious that the primary object of her brain-racking is not to cement her friendship with the handful of fellow Chinese students. Jade Snow is unlikely to forget that she enters exclusive Mills College under the patronage of its president, who "has had a lifelong interest in Oriental people" (148). Her scholar's status may distinguish her from the "entirely Chinese" kitchen staff, "some of them descendants of the first Chinese kitchen help who worked for the founders of the college" (158). However, her acutely felt sense of inferiority to the white students, who are there "naturally," unbeholden to well-meaning Christian sponsors, places her closer to the kitchen help than she might care to admit. Her statement that "Mills living [is] democratic living in its truest sense" (158) leaves one wondering what role kindness to subordinates plays in her definition of true democracy.

When Fred Eng in *The Year of the Dragon* speaks bitterly of writing "a book of recipes telling the story of a Chinatown family" (86), he is obviously alluding to *Fifth Chinese Daughter*. In his 1978 short story, "Railroad Standard Time" (rpt. 1988), Frank Chin sums up his impressions of *Father and Glorious Descendant*, *Fifth Chinese Daughter*, and Virginia Lee's *The House That Tai Ming Built* (1963) with a caustic tirade against the popular "Chinatown book" filled with food—and cultural—pornography:

> Part cookbook, memories of Mother in the kitchen slicing meat paper-thin with a cleaver. Mumbo jumbo about spices and steaming. The secret of Chinatown rice. The hands come down toward the food. The food crawls with culture. The thousand-year-old living Chinese meat makes dinner a

safari into the unknown, a blood ritual. Food pornography. Black magic. Between the lines, I read a madman's detailed description of the preparation of shrunken head. (F. Chin 1988:3)

FOOD AS ETHNIC SIGN: AN EXCURSUS ON READING AND ETHNIC SEMIOSIS

The very concept of food pornography raises an interesting issue: since Asian food necessarily differs from mainstream American food, perhaps one cannot even make a factual description of the former, let alone serve it to an "outsider," without seeming to point up the contrast. Which would mean, then, that our food pornographers could be innocent, their alleged complicity having been read into an originally matter-of-fact narrative moment. This is especially true of the autobiographers, who work with a form commonly defined by its referentiality. In the case of *Father and Glorious Descendant*, for example, the Cantonese are indeed partial to "tonic foods" (*bupin*), wildcat and snake among them. And unlike the restaurant meals on Fred Eng's tours, the birthday banquet exists as a cultural institution cementing relationships *within* the ethnic group; symbolic foods (like noodles for longevity and sweetmeats for "sweetening one's life") communicate clearly understood messages between participants. As cultural anthropology, Lowe's book is quite accurate. In *Fifth Chinese Daughter*, when the mother teaches Jade Snow how to cook rice, she does so as an expert-insider passing her cultural competence on to an apprentice-insider; a simple, mimetic narrative reprisal of the act would have produced the "pornographic" episode that incenses Frank Chin so much.

It is a commonplace in foodways studies that food is an ethnic sign. As Brown and Mussell note in the Introduction to their anthology, *Ethnic and Regional Foodways in the United States: The Performance of Group Identity* (1984):

> Foodways bind individuals together, define the limits of the group's outreach and identity, distinguish in-group from out-group, serve as a medium of inter-group communication, celebrate cultural cohesion, and provide a context for performance of group rituals. (5)

> Mainstream Americans frequently use foodways as a factor in the identification of subcultural groups and find in the traditional dishes and ingredients of 'others' who eat differently from themselves a set of convenient ways to categorize ethnic and regional character. (3)

(One should add, too, that foodways stereotyping occurs both ways: ethnic Americans are just as fond of ridiculing mainstream Americans' taste in food, or their lack thereof. This is especially true in an era when consuming highly processed prepared foods is identified by many immigrants with an "American" way of life, one notably long on technical wizardry but short on felt quality.) In this light, it seems inevitable that any representation of food practices in ethnic literature would involve an element of display. Furthermore, in autobiographical discourse, the narrator naturally assumes an explicatory stance toward the reader. If an Asian autobiographer writes in English at all, the intended audience must include white readers, so that accounts of ethnic foods and eating habits may well be seen as an exercise of authorial responsibility. On what basis, other than intuition, does one identify the workings of food pornography? Is food pornography "read into" the text or "read out of" it? The question concerns more than "fairness" toward the characters and/or the authors. Ultimately it concerns ethnic semiosis; how one conceptualizes the operations of ethnic signs will shape how one approaches ethnic American literature as a reader.

The question may be answered from three perspectives, corresponding to the three modes of reading already touched on at the beginning of this chapter, in connection with the image of stone bread. To begin with, food pornography may be identified *intra*textually. One may, for example, examine the phrasing in descriptions of ethnic foodways, to determine the character's stance toward the guest or the author's stance toward the reader. In *Father and Glorious Descendant*, when Lowe writes of Chinese New Year's: "Instead of a one-day feast as at Thanksgiving, we had then fourteen consecutive days of feasting" (69), it is apparent that he is not simply reminiscing about childhood but is illustrating a point of cultural contrast for an American audience. When he refers to "the Chinese prototype of *Sukiyaki*" (70), eschewing the Cantonese term *da bin louh* (in Mandarin *huoguo*) or even the translation "hot pot" or "firepot" (*huoguo*), he is obviously not trying to avoid cluttering up his storytelling with foreign words. *Sukiyaki* is itself foreign; the adoption of one Asian term to gloss another betrays a concern for the mainstream reader's mental comfort, since Japanese sukiyaki happens to be more familiar to the American public (probably as a result of U.S. involvement in Asia during World War II and the occupation of Japan afterward). Nor can the word choice be motivated by a desire for conciseness; at other times, for comic effect, Lowe is quite free with lengthy circumlocutions based on excessively literal translations from the Chinese (e.g., 227, 247). Textual clues such as these hint at a "tourist guide" habit of mind on the part of the author: to supply the white reader with amusing but not too taxing glimpses of the mysterious ways of the Chinese. An intratextual approach is hardly novel—if anything it may smack of regressiveness when applied to the literatures of people of color—yet its role bears reiteration, for Asian American literature has only recently begun to be read with the kind of attentiveness to detail traditionally accorded the Anglo-American canon.

The presence of food pornography is also determined *inter*textually, with the prototypic Fred Eng supplying a point of reference for the weaker versions of the food pornographer. Each component of the intertextual cluster alludes to, comments upon, clarifies, and qualifies the others. As the distinct motif coalesces from this process, it simultaneously reinforces each supporting example by sharpening the common core meaning. What in isolation appears inchoate or tangential is now given focus, gains a dimension of significance. For instance, Fourth Jane is a marginal specimen of the type; the issues of ethnic identity implicit in her duck-roasting emerge with greater clarity only when her action is read alongside those of other, more clearly Asian American and often more unabashed food pornographers. Yet the example from *Crossings* is not merely parasitic: rather, the European setting of the episode, the anti-American bias of the white lover, Fourth Jane's upper-class émigré background, all so different from what one finds in the other examples of food pornography, accentuate the prevalence and inveterateness of the practice among Asian Americans all the more. This in turn amplifies the *Crossings* example, lifting it from the stream of minutiae that document the disintegrating romantic relationship.

Finally, and perhaps most importantly, *con*textual considerations are crucial to a proper identification of food pornography, as they are in any attempt to interpret literary representations of ethnic foodways. Food pornography consists not in any particular menu of intrinsically "pornographic" or even intrinsically "ethnic" items but in a certain posture of presentation. This ingratiating posture, having arisen in response to a set of oppressive interracial relationships, cements it in turn by reassuring the patron that the unsettling implications of "eating ethnic" can be arrested. Mary Douglas writes in her seminal essay on the semiotics of food, "Deciphering a Meal":

> If food is treated as a code, the messages it encodes will be found in the pattern of social relations being expressed. The message is about different degrees of hierarchy, inclusion and exclusion, boundaries and transactions across the boundaries. Like sex, the taking of food has a social component, as well as a biological one. Food categories therefore encode social events. (1972:61)

To determine whether a literary act of food-sharing across ethnic boundaries is "pornographic," it is essential to attend to the place in the American "hierarchy" occupied by each of the ethnic groups; the way each is empowered to exercise "inclusion" and "exclusion"; and the extent to which the characters in the transaction embody these social forces at work. It is because Asian Americans have been assigned to a specific position and set of symbolic functions in the American hierarchy of ethnic groups—not merely because their food is "different" from mainstream American food—that food pornography becomes a concern for the authors. Alone, the term *difference* is insufficient to capture the many issues of "hierarchy" that may be expressed in interethnic food transactions.

This more dynamic and contextualized perspective on the meaning of food as ethnic marker may be illustrated in two ways: through a transcultural historical account of "exotic" Asian food of the kind frequently featured in literary food pornography; and through contrast with a European ethnic example.

If Lowe's "pornographic" wildcat soup is reminiscent of Brave Orchid's Necessitous turtle or skunk, the association is not fortuitous. Both are links in a long process of alimentary evolution originating in the eating habits of the old country. It has often been said that China's poverty is responsible for the inventiveness of its cuisine: according to Jacques Gernet, "undernourishment, drought and famines" have compelled the Chinese to "make judicious use of every possible kind of edible vegetable and insect, as well as of offal" (quoted in K. Chang 1977:13). Though some experts are dubious of a simple cause-effect relationship, it is safe to say that even those food practices born of privations have in time been absorbed into a sophisticated gastronomic "high culture," whose excesses have outraged many Chinese themselves. When the Chinese emigrate to America, the eating of "unusual" foods, with its dual connotation of brutalizing poverty and refined gourmandism, is not only encouraged by actual physical hardships (as noted above in the section on "big eaters") but dovetails into the American symbolic economy. The former connotation reinforces the white stereotype of Chinese as an outlandish, almost subhuman, race; the latter fits into the image of an overripe civilization that can teach the puritanical young nation a thing or two about sybaritic pleasures. Food pornography is born and sustained in such a context. Frank Chin sums up this complex development in "Railroad Standard Time":

> I read a list of what I remembered eating at my grandmother's table and knew I'd always be known by what I ate, that we come from a hungry tradition. Slop eaters following the war on all fours. Weed cuisine and mud gravy in the shadow of corpses. We plundered the dust and fungus. Buried things. Seeds plucked out of the wind to feed a race of lace-boned skinnys, in high-school English, become transcendental Oriental art to make the dyke-ish spinster teacher cry. (1988:3)

The same "unusual" food, then, can assume multiple meanings both within the Chinese tradition and in the Chinese American setting. Even such a historicized understanding, however, cannot exhaust the symbolic uses to which food may be put in the "micro" context of person-to-person interactions. As Kalcik notes in her enlightening discussion of ethnic foodways, "The symbol system is flexible in that symbols can be replaced, different symbols can perform the same function, and the same symbol can change its function" (1984:45). Thus in *The Joy Luck Club*, we find an episode in which food pornography is turned on its head to signal its antithesis: resistance to exoticization. As a child, Waverly Jong roams the streets of Chinatown, where she has to suffer endless camera-touting tourists. Once, after a particularly obnoxious Caucasian man has posed her and her playmates with a roast duck ("its head dangling from a juice-covered rope"), Waverly wreaks her revenge by recommending an authentic Chinese restaurant. When the intrigued tourist asks what it serves, Waverly shouts "Guts and duck's feet and octopus gizzards!" and runs away shrieking with laughter (Tan 1989:91). Waverly's list, though "pornographic" in appearance and also colored by the child's natural glee at the chance to gross out adults, represents in fact an act of ethnic counteraggression. It mixes factual description ("guts" and "duck's feet" are perfectly normal fare to the Chinese) with deliberate exaggeration (there is no such thing as "octopus gizzards") to convey the speaker's spite at the cultural voyeur. Like the restaurant menu printed only in Chinese, it is used to exclude the unwelcome intruder.

Later in Waverly's life, at the Wu family's crab feast, Mrs. Lindo Jong challenges Waverly's Caucasian fiancé to eat the crab butter, a delicacy to the Chinese. "Why you are not eating the best part?" she demands of Rich and promptly proceeds to demonstrate how to pick the brain out of the shell (203). As expected, both Rich and Waverly react with disgust, which is precisely what Lindo intends to draw out. Under the "pornographic" guise of educating her future son-in-law in Chinese gourmandism, Lindo is actually showing her displeasure at the interracial union: she wants to emphasize the cultural chasm between the two young people, imply that Rich is not sincerely interested in her daughter (otherwise he would have learned to eat Chinese), expose Waverly's poor judgment, maybe even disclaim responsibility before her Joy Luck Club friends for Waverly's failure to remain Chinese. Lindo's flaunting of (to whites) "revolting" food habits, if more subdued than Waverly's, is no less than hers a gesture of exclusion.

In response to Lindo's statement, "See how this one doesn't know how to eat Chinese food," Waverly retorts, "Crab isn't Chinese" (203). The daughter is right, of course, in a technical sense; what she misses (perhaps intentionally, since such things are notoriously immune to rational counterargument, especially when they come from one's mother) is the fact that food is not inherently or statically "ethnic." Rather, food may be *used* either ethnically or nonethnically, as the participants see fit and the nature of the social relationship dictates. Lindo exemplifies what Kalcik calls the "performance of [ethnic] identity"—an interactive process in which the ethnic identities of the participants are advertised, communicated, negotiated, compared and contrasted, defined and redefined, through foodways (1984:37, 44). Despite the "pornographic" associations of the crab butter, then, Lindo is not a food pornographer. Only context allows us to determine this with reasonable assurance; a fixed "menu" is of little help. As William Boelhower repeatedly stresses in *Through a Glass Darkly* (1984), "Context and not content must ultimately serve as the epistemological touchstone" (1987:33). Ethnic discourse is ethnic not because it partakes of a cultural "encyclopedia" semantically, but because pragmatic realization by the subject creates a "spatio-temporal moment of ethnic semiosis" (what Boelhower calls the "frame") (90, 92).

Boelhower's concept of the "ethnic feast" provides another occasion for clarifying the central role of context in the reading of alimentary images in Asian American literature; this time, however, his discussion serves a contrastive, not confirmatory, function. Boelhower sees the ethnic feast as "perhaps one of the best and most transparent literary *topoi*" for examining the grammar of ethnic sign production (1987:113). Drawing on Italian American examples, he characterizes the ethnic feast as a codified event where ethnic identity is "positively affirmed and socially reinforced" (113), the "raw data" of the ethnic encyclopedia is transformed for communal consumption (114), and the American-born children are put through an "apprenticeship" in "ethnic know-how" as manifested in recipes and rituals (115). He also notes that the ethnic feast can be "put to various *ad hoc* uses," mainly for the edification of the second generation (116).

Much of this, of course, is reminiscent of *Father and Glorious Descendant* or *Fifth Chinese Daughter*, to the extent that Italian Americans and Chinese Americans are both "ethnic," their cultural institutions share certain affinities. But from Boelhower's list of ad hoc uses of the ethnic feast, the "pornographic" is conspicuously absent, for the obvious reason that Italian Americans as a group, despite having been subjected to stereotyping and discrimination, have not been called upon to justify their very existence by the purveyance of exoticism. In contrast, Asian Americans, especially Chinese Americans, have been routinely reduced to such a role. The topos of the feast in Italian American literature thus appears more purely celebratory; the ethnicity-affirming tone in the instances of Asian American food pornography, on the other hand, often contains traces of ingratiation. Boelhower describes the ethnic feast as "a rather clearly circumscribed ethno-semiotic activity" (117), but for an ethnic group whose every move is in danger of being viewed as a picturesque tourist attraction, the circumscription is perhaps more apparent than real.

Though rightly preoccupied with context in his theoretical generalizations, in his actual reading of Italian American representations of food and eating Boelhower has imperceptibly shifted his attention from the surrounding society (matters of "hierarchy" and "boundaries") to the internal cohesion of the ethnic community. One can perhaps afford to do so with the literature of European ethnics, for whom "genealogical ordering and interrogation" (112) is judged by the mainstream to be an honorable, even enviably enriching, project, but for Asian Americans a different set of pressures obtains. Given this fundamental difference in sociohistorical context, Asian American alimentary images have acquired unique nuances of meaning, such as those of food pornography, which would be obscured by an essentialist mode of reading that scans the text for static markers of ethnicity.

OF DOUGHNUTS AND HOT POTS: VISIONS OF "RIGHT EATING"

With alimentary images being the focus of so much negative energy, one may justifiably wonder whether Asian American literature offers representations of food and eating that exemplify free choice, wholeness, communality, dignity. If, as we have seen, alimentation represents "a manner of interpreting the world and integrating oneself with it" (Tucker 1984:4 n. 11), a vision of what might be called "right eating"[30] would in fact imply a vision of an America in which Asian Americans are no longer plagued by a painful dialectic of outside/inside, foreign/native, other/self, but are free to fulfill a natural appetite in a natural place among equals.

The very posing of such a possibility, of course, already presupposes a fall from grace: it is precisely the imputation of foreignness, outsiderhood, otherness to the group that has precipitated this sense of disequilibrium in Asian American literature. For this reason ethnic "comfort food," lovingly recalled in a number of Asian American literary works (e.g., Sone 1979:75–77; D. Lum 1980:38–43: Ng 1986:335–37; W. Lum 1987c:91–92), cannot be the endpoint of the search for right eating as long as it is thought of as a counterpoise to "American" eating. At best it can only catalyze a meditation on the nature of such a desire. The narrator in Ng's "A Red Sweater" retains tenuous gustatory links to her ethnic culture, but her memories of Chinese food are too enmeshed in memories of painful Necessity to reinstate her in existential plentitude. The only alternative she can conceive of is dining out Western style: letting the trappings of material luxury mask any misgivings she may have about the spiritual poverty of her assimilated life.

> The food isn't great. Or maybe we just don't have the taste buds in us to go crazy over it. Sometimes I get very hungry for Chinese flavors: black beans, garlic and ginger, shrimp paste and sesame oil. These are tastes that we grew up with, still dream about. Run around town after. Duck liver sausage, beancurd, jook, salted fish, and fried dace with black beans. Western flavors don't stand out, the surroundings do. Three pronged forks. Pink tablecloths. Fresh flowers. Cute waiters. An odd difference. (336)

The list of the family's favorite foods, similar in structure to the lists of "marginal" foods we have encountered, here serves an incantatory purpose. The two sisters toss out names of dishes at each other—"Johnny Walker in shark's fin soup," "squab dinners" (335), "hung toh-yee-foo-won-tun" (336)—in an attempt to trigger pleasant recollections. But this restorative litany is of limited magical powers. Likewise, the list of the "American" restaurant's virtues lacks efficacy. Both are governed by the terms of a fallen world in which Chinese and American, home and world, self and other have been dichotomized and made antagonistic. Native and foreign have become inverted in the course of the narrator's induction into mainstream society: the Chinatown culture once native to her is now foreign, to be revisited in an annual ritual. "An odd difference" is as far as the narrator can go in her meditation; she sees no possibility of integration.

Hawaiian writer Darrell Lum's "Yahk Fahn, Auntie" (1980) features an assimilated protagonist who, like the narrator of "A Red Sweater," hungers for the "comfort food" of his Chinese heritage but can only manage partial and erratic reconnections with it in adulthood. For Jimmy the fall occurs at a young age: early in his life he has learned to abandon chopsticks and bowl for fork and plate (40). After the death of his favorite elder, Auntie Tsu (a virtuoso of Chinese cooking, of course), Jimmy makes valiant attempts to attain right eating, such as ordering chow mein in his broken Cantonese. At the end of the sketch Jimmy is shown dining out with an even more "haole-ed" date who orders steak and potato; in front of her it becomes a point of honor for him to insist on eating rice with chopsticks. Mentally contrasting Chinese rice—the real thing, so to speak—with "haole rice," Jimmy scoops some rice over the girl's baked potato. Whether meant to convince himself of the possibility of redemption, to show off his meager superiority in retention of things Chinese, or to convey a sense of shared inadequacy with her fellow cultural exile, this gesture is fraught with irony, and Jimmy knows it.

Auntie Tsu would have laughed because she had once written to ask whether he had met any nice Chinese girl in New York. And here he was back home [for Auntie Tsu's funeral] with a nice Chinese girl and a baked potato.

"Yahk fahn, Auntie," Jimmy said softly. (43)

"Yahk fahn," literally "eat rice," is a Cantonese formula one utters at the beginning of a meal, to urge fellow eaters to start; good manners requires it, especially of children in the presence of elders. In murmuring the phrase to a deceased mother surrogate, Jimmy is trying to invoke a lost world of innocence that has, in fact, never really existed. Except perhaps in infancy, he has always lived as a "haole-ed oriental" (43). The hopelessly crossed jumble of ethnic signs now confronting him cannot be simplified into order by regression to oblivion. The moment certain foods are recognized as "Chinese," *different* from what "Americans" eat, a breach has already occurred in one's sense of wholeness. Time, too, is fallen: an outmoded, parochial past is set up against a modern, cosmopolitan present from whose homogenizing demands there is presumably no escape. (In this light, even Wing Tek Lum's paean to Chinese rice gruel, "Juk," though not ethnically marked, still belongs to the world of ethnic polarization, since its affectionate lingering over physical details is based on nostalgia. "No one has made as good / a juk since then.")

Despite such examples of frustrated effort, a vision of prelapsarian right eating does exist in Asian American literature, in Toshio Mori's "The Woman Who Makes Swell Doughnuts," a short sketch in his collection of short stories, *Yokohama, California* (1949; rpt. 1985). While the promise held out by this vision was betrayed by the internment of Japanese Americans only a few years after *Yokohama, California* was accepted for publication in 1941 (Inada 1985:xviii), its very existence suggests that the kind of reconciliation sought by displaced eaters like Ng's narrator and Jimmy is imaginable, that their groping meditation has a theoretical endpoint.

"The Woman Who Makes Swell Doughnuts" concentrates, in barely four pages, all that one might desire of body and soul, in a language resonant with religious connotations yet devoid of doctrinal propositions. The nameless Issei woman on Seventh Street (known simply as Mama to everyone) has lived a full life and now enjoys a ripe old age. A humble soul who will never make it into history books, she yet turns out doughnuts that are "the tastiest doughnuts this side of the next world" (24). To the narrator they are "in [a] class by itself, without words, without demonstration" (23). She represents rest: "inside of her she houses a little depot" (25); she is the center of her "little circle," her "little world" (24, 25). She may be identified with the still point of the turning world of which mystics speak, the motionless prime mover that powers the cosmic dance, "the dancing of emotions before our eyes and inside of us, the dance that is still but is the roar and the force capable of stirring the earth and the people" (22). Mama is, in fact, godlike, her doughnuts a sacrament through which the celebrants can absorb her essence. "Perhaps when I am eating her doughnuts I am really eating her" (23). A visit to her is a foretaste of "immortality" (22). (Note also that the circle is a symbol of perfection commonly found in religious iconography.)

Whence all this lavish praise for a doughnut maker? Read in isolation, Toshio Mori's heavily spiritual language might seem puzzlingly unmotivated, disproportionate to the modest subject matter—a curious case of a hagiography unanchored to any religion. Yet if "The Woman Who Makes Swell Doughnuts" is read intertextually with other Asian American alimentary images, its import becomes almost too transparent. Here is food and eating as they should be before the fall into a fragmented world of interethnic oppression and discord. The doughnut is "American,"[31] but the sketch makes nothing whatsoever of this fact. This differs noticeably from numerous other Asian American literary works that imbue food with almost stereotypic ethnic significance: a preference for Japanese pickles betokens stubborn refusal to assimilate; for hamburger, forsaking of Chinese roots; and so forth.[32] Unlike other fictional mothers whose provision of sustenance is inextricable from the demands of Necessity, Mama's bounty has no emotional strings attached and calls forth no memory of pain. If cannibalism is hinted at, it connotes not insensitivity and destructiveness but love: Mama is like the gods of ancient cultures (Frazer 1964:543) of whose flesh one partakes to renew vigor and faith. Moreover, her nurturance is not a one-time mythical event, the loss of which sets in motion the desire to regain paradise, the need for the intervention of transformative language. Her bounty is a condition of being that overcomes flux and banishes nostalgia; in it the "ethnic" is become universal. In fact, Mama sounds somewhat like an Asian American version of what Crevecoeur calls "our great *Alma Mater*," the American earth-goddess (Sollors 1986a:75–78): "I take today to talk of her and her wonderful doughnuts when the earth is something to her, when *the people from all parts of the earth may drop in and taste the flavor, her flavor, which is everyone's and all flavor*." (Mori 1985:25; my italics).

"The Woman Who Makes Swell Doughnuts" was the product of a narrow window of confidence in Japanese American history when full participation in American society seemed within reach. As Lawson Inada notes in his introduction to the 1985 edition of *Yokohama, California*, "This was . . . a time of hope and optimism, of established communities, of flourishing culture, of the new generation getting on with America. This was a time of pride and accomplishment. The people quite obviously believed in themselves, in what they could do, were doing, in America" (x).

Unlike early Chinese immigrants, who were subjected to systematic exclusion designed to prevent the group's perpetuation, early Japanese immigrants did establish families. By the 1930s the Nisei generation had come of age. For a while it appeared that the Japanese American community was destined to duplicate the successful assimilation of white immigrants—for a price, it is true, in ethnic pride, but no higher than what others had to pay. Yet Toshio Mori's stories in *Yokohama, California*, written in the 1930s and 1940s, provide snapshots of a way of life before internment capable of serving as a touchstone of at-homeness in America. No other Asian American writer since has been able to match Mori's community portraits for mellowness: internment is too bitterly emblematic an event to leave room for equanimity, not only for Japanese Americans but for others of the "yellow" race. By the same token, no other Asian American writer since has been able to present images of perfect sustenance.

What of the future? If "The Woman Who Makes Swell Doughnuts" represents paradise lost, can paradise be regained?

As Werner Sollors notes in *Beyond Ethnicity* (1986a:81–86), Israel Zangwill's *The Melting-Pot* employs an explicitly religious rhetoric indebted to the New Testament; the reason is that "descent is secular and temporal, consent is sacred and eternal" (74). The sacramentalization of quotidien experience in Mori's sketch parallels, in a sense, the alchemical emphasis of the melting pot myth: the possibility of transformation by America is affirmed and demonstrated. What internment did—and the same goes for other canonical Asian American historical experiences of discrimination, such as exclusion for the Chinese—was to block transformation, insist on the immutability of Asian descent, invalidate Asian consent. After this fall, an alternative vision of right eating—and of America—must be fashioned; the prelapsarian one, though timelessly present to its author, is now lodged in the past, irretrievable.

Wing Tek Lum presents just such an alternative vision in a short poem, "Chinese Hot Pot," collected in *Expounding the Doubtful Points* (1987a).

> My dream of America
> is like *da bin louh*
> with people of all persuasions and tastes
> sitting down around a common pot
> chopsticks and basket scoops here and there

some cooking squid and others beef
some tofu or watercress
all in one broth
like a stew that really isn't
as each one chooses what he wishes to eat
only that the pot and fire are shared
along with the good company
and the sweet soup
spooned out at the end of the meal.

(105)

Wing Tek Lum's conceit is not necessarily original; Kalcik notes that the metallurgical melting pot is frequently replaced by the stewpot in the popular imagination (1984:60). Yet it is an extraordinarily potent one. Although, as a national symbol, the melting pot has lost some of its sacrosanct air since the 1960s (if not earlier), Lum's depiction of *da bin louh* is bold in its play upon the received image; what is more, it sets up many thought-provoking resonances with other alimentary images we have encountered in Asian American literature. "Chinese Hot Pot" reverses the sacramentalism of "The Woman Who Makes Swell Doughnuts" and secularizes the melting pot myth. Although alchemy and cooking are both transformative, the former, in distinguishing between gold and dross at all, assumes a discriminatory and destructive aspect. On the other hand, the cooking of *da bin louh* is purely constitutive. The centerless format of the *da bin louh* table also contrasts with the centering of Mama in her house: if the "ethnic" cannot be universalized without violence, then let everyone be equidistant from a center whose only function is to facilitate nourishment and fellowship. Thus "Chinese Hot Pot" offers at once a critique of and an improvement over Mori's prelapsarian vision. Necessity has been cast aside: "each one chooses what he wishes to eat." There are no involuntary swallowers, food prostitutes, or food pornographers at the *da bin louh* table.

Such is the poet's "dream of America." Unmistakably postlapsarian but hopeful nonetheless, it recognizes right eating for Asian Americans as contingent upon radical revisions of all outside/inside, foreign/native, other/self relationships—in short, a reordering of the entire American body politic.

Chapter Two

ENCOUNTERS WITH THE RACIAL SHADOW

AS OUR ANALYSIS of "big eaters" in chapter 1 suggests, many Asian American writers use the motif of eating to symbolize a survival-driven act of assimilation, with the word *assimilation* reinterpreted (however obliquely and implicitly) to oppose the meaning most common and expected in the minority context. Instead of *assimilating to* the dominant society—that is, allowing the circumstances controlled by those in power to overwhelm them—the experts in "eating bitterness" *assimilate* even the most unpromising material for their own sustenance. Thus is the external transformed into the internal, the alien overcome, and life, continuity, ensured. Yet there is such a thing as having to swallow too much, until one can no longer hold in the pain and humiliation. A large number of images of overstuffing, gagging, bursting, and vomiting testifies to the Asian American writers' concern with the limits of endurance.[1]

The motif that forms the subject matter of this chapter—the double, variously known as the alter ego, the shadow, the Doppelgänger, the second self, the anti-self, the opposing self, and the secret self, among others (J. Berman 1988:963)—seems at first glance unrelated to the motif of eating. However, a certain logic links their manifestations in Asian American literature, for both derive ultimately from the Asian American experience. One of the bitterest Necessities for Asian Americans is having to contend with total devaluation of their Asian ethnicity. If they stomach it, they get caught in a cruel bind: to become acceptable to a racist society, one must first reject an integral part of oneself. In a 1972 essay entitled "Racist Love," Frank Chin and Jeffery Paul Chan note that Asian Americans often adopt internalization of white judgment as an "expedient tactic of survival":

> For the subject to operate efficiently as an instrument of white supremacy, he is conditioned to accept and live in a state of euphemized self-contempt. This self-contempt itself is nothing more than the subject's acceptance of white standards of objectivity, beauty, behavior, and achievement as being morally absolute, and his acknowledgment of the fact that, because he is not white, he can never fully measure up to white standards. (1972:67)[2]

Swallowing negation creates an unfillable hole in the very core of one's being. To preserve the illusion of psychic wholeness indispensable for sanity, then, one must resist the realization of so impossible and humiliating a demand. Projection, a psychological process that (like bursting and vomiting) reverses the symbolic directionality of eating (introjection), keeps at bay the threatening knowledge of self-hatred. By projecting undesirable "Asianness" outward onto a double—what I term a *racial shadow*—one renders alien what is, in fact, literally inalienable, thereby disowning and distancing it.

As will be seen in the following chapter, Asian American literature abounds in encounters with the racial shadow. Although, at a very high level of abstraction, the defense mechanisms of repression and projection may safely be considered universal, I contend that traditional concepts of the double are inadequate for bringing out the distinctness of instances of the double in Asian American literature. To fully understand the psychological and sometimes physical violence that characterize these encounters, one must read them against each other in their sociopolitical context. The universalistic theories that have informed readings of Western classics of double literature are not so much wrong as partial; they must be modified before they can be of use to students of Asian American literature.

Torture in the School Lavatory: A Test Case for Theory

In "A Song for a Barbarian Reed Pipe," the last chapter of Maxine Hong Kingston's *The Woman Warrior*, the narrator recounts her torture of a quiet Chinese girl in the school lavatory. The vocabulary of double literature has been applied to this well-known scene by more than one critic. Elaine Kim, for example, calls the quiet girl the protagonist's "anti-self" and "alter-ego" (1981:153). David Li also uses the term "alter-ego," as well as the German term *doppelgänger* (1988:509).

To identify the silent girl as Maxine's double does not in itself raise theoretical issues for the student of Asian American literature. As Albert J. Guerard notes, "the word *double* is embarrassingly vague, as used in literary criticism" (1967:3). Guerard's opinion has been either cited or echoed by virtually every student of the double since. Clifford Hallam observes, "In the broadest sense of the idea, 'double' can mean almost any *dual*, and in some cases even multiple, structure in a text" (1980:5). In contemporary criticism, therefore, one is free to describe as a double any character who shares a facet of the protagonist's personality and has an intense relationship with him/her; the nature of the shared facet and the relationship may be left vague. The practice most likely results from a natural trickling-down of critical vocabulary (in general, the more established a term, the greater the tolerance for a broadening of its meaning and an obscuring of its original sources) and is not necessarily a sign of sloppy thinking.

Thus to label the quiet girl as Maxine's double is to provide merely localized illumination for one part of one work by one Asian American author. Unless its theoretical ramifications are pursued, the observation could remain on the level of an offhand remark. Assuming a more than casual use of the term the *double*, as implied by the aforementioned co-incidence of critical opinion, we might ask more global and challenging questions: What enables critics to recognize, in a contemporary work of Asian American literature, a motif most frequently associated with nineteenth-century Romantic and post-Romantic fiction? Is the occurrence of the double in *The Woman Warrior* a fluke or does it have analogs in other works of Asian American literature? Hallam has cautioned, "the terms 'Doppelgänger,' 'Double,' 'alter-ego,' and so forth, without further clarification or restriction, are virtually meaningless as a critical tool" (1982:18). If a cluster of double figures can be identified in Asian American literature, what new "clarification and restriction" of the term's traditional usage, derived from European and Anglo-American literature, must be made? Can we arrive at a reconceptualization of the double useful to students of marginalized literatures?

A Brief Survey of Existing Scholarship

In what sense is the quiet girl Maxine's double? This seemingly straightforward question is actually quite difficult to answer, for a wealth of scholarship exists on the double, offering a bewildering variety of theories and taxonomies.

To begin with, there is the matter of naming. While terms like the *double*, the *doppelgänger*, the *shadow*, the *second self*, and the *alter ego* are often used interchangeably, their connotations do not entirely overlap. The word *doppelgänger* is steeped in the German tradition[3] and is associated with German Romantic prose fiction of the fantastic as exemplified by E. T. A. Hoffmann. The *shadow* shares with *doppelgänger* the sense of haunting, but both its occult connotations and its connection to a specific historical-literary milieu are weaker. The *double* is even more generalized in meaning: it does not oppose the solid to the insubstantial, the dominant to the derivative, leaving open the nature of the relationship between the coupled entities. The *alter ego* is probably the least clearly defined usage for literary criticism, while the *second self*, the *anti-self*, and the *secret self*, adopted by some specialists, are the least current in everyday speech.

In the following analysis, the *double* and the *shadow* will be used the most frequently; the *second self* is preferred when there is a contrast with the protagonist, who is the *first self* or *host character*.

Besides the terminology, one is also confronted with an array of theoretical approaches on the double. A student of Asian American literature must carefully evaluate this assortment of critical apparatus for useful points of contact with the episode in *The Woman Warrior*.

To even begin to make this task manageable, many phenomena of potential interest to the scholar of the double, such as those listed in Tymms (1949:15–27) and Rogers (1970:7–14), have to be omitted from discussion. I have also decided to exclude cases of so-called split, dual, or multiple personality, which typically involve dissociated elements of the self *alternating* with each other and kept apart by amnesic barriers (Hawthorn 1983:3). Such cases are frequently alluded to in studies of the double; indeed, mention of R. L. Stevenson's *The Strange Case of Dr. Jekyll and Mr. Hyde* (1866), which conforms in no small part to clinical definitions of the split personality, is almost obligatory. However, the *temporal* alternation of the split personality seems sufficiently distinct from the *spatial* coexistence of selves (whether "real" or "imagined") in the double to merit separate analysis.[4]

Even after eliminating tangential topics, existing scholarship on the double remains voluminous. Through its many variations in definitional stringency and emphasis, one might distinguish several at times overlapping approaches: the psychogenic, the taxonomic, and the diachronic.[5] A quick survey of these underscores the predicament of the student of Asian American literature, who, because of the group-specific demands and the newness of her discipline, cannot avoid drawing on critical precedents whose usefulness to her work is to be negotiated rather than assumed.

A psychogenic approach is one that speculates on the psychological dynamics that may have led to perception of the double or depiction of it in literature. It may be said to originate with Otto Rank, who in 1914 first linked the double to a narcissistic, guilt-evading phase in ego development (1971:76), then later in 1941 connected the double to man's fear of death and desire for a symbol of the immortal soul (1958:81). Another classic of the psychogenic approach is Freud's well-known essay "The Uncanny" (1919), which argues that confrontation with the double is one of many avenues for the return of the repressed, which, by virtue of removal from consciousness, has come to appear unfamiliar and terrifying (20–28). Clifford Hallam's "The Double as Incomplete Self: Toward a Definition of Doppelgänger" (1980) elaborates on parallels between the double and the Jungian shadow, both of which can take either a "personal" or a "collective" form (1980: 16–17).

After Rank and Freud, virtually all studies of the double have a psychogenic component. However, some are notably less interested in reconstructing hypothetical mental processes than in constructing taxonomies to cover actual manifestations of the double in literature. Robert Rogers's *The Double in Literature* (1970) proposes a fourfold set of distinctions with which to classify the double (4) and organizes examples of the double by type like "the mirror image," "the secret sharer," "the opposing self," or the fair maiden vs. the femme fatale. C. F. Keppler's *The Literature of the Second Self* (1972) also lists common types of the double, such as the Twin Brother, Pursuer, Tempter, Vision of Horror, Savior, and the Beloved. Nevertheless, unlike Rogers, who is less concerned with purity of type than with accommodating diversity, Keppler offers a much more stringent, a priori definition of the double as a "second self" midway between reality and imagination (6–10). Masao Miyoshi's study of Victorian literature, *The Divided Self* (1969), though primarily a delineation of the Victorian Zeitgeist, does offer a tripartite typology of the double—the formal, the thematic or ideological, and the biographical (ix–xi)—and may therefore be included in the taxonomic group as well.

The diachronic approach examines literary examples of the double in their sociocultural context and traces their development in several national literatures over time.[6] Ralph Tymms's *Doubles in Literary Psychology* (1949) focuses closely on Romantic and post-Romantic fiction and its formative influences in contemporary psychology. Theodore Ziolkowski's *Disenchanted Images* (1977), an iconological study of animated statues, haunted portraits, and magic mirrors as they develop through the period of "disenchantment" or secularization in Western civilization, contains a section on the fortunes of the double (175–201). Karl Miller's *Doubles: Studies in Literary History* (1985) reflects on Romantic and modern duality as manifested in the related images of orphaning, stealth, anonymity, and flight. Paul Coates's *The Double and the Other: Identity as Ideology in Post-Romantic Fiction* (1988) examines, in a "decentered," nonmonographic manner, the double and its role in the emergence of modernism. While differing vastly in scope and method, all these studies see the double theme as constantly evolving in response to changes in the sociocultural milieu.

The works surveyed above represent only part of the extensive scholarship on the double (which also includes useful brief overviews such as A. J. Guerard and C. Rosenfield). A feminist study such as Joanne Blum's *Transcending Gender: The Male/Female Double in Women's Fiction* (1988) is likely to add a new gender-linked subcategory to the scholarship on the double. Faced with such a proliferation of analytical frameworks, then, how are we to recognize a double in any given work, not to mention a modern Asian American work apparently so far removed from the nineteenth-century European context in which the doppelgänger figure first crystallized?

"Disowning": A Common Denominator

As a first step in answering this question, we might attempt to seek a lowest common denominator in the views of various students of the double.[7]

Despite widespread disagreement on many other theoretical issues, students of the double are remarkably consistent on one point: the central role of psychological "*disowning*" in the formation of the double. Although only some scholars directly invoke the language and the authority of psychoanalysis, all would agree that the double is formed through repression and projection, in a general defensive process known variously as splitting, dissociation, decomposition, or fragmentation. The double is symptomatic of a crisis in self-acceptance and self-knowledge: part of the self, denied recognition by the conscious ego, emerges as an external figure exerting a hold over the protagonist that seems disproportionate to provocation or inexplicable by everyday logic.[8]

This model of the etiology of the double can be discerned in a broad range of wording employed by scholars of differing persuasions. Rank describes the modern form of the double as "an opposing self, appearing in the form of evil which represents the perishable and mortal part of the personality repudiated by the social self" (1958:82). Freud, as mentioned above, considers defamiliarization through repression central to the double. Tymms calls the double figure "a figment of the mind, to which one attributes the promptings of the unconscious self, now dissociated from the conscious personality" (1949:97). To Guerard, the double is "a personality we have attempted to disown" (1967:8).

> One of the recurrent preoccupations of double literature is with the need to keep a suppressed self alive, though society may insist on annihilation: to keep alive not merely a sexual self or a self wildly dreaming of power or a self capable of vagrant fantasy, the self of childhood freedom—not merely these, but also a truly insubordinate, perhaps illusory, original and fundamental self. (2)

Similarly, Rosenfield suggests that "each of us has within us a second or shadow self dwelling beside the eminently civilized, eminently rational self, a Double who may at any time assert its anti-social tendencies" (1967:311). "The novelist who . . . exploits psychological Doubles may either juxtapose or duplicate two characters; the one representing the socially acceptable or conventional personality, the other externalizing the free, uninhibited, often criminal self" (314). Rogers sees the double as a result of "essentially intrapsychic or endopsychic" conflict (1970:4) writ large. The type of conventional double Rogers calls the "antithetical" (2) or "opposing self" (60–85) results from the interrelated defense mechanisms of projection, displacement, repression, regression, reaction formation, and turning against the self (64). Keppler defines the second self as "a cluster of rejected or inadmissible mental states" (1972:6), "the self that has been left behind, or overlooked, or unrealized, or otherwise excluded from the first self's self-conception . . . the self that must be come to terms with" (12). Citing Jung, Keppler speaks of the shadow as "the personified sum of all the inferior, less respectable, even criminal potentialities of one's own psyche" (203). Analyzing Dostoevsky's *The Double*, Ziolkowski calls the double "an extension of the suppressed aspects of [Golyadkin's] own personality" (1977:184). Hallam calls the double an individual's "hidden (repressed) self" that he "has not come to terms with" (1980:17); the double represents a "lost, hidden, or denied aspect of the personality" (18–19). Miller speaks of "an attempt to disclaim responsibility for events and crises which are internal to the individual but in which his environment will always seem to take part" (1985:416). Last but not least, Coates relates the double to the attempt "to disavow the knowledge of the inner corruption of the self" (1988:34).

Articulated by critics with divergent theoretical agendas and foci, all these views on the double in literature postulate a common operation. The resulting double figure may be a separate, autonomous character in the fictional world, or it may be a hallucination; some writers work within conventions of narrative verisimilitude, while others exploit the protagonist's psychological instability and emphasize the double's ghostly and ambiguous status. But a plurality of literary approaches is possible.

Such a bare-bones formulation of the double has several advantages. The criterion of "disowning" effectively distinguishes the double from what Eder terms the "foil," a character contrasting with the protagonist but functioning more as a literary device than a concretization of psychodynamics (1978:585–94). Focusing on disowning also gives us greater flexibility in recognizing transformations of the motif in works exhibiting great disparities in setting and mood. We will see, for example, how the "component of terror" or "*frisson* of the uncanny" (Guerard, 1), though typical of many well-known tales of the double, is not an essential ingredient in all of them.[9] The sense of the uncanny is not an autonomous element but a measure of the severity of the dissociation. As Hallam notes: "The form of the shadow and his relative wickedness depends on the nature and on the intensity of the individual's repressions: that is, the more repressed the more 'alien' the shadow will appear when projected into the world" (17). Eeriness of mood is therefore not normative. To identify a double, it is perhaps more fruitful to ask whether the protagonist's feelings toward the figure in question are considered *disproportionate* by everyday standards. Since repression and projection are unconscious defenses, the protagonist's reactions, be they extremely negative (repulsion, fear, violence, and so on) or extremely positive (fascination, love, indulgence, and so on) are not amenable to rational analysis and control.

Finally, a concept of the double with disowning as its nucleus captures the simultaneous sameness and difference of the double with regard to the first self, giving us a less dogmatic perspective on the subject than theories preoccupied with the morphology of the double. As Keppler puts it so aptly, the double is "the Other who is also the I" (199). At times superficial sameness obscures deep-seated differences disclaimed by the first self; at times the opposite is true, with superficial differences concealing a fundamental kinship with the double that the protagonist wishes to deny. What Tymms identifies as the two subtypes of the double, "double-by-duplication" and "double-by-division" (16)—the distinction has been adopted with modification by Miyoshi (1969:xii), Rogers (4), Rosenfield (314), Eder (570), and others—reflect the two main forms taken by disowning. Neither is more "true" than the other. In this light, canonical tales involving exact replicas, such as Dostoevsky's *The Double* or Poe's "William Wilson," need not be held up as exclusive yardsticks. Such a practice may blind us to the multifarious ways in which the double may appear in literature.

RETHINKING THE "UNIVERSAL" DOUBLE

The definition of the double yielded by this theoretical excursus has the advantage of "universality": it may be presumed to be based on a fairly uncontroversial theory of human nature. As Rogers notes, "The phenomenon of decomposition in literature has its origins in so fundamental a stratum of mental activity that it has analogs in other quite different realms of human concern," including such commonplace expressions as "I'm not myself today" (5). In post-Freudian times, even the most ardent proponent of materialist determinism or cultural relativism would concede that nobody is totally exempt from inner conflict or innocent of defense mechanisms like repression and projection. Furthermore, one hardly needs to be an adherent of psychoanalysis to agree with Freud that "a most natural way for art to depict endopsychic conflict is to picture it as being interpersonal conflict, the seemingly separate characters representing the psychological forces at odds" (*The Interpretation of Dreams*, 507; cited in Rogers, 64). A generalized model of the double is not tied to any national culture, period, or genre and leaves the critic enough room to explore novel versions of the double. One could therefore apply the model to any text—the torture episode in *The Woman*

Warrior for instance—and look for points of contact between the theory and the illustration.

On the other hand, the very strength of such an account of the double is also its chief shortcoming. In attempting to fix the minimal commonality of all literary uses of the double, it fails to address the crucial question: *"Precisely what, in any specific version of the double, has been disowned, and why?"* Even if the double were indeed archetypal, as Jungian critics claim, in literature it must still take a concrete form conditioned by complex, interacting material forces. That endopsychic conflict is representable as interpersonal conflict is not due solely to the innate organization of the human mind or the exigencies of verbal art; rather, the former must also have arisen from prior human conflict, which are inextricably embedded in sociohistorical particulars.

The Asian American student of the double is compelled to take sociohistorical particulars into account because, for a marginalized group, the terms that figure so prominently in existing scholarship, such as "personality," "the civilized self," or "antisocial tendencies," have never been neutral or unmarked. American minorities have never had the power to define their own "personality" or the full freedom to participate in the "society" or "civilization" in which they find themselves. A major controversy dividing students of Asian American psychology is, in fact, whether there is an identifiable "Asian American personality," with its many (by white standards) "antisocial" traits; and if so, whether it results from dysfunctional "cultural baggage" or from societal stereotyping and acquired survival tactics against racist policies (Suzuki 1977: 35–38). Thus an Asian American student of the double, aware of the inscription of ideology in even the most "universal" psychological terms of analysis, cannot be content with appreciating a work's compelling realism or the author's masterful evocation of the frisson. Constructing an uncontextualized concept of the double from existing scholarship, as has been done here, is only a heuristic device.

Existing analyses of the double, devoting varying amounts of attention to sociohistorical particulars, are helpful to the critic to varying degrees as she attempts to ascertain the nature of the disowning found in the torture episode from *The Woman Warrior*. Psychogenically oriented students are quick to recognize the intricate operations of defense mechanisms, but tend to flatten the materially shaped contours of a double story to quasi-mythic patterns. Taxonomic studies, characterized by inclusiveness, are in one sense sensitive to diversity. On the other hand, since these are usually prompted by almost encyclopedic theoretical ambitions, and since types of the double can only coalesce when similarities are foregrounded, sociohistorical specificity is again given short shrift.[10] Students using the diachronic approach are most alert to the dangers of decontextualization: proceeding as they do from the axiom that the treatment of any literary motif is culturally governed and evolves with changing times, they set their sight beyond the individual psyche. To that extent, their methods can inspire. Nevertheless, they, like practitioners of the other two approaches, draw their examples all but exclusively from European and Anglo-American writing.[11] As a result, they are preoccupied with the European and Anglo-American traditions, and what they have to offer to students of ethnic American literatures is at best indirect.[12]

Accordingly, our investigation of the disowning found in *The Woman Warrior* calls for a further step, a raising of the power of the lens, so to speak. We will read the text closely against existing theoretical concepts on the double, especially the "lowest common denominator" model, then against other episodes in Asian American literature displaying a similar psychological gestalt. Through the teasing apart of affinities and contrasts, we may be able, eventually, to formulate an understanding of the double that does justice to the uniqueness of the Asian American experience and its literary expressions.

READING THE RACIAL SHADOW: A PLACE FOR RACE

The torture incident in *The Woman Warrior* is of singular interest because it can be recognized as an instance of double literature by a number of criteria, even those that might be secondary or else peculiar to individual scholars. In terms of mood-setting, the scene has an air of foreboding and mystery of the type traditionally attending the apparition of the double. Though supernatural events (whether rationalizable or not) are absent, Maxine's encounter with the quiet girl is set in a deserted schoolyard, in a crepuscular half-light reminiscent of many classic tales of the doppelgänger. Twilight, that transition between day and night, signals that the protagonist is in between orders of reality, about to cross proscribed boundaries or receive an unusual visitant:

> The day was a great eye, and it was not paying much attention to me now.
> I could disappear with the sun; I could turn quickly sideways and slip into
> a different world. It seemed I could run faster at this time, and by evening
> I would be able to fly. As the afternoon wore on we could run into the
> forbidden places. (Kingston 1977:203)

The bright eye of reason is turned away. In another intimation of an impending confrontation with the irrational, the protagonist recalls "a giant thing covered with canvas and tied down with ropes," which the children thought was a "gorilla in captivity" held outside the reassuring borders of authority and order, the school fence (203). Maxine also experiences physical descent, which in many folktales and myths symbol-izes the self's perilous, unescorted journey into its own depths (Keppler, 204): the lavatory, which serves the "lower" functions of the human body, and the playroom, where the logical mind ceases to hold sway, are both located in the basement (Kingston, 202).

Is the quiet girl, then, a "second self" in Keppler's sense: a figure of fantasy? Even if we do not subscribe wholesale to Keppler's concept, it is evident that the beating-up incident, taking place unwitnessed, could very well have been imagined. Notwithstanding some observable conse-quences for Maxine, she is never called to account by another. The quiet girl, to be sure, has a more definite ontological status than the figure of the "hulk" (226–29, 233, 239), who seems to have been called up to mirror what Maxine perceives as the villagers' humiliating underestima-tion of her intelligence and attractiveness. The mentally retarded, por-nography-reading "huncher" disappears the day after Maxine blurts out her complaints to her mother (239)—an improbability that is the hall-mark of hallucinations. However, both the quiet girl and the hulk do inhabit an uncertain realm between objectivity and subjectivity, the locus of many alleged events in *The Woman Warrior* (the death of an older sibling, the cutting of the tongue, the mother's conquest of the sitting ghost, Moon Orchid's husband-reclaiming in Los Angeles). (Maxine, we recall, is a susceptible child who hears voices in motors and sees cowboy movies on blank walls [221].) To the extent that Maxine's encounter with the quiet girl can neither be confirmed nor denied, it matches Keppler's concept of the "second self."

The fit between concept and example is even more striking if we apply the criterion of simultaneous identity and difference. However reluc-tantly, Maxine concedes important similarities between herself and her victim: if the quiet girl is better protected by her family, "in other ways we were the same" (200). "In sports we were similar": "I hated her when she was the last chosen for her team and I, the last chosen for my team" (200–201). Both tormenter and victim suffer from an inability to make themselves heard. Maxine has on her record three years of total silence at school (192) and speaks with an ugly "pressed-duck voice" (223). The quiet girl, who cannot speak up even in Chinese school (200), produces pathetic "wheezes" out of her plastic flute at music time (202). Maxine admits, "people and she herself probably thought I was her friend. I also followed her sister about" (201). (And if the two share a sister, they might as well be sisters too.) Yet despite common prob-lems, Maxine obviously regards the quiet girl as sufficiently different from herself to be an object of her lunchroom gossip (201) and a target of violence.

Disproportionateness of response, one of the corollaries of the "lowest common denominator" model, characterizes the entire episode. The torturer unleashes violence on her victim without any provocation whatsoever; or rather, the quiet girl's very lack of provocativeness serves to provoke Maxine to new heights of hatred and hysteria. If, as a rule, the intensity of response to the double betrays the intensity of "disowning," the victim must have a great deal in common with the perpetrator. The question is, what exactly is she repressing and projecting as alien? What does she need to come to terms with?

Here is where formulations of the double derived from European and Anglo-American works begin to prove inadequate. For what the quiet girl stands for cannot be entirely explained in terms of the structure of the individual psyche. Listing specific attributes shared by the two girls—awkwardness in sports, silence, shabby appearance—does not get us very far. Despite hints of the Freudian id in the image of the gorilla held in check, the girl cannot, in the usual sense, be described as antisocial or criminally inclined, some primordial self lurking beneath the eminently "civilized," "rational," "socially acceptable," and "conventional" self. Unlike Dorian Gray, Leggatt, Hyde, William Wilson, or Ivan Karamazov, she has not broken any laws or ethical rules. She is, in fact, supremely well behaved, given to neither protest nor aggression. If Guerard's and Rosenfield's generalizations about the double still hold true, it is only because she is "antisocial" in a very specific sense: she acts Chinese in a society where acceptability is synonymous with assimilation to white standards. Indeed, by the codes of the patriarchal Chinese culture in which she spends her time outside school, the quiet girl is the civilized one, while the loud and assertive white Americans are the "barbarians" and "ghosts."

There are other intriguing contrasts. In most canonical tales of the double, the protagonist is cast in the role of the apparently sensible, socially adjusted first self or host character, haunted by the inadmissible impulses of the double. Hence the frequent antipathy between the two. Where the first self recognizes a spiritual affinity with the double, the relationship is usually one of sympathy or indulgence (the young captain and Leggatt, Mrs. Dalloway and Septimus Smith, the lawyer and Bartleby the Scrivener). In "A Song for a Barbarian Reed Pipe," though, we see a different configuration: it is the protagonist who exhibits "criminal tendencies" in an uncontrollable fit of pinching, twisting, squeezing, and hair-pulling. What is more, the violent outburst is motivated not by awareness of dissimilarity but by awareness of kinship. Maxine and the quiet girl are not set apart by categorical opposites—articulateness, for example, versus silence, or agility versus klutziness. Rather, their difference is merely one of degree, detectable more to Maxine than to others—the double is "the girl who [is] *quieter than I*" (201; italics mine).

If we try to apply Hallam's idea of the "incomplete self" (1980:20) or Eder's concept of the "antithetical complement" (1978:583, 600), to see if protagonist and double form an integrated personality when put together in the interpretive act, we will see that individual attributes are not really the issue—the two girls are too alike. The quiet girl is "antithetical" to Maxine only in the latter's deluded self-image; thus the powerful influence of others—the context in which such a self-image is acquired—must be brought into the analysis.

The idea of "personality" underlying much (though not all) existing scholarship on the double is that of a collection of drives and traits. This discrete package may play out some deterministic psychosexual principle, or be propelled into interpersonal conflict by the inexorable logic of its inherent flaws, but it is not readily seen as historically contingent. The example from *The Woman Warrior* suggests that the terms of analysis must be expanded to include not only an individual's psyche but also the way it functions in the social and cultural matrix and the way resulting behavior is interpreted. The dynamics of power, rather than ethics or psychology—"human nature" in the abstract—must become the focus of our inquiry. As the desperate Maxine tells her alter ego, "If you don't talk, you can't have a personality. You'll have no personality and no hair" (210). Talking means having the power to define oneself, to resist the definition of others. The quiet girl is hateful because she does not have power ("I don't like the way you can't make a fist for tetherball. Why don't you make a fist?" [208]). She does not have power because she is female and, ultimately, because she is Chinese in a white society.

At this point in her growth, the protagonist still believes that assimilation will gain her social acceptance, defined as a chance to become a cheerleader and pompon girl, to get dates and get married (210). In her conscious mind, she considers herself more assimilated than her victim; and in a very limited sense, when hidden away from the arbitrating gaze of the public, she is, indeed, more powerful. But of course Maxine's sense of superiority is imaginary. In truth she cannot "run faster" than in the sober light of day (let alone "fly"). However scrupulously she insists on her difference, the larger society will not bother to distinguish between the two. Even though the protagonist has "invented an American-feminine speaking personality," and even if, in a cultural sense, she continues to adopt "mainstream" ways, she will never be accepted as a member of the dominant group. Being of Chinese descent, she will always be Other.

We are now ready to return to the question of what the protagonist must be repressing and projecting onto the double. The quiet girl represents that residue of racial difference which dooms Chinese Americans to a position of inferiority in a racist society. It is this very irreducibility that most infuriates the protagonist: the quiet girl is immune to either threats or bribery, does not respond to effort, seems indifferent to the promised benefits of assimilation, cannot be done away with: "I met again the poor girl I had tormented. She had not changed. She wore the same clothes, hair cut, and manner as when we were in elementary school, no make-up on the pink and white face, while the other Asian girls were starting to tape their eyelids" (212).

When Maxine forces the girl to speak up, she is seeking confirmation that her own meager, fragile achievements in assimilation would guarantee a hopeful future. A recent and insecure convert to Americanization, she cannot tolerate counterexamples. A single hopeless case of unassimilability would throw the inevitability of her entire undertaking into doubt, obliging her to seek another redemptive alternative. The violence she discharges onto the girl escalates in proportion to her growing realization that, in a profound sense beyond issues of specifiable, modifiable behavior, they are "the same" to the non-Chinese. Manners can be changed, but not skin color; as the Other, Chinese Americans will always, to some degree, be spurned. In this light, the gorilla held under canvas is not so much any individual's id as American society's potential for institutionalized racist violence, of which the protagonist temporarily becomes a deputy.

When even brutality fails to eradicate the evidence of her racial difference, Maxine knows subconsciously that the accommodationism to which she has committed herself does not offer a true solution to her identity problem. That immediate options are nonetheless lacking is a thought too frightening to admit to awareness. Through a process psychiatrists call "somatization," the protagonist develops a mysterious illness whose sole purpose is to remove her from any further occasion for conflict, any further reminder of her defenselessness. At once punishment and reprieve, the year-and-a-half of invalid seclusion allows her to act even more passive than the quiet girl, with total impunity. However, as implied by the image of "the middle line in [her] left palm [breaking] in two" (211), refusal to face her American environment will no more heal her inner split than denial of her Chinese origin. Eventually she will have to return to the demands of the larger world and learn to fashion a viable, integrated Chinese American self.

Obviously the protagonist of *The Woman Warrior* suffers from fragmentation. But it is important to remember that the split in her Chinese American identity is not inherent in the order of things; rather, it is a result of *definition*. Coates's remarks, recalling Chin and Chan's discussion of "self-contempt" quoted at the beginning of the chapter, are relevant:

> Ideology socialises the individual by bringing him or her to internalise the dividedness of a class society in the form of the structure of "objective,

value-free judgment"—thereby enabling the system to rule the subject, by dividing it. The antithesis between the "here" of the individual and the "there" of others is translated into internal space. (1988:5)

If it seems natural for us to speak of the quiet girl as a projection of "the Chinese part of the protagonist," it is because we have become accustomed to society's prevailing way of conceptualizing racial minorities as composites or hybrids—namely, not fully "American." (This wording has in fact become so rooted in the language that avoidance would create great inconvenience; it will continue to appear in this chapter, but always in quotation marks to indicate its provisional nature.) Asian Americans, like other immigrants and descendants of immigrants in American history, engage and are engaged by their sociocultural environment, becoming in the process different from Asians in Asia. Yet this fact is all too often disregarded in favor of the ahistorical view that Asian Americans are forever marked by some untransformable alien element. Thus an identity that has been formed like a chemical compound, in that complex, irreversible process called living, is forcibly broken apart, treated as if it were a physical mixture with readily sorted-out ingredients.

It is true that in *The Woman Warrior*, the first-generation Chinese Americans are shown as doing their share of splitting and projecting: they refer to non-Chinese as "ghosts" and attribute to them all manner of immoral ideas and outlandish practices. To that extent minority and majority can be said to share "universal" defense mechanisms. Yet there is a crucial difference between this process—a side effect of relocation to new surroundings—and the one that leads to the formation of the racial shadow. Whereas "ghosts" become substantial and human upon familiarization (witness the second generation's gradual shift in perspective), the power differential that defines Asian descent as alien cannot be abolished upon closer association with whites. In fact, if anything, further incorporation into American society only exposes the impossibility of the agenda set for Asian Americans: that they are expected at once to lose their offensive "Asianness" and to remain permanently foreign. We might note that it is the American-born Maxine who is troubled by an alter ego; the psyche of her immigrant mother remains relatively intact, despite a trying physical existence.

Our reading of the torture episode from *The Woman Warrior* compels a reformulation of the "lowest common denominator" model of the double: race must be prominently inserted into any analysis of the double in Asian American literature. Such a move is amply supported by a growing literature on the representation of the racial Other.[13] Comparative studies of the double focusing on European and Anglo-American national literatures have never included Asian American cases; this, added to the fact that such studies have been insufficiently articulated with the scholarship on Otherness, may have obscured the place of race in the formation of the Asian American double.

Rogers is one of the few students of the double to theorize overtly on race. He writes:

> The inclination of the racist to make an invidious division of all people into superior whites and inferior blacks presumably stem not so much from simple-mindedness as from an inner, emotional split, an ambivalence generated out of his own confusion about his identity. The racist adopts social myths as a mode of dealing with his own inner tension and insecurity, just as the neurotic does. Similar dichotomous tendencies prevail among competing social, political, and economic ideologies. (1970:6)

Rogers's insight can be extended to the double in *The Woman Warrior*, with this important modification: the "good" and "bad" halves of the ambivalent self are distributed not in two visibly different races but in two unequally assimilated characters of the same race. It is not merely the rabid racist who "adopts social myths" to deal with "inner tension and insecurity." In fact, such phrasing misleadingly implies, first, that some idiosyncratic, culture-independent malaise precedes the adoption of "social myths," and second, that the "social myths" exist in an inexplicably ready-made form waiting to be made use of in various ways (presumably some neurotic and some wholesome). It is much more accurate to say that double-producing myths of racial superiority *are* themselves a malaise of a society split by political and economic inequities. Individuals do not *adopt* them to assuage other ills; they *enact* the myths. Assimilated Asian Americans like the protagonist in "A Song for a Barbarian Reed Pipe" act out the paradoxical status they occupy in American society through encounters with the racial shadow.

Besides the torture incident in *The Woman Warrior*, I argue, there are a convincing number of episodes or stories in Asian American literature that embody this recurrent pattern of the double: a highly assimilated American-born Asian is troubled by a version of himself/herself that serves as a reminder of disowned Asian descent. The racial shadow draws out mixed feelings of revulsion and sympathy from the protagonist, usually compelling a painful reassessment of the behavioral code which has thus far appeared to augur full acceptance into American society. These examples, of varying elaborateness and thematic explicitness, constitute a distinctive subtype of the double, one that cannot be adequately accounted for by the approaches we have described as psychogenic, taxonomic, and diachronic. The racially linked subtype confirms the need for a more rigorous revision of traditional theories of the double, in the direction of greater sociopolitical emphasis.

The "Asian" Kinswoman

The torture incident in *The Woman Warrior* bears an interesting resemblance to a seldom-remarked-upon scene in Monica Sone's 1953 autobiography, *Nisei Daughter*. The young protagonist, Kazuko, visits her father's family in Japan, and meets her older cousin Yoshiye, who is described as a proper Japanese young lady with "restrained, delicate movements" (1979:92). Yoshiye refuses to give a kimono to Kazuko; that night, when the young girls are put into the same bedroom, a quarrel breaks out.

> Thick, padded quilts were brought out from built-in shelves and put on the floor. Yoshiye laid her head on a cylindrical padded roll. The nape of her neck rested on this pillow and her head hung back slightly over it. Lying there with her eyes closed, she looked to me as if she were waiting for an executioner's ax to fall. I pushed my pillow aside. Yoshiye and I simmered silently in the dark for a while. Then I burst out impulsively in English, "You know, I think you are awfully selfish."
>
> "You talk so funny," she laughed.
>
> I flung the covers back angrily. When she sat up, surprised, I slapped her face. Then I raised my arms around my neck, waiting to be thoroughly pummeled. But nothing happened. Yoshiye just sank down on her quilt and cried. (93)

The mothers of the girls come in and separate them. Kazuko notes: "Although I was not sorry I had slapped my cousin, it had been an odd sensation. It was like striking a sack of flour. There had been no resistance or angry response, only a quiet crumbling away" (94).

Hardly a writer given to the pursuit of subtleties and implications, Sone quickly drops this scene for more colorful events to narrate. Sketchy as it is, though, to a contemporary reader of Asian American literature this episode reads almost like an embryonic version of Maxine's encounter with the quiet girl; between the two incidents there are some minor differences but also several crucial parallels. What in *The Woman Warrior* appears as symbolic sisterhood is here a matter of blood ties, an even stronger reminder that the protagonist's right to full participation in American life is no better than presumptive. *Nisei Daughter* opens with Kazuko's discovery of "a shocking fact of life" (the title of the first chapter): "One day when I was a happy six-year-old, I made the shocking discovery that I had Japanese blood. I was a Japanese" (3). Since her early fall from the "amoebic bliss" (3) of ethnic ignorance, optimistic Kazuko has attempted repeatedly to protect her faith in assimilation by dissociating herself from the image of the submissive Japanese maiden, "quiet, pure in thought, polite, serene, and self-controlled" (28). Kazuko pictures herself as a rambunctious "Yankee" tomboy dashing happily in and out of the back alleys of Seattle's skid row, much like the young Maxine exploring the school's deserted playground, imagining limitless power and freedom.

For both Kazuko and Maxine, the racial shadow is a slightly older "kinswoman" whose very presence constitutes a challenge to the universal validity of American values. Yoshiye's taunt about "funny" speech is superimposed on the account of an earlier stage in Kazuko's life, during which she innocently thought that it was the white people, not the Japanese Americans, who "spoke a strange dialect of English" (18). Though the disabusing process—which most likely included ridicule of "funny" Japanese-accented English—is not portrayed in *Nisei Daughter*, its end product is clear from Kazuko's later (and self-contradictory) characterization of her childhood years: "For eight years at Nihon Gakko [the Japanese language school], Bailey Gatzert and Central Grammar, I had done only what I was told by my teachers. I opened my mouth only in reply to a question. I became a polished piece of inarticulateness" (131). Thus the contrast between Japanese and American schooling so carefully drawn in the early chapters of *Nisei Daughter* turns out to be fraudulent. It is in fact Kazuko's minority status as an American of Japanese ancestry which has caused her silence:

> Some people would have explained this as an acute case of adolescence, but I knew it was also because I was Japanese. Almost all the students of Japanese blood sat like rocks during discussion period. Something compellingly Japanese made us feel it was better to seem stupid in a quiet way rather than to make boners out loud. (131)

Kazuko's discovery parallels Maxine's: "The other Chinese girls did not talk either, so I knew the silence had to do with being a Chinese girl" (Kingston, 193).

In acting so Japanese—applying Japanese standards of acceptability with blithe disregard for American ones—Yoshiye subverts Kazuko's as-yet-untested conviction in the rightness of her American self-image. Even more disconcerting than Yoshiye's scorn for American speech is her inability to be roused to anger, aggression, and resistance: precisely the same quality in the quiet girl that infuriates Maxine. The weak neck, the yielding flesh, the passive anticipation of hurt, the "quiet crumbling away," here concentrated in the body of one Japanese individual, emblematize the collective vulnerability of Japanese Americans in a society that proves capable of singling them out for wartime internment solely on the basis of their race. With a sort of subconscious imagistic logic, Sone (generally a rather literal-minded writer) picks out one physical detail in the Japanese furnishing—the thick padded bedding—that seems to epitomize the mentality of some (obviously not all) Japanese Americans. Like psychological acceptance of a position of weakness in white society, the thick padding absorbs blows but also deadens, neutralizes, and confines. In a sense it even readies the victim for greater injury: the roll presents the neck on which the ax may fall. Sone's unelaborated images of the padded quilt and flour sack, and Kingston's excruciatingly detailed delineation of the quiet girl's soft, stretchy, shapeless flesh, together adumbrate certain distinguishing characteristics of the racial shadow in Asian American literature.

Are we confusing issues, guilty of conflating Asian American and Asian, when we read Kingston's and Sone's accounts against each other? No. The point that emerges from the similarities between the two episodes is precisely that white society's refusal to distinguish between Asian American and Asian has been internalized uncritically by both Asian American protagonists. As a result, both are plagued by a misgiving that they are tainted by an indelible "Asianness"; this "Asianness" is projected onto external figures of the same racial background and then recognized with dismay, even repugnance. In the case of Japanese Americans, internment dramatizes more unequivocally than ever how ready white society is to equate the Japanese in America with those in Japan. Yet exactly like Yoshiye, Kazuko fails to fight back against injustice. To the accusation that the Enemy has been within her from the beginning—that the Enemy is, in fact, her Japanese blood, which no amount of assimilation can obliterate—Kazuko's response is passive resignation. "In the privacy of our hearts, we had raged, we had cried against the injustices, but in the end, we had swallowed our pride and learned to endure" (124).

In the end, Kazuko turns out to be as immobilized as the *odori* dancer she has despised in childhood, a figure "completely entombed like a cocoon, under layers of garment and miles of sash" (45). (Recall the imagery of padding.) Her expectations of untrammeled development as an American are as illusory as her childhood dream of becoming a leaping, whirling ballet dancer.

A CRITIQUE OF CULTURALISM

Thus far, my analysis has emphasized the role of an interracial power differential in the formation of the racial shadow. Yet since both episodes from *The Woman Warrior* and *Nisei Daughter* involve female characters, and both suggest Asian cultural restrictions on women as a possible cause of the protagonists' silence and passivity, a question naturally arises: to what extent can Maxine's and Kazuko's encounters be explained simply in terms of gender and culture? Why can't we attribute the friction between the Americanized and "Asian" girls to cultural differences alone? Why is it necessary to invoke repression and projection as underlying psychological processes?

In addition to the Yoshiye incident, *Nisei Daughter* relates another encounter, this time with two Nisei young women, in which cultural differences are offered explicitly as an explanation for Kazuko's sense of alienation from white society. Kazuko enters a sanitarium for tuberculosis and soon learns something about herself analogous to her discovery of Japanese blood:

> At the sanitarium, I noticed that I was not quite in step with my companions. These discrepancies came as tiny shocks to me, for I had been so sure of my Americanization. I had always annoyed Father and Mother with my towering pride on this point. I could speak English much better than they could. I felt no hesitation in wearing blood red nail polish or violent purple lipstick. But here I started to lose my confidence. (140–41)

The incompleteness of her Americanization is brought home when she notices two Nisei patients "[sitting] by themselves at the far end of the room as if they were trying to remain inconspicuous" (140). Only after trying to start a conversation with them does Kazuko realize that, as assimilated and outgoing as she imagines herself to be, to her white friends she too is just a typical Japanese young lady, decorous, reserved, aloof, *foreign*. "The girls had not meant to be unkind even though they had made me feel as if I were a spy at large. Their response was typically Japanese, and that was the way I had behaved with Laura. No wonder Chris and Laura thought I had been deliberately impolite" (141).

Kazuko's meeting with the two Nisei patients, though not violent, recalls the torture episode in *The Woman Warrior* in that it too reveals radical dissonance between the protagonist's flattering self-image and the rude reality of her inadequate qualifications for full membership in white society. Like the quiet Chinese girl, Nami and Marie are perceived by the protagonist as different from herself, yet the favorable judgment is contradicted by white treatment. We might thus consider Nami and Marie diluted versions of the racial shadow. For author Sone, however, the main cause of Kazuko's disaffection is not her minority status but cultural differences, which are to be resolved by greater effort on the part of the minority and greater tolerance on the part of the whites.

Is a culturalist reading of interethnic encounters compatible with an interpretation that stresses inequality in power relationships? Which is more valid? One way to approach the issue is to examine usages of the word *difference*. From a perspective of cultural relativism, which would allow us to bypass political terms of analysis, two codes of behavior are different *from each other*; lack of mutual understanding and acceptance results from the clash of codes, and neither side is favored. Yet to Sone, difference is evidently conceived of as difference *from white standards*: the unstated reference point is always white. It is such an implicit norm that gives the lie to Kazuko's rhetoric of individual human decency. At the end of her stay at the sanitarium, Kazuko notes with relief and gratitude that she is finally one of the girls. "[My companions] had accepted me into their circle as I was. They did not care that I looked different, said or did a few odd things, because basically we liked each other. For the first time in my life I felt sheer happiness in being myself" (143).

The patent absurdity of defining "being oneself" on other people's sufferance seems to escape the protagonist. Thus Sone's inventory of cultural differences, her little comparative treatise on feminine deportment (142), is in truth an inventory of Japanese American deficiencies. The superficial persuasiveness of her list, with its air of insider's authority, only disguises the bitter political realities of the Japanese American situation. Kazuko's stance fits Arif Dirlik's characterization of culturalism: her belief in the autonomy of culture "reduces all realms of social experience (from the economy to ideology) to the question of culture; cultural change then appears as the key to social change" (1987:15). The fact is, culture is not "exterior to the socio-political relations and logically prior to them"; rather, culture is itself "an ideological operation crucial to the establishment of hegemony" (15).

It would be foolish to deny that cultural differences influence the form taken by the racial shadow. However, a strictly culturalist reading cannot adequately account for the distaste with which the double is consistently viewed, or the readiness with which the first self assumes blame for her sense of self-division. Further, it cannot adequately account for the remarkable similarity between Kazuko's responses as a culturally different individual and as a member of a politically oppressed racial group. When Kazuko and her family and friends obtain leave from camp to go shopping in town, they try to see themselves through the eyes of hostile whites and adjust their behavior accordingly, acting "like children out on a spree not to be seen or heard":

> Somehow we felt we ought not to travel in droves or congregate in public in large groups. One Japanese face was conspicuous enough, and a party of them might be downright obnoxious. . . . We walked timidly [into a restaurant], hoping that we would not attract too much attention. . . . We made for the corner where we huddled close against the wall, trying to blend into the wallpaper design. (204)

It would seriously strain credibility to argue that victimization to the point of infantilization is a natural corollary of cultural differences, and that power plays merely an incidental role in the kind of interracial relations that find embodiment in the double in Asian American literature.

Diana Chang's 1989 short story, "The Oriental Contingent," provides ancillary evidence that culture is a relatively insignificant factor in Asian American versions of the double. This story explores the ambivalence of American-born Chinese who feel *inferior* for being assimilated. Connie Sung, a third-generation pianist, meets a Chinese American woman with the name of Lisa Mallory, which Connie assumes comes from marrying a Caucasian. For three or four years after their first meeting, Connie is plagued by bewilderment at Lisa's aloofness. Considering herself a "failed Chinese" (174), Connie concludes that Lisa must be "Chinese-Chinese" (173); the latter's reticence must be a matter of tact, to protect the feelings of the less fortunate.

Finally, at a chance encounter, Lisa confesses to Connie that she was born in Buffalo and adopted by white parents. The two women have in fact been feeling defensive toward each other, each believing the other to be more Chinese, each trying to hide her own lack of cultural authenticity. They have been each other's ethnic "secret sharer," so to speak. Lisa exclaims: "The only time I feel Chinese is when I'm embarrassed I'm not more Chinese—which is a totally Chinese reflex that I'd give anything to be rid of!" Connie knows that "none of this matters to anybody except us" but cannot help feeling cursed.

> "It's only Orientals who haunt me!" Lisa stamped her foot. "Only them!"
>
> "I'm so sorry," Connie Sung said, for all of them.
>
> "It's all so turned around." (177)

While Chang's short story is so sketchy that all our inferences must be tentative, the sense of tension, fascination, and haunting that the two characters feel toward each other suggests a possible reading of the story as one of the double, with this critical difference: that everything about the two main characters is "turned around," a mirror image of the situation in *The Woman Warrior* or *Nisei Daughter*. Connie and Lisa feel stigmatized and diminished for being too Americanized. They have internalized the disdain that "Chinese-Chinese" hold for the American-born. Each woman projects onto the other all the strengths that she wishes she had: direct access to the Chinese community, familiarity with Chinese culture, self-assurance, security of identity. The "Asian" side of the self, not the "American," is the favored one.

Now if cultural conflict could adequately account for the phenomenon of the racial shadow, we would expect to see more stories like "The Oriental Contingent," for then both the "Asian" and the "American" aspects of the self would have an equal chance to be repressed and projected. What we find instead is that the theoretical possibility hinted at in "The Oriental Contingent" is hardly ever actualized in Asian American literature, for the simple reason that the prevailing asymmetry in interracial relationships makes such actualization unlikely. For Asian Americans, incomplete assimilation to white standards is more liable to create embarrassment or insecurity than lapses from Asian standards, which are not taken into account by those who dominate the power structure of the country.

GENDER AND THE RACIAL SHADOW: MALE PARADIGMS

What about gender then? How does gender fit into a theory of the racial shadow in Asian American literature? All our illustrations thus far feature female characters. Is the double merely a function of gender, the protagonist's inner split having been caused by disparities between white American and Asian ideas on the nature and status of women?

To the extent that being female (in Asian and white American cultures) and being Asian (in American society) both entail subordination, race is a "gendered" term of analysis. Thus the double is not so much *merely* as *necessarily* a function of gender. The copresence of female gender and Asian descent results in a sort of synergy of oppression; "male" works of Asian American literature elucidate internalized self-rejection in other ways. Lonny Kaneko's short story "The Shoyu Kid" (1976), like sections of *Nisei Daughter* set in a World War II internment camp, portrays an encounter with the double which uncovers the role of gender in the formation of the racial shadow. This role is markedly different from what one might expect from universalistic psychological interpretations of the double, such as Hallam's incorporation of the Jungian animus and anima, Rogers's Freudian reading of *Pierre* (1970:133–37), and Blum's study of the male/female double informed by current feminist psychosexual theory (1988:1–10), or even Coates's more contextualized interpretation of the fin de siècle double as mirroring the breakup of traditional gender roles (1988:4–5).

The preadolescent narrator and his gang operate on an unstated syllogism distilled from the experience of political subjugation: being Asian means being weak; being female also means being weak; therefore being Asian is like being female.[14] In submissively performing homosexual services (acting "female") for a white camp guard, the Shoyu Kid scandalizes the gang members, provoking a violent and merciless attack. At the same time, as is typical of the double, the Shoyu Kid is living proof of their complicity in weakness; the story ends with the stunned gang members silently pondering their kinship with the despised "queer."

The doubling in "The Shoyu Kid" is considerably more complex than that found in the examples discussed so far in this chapter. There is no single first self, though there is a first-person narrator, Masao. In a case of doubling by duplication, Masao, Jackson (Hiroshi), and Itchy (Ichiro) are depicted as all but interchangeable members of a hunting pack, their prepubescent insecurity over both sexual and racial identity calling for compensation in the form of mutual reassurance. A simple code, constantly reinforced by mutual egging-on, underlies their feeble gestures of defiance: avoid appearing weak—that is, Japanese and "queer"—at all costs. They replace their Japanese names with American nicknames and give the finger to Issei women behind their backs. They strike dramatic poses learned from cowboy and war movies (2, 3, 7), imitating "macho" authority figures such as John Wayne, cavalry colonels, police interrogators, and army intelligence officers (7). They call each other's bluff on sexual prowess, discoursing abstractly on naked girls and hard-ons. The gun that the red-headed guard points at them (4) symbolizes their obsessive but frustrated aspiration: to be more American and more masculine than young Japanese American males seem entitled to be at this juncture in history.

The Shoyu Kid is the racial shadow of the gang members in that he mirrors their inadequacies as both Americans and as men. His trademark brown snot is to them a loathsome indicator of "Japaneseness": "Jackson's older brother told him the reason the Kid had brown snot was because he used too much soy sauce, and it just dripped out of his nose. We all stopped using shoyu when we heard that" (5).[15] The narrator, Masao, comments that the Kid's snot "didn't used to be [brown] when he trailed after us." In other words, the Kid's "Japaneseness"—his inferiority—is not noticeable to the gang members as long as he serves them as loyal hanger-on and gofer, which enables the four boys to function more or less as a single psychic unit.

The Kid, being the weakest of the lot, gives the other boys an illusion of power. Nevertheless, once he attaches himself to the red-headed soldier, who personifies the entire power structure that has placed Japanese Americans behind barbed wire, it becomes impossible for the three gang members to remain blind to the parallel between themselves and the Kid. That which they hate in themselves has become externalized, projected, visible. The brownness of the Kid's snot is a sign of some ineradicable congenital taint; however, unlike the birthmark of original sin in Hawthorne's "The Birth-Mark," it pertains to a specific historical situation rather than an abstract realm of universal morality.

The three boys' doubts about their "Americanness" are inseparable from their sexual anxieties, of which the Kid again serves as a constant reminder. From the gang members' vehement denunciation of all forms of "queerness," one might expect them to express nothing but revulsion upon discovering the Kid's relationship to the soldier. Yet their actual responses are much more complex and revealing. When the gang asks Ichiro what he has seen behind the garage, he keeps quiet, changing the topic to divert his friends' attention. This curious protectiveness suggests a tacit acknowledgment of complicity in the Kid's shameful act. After Jackson has tortured the Kid into telling the truth, Ichiro asks, "Do you think the Kid will squeal?" While the sentence can be interpreted to mean squealing about the torture, the context makes it clear that Ichiro is at the moment preoccupied with sexuality. Ichiro appears afraid that exposure of the Kid's "queerness" would somehow implicate them all. To the extent that the three boys are as deficient in "masculinity" as the Shoyu Kid, Ichiro's apprehension certainly makes much symbolic sense. The "pantsing" of the Kid is a shocking moment of revelation that confronts the tough-talking boys with graphic proof of their own impotence: "There staring at us with its single eye squinting in Jackson's face was a little prick like a broken pencil between equally white but shapeless thighs. Jackson was immobilized, his face slack in surprise and Itchy moved away" (8).

That impotence in Asian American literature has both a physical and a political meaning is much more apparent in "The Shoyu Kid" than in "A Song for a Barbarian Reed Pipe" because of the gender difference in the characters as well as the wartime setting of the former. However, as illustrations of the theme of the double, the two torture episodes are in fact markedly similar. In both cases, the protagonists' attempt to make the racial shadow "talk" hurts *them* even more: instead of eliciting validation of their superiority, it compels them to admit affinity with the weak. The "first self's" response toward the double betrays not only abhorrence, as professed and as expected, but also a devious sort of solicitude. Ichiro, eyewitness to the Kid's disgrace, keeps silent. The gang members release the Kid at the moment of bitterest disgust, which one might suppose to be also the moment of fiercest persecution. Likewise, in *The Woman Warrior*, brutality alone is not sufficient to describe Maxine's effort to extort words out of the "sissy-girl" (Kingston, 204). As she begins to suspect failure, her demands for verbal performance de-escalate, from spirited protest to a brief "Let go," to "just screaming," to a nonsensical *a* or *the*. Maxine adds a series of increasingly attractive bribes to her threats; eventually she herself breaks down into unstoppable sobs. Needless to say, all the above seemingly surprising gestures of leniency and softness are simply signs that the racial shadow is an undeniable facet of the protagonist.

A meticulously wrought moral allegory, "The Shoyu Kid" takes pains to make the point that the potential for domination and violence is universal, found within even the weakest and most oppressed. Author

Kaneko inserts an obviously symbolic hunt sequence in the middle of the story, in which the internees, themselves trapped, band together to trap a small animal of indeterminate identity—maybe a vile rat, maybe a harmless rabbit. (Are the Japanese Americans lurking spies or loyal citizens?) Thus the pattern of violent encounter is repeated hierarchically: white society, Japanese Americans, the "American" gang members, the "Japanese" Shoyu Kid, the Kid's dog (named Kraut, after the more remote enemy) sent in for the hunt, and the hapless prey.

Kaneko's generalizations about human nature, however, do not discredit a reading of "The Shoyu Kid" that highlights ethnicity-bound repression and projection; disowning is by no means inevitable in all works that explore "universal" human frailties. That "The Shoyu Kid" is not simply a parable of human evil will become apparent if we contrast Kaneko's hunt sequence with the chicken-killing episode in Joy Kogawa's *Obasan* (1982:155–56). In the latter, a group of preadolescent Japanese Canadian boys, uprooted victims of wartime relocation, gather outside the schoolyard to kill a white chicken. Like the internees who cheer "Get him!" "Kill him!" the boys torture and slaughter the chicken in a bloody ritual, saying "Got to make it suffer" and "Kill it." Nevertheless, though Kogawa would no doubt agree with Kaneko that the oppressed tend to imitate their oppressors and repeat the violence that has been done to them, the Japanese Canadian boys are simply motivated by revenge. The only psychological subterfuge is the displacement of hatred from powerful white people to the defenseless white chicken. There are no hints of psychic decomposition, no signs of a racial shadow.[16]

Ashley Sheun Dunn's "No Man's Land" (1978) resonates well with "The Shoyu Kid." Both are "war stories," concerned with the effect on American-born Asian men of wars in which an Asian nation (Japan, Vietnam) becomes America's enemy. Like "The Shoyu Kid," "No Man's Land" modulates the canonical encounter with the racial shadow in a number of intricately interlocking episodes; in both cases the racial shadow is a pathetic figure who yet haunts the imagination of the stronger protagonist(s). The characters representing the first self and second self are joined in a sort of brotherhood. In "No Man's Land," these roles are played out between two unrelated Chinese American soldiers in the Vietnam War, one American-born and one immigrant. However, the first self's blood brother, the narrator, may be considered a "latent" double, to use Rogers's term (1970:4); like Conrad's Marlow, he vicariously participates in the extreme experiences of someone thrust into moral disorientation.

The older brother, Stuart, fits into a by now familiar mold. Born in the United States, devoted to hamburgers and TV dinners, a master storyteller in urban slang, Stuart is filled with contempt and hostility toward the type of impoverished, unassimilated Chinese who would invite derision from whites. He is a misfit in his immigrant parents' permanently makeshift Chinatown world. Though he knows some Chinese, his place in the Chinese American community is no less marginal and ambivalence-ridden than that of the Asian American soldier in Vietnam:

> It's a funny thing, there you are in a place where everybody around you looked just like you, only you couldn't understand a word they say, everything they do is strange. I mean it made you feel lonely as hell, just like if you were down at Playland with no money at all, and you just had to sit there and watch everyone have a good time. (118)

The "good time" from which he is excluded is a sense of organic connection to the community, accompanied by a natural respect, undistorted by socially instilled shame, of its "different" way of life and cultural values.

In contrast to the defiant, tough-talking Stuart, Sam looks and acts exactly like a white caricature of the meek Chinaman, virtually a textbook example of the racial shadow: "You know, he's the type with the black horn-rimmed glasses, buck teeth. When he stood up it always looked like he was about to bow or something" (112). His "fresh-off-the-boat" accent and "gawky Hong Kong ways" (117) are an acute embarrassment to Stuart. Yet Stuart somehow feels drawn to the piteously ugly man and voluntarily accompanies him on his pearl-buying and duck-stealing missions. On both trips Sam proves himself a laughing-stock. The pearl merchant not only cheats him but also spits in his face; when the duck owner chases the thieves with a meat cleaver, Sam throws up his hands in surrender and shits in his pants. Stuart sums up: "I swear to god if I ever met a dumber Chinaman" (112). Such stupidity deserves to be annihilated to spare the sensibility of those with better judgment: "I would have shot the guy if I didn't know he was in our army" (120).

Ironically, it is Sam who emerges from the story with dignity, for his culturally rooted sense of right and wrong has not been warped by anticipation of condescending non-Chinese opinion. After being cheated, Sam buys a real pearl with his own money for a black army buddy (who doesn't even bother to thank him). He empathizes with the needy duck owner and returns to his hut every week with some small gift, socializing with the Chinese-Vietnamese family even though they speak different dialects. Thus unlike Stuart, who is exasperated by such useless, apparently self-sabotaging behavior and considers himself insulted by implication, Sam has access to the "good time" of human bonds. When Sam yells in anger for the first time, it is to remind Stuart of his obligations to the ethnic community: "You know, you're not very Chinese. If you were, you'd go back there and apologize. They don't even think that you're a Chinese! They think you're Japanese, or even Mexican!" (121).

Through the agency of Sam, Stuart experiences more encounters with the double. When Stuart is sent by the sick Sam to visit the duck owner, he brings the fake pearl set in a cheap ring as a gift, unaware that the old man would interpret this as a marriage proposal for his daughter. The culturally ignorant Chinese American man doesn't realize his mistake until the wedding day. The lowly peasant girl he is supposed to marry is reminiscent of Maxine's mentally retarded "hulk"; that someone could even imagine such a girl to be a suitable mate must be an unbearable affront to Stuart's Americanized ego. Standing there awkwardly in a "drooping red and gold cheung sam" (123), she is a living specimen of his "unhip" Asian origin: "Oh man was she ugly! Pimples all over her face, with these thin squinty eyes and hairy underarms! She was real pathetic!" (122).

Stuart narrowly escapes reintegration with his racial shadow by fighting his way through the crowd of wedding guests; this act, which brings irremediable public humiliation to the duck owner, cuts Stuart off forever from the unified cultural world that could have anchored and sustained him. When he returns to the hut a month later to apologize, urged on by Sam, he notices his alienation. "Before it smelled, well . . . like a home, or like the country. All these different smells like food and mud and fertilizer, together they smelled good. But that time I drove back there it just smelled like shit and junk and bad breath" (124). The old man charges at Stuart with his meat cleaver. Stuart knocks him down and leaves his motionless body in the mud; without checking whether he is dead, the young man drives off in his jeep. In this third confrontation with the racial shadow, the murderous intensity of Stuart's disowning is clearer than ever. When the narrator shows concern for the fate of the old man, Stuart screams: "I'm your brother! He's a stranger! You don't even know the guy! He's just like any stranger around here!" (125).

Features of this scene are recombined in a fourth encounter with the racial shadow. This time the double is Uncle Fish, a figure somewhat reminiscent of the ever-hungry eccentric loner, Uncle Kwok, in Jade Snow Wong's *Fifth Chinese Daughter* (1945:46–49). Uncle Fish used to be a doctor in China but is now unemployed, having failed the American certification test seven times; impoverished and alone, he is reduced to sponging on sympathetic Chinatown families. The customary Chinese title "uncle," to show respect for older men, bespeaks a sense of community that extends beyond blood ties. Yet by Stuart's code Uncle Fish has no more claim on his kindness than the duck owner: both are just "strangers," and all losers infuriate him. Touched off by Uncle Fish's indirect but culturally acceptable begging for food, Stuart explodes into savagery. He threatens the helpless man with a meat cleaver, shouting: " 'If I find you anywhere, begging for anything, I'll cut your head off! Don't ever come here again! I can't stand all you goddamned peasant chinks crawlin' up Jackson Street like a bunch of slaves!' " (Dunn, 127).

Although the origin of Stuart's parents is unspecified, judging from their dialect it is most likely that they too come from a "peasant chink" background. Symbolically, then, Stuart is thrice guilty of attempted patricide. He is also guilty of imagined fratricide; even after Sam's death in a car wreck, Stuart feels like "[killing] him right there and [saving] him the trouble of killing himself off" (131). Ultimately his fantasy of killing extends to all unassimilated, downtrodden elements of the Chinese American community:

> old people walking up those streets with a look on their faces like they were goddamned fish floating in those tanks at the butchers; or those people who come from China, they come here when they're forty years old! What the hell sense does that make! . . . Sometimes I wish that there'd be this huge car accident, like that truck that came tearing down Sacramento Street once, and it would kill off all those old people and all those people who couldn't mumble a word of English if they had to. (131)

Having sinned against life, Stuart acts like an obsessed Ancient Mariner: the "great storyteller" (125) confesses to the narrator, then wanders off on a Greyhound bus to unknown destinations.[17] The apology owed to so many people and postponed for so long he finally utters to his blood brother, "I'm so goddamned sorry" (132).

The versions of the racial shadow in "No Man's Land," recalling the images of slaughter such as the dead duck at the wedding or the fish in Chinatown butchershop tanks, are in a sense sacrificial offerings: they make possible Stuart's eventual self-knowledge. The morning after his return to San Francisco, Stuart is asked by his father, "So, what did you learn over there?" (116) Without consciously recognizing it, Stuart has actually learned a great deal. Like many protagonists of classic tales of the double, from Hoffmann's *The Story of the Lost Reflection* to Poe's "William Wilson" and Wilde's *The Picture of Dorian Gray*, Stuart has learned that, metaphorically speaking, he cannot kill his double without also killing himself. As Hallam observes of such protagonists, through murder "the narrator destroys a part of his being," thus committing "psychological 'suicide' " (1980:22). After his homicidal tirade against his victimized people, Stuart admits, "I miss him [Sam]. I miss my wife. I miss that old man with his fucking meat cleaver, I miss everything. . . . I start to miss myself. Sometimes I almost cry just thinking, 'Poor old Stuart, he ain't never coming back' " (Dunn, 131). This admission makes possible an even more unsettling insight: "You know it's funny,

in a lot of ways me and Sam were the same. Shit, you look at those hon-
kies and you know they can do whatever they wanna do, no one's gonna
stop them. But me and Sam? We don't have any choice" (132).

It is no accident that the wretched FOB ("fresh-off-the-boat," or immigrant) is given a name conventionally used to designate the United
States. Sam is not an outlandish importation from China irrelevant to
the world of American-born, American-bred Stuart. Both of them are
Chinese in America, which is why, in spite of vast disparities in upbringing, manners, and values, they are both cursed with the "Chinaman's
chance" in life. Racially based victimization does not respect individual
differences.

Sam has given Stuart something that looks as phony and cheap as the
fake pearl but is in fact invaluable. The comically stereotypical Chinaman with his cultural rootedness and moral integrity is in possession of
a "pearl of great price." Once Stuart proves worthy of inheriting it, it
will become his means of healing the breach within himself and between
him and his community: "disowning" will give way to "owning." The
plastic pearl returns to the United States set in Stuart's buck knife; unlike the stark pointed gun in "The Shoyu Kid," the emblem of phallic
aggression that Stuart has brought back from the war in Vietnam has
been tempered by Sam's instinctive decency and compassion. The pearl
is ready to be set in a wedding ring for a second time. When Stuart lies
to his parents about dating a nice Chinese girl, he is not motivated by
wanton deceitfulness; his confusion is genuine. Getting the ring back is
important to him because it symbolizes the potential of psychic wholeness, but at this point he is not yet ready to realize it. His bus trip is at
once self-exile, penance, and quest. At the end of the story the narrator
pictures Stuart finally reverting to his "best and gentlest Chinese," to
acknowledge Sam's friendship and mourn his death.

FOB: A CONTEMPORARY PARABLE

With its carefully constructed thematic repetitions and its concentrated
doses of psychological and physical violence, Dunn's "No Man's Land"
may be considered a paradigmatic story of the racial shadow. However, it is important to remember that the division-inducing stresses in
the Asian American condition portrayed in "No Man's Land" are not
peculiar to extreme circumstances or conspicuously volatile characters.
David Henry Hwang's 1979 play *FOB* centers on the enmity between a
modern-day FOB, Steve, and an ABC (American-born Chinese), Dale.
Deliberately contextualized through historical flashbacks, the play suggests that for Asian Americans the struggle for self-acceptance and self-
integration is an ongoing one.

The FOB of the title, Steve, is a very different type of immigrant from either the working-class Issei in the Japanese American tales or the rural Cantonese oldtimers of *The Woman Warrior* and "No Man's Land." He is from a well-to-do Shanghainese businessman's family, grew up in the British colony of Hong Kong, listens to American pop music, and studies at UCLA; he does not live in the isolation and squalor of an ethnic ghetto. Grace, the young woman mediating between Steve and Dale, remarks: "The people who are coming in now—a lot of them are different—they're already real Westernized. They don't act like they're fresh off the boat" (1983:43). Yet as long as American society continues to view Asian Americans as the Other, the actual, absolute degree of their Westernization is beside the point; it is the function they serve—as incarnation of racial difference, always defined relatively—that provokes contempt in whites and insecure assimilated Asian Americans. As mentioned earlier in my analysis of the torture episode in *The Woman Warrior*, specifiable, modifiable behavior is not the issue. Steve, with his trappings of affluent international urban culture, is different enough from the quiet girl with her homemade clothes and China doll haircut. Yet as Dale would say, "But they're still FOBs" (43).

The psychological mechanisms of repression and projection operate as forcefully as ever in Dale's mind, giving rise to the racial shadow. Dale subscribes blindly to the most superficial, materialistic version of the American dream, conceiving of success solely in terms of conspicuous consumption and popularity based thereon. As is typical of first selves, he displays an inflated self-image that is constantly undercut by inadvertent admissions of failure: "I am much better now. I go out now. Lots. I can, anyway. Sometimes I don't ask anyone, so I don't go out. But I could" (36). What he is "much better" than, Dale does not say; it could be his earlier, less assimilated phase as a child of immigrant parents, or it could be his parents themselves, who, he laments, "don't know anything about the world." By calling them "yellow ghosts" who try to "cage [him] up with Chinese-ness," Dale indirectly expresses a wish to see them relegated to the realm of the dead; in this he is at one with Stuart. Like Kazuko, he betrays an exaggerated concern for the opinion of whites, the "normal" human beings who may grant to or withhold from him the right to be himself: "I've had to work real hard—real hard—to be myself. To not be a Chinese, a yellow, a slant, a gook. To be just a human being, like anyone else" (36). What Dale refuses to see is the fact that, as a person of Chinese ancestry in race-conscious America, to be "like anyone else" is an unrealizable dream.

With knowledge of his self-defined deformity repressed, Dale directs all his pent-up spite toward the FOB, whom he describes in a lecture-like prologue:

F-O-B. Fresh Off the Boat. FOB. What words can you think of that characterize the FOB? Clumsy, ugly, greasy FOB. Loud, stupid, four-eyed FOB.
Big feet. Horny. Like Lenny in *Of Mice and Men*. Very good. A literary
reference. High-water pants. Floods, to be exact. Someone you wouldn't
want your sister to marry. If you are a sister, someone you wouldn't want
to marry. That assumes we're talking about boy FOBs, of course. But girl
FOBs aren't really as . . . FOBish. Boy FOBs are the worst, the . . . pits.
They are the sworn enemies of all ABC—oh, that's "American Born
Chinese"—of all ABC girls. Before an ABC girl will be seen on Friday night
with a boy FOB in Westwood, she would rather burn off her face. (7)

While this description is reminiscent of the portrait of Sam in "No
Man's Land," the playwright gives an interesting twist to the double
theme by making Steve an active, indeed cunning, warrior against abuse
by the self-righteously Americanized. Through leaps between realms of
reality created by stage effects, Hwang provides us access to the workings of Steve's mind and identifies him with Gwan Gung, the famed warrior of Chinese history revered as a god. Steve arms himself by acting like
the stereotypical FOB, which he in fact does not resemble. In other
words, he is merely playing the racial shadow. As he explains to Grace,
who is puzzled by his sudden shifts between nativelike and accented English, "Gwan Gung will not go into battle without equipment worthy of
his position" (26). He pretends to be the dumb Chinaman only to draw
out the ABC's worst prejudices; his strategy is to trap Dale into smug-
ness, then shock and confound him with unexpected behavior. Rather
than resort to physical violence, Steve clashes with Dale in metaphoric
combat, such as verbal duels, an eating contest (see previous chapter),
and a ritual battle between the one-legged bear and Gwan Gung in the
Group Story game. At the end of the play, a disoriented Dale confesses
to Steve, "You know . . . I think you picked up English faster than anyone I've ever met" (56). By the time we reach the play's coda, which is
a truncated version of the prologue, Dale has lost his obnoxious cer-
tainty; he is unable to finish his zoological lecture on the FOB.

Steve, then, is an unusual, because role-played, variant of the racial
shadow. In the Asian American stories we have examined up to *FOB*, the
double is always seen solely from the outside; not so Steve. Does
Hwang's focus on the inner operations of Steve disqualify the latter
from being a racial shadow? The term *shadow* has connotations of parasitism and secondariness, which certainly do not describe Steve's *actual*
position relative to Dale. Nevertheless, what counts in this question is
his *perceived* status and attributes in Dale's eyes. While confinement to
the first self's viewpoint follows naturally from the essence of projection,
Hwang's treatment underscores even more clearly that the double is always, to some extent, a figment of the first self's imagination.

Steve also stands out in the deliberateness with which he teaches Dale a lesson. All the encounters with the double we have studied result in what Keppler terms the "growth of the first self." However catastrophic the harm done to the first self by the second self, "it is a harm that stirs awake, that lances through the comfortable shell of self-complacency or self-protection, that strips away all masks of self-deception, that compels awareness and in the agony of the process brings self-enlargement" (Keppler, 194–95). Nevertheless, with the quiet girl, cousin Yoshiye and the Nisei patients, the Shoyu Kid, as well as the doubles in "No Man's Land," participation in the spiritual and political education of the protagonist(s) is unwitting. In contrast, Steve takes on a conscious mission to expose Dale's confusion and self-contempt. When Dale tries to "help" Steve to become "a little more normal," the latter smiles a lot and keeps interrupting with inconsequential remarks, until Dale is driven to articulate the absurdity of his own undertaking: "I'M TRYING . . . TO MAKE YOU LIKE JOHN TRAVOLTA!" (38). When Dale concludes a caustic speech on FOBs with the remark, "Yeah—great things come to the U.S. out of Hong Kong," Steve comes back with "Such as your parents?" (30). This is the kind of moral that Stuart in "No Man's Land" has to deduce on his own from traumatic experiences.

It is true that Hwang's overt didacticism differs substantially from the kind of subtle and strenuous psychological drama that gives many traditional stories of the double their special flavor. Moreover, learning in *FOB* is not limited to Dale but is experienced by Steve as well; their common teacher is Grace, an ex-FOB who has had time to "thaw out" (40) and attain self-acceptance (34–35). By the end of the play both young men have lost some of their rigidity and gained receptiveness toward the opposite persuasion. *FOB* thus branches off in more directions than most of the episodes and stories examined in this chapter. On the other hand, the structural constituents derived from other examples of the racial shadow are unequivocally present in *FOB*: an American-born, assimilated first self; internalization of white judgment and disowning of one's Asian identity; psychological and/or physical violence against a character who personifies inferior "Asian" qualities; and forced questioning, if not revision, of the first self's original concepts of acceptability. By this set of criteria Steve is a racial shadow.[18]

FURTHER HISTORICIZING OF THE RACIAL SHADOW

Identifying the racial shadow in Asian American literature, as with all acts of classification, entails mindful movement between levels of generality. Having established the distinctiveness of the type through a temporary and strategic exaggeration of commonalities, we can now concentrate on deepening the historicization process. What does it mean, we may ask, to find a calculatedly instructive variant of the racial shadow like Steve? Is its existence to be attributed solely to the playwright's artistic inventiveness or are larger sociohistorical forces implicated? Among various encounters with the racial shadow depicted in Asian American literature, can we discover nuances that can be correlated with the particular historical junctures at which they appear?

If "the nature of the Asian presence in America has been one of a constant positioning and re-positioning according to the shifting, yet constant needs of American ideology" (Palumbo-Liu 1988), the racial shadow will likewise exhibit both constancy and shift. The Asian presence has been exploited to exemplify a perennially unassimilable Other, somewhere between the deserving melting-pot-readiness of white immigrants and the irredeemable negativity of black slaves (and their respective descendants). However, the material means by which the "alienation"—literally, making alien—of Asian Americans is effected have fluctuated with America's economic and political needs, as well as with the legislative mobilizations that express them (Lesser 1985–86). These implementations, by altering the composition and ethos of Asian American communities, have discernibly (if indirectly) influenced the manifestations of the racial shadow in Asian American literature.

Two sets of contrasts in the handling of the racial shadow bear out this point: Sone's fetishization of cultural differences, which stands out from the more critical presentation of the other authors; and Hwang's "deconstructivist" thematization of disowning, which differs from treatments based on the first self's standpoint.

Two major historical "alienating" events fed the self-alienation depicted in Sone's *Nisei Daughter*. The first was the Immigration Act of 1924 barring entry of those "ineligible for citizenship" (among them Japanese), which climaxed earlier anti-Japanese efforts mounted by economically threatened whites.[19] Unlike in Euro-American communities where continued immigration "diluted the impact of the American born," the Japanese American community found the Issei "frozen" not only in numbers but also in legal outsiderhood, while the Nisei were discretely set apart. As a result, the latter experienced magnified pressures toward assimilation and intensified intergenerational conflict (Daniels 1988: 172).[20] The second "alienating" event was, of course, the wartime internment of over 110,000 Japanese Americans, some 70,000 of them American-born citizens. By this act of betrayal by one's own government, the ideology of Americanization so enthusiastically espoused by the Nisei was radically called into question.

It is against this background that the encounter with the racial shadow in *Nisei Daughter* should be understood. Kazuko's unreflecting

self-fragmentation and absolutizing of cultural differences are symptomatic of an endeavor to fashion an alternative mythology, one capable
of explaining away, in a depoliticized (hence less menacing) manner,
the contradictions revealed by internment.[21] Published in 1953, *Nisei
Daughter* bears the mark of recent trauma in that the workings of psychological defenses, though leaving numerous traces in the narrative,
appear to have gone totally undetected by the author herself.[22] In contrast, Kaneko's treatment of the racial shadow in "The Shoyu Kid" is a
critical one. The characters' confusions are transparently not the author's; it is precisely because the author is distanced both temporally and
emotionally from self-hatred that he is able to allegorize about it so elab-
orately. In his critical stance Kaneko not only differs from Sone but resembles the other authors discussed in this chapter. Dunn, Kaneko,
Kingston, and Hwang are all beneficiaries of the Asian American consciousness movement of the 1960s, having learned to be suspicious of
both the rhetoric of ethnic uplift ("best of both worlds") and ethnic
schizophrenia ("torn between two cultures").[23]

One of the factors that prompted a fundamental rethinking of the
Asian American condition is the immigration reform of 1965, which
dramatically transformed the makeup and dynamics of Asian American
communities by lifting earlier provisions favoring Northwestern European immigrants and allowing a resumption of massive immigration
from Asia (Reimers 1985, esp. 11–38, 63–90, 91–121). Curtailment of
Asian immigration or outright exclusion, the overtly racist forms in
which white domination was earlier embodied, were superseded after
America's postwar economic needs and world role changed (Reimers,
11–13). Instead of battling explicitly racist legislation, Asian Americans
now have to contend with indirect pressures, chief among them renewed
promotion of the Horatio Alger myth and selective celebration of successful Asian Americans in order to justify continued social stratification.
The growing heterogeneity and tension within the ethnic community—
a large segment of which is still disenfranchised (Takaki 1989:475–
76)—are precisely those conditions most conducive to formation of the
double. The vehemence with which Stuart in "No Man's Land" lashes
out against the hordes of immigrants in Chinatown reflects, to a certain
extent, the way in which the assimilative expectations of the American-
born were frustrated, and their sense of alienation exacerbated, by an
influx of diverse immigrants at the very moment the "model minority"
is being touted.[24]

But the most pronounced mark left by post-1965 demographic
changes is Hwang's treatment of the racial shadow in *FOB*, which directly pits ABCs against a new type of Chinese Americans: well-to-do,
urbanized, educated, and already somewhat Westernized immigrants.

This group constitutes one end of a bimodal economic structure within the Chinese American community, the other being "have-nots" stuck in menial positions in crowded Chinatowns (Chen 1981:223–38). The presence of the former group inflates statistics of Asian American achievement (Kan and Liu 1986:22) and feeds the myth of the "model minority," which, by its flattering appearance (Osajima 1988), deceptively transposes social conflicts onto the personal plane. In *FOB*, Hwang has chosen to assume the racial shadow's hitherto insubstantial (because projected) vantage point. He is thereby able to flesh out a presence elided in "mainstream" ideological discourse and deconstruct roles and interactions too often seen as conforming to unalterable cultural laws. Hwang's handling of the double may, in part, be attributable to insights gained from his own background: his immigrant parents and Steve's belong to the same privileged sector. But a more historically informed explanation would consider how a deepening of self-understanding in a much-altered Asian American community has facilitated deconstruction of the racial shadow.[25]

AN EXTRAVAGANT LOOK AT THE HYPHEN

A number of scholars of the double have suggested that self-reintegration is the goal toward which the first self gropes. Rosenfield speaks of "personal coherence" (319); Hallam, of "psychic integration" (20). Eder maintains that "if doubles are successful, a therapeutic exchange of characteristics or reintegration of personality is effected. . . . The drive of double literature is toward the reunification of the selves who have been split" (597). Keppler goes so far as to assert that "every second-self story, so far as the first self is concerned, is to one degree or another a story of shaping, a *Bildungsroman*" (195); the aspiration is toward "expanded rather than contracted being" (208). Apparently, once galvanized into awareness by a confrontation with the double, the protagonist is then free to reabsorb the denied and externalized aspects of the self. All the Asian American examples of the double investigated in this chapter point in the direction of eventual wholeness, yet success seems elusive. The most we can say of the protagonists is that they are made ready for self-reintegration by the various states of discomfiture in which the fateful encounter has left them: shock, anger, inexplicable shame, bewilderment, a sense of defeat, an urge to withdraw. How resolution is to be achieved is usually left open.

An ostensible exception to this pattern is provided by Sone in *Nisei Daughter*. As a young girl Kazuko feels that "being a Yankee and Japanese at the same time" is "like being born with two heads." It sounds "freakish and a lot of trouble" (19). After the experience of internment and then dispersal into the white world of the Midwest, Kazuko says to her parents, "I used to feel like a two-headed monstrosity, but now I find that two heads are better than one" (236). The book ends on a celebratory note: "I was going back into its mainstream, still with my Oriental eyes, but with an entirely different outlook, for now I felt more like a whole person instead of a sadly split personality. The Japanese and the American parts of me were now blended into one" (238).

Is this, then, an inspiring instance of doubling reversed, the split healed, the racial shadow reincorporated? As we may have learned to expect of Kazuko, her phrasing often undermines the content of her utterances. In this case, the phrase "still with my Oriental eyes" betrays the same preoccupation with deviance from white norms which causes her to worry about her ruined hairdo on the momentous morning of the relocation (167). As for the "Japanese parts" of self, these have not been mentioned since her account of burning Japanese mementos (154–56). Thus a vivid experiential sense of internal division and deformity, whose sources Kazuko has chosen not to investigate, has been domesticated with a reassuringly banal cliché.

Kazuko's professed attainment of self-reintegration, which is probably not uncommon among Asian Americans, is parodied in Maxine Hong Kingston's *Tripmaster Monkey: His Fake Book* (1989). In "Bones and Jones," one of the chapters detailing the encyclopedic and climactic "Magic Theater" performance staged by protagonist Wittman Ah Sing, Sone's facile idea of the "whole person" is concretized in a pair of Siamese twins—a "two-headed monstrosity" if ever there was one. They are "verbal twins in green velveteen connected suits": "Chang and Eng, the Double Boys, pattering away in Carolina-Siamese, Chinkus and Pinkus" (Kingston 1989:290). The two try out ideas that would make them "more like the normal American person," including intermarriage. The brothers dance with "lovely white ladies of the wider American world" as well as famous pairs of Chinese American sisters—Lin Yutang's daughters, Adet and Anor; the Eaton sisters, Sui Sin Fah[26] (Edith) and Onoto Watanna (Winnifred) (291). The twins are simultaneously accused of having lost his/their identity and being assimilated (292), and, like Japanese Americans during World War II, they are wanted by the United States Army (293), presumably "to make a more perfect union" (292).

The circus crowd rushes the stage, shouting "Let's have a look!" "Let's see! Let's see!" A doctor inspects the twins and pronounces him/them "as human as the next American man." After a riot, the twins are jailed, and Chang yells at the audience through the bars:

We know damned well what you came for to see—the angle we're joined
at, how we can have two sisters for wives and twenty-one Chinese-Carolin-
ian children between us. You want to see if there's room for two, three
bundling boards. You want to know if we feel jointly. You want to look at
the hyphen. You want to look at it bare." (293)

All the Asian American works on the double cited in this chapter are
attempts to "look at the hyphen." Their scrutiny is serious rather than
prying; failure to "feel jointly" is no joking matter. However, after a sustained inquiry into the painful Necessity of self-alienation, it is perhaps
fitting to be reminded again of the power of Extravagance. In Kingston's irreverent comic imagination, absurdity, like a good Zen koan, re-
solves the problem by dissolving it into unformulability. Winnifred
Eaton, aka Miss Watanna, condescends to the twins, gushing: " 'I'm so
sorry for your sad life and persecution, and your loneliness. I sympa-
thize.' " At which Chang-Eng, never deprived of each other's company,
exclaim(s) in surprise, " 'Loneliness?' " When Miss Watanna advises assumption of a Japanese identity and a career in exoticism like her own,
"He are baffled. 'Identity?' " he/they echo(es). Identity? What identity?
Haven't the two always been one?

The relief afforded by such zaniness is momentary—the sociohistorical forces that give rise to the racial shadow are unlikely to disappear
anytime soon, which is probably why reintegration is merely hinted at by
most of the authors. But the verbal paralysis brought on by the Chang-
Eng duo exposes, as refreshingly as ever, the constructedness of the
"Asian American identity problem."

CONCLUSION

The configuration of the racial shadow that has emerged from the foregoing analysis demonstrates both the "universality" and uniqueness of
Asian American literature. This literature is found to share a motif—the
double—with works in the European and Anglo-American traditions,
some quite remote from it in both subject matter and tenor. Nevertheless, careful intertextual reading reveals that the motif takes a particular
form determined by the place Asian Americans have been occupying in
the United States. Asian American examples of the double are not—perhaps cannot afford to be—parables of human nature in the abstract or
case studies in the intricacies of human psychology. Not that history is
not sedimented in their European and Anglo-American counterparts:
the scholars of the diachronic school have convincingly demonstrated
otherwise. Still, in Asian American literature, depoliticization of the
double is less fully veiled, and historical contextualization much more

essential to profitable reading, than in Western "mainstream" literature. (This is true even of the torture episode in *The Woman Warrior*, which more than the others partakes of the extreme subjectivity and eerie atmosphere typical of canonical tales of the double.)

Without an awareness of Asian American literature's continuities with its counterparts in other cultures, the double theme may go unrecognized. On the other hand, without a race-aware framework for reading it, critics may simply be reduced to testifying to the "humanness" of Asian American characters—how a common set of psychological mechanisms operate in us all—hardly a stimulating or inspiring project. A group-specific framework, far from a product of the kind of facile biological insiderism decried by Sollors (1986a:11), requires informed selectivity and scrupulous attention to text, context, and intertext alike. But once devised, such an approach to the double theme may suggest many further subjects for study in American literatures of people of color.[27]

Are there counterparts to the Asian American racial shadow in other American traditions, and if so, what are they? In the symbolic economy of African American works that explore enforced self-fragmentation, for example, is gradation of skin color the counterpart of degree of assimilation in Asian American works: an encoding of white-defined acceptability within a group grossly designated by a single label—more physical in manifestation, perhaps, than assimilation, but an ideological construct nonetheless? If there is an African American version of the racial shadow, what are its characteristics, and what is the typical interaction between it and the first self?

The recurrent "tragic mulatto/mulatta" figure (Christian 1985:3–5, 8, 166–67; Carby 1987:88–91, 135–37, 140–41, 171–74); the appearance of the black-skinned wife in Charles Chesnutt's "The Wife of His Youth" (1898); the relationship between Irene Redfield and Clare Kendry in Nella Larsen's *Passing* (1929); the narrator's gravitation toward Trueblood in Ralph Ellison's *Invisible Man* (1952); the way Pecola in Toni Morrison's *The Bluest Eye* (1970) absorbs the scorn and hatred of the lighter-skinned blacks in her community—these examples all strongly suggest that the racial shadow could be a useful concept for reading African American literature. The narrator of *The Bluest Eye* says of Pecola:

> All of our waste which we dumped on her and which she absorbed. And all of our beauty, which was hers first and which she gave to us. All of us—all who knew her—felt so wholesome after we cleaned ourselves on her. We were so beautiful when we stood astride her ugliness. Her simplicity decorated us, her guilt sanctified us, her pain made us glow with health, her awkwardness made us think we had a sense of humor. Her inarticulateness

made us believe we were eloquent. Her poverty kept us generous. Even her waking dreams we used—to silence our own nightmares. She let us, and thereby deserved our contempt. We honed our egos on her, padded our characters with her frailty, and yawned in the fantasy of our strength. (163)

This passage describes a "general" projective basis of double formation, superficially unmarked for race; at the same time, each of the attributes listed (beauty, simplicity, pain, etc.) is realized in the novel in racial and class terms—especially racial. The title of the book is a constant reminder of the racial formation obtaining in Pecola's world: in the phrase "the bluest eye," the definite article and the singular form of the noun combine to indicate the objectification of arbitrarily valorized physical features—the creation of racially marked "types"—as an external correlative of innate desirability.

In other literatures of people of color as well, the figure of the racial shadow may be recognized. For example, in Chicano literature, Ana Castillo's exploration of feminist and cultural nationalist intersections, *The Mixquiahuala Letters* (1986), exhibits an interesting pattern in which two women protagonists—one light-colored and of Spanish stock, the other darkly Indian in origin and appearance—haunt each other's life and imagination with neither predominating as a first self. In Native American literature, mixed descent in such works as Emily Pauline Johnson's *The Moccasin Maker* (1913), Mourning Dove's *Co-ge-we-a, the Half-Blood* (1927), John Joseph Mathews's *Sundown* (1934), and D'Arcy McNickle's *The Surrounded* (1936) appears to function, like skin color and cultural trait, to embody the tensions experienced by the colonized. In Louise Erdrich's *Love Medicine* (1984) and *Tracks* (1988), the mixed-blood Pauline/Sister Leopolda shows a combination of fascinated obsession and malicious persecution first toward Fleur, the un-Christianized Indian woman of power, then toward Marie, the illegitimate daughter Pauline has abandoned and never acknowledged. The doppelgänger pattern is readily recognizable from its "classic" characteristics, including hints of occult powers and Pauline's unstable mental state. Yet individual psychopathology is shown to be inextricable from—in fact exacerbated and given frighteningly violent shape by—the history of Native American subjugation through force and deceit, treaties and government agencies, missionary schools and convents, land appropriation, the plunder of natural resources, the imposition of a cash economy, the destruction of the Indian's self-sufficiency and self-respect—all vividly but unobtrusively evoked in Erdrich's lyrical prose.

In addition to the racial shadow, related phenomena outside the scope of this chapter, such as doubling by multiplication, or the idealizing (as opposed to disowning) type of projection, may also be studied. The former concept may provide fruitful ways to read works like *The Woman Warrior*, *Obasan*, or Ellison's *Invisible Man*, where differing versions of a basic figure are offered to the protagonist faced with a race- and ethnicity-linked identity crisis. The latter is found in works as disparate as Bienvenido Santos's fiction on Filipino Americans ("Scent of Apples" and "The Day the Dancers Came," in *Scent of Apples*, 21–29, 113–28), in which youthful Filipinos, in memory or in the flesh, are deified to represent a prelapsarian (preimmigration) perfection (Cheung 1986); and Toni Morrison's *Beloved* (1987), in which the Protean, ghostly Beloved takes shape as the "best thing" of each of the characters traumatized by racial violence and hungry for healing. As with the racial shadow, precisely *what* gets projected as desirable goes beyond idiosyncracies of the individual personality or the logic of philosophical tenets; understanding it calls for a mobilization of our knowledge of American realities, historical, racial, economic, and more. The possibilities for comparative study appear numerous and promising.

Chapter Three

THE POLITICS OF MOBILITY

AMERICA IS FOUNDED on myths of mobility. Not only have the ocean crossings of the Pilgrims been elevated to a national fable, affirmed anew every time an immigrant voyage is celebrated as its reenactment (Boel-hower 1982:27–28; Stout 1983:4; Sollors 1990b); but the Puritan "er-rand into the wilderness"[1] is predicated upon the possibility of move-ment, however charged with ambivalence, between "civilization" and "nature." Of course, different regional emphases existed of the colonial project, as in the case of the Virginian settlers, whose motives were more nostalgic than utopian (Allen 1969:39). Nevertheless, the powerful metaphor that informed the Puritan vision provided the terms to define the national drama and colored much subsequent thinking on the dis-tinctiveness of the American spirit. Frederick Jackson Turner's influen-tial "frontier thesis" regards the availability of free land—presupposing unconstrained mobility to take advantage of it—coupled with equality of opportunity, to be crucial determinants of American character and the source of American democracy, through a process of "perennial re-birth" (1963:28). In the "crucible of the frontier," that meeting place of "savagery and civilization," a uniquely American "composite national-ity" emerges: "the immigrants were Americanized, liberated, and fused into a mixed race" (44, 28).

Since its publication in 1893, the inadequacy of Turner's thesis has been exposed by the events of history as well as the alternative analyses of historians (Smith 1970:295 n. 3; Simonson 1963:17–20). Yet the idea that the essence of America consists in freedom, in both a physical and a spiritual sense, has worked itself deep into the national imagina-tion and continues to exert a potent hold on the American imagination (e.g., Clough 1964:81; Allen 1969:56). Since its birth as a political and social entity, it is safe to say, America has customarily defined its unique-ness in terms of the enhanced mobility it can offer: the opportunity to go where one wants, do what one wants, shape life anew.

Given the importance of mobility in the ideological underpinnings of America, it is hardly surprising to find that American literature, too, has from its beginnings been "a literature of movement, of motion, its great icons the track through the forest and the superhighway" (Stout 1983:3). Some of the most revered classics of American literature, such as Cooper's *Leather-Stocking Tales* (1823–41), Hawthorne's *The Scarlet*

Letter (1850), Melville's *Moby-Dick* (1851), Whitman's "Song of the Open Road" (1856) and "Pioneers! O Pioneers!" (1865) from *Leaves of Grass*, and Twain's *The Adventures of Huckleberry Finn* (1884), either celebrate ceaseless movement into new realms or, where it is not fully realized, are at least preoccupied with the possibility or else permeated by the vocabulary of travel and exploration.[2] Later writers such as Jack London (*The Road*, 1907), John Steinbeck (*The Grapes of Wrath*, 1939), Jack Kerouac (*On the Road*, 1957), John Updike, (*Rabbit, Run*, 1970), and Joan Didion (*Play It As It Lays*, 1970) are likewise drawn to images of motion expressing a range of now overlapping, now contradictory, meanings—adventure, exploration, escape, home-seeking, quest, aimless meandering. Travel literature and its cousin, nature writing (Lyon 1989), are important narrative subgenres in American letters, as is the Western, populated by men on horseback roaming about expansive spaces (Folsom 1966).[3]

On the whole, despite qualifying variations such as countermovements of repatriation and self-exile in Europe (Stout 1983:5), and despite a growing sense of futility and exhaustion of will in twentieth-century fictions of flight (Bluefarb 1972:3; Zink 1956:287), one can say that a controlling influence in American literature has been the perception of an open continent and the limitless opportunities it implies—to shed corrupt European culture, to recover lost innocence, to rejuvenate self and society, to discover or invent personal identity, to realize individual potential, to commune with Nature, to appropriate abundant resources, and a host of other physical or spiritual options. In the words of R. W. B. Lewis, the archetypal American hero is a "hero in space," his "initial habit [being] space as spaciousness, as the unbounded, the area of total possibility" (1955:91). "The frontier, the movement westward, remains the great image of the American sense of possibility" (Allen 1969:58).[4]

This, then, is the mainstream understanding of mobility, a cultural axiom that has governed popular myth-making from the cowboy's lonely ride into the sunset to the stirring rhetoric of the space program (e.g., Carter 1988; Mazlish 1965; Michaud 1986; Taylor 1974). Yet the Asian American has been conspicuously absent in existing generalist formulations of a presumably universally applicable theory of American mobility; none of the major studies on the American landscape, the frontier, or the journey motif makes a place for the group (e.g., Clough 1964; Fussell 1965; Hazard 1927; Marx 1964; Smith 1950; Stout 1983).

The absence of Asian Americans in the literary scholarship on American mobility must be deemed a serious, if historically explainable, omission. For Asian American literature, from its very inception, has also been "a literature of movement, of motion." Carlos Bulosan's *America Is in the Heart* (1943), one of the first Asian American works to reach a mainstream audience and a classic in the Asian American canon (E. Kim 1982:45), chronicles the constant displacement of migrant Filipino farmworkers. Dislocation is a key theme for Japanese-ancestry writers in the United States and Canada from John Okada to Joy Kogawa. Images of incessant motion abound in the works of Frank Chin and Shawn Wong, for whom the railroad and the highway are obsessive loci of experience. The first modernist Asian American novel, by Chuang Hua, is entitled *Crossings* (1968), referring to the deracinated protagonist's trans- and intercontinental wanderings. Recent writers continue to create characters who are "on the road": Nieh Hualing's *Mulberry and Peach* (1981), Cynthia Kadohata's *The Floating World* (1989), and Bharati Mukherjee's *Jasmine* (1989) all feature female protagonists restlessly traversing the American landscape. Theresa Cha's postmodernist *Dictee* (1982) so incessantly and hauntingly evokes dislocations and border-crossings that physical movement and state of mind become indistinguishable. In a lighter vein, in Gish Jen's *Typical American* (1991), America's glorious promise to the (soon-to-be-disabused) immigrant is symbolized by a joy ride in a commandeered convertible (100–102).

An examination of the mobility theme in Asian American literature would obviously be worthwhile for the group's self-understanding, but it should not be considered a "special interest" project. Rather, by reinstating previously suppressed or neglected viewpoints, it can reveal the workings of dominant discourse and provide a corrective to its oversimplifications. An ethnic group-specific approach to the mobility theme gains support from recent scholarship on the sexual symbolism of the American landscape, which has demonstrated how gender-linked assumptions may have operated undetected in the putatively natural and objective process of developing a common American identity. Continuing a line of inquiry adumbrated as early as 1964 by Leo Marx (29) and taken up by Richard Slotkin (1973), feminist critic Annette Kolodny, in *The Lay of the Land* (1975), makes explicit the concealed role of gender in the American "pastoral impulse"—"a yearning to know and to respond to the landscape as feminine" (8). In *The Land Before Her* (1984), Kolodny furthers her inquiry to identify a tradition of white pioneer women's responses to the west, distinct in imagery and tenor from the men's (which have been taken to represent a quintessentially American mentality). Thus even within the dominant group—the white settlers—heterogeneity of attitude is found to be significant enough to compel an amendment of received wisdoms. Race and ethnicity are at least as instrumental as gender (if not more so) in shaping perceptions of the American land, since they form the basis of a long tradition of legislative, not to mention informal, circumscription of spatial possibilities for certain groups. In fact, if, as bell hooks puts it in *Yearning: Race, Gender, and Cultural Politics*, "sexuality has always provided gendered metaphors for colonization" (1990:57), race and ethnicity should always be considered with gender when analyzing the discourse of American settlement. An examination of Asian American images of mobility, apart from advancing our sense of a distinct Asian American literary tradition, would foster a more nuanced understanding of the nature of the American enterprise in the New World.

What does mobility mean in Asian American literature? How do writers conceptualize the Asian American's relationship to the American landscape? What, in their works, are the spatial expressions of the Asian American's "place" in the overall social structure? What aspects of mobility preoccupy the writers, and how do they represent these preoccupations? Do Asian American thematizations of mobility differ noticeably from those in mainstream writing, and if so, in what ways? Does Asian American literature offer any oppositional mobility myths to the dominant ones? These are some of the questions to be explored in this chapter (which will, like the rest of the book, be partly structured by the master concepts of Necessity and Extravagance).

MOBILITY AS NECESSITY

One striking difference presents itself upon even the most cursory comparison between mainstream and Asian American discourses on mobility. In the former, horizontal movement across the North American continent regularly connotes independence, freedom, an opportunity for individual actualization and/or societal renewal—in short, Extravagance. In the latter, however, it is usually associated with subjugation, coercion, impossibility of fulfillment for self or community—in short, Necessity.

Of course, since Necessity and Extravagance are contrasting positions on a continuum rather than mutually exclusive categories, a broad observation like the above must be scrupulously calibrated as soon as it is offered. In point of fact, America's first settlers were not as purely motivated by Extravagance as cultural clichés and patriotic pieties later made them out to be. It has been said that Puritan pioneer was "both a mystic and a bargain hunter," combining "the endurance of the zealot with the enthusiasm of the realtor" (Hazard 1927:4, 9).[5] Land hunger and disenfranchisement in the Old World were intertwined with a sense of divine mission. In that sense, even the most lavish pioneer rhapsodies must not be taken entirely at face value. The issue is not the absolute absence of Necessity in their experiential origin—as drastic a step as emigration is seldom prompted by Extravagance alone—but the way they express a group-sanctioned ideological direction and the remarkable extent to which they contrast with Asian American representations of mobility. A similar point may be made about the character of the first Puritan communities, which, from most accounts, was rather joyless, repressive, and intolerant (Hazard 1927:14–15, 19–21; Allen 1969:30–32). What is of interest is not this particular historical fact, but the evolution of Extravagant national myths that have come to overshadow their literal origin.

A corollary of the first point is that a number of mainstream texts using motifs of mobility imply an endpoint of immobility, but immobility of a desirable kind: that of having created a permanent home and cast down roots. Such a pattern is seen in a subtype of American journey narrative, the home-seeking or home-founding narrative, identified by Stout (1983:41–64).[6] The immobility of the settler is not a negation of freedom but a realization of it: the result of being able to exercise it to the full. To prevent confusion with the kind of immobility imposed by external force, this kind will be designated as at-homeness, rootedness, or centeredness.

Notwithstanding the existence of home-seeking narratives, the traditionally recognized westward errand has never been free of ambiguity.[7] It mixes "elements of progress with impulses of infantile regression" (Sanford 1961:56). If this movement suggests Extravagance, it is a somewhat compromised Extravagance, shot through with misgivings about its unsettling implications. Fussell summarizes the contradiction thus:

> Those exhilarating analogous progressions from East to West and from present to future were surcharged with teleological nationalism cartographically advancing from right to left, Old World to New, reality to beatitude. Yet paradoxically the American West—as chaos, matrix, or embryo—was also "earlier," and therefore the past. . . . Westward progress meant cultural regress. (1965:13–15)

Hence the linguistic indecision betraying conflicting notions of "back" ("backwoodsman") and "front" ("frontiersman") (Fussell, 15). Manifest destiny flaunts the banner of progress, but the serious writers in the dominant tradition have always communicated some unease about the national program of betterment through motion.

These, then, are some of the countervailing considerations to bear in mind when we heuristically invoke a mainstream understanding of mobility to help us define an Asian American one. Yet the former is far from being a straw man, erected only to be knocked down in order to exaggerate Asian American differences. Though the conventional vocabulary of mobility has lost much of its exuberance in twentieth-century mainstream literature and is frequently subjected to ironic manipulation, this crisis of confidence is the direct result of a lengthy, actual national experiment: it is from *having had* the chance to realize the promises of mobility but coming up against its limitations that the nation has fallen into a somber mood, which in turn has given the modern literature of mobility a defeatist cast. In Asian American literature, in contrast, there has from the beginning been a keen collective awareness of immobility as a historical given rather than a private frustration or temporary setback remediable by further ventures into virgin space. The writers' preoccupation with mobility often takes the form of images of *im*mobility: the coerced movement alluded to earlier can quite arguably be read as a kind of immobility as well, not as blatant as imprisonment but no less damaging. The Necessity-linked configurations of mobility images coalesce when Asian American texts are read not only *with* each other but also *against* the public discourse of mobility, for it is the group's exclusions (often rendered invisible) from "general" patterns of American mobility that has given rise to divergent representations.

Several such exclusions, together with some indication of their manifestation in literature, can be outlined here. These all pertain to the North American mainland.[8] The most salient of the exclusions is perhaps the passage of alien land laws prohibiting "aliens ineligible to citizenship" from buying and owning land. The California laws were passed in 1913 and 1920,[9] originally to check the influence of successful Japanese farmers, but were soon extended to cover all Asian immigrants, and were copied in Arizona, Idaho, Oregon, Washington, and Montana (Lai and Choy 1973:99).[10] The laws were not declared unconstitutional until after the Second World War.[11] Although the first alien land law was enacted some two decades after the "official" closing of the frontier, Asian groups, given their relatively recent immigration history and their typical movement from the Pacific Coast eastward (the reverse of the European settlers'), really had not benefited collectively from the availability of cheap land before their presence in the West was contained by unabashedly racist restrictions (Takaki 1989:203–204). Thus the homestead, whether as a legal entity or as a key item in American cultural iconography, was largely irrelevant to the Asian American experience; likewise the genre of the home-founding narrative, in which movement culminates in an abiding place of rest.

Ruthanne Lum McCunn's *Thousand Pieces of Gold* (1981), a historical novel based on the life of Lalu Nathoy, later known as Polly Bemis (1853–1933), is perhaps the only Asian American text with clear and self-consciously wrought analogs to mainstream images of the frontier and the homestead.[12] After traversing the ocean as a kidnapped slave girl and enduring an uncertain mule ride into Idaho mining country, the Chinese prostitute-turned-pioneer woman engages in the exemplary activities of cabin-building, claim-staking, garden-planting, bread-baking, home nursing of sick children, and improvised surgery on gunshot wounds. Yet conformity to pioneer models is not the only or even main source of Bemis's epic stature; it is what she manages to create despite a crucial *difference in legal status* from her white counterparts that makes her a true Asian American heroine. In a conversation with Charlie, the white man who wins her in a poker game and later marries her, Bemis is rudely awakened to the fraudulence at the heart of America's official idealism, the attractive expansionist slogans of free land and equal opportunity.

> "A Chinaman can't own land," he said, so softly she could barely hear him.
> "But you say America have land for everyone. That people from all over the world come for the land. Rich. Poor. All the same. Anyone can have land. You said."
> "Any American. You're from China." . . .
> "You not understand. I never go back to China. I become American.". . . .
> "The only way a Chinaman can become an American is to be born here."
> (162, 164)

And the only way Bemis can be guaranteed freedom from eviction is to take advantage of a loophole in the alien land laws by filing a mining claim, which allows her to possess the surrounding land (228). In reconstructing Bemis's story, McCunn is far from lending greater credibility to the frontier myths by showing how they apply even to the Chinese. Nor is parity-claiming ("We, too, have our pioneer women") the decisive issue, for Bemis's case is admittedly atypical. Rather, the point is to insert a forgotten presence and a reminder of contradiction into the prototypical American home-founding narrative.

GROUP-SPECIFIC PATTERNS OF MOBILITY

In addition to sharing an ambiguous and ambivalent relationship to the American land (it was simultaneously home, object of one's cultivation and attachment, and not home, since one's claim to it had to be established through legal subterfuge, if at all),[13] Asian American subgroups each had specific historical experiences that affected their visions of mobility.

For the Chinese, who among Asians have been in America the longest, the idea of mobility possesses an especially ironic poignancy that writers like Shawn Wong and Frank Chin are quick to appreciate. The early immigrants' contribution to railroad building, which opened up the continent and enabled the allure of manifest destiny to take hold, led not to a corresponding social participation but to immobilization. The laborers' absence from the 1869 Golden Spike ceremony, which marked the completion of the transcontinental railroad, betrayed the inapplicability of mobility myths to the Chinese and foreshadowed their subsequent scattering across the land. The disbanded railroad workers, unwelcome as settlers, encountered a series of violent "driving-out": coerced movement; many found themselves confined to urban Chinatowns, hemmed in by harassing laws and taunting, stone-hurling white men.[14] This de facto imprisonment later took an overt, legislative form, as prospective Chinese immigrants were routinely detained at the Angel Island immigration station in San Francisco Bay from 1910 to 1940, during part of the Exclusion period. As an anonymous poem on the Angel Island barrack walls intimates, the moment of landing in America, made to signal an exhilarating fresh beginning in popular myths of the immigrant experience, meant to the Chinese not enhanced mobility but its very opposite:

> The moment I hear
>   We've entered the port,
> I am all ready:
>   My belongings wrapped in a bundle.
> Who would have expected joy to become sorrow:
>   Detained in a dark, crude, filthy room?
>
> (Hom 1987:75)

The arbitrary confinement on Angel Island has become a standard (or canonical?) subject in Chinese American literature, inspiring many American-born writers to recreate the experience (e.g., Shawn Wong 1979: 102–10; Kingston 1981:50–57; Hwang, 1983:23–24 [FOB]; Genny Lim 1991 [Paper Angels]).[15] Detention of Chinese immigrants ended in 1940, but their and their children's social confinement to the ethnic ghetto persisted well after the Second World War, so that even writers in the post-1965 period continue to be absorbed by the mobility theme.

The pivotal Japanese American exclusion from American mobility is, of course, internment during the Second World War, which constitutes a recurrent theme in the literature: a nightmarish "sticking point," so to speak, to which generations of authors feel compelled to return repeatedly, searching for answers. Unlike the "driving-out" of early Chinese Americans, which were carried out mainly by mobs (though sometimes with the abetting of government officials; see Tsai 1986:71 and Daniels 1988:62–63), the internment was premeditated and systematic, involving the entire state machinery.[16] It included both the indirect immobilization of coerced movement and the direct one of incarceration (first in temporary assembly centers—holding pens, rather, some hastily converted from horse stables—then in remote inland camps surrounded by barbed wire and armed guards). (In the Japanese Canadian case, no large-scale concentration camps were set up, but the serial exile at short notice, based on arbitrary criteria, was more disorienting and in some sense even harsher than the American arrangement.)

Central as the internment experience is, it must be remembered that, for a brief period before the war, many Japanese Americans had settled on the land with at least an unconscious expectation of permanence and hope of eventual full participation in American society, through their children if nothing else. Early Japanese immigrants were backed by a strong Japanese government and were, moreover, allowed to come with (or bring in) wives.[17] For a while, they seemed to have created a pattern of stable living close to the land reminiscent of certain elements of the homestead. Some of the stories of Hisaye Yamamoto ("Seventeen Syllables," "Yoneko's Earthquake," "Life Among the Oil Fields, A Memoir") and Wakako Yamauchi ("And the Soul Shall Dance," "Songs My Mother Taught Me") set in rural California evoke a sense of immersion in the seasonal rhythms of farm work and the human drama of an isolated community, making scant explicit references to the Japanese American's place in the larger polity. Yet even these works are never free from implicit irony, given the existence of alien land laws: if strictly enforced, the laws could undo the life's work of the Issei overnight. Whatever at-homeness the Japanese immigrants and their children managed to attain was illusory, and forced dispersal turned out to be the group's true fate, as it had been for the Chinese.

The Filipino Americans' mobility pattern on the mainland was shaped by the colonial history of their place of origin and the pre-Philippines Independence immigrants' special status as "nationals" of the United States, midway between aliens and citizens, between exclusion and inclusion. Carrying American passports and not subject to deportation like other Asians, Filipino immigrants were at the same time denied the full rights of citizenship (Melendy 1981:46–57). They were relegated to the most menial, lowest-paying occupations, a succession of which was often needed to eke out an living. Migrant seasonal work was typical of the Pinoys who immigrated to the U.S. mainland during the 1920s. As we will see in the section on Carlos Bulosan (below), the repetitive, unremitting nature of the work, with no home in sight, deprived ceaseless motion of any overtone of epic adventure or spiritual reinvigoration.

One of the characters in Bienvenido Santos's short story "The Day the Dancers Came" (1967), an aging, family-less immigrant from Bulosan's generation, is obsessed with discovering how to "keep floating indefinitely" (1979:123). This sense of terminal stranding and paralysis seems a principal component of the Filipino American understanding of mobility. Even Santos's recent work, *What the Hell For You Left Your Heart in San Francisco* (1987), which portrays post-1965 urban, middle-class Filipino immigrants, echoes the constant ramblings of the farmworkers in the person of a homeless protagonist searching for his lost father. In Filipino American literature, inability to break out of endless looping seems to be associated with inability to sustain a home and achieve a communal culture, which is one of the most unfortunate legacies of American colonialism.

The above profiles by no means exhaust the meaning of Asian American images of mobility,[18] but even so synoptic a survey has made one point clear: the idea of discovering a common direction of movement for this body of works, intellectually attractive as it is, must be eschewed, and the common thread among Asian American mobility narratives otherwise sought. Collectively, they exhibit no canonical direction of geographical movement; rather, they trace a multiplicity of routes, some linear and coherent, others defying patterning. Perhaps the only generalization we can safely make about directionality is that, when an Asian American mobility narrative consciously alludes to Westward movement as a possible structuring principle, the effect is typically ironic, as in Nieh's *Mulberry and Peach* and Mukherjee's *Jasmine*. In the former novel, a Chinese refugee woman suffering from split personality wanders vaguely Westward from New York in quest of peace of mind; after crisscrossing the interior, she decides to go to California in a gesture of hope but is haunted by tales of cannibalism about the Donner Party. The heroine of Mukherjee's *Jasmine*, an illegal alien like Mulberry/Peach, lands in Florida and eventually makes her way to Iowa, but finds no place in America, not even the heartland, that is sound or safe from decay and violence. At the end of the novel, a former lover persuades her to leave for California, in yet another reenactment of the American myth of self-making; her confident, forward-looking rhetoric is undercut, however, by the trail of disasters she has left thus far. In both these cases, it is significant that the authors have chosen to position their heroines initially on the East Coast, making possible troping on the myth of Westward movement, when a West Coast city would have been the most likely landing point for immigrants from Asia.

Instead of any clear-cut directional axis, the organizing spatial dimensions I have found useful are the horizontal and the vertical; within this general framework, contrapuntal readings of the Asian American texts bring out contrasts in the meanings of the cardinal directions. The reading stance I adopt acknowledges the group-specific historical conditions whose traces surface in varying degrees in individual texts. On the other hand, the relationship posited is not one of empirical determinism: there is never any claim that Asian American writers, given the circumstances, could only have written certain types of mobility narratives or that the existing ones must have flowed from some self-propelled historical imperative, for which the authors are merely passive vehicles. One obvious case in point is that, despite the enormity of Japanese American internment, there is as yet no single book-length treatment of it comparable in range and intensity to Joy Kogawa's novel on Japanese Canadian relocation, *Obasan*. And no one quite knows why. Each text represents a unique convergence of historical processes, cultural parameters, literary mediations, market forces, individual intent, and individual talent, among other accidents and idiosyncrasies; it is always, to some extent, a mysterious amalgam.

But the critical act performed on the produced texts, if always a post hoc accounting, is not just an ad hoc assemblage of single-text-bound observations. The following readings of specific Asian American images of mobility proceed on two consistently applied assumptions: that creative writers are often intuitively responsive to certain aspects of mobility congruent with collective focal experiences; and that meaningful patterns would emerge through an interpretive process that is simultaneously an attentive uncovering and an active construction. Finally, mobility is deemed a particularly intriguing motif to study because its constitutive temporal/spatial progressions lend themselves naturally to structural functions. (In comparison, the two motifs examined so far, alimentation and the double, tend to be more locally applied; the former is in fact hardly ever used to organize sustained narratives.) Whether a writer chooses to exploit them, and if so, in what ways, is itself capable of revealing a great deal about his/her sense of the world's scope and order (or disorder).

MAP-MAKING AND THE MOBILITY NARRATIVE

In the sections to follow, the readings of several Asian American texts on mobility will incorporate "map-making" as an instrument of textual analysis and historical understanding. This procedure might strike some as whimsical, but there is a rationale for it.

We are accustomed to thinking of narrative structure as temporally organized, but in a mobility narrative, place names and the way they are sequenced could also be indices of narrative structure, for mobility by definition involves changes in both temporal and spatial dimensions.

Mobility on any reasonably large scale would generate a map, a spatial correlate of completed and contemplated moves as well as a representation of one's mental patterning of the world. Thus plotting a map for a mobility narrative, whether "documentary" or "fictional," would be one interesting way to discover the author's vision of the land's possibilities and proscriptions, as derived from historical experience.

Map-making, as Boelhower reminds us, is in fact a process imbued with cultural and ideological values, especially in the New World context. The imperialistic maps of America made by European colonists were, for example, primarily "political and juridical" in spirit, despite their seemingly neutral scientific trappings.

> The function of the first maps was not at all to report a place, but to impose an *idea* of place on the new continent. . . . The map was above all a national signature of possession and a public declaration of the right to settlement. This is ultimately why the colonist and the explorer did not really see the Indian as much as they saw through him. (Boelhower 1987:49)

(A similar point is made forcefully by Edward Said when he describes the practice of modern geography as "geographical violence through which virtually every space in the world is explored, charted, and finally brought under control" [1989:10; cited in Kaplan 1989].) It is not that the Indians did not have maps; theirs were in fact impressively accurate and relied upon in war or hunting councils. But Indian maps were "chorographic," focusing on exact local details, unable to take in the continent at a glance and therefore vulnerable to the global plotting (in both a cartographic and political sense) of the Europeans. "What [the Indians] lacked was a map to produce a rival cultural discourse" (Boelhower 1987:50).

Boelhower is concerned with what might be called "first-order" map-making, with real topography as its referent, whereas a map of a narrative is a "second-order" schematization. But his point concerning the ideological meaning and revelatory capacity of maps remains valid.[19] We do not know what kind of first-order maps early Asian immigrants constructed or worked from, so this kind of "cultural discourse" is lost to us. But we do have a wealth of mobility narratives attempting or offering a "rival cultural discourse" for which second-order maps can be charted. In her 1989 paper "Remapping or Retelling History: The Politics of Location and the Poetics of Displacement," Caren Kaplan, noting a recent explosion of interest among humanists in space, maps, and boundaries, challenges students of minority discourse to create "geographies of history and histories of geographies."[20] The mapping of Asian American mobility narratives may be considered one modest effort in such a critical project.

BULOSAN'S "BE AMERICAN": CIRCULATIONS

Carlos Bulosan's *America Is in the Heart*, arguably Asian America's first major mobility narrative, promises an interesting point of entry for an investigation of the Asian American's peculiar situation—if for nothing else but its intriguing resistance to map-making efforts. Before we turn to this valued but highly problematic text, however, let us first ponder a shorter piece by Bulosan that sets out many of the book's images and concerns.

In a short story entitled "Be American" (1977),[21] whose central character Consorcio (the narrator's cousin) is a naive, illiterate peasant immigrant turned union organizer and war hero, Bulosan writes:

> We are a wandering people, due to the nature of our lowly occupations which take us from place to place, following the seasons. When I received a box of grapes from a friend, I knew he was working in the grape fields in either Fresno or Delano, depending on the freight mark. When I received a box of asparagus, I knew he was working in Stockton. But when it was a crate of lettuce, he was working in Santa Maria or Salinas, depending on the freight mark again. And in the summertime when I received a large barrel of salmon, I knew he was working in the salmon canneries in Alaska. (1977:160)

Here place names mark the limits of the early Filipino immigrant's world. They signal the dictates of not only nature (the labor demands of seasonal crops) but also the political and economic constraints placed on the Pinoys. Until after the Second World War, Filipinos were not allowed to naturalize (a fact that, rather improbably, the narrator claims to have withheld in order to better educate his overeager cousin). The Filipinos' lack of citizenship further legitimized Depression-era employment discrimination and vigilante violence directed against them, turning their drifting and fleeing into a permanent state of dispossession. A laconic exchange between the narrator and Consorcio, at a reunion before the latter's eventual conversion to labor causes, hints at the depth of the disillusionment from which the American dream must be rescued.

> "Been wandering everywhere." [Consorcio said.]
> "No job."
> "Nothing anywhere."
> "Where have you been all these years?"
> Silence.
> "No finished school?"
> Silence.
> "Not American citizen yet?"

"You should have told me."

"Told you what?"

"Filipinos can't become American citizens."

"Well, I could have told you. But I wanted you to learn."

"At least I speak better English now."

"This is a country of great opportunity."

Silence.

"No work?"

"No work."

"How long?"

"I have forgotten."

"Better times will come."

"You have a wonderful dream, cousin," he told me and left. (161)

As the terseness of this conversation suggests, the early Filipino immigrant's disenfranchisement is deepened by discursive exclusion. The men who communicate by boxes, crates, and barrels send "no letters, no post cards—nothing" (160), not only because migrant workers have no return addresses, not only because they are poorly educated, but also because, in a dehumanizing economic order, they have come to be equated with—reduced to nothing but—their labor. Until they learn to enter the circulation of verbal signs that spells power in this society, like Consorcio appropriating the oppressor's language (improving his English, learning to read, writing letters and articles, eventually publishing a union newspaper), the food they help to produce would remain the only tangible sign of their presence: they would continue circulating as commodified labor.

"Be American" is a seven-page short story, but it contains a microcosmic model of the concept of mobility that informs *America Is in the Heart*: mobility is strenuous, chronic, directionless, dependent on external factors (both natural and man-made, the latter being the more onerous) over which the individual has little control. The narrator may try to put the best face on the situation by stressing the spiritually nourishing aspect of the circulating packages ("the best letters in the world" [160]), but as a literate, informed mentor of the greenhorn and guardian of American ideals, he has surprisingly little to offer his unlettered friends in return. He can only send out "unsealed envelopes bursting with the colored pictures of actresses and other beautiful women" (160) addressed to poolrooms and restaurants where lonely Filipino men congregate: that is to say, wish-fulfilling fantasies and icons of the culture industry, communally appreciated because they speak to a collective deprivation. (*Bursting* bespeaks barely contained desires.) Individual anonymity is the dark side of the communality of experience celebrated in

"Be American." The Pinoys are constantly threatened by erasure from the white consciousness, through dismissive accusations of savagery, immorality, and shiftlessness (Melendy 1977:46–97). Hence the hagiographic overtones of the cousin's brief life—the representative martyr must be memorialized in words, to redeem the entire group from the oblivion of "un-Americanness."

Yet even the heroic Consorcio apparently dies without a wife, a family, or a home—that is, without symbolic consummation of his relationship to the American land. Consorcio immigrates as a single young man, joining a bachelor community with a highly unbalanced male-female ratio (cf. Melendy 1981:42); but the land that he works on belongs, on the whole, to the whites,[22] and he is forbidden by law from marrying any white woman. (Anti-miscegenation laws were in effect in several states and remained on California's books until 1948 [Melendy 1981:52–53].) Though the narrator makes much of Consorcio's creating a kinship by choice with his fellow workers, his vindication of American democracy requires some mental gymnastics, some suppression of the term's most obvious (i.e., ideologically dominant) meaning: American democracy must be discerned through its violations and is best exemplified by someone who continues to have faith in it despite being, by all other indications, a victim of its deficient implementation (162–63). Only in its failures can its true success be seen.

In this light, the narrator's paean to the American land toward the end of the story rings a little hollow:

> Rolling like a beautiful woman with overflowing abundance of fecundity and murmurous with her eternal mystery, there she [the American land] lies before us like a great mother. To her we always return from our prodigal wanderings and searchings for an anchorage in the sea of life; from her we always draw our sustenance and noble thoughts, to add to her glorious history. (162)

In deploying this exalted rhetoric of the American land as at once nurturing mother and inviting consort (the subject matter of Kolodny's *The Lay of the Land,* alluded to earlier), whose venerable genealogy is virtually coextensive with the continent's development by non-Indians (Sollors 1986a:75–81), author Bulosan claims a fervently adopted American lineage. But judging from his inadvertent midsentence shift in metaphor ("sea of life"), the Filipino's connection to the American land is hardly as solid as he would like to believe. (What color, anyway, is this welcoming female figure? She can no longer be Native American, as in the symbology of the first European settlers. Is she white? Can there be a "colorless" personification of the American land? We know a "genderless" one is impossible.) The Filipino laborer's involuntary, nomadic looping is not the European colonist's entrepreneurial penetration. Instead of virgin territory (pesky Indians aside, of course) awaiting his naming, the Filipino confronts a world already mapped for him. His range has already been circumscribed. What he is allowed to add to America's "glorious history" is chiefly inglorious servitude, whose merit has to be painstakingly established and jealously defended.

AMERICA IS IN THE HEART: THE IMPOSSIBLE MAP

When the themes of "Be American" are transposed to a larger canvas in *America Is in the Heart*, the short story's teleological clarity of line dissipates: though the book-length work still ends with a declaration of undying faith in America, the events leading up to it are a confusing blur that is virtually impossible to chart. Ultimately, through their sheer amorphousness, through the formal unintelligibility of the professed transformation, the narrator/protagonist Carlos's experiences belie his passionate tribute to American ideals.[23] If the tribute remains profoundly affecting, it is less from the reader's conviction of its inevitability than from marvel at such single-minded devotion. This curious enhancement through detraction is not a calculated artistic effect but a symptom of the fierce ideological contestations taking place in the text, contestations that appear manageable in "Be American" because masked by the subduing brevity of the short story form.

One of the most glaring and instructive contestations is that between the book's title, *America Is in the Heart*, and its mind-numbing proliferation of place names in parts two to four, especially two (part one is set in the Philippines). One count of place names yields (roughly from north to south and ignoring the countless repetitions): Alaska; (in Washington) Seattle, Bremerton, Spokane, Yakima, Moxee City, Toppenish, Sunnyside, Grandview, Pasco, Kennewick; (in Oregon) Hood River, Portland, Salem, Eugene, Medford, Klamath Falls; (in California) Redding, Marysville, Sacramento, Lodi, Walnut Grove, Stockton, Oakland, San Francisco, Niles, San Jose, Salinas, Monterey, Fresno, Visalia, Bakersfield, San Luis Obispo, Pismo Beach, Guadalupe, Lompoc, Nipomo, Santa Maria, Solvang, Buellton, Santa Barbara, Ventura, Oxnard, Los Angeles, San Fernando, Pasadena, San Bernadino, Riverside, San Diego, Coronado, Calpatria, Brawley, Holtville, El Cerrito, Calexico; not to mention scattered points in Idaho, Montana, Wyoming, Nevada, and New Mexico.[24] *America Is in the Heart* (the title bearing a single place name) betokens a promise to undo the hurt of Necessitous mobility, to subsume the unruly Many of specific injustices into the liberating One of a heartfelt, shared creed. The place names crowding the pages, on the other hand, threaten to undermine this reassurance by contrasting with its insubstantiality: if America is in the heart, doesn't it mean that it is nowhere, that its rallying aspirations have not been realized in any of these actual places?[25] If they had been realized, the narrative would have shown a meaningful arrangement of place names, a trajectory of struggle and triumph. Yet there is no blazed trail, only chaos, a senseless jumble of brutalities.

Plotting a map for *America Is in the Heart* is, of course, not impossible in the literal sense; given sufficient time and patience, pens of many colors, perhaps transparent overlays to sort out different time periods in Carlos's life, it could be done. But the operation is impossible in the sense that, even if such a diagram were made, it would mean little: one could detect neither rhyme nor reason in the criss-crossing lines, could see no design in the connect-the-dots frenzy (not even a retrospectively imposed one such as the first-person point of view would encourage). Certain place names do stand out in frequency of appearance, such as Seattle, where the narrator first lands, and Los Angeles, where one of his brothers lives and where, toward the end of the book, the bedridden Carlos stays put for once, reading to improve his mind and learning to become a writer. But even these place names hardly represent beacons of sanity and peace, nor are they clearly associated with a feeling of belonging. They too are stops along the way, just more frequently visited stops; as such they are devoid of genius loci. Carlos is continually walking, running, hopping freight trains, taking buses, hitching rides, shuttling back and forth. He is forever making on-the-spot decisions to go somewhere but repeatedly diverted from his destinations, propelled by a host of reasons ranging from the rational to the fortuitous: availability of work (or rumors thereof); racial and/or union-busting violence (or threats thereof) in the form of Filipino-hunting, vigilante executions (in one case tar-and-feathering and near-castration); harassment by police and railway detectives; nasty encounters with rapists, perverts, gamblers, prostitutes, petty criminals, drunks, wife-beaters, and other assorted riff-raff; loneliness in a strange place; chance meetings with acquaintances; happening to miss his brother at home; junky cars breaking down on the road.

The meticulousness with which the author records the place names along the narrator's accidental itineraries contrasts strangely with his perfunctory characterization and emplotment. Key figures like Carlos's brothers or socialist mentors or female benefactors are scarcely more developed than casual acquaintances. Emotions and motifs are attributed without elaboration. Events that should, in commonsense logic, vary in significance are indiscriminately described in an unmodulated prose. Amount of detail is not proportionate to the event's alleged developmental import. Even Carlos's momentous discovery of his mission as a writer and conversion to socialism, a turning point if there ever is one, are swiftly disposed of in a few sentences: "When the letter was finished, a letter which was actually a story of my life, I jumped to my feet and shouted through my tears: 'They can't silence me any more! I'll tell the world what they have done to me!' "(180); and, upon being invited to help by a newly met union organizer, "I could not find words to express my joy. Here was the answer to my confusion" (182).

Unless one consciously looks out for them, the milestones in Carlos's inner journey would be easily missed. And his new calling does only a little to slow down the rushing montage; his later business trips on behalf of union activities are recounted in an undifferentiated voice, continuing the litany of place names. His newfound purposiveness has no appropriate formal expression. The promise of language to order experience, assert presence, and counteract the Pinoys' circulation in the nation's material economy, so enthusiastically extolled in "Be American," has failed Bulosan here.

Our thwarted attempt to construct a map for *America Is in the Heart* points up an odd phenomenon: the succession of place names almost serves as a covert countertext to the content-driven narrative; they keep leveling and casting into doubt whatever redeeming bildungsroman features the author advances in the form of announced resolutions. The story of unrelieved Necessitous mobility competes with (instead of complementing and reinforcing) the story of spiritual awakening and political commitment, with the former providing the more intrusive toponymic punctuation marks. Bulosan seems to be insisting on imposing a direction on the directionless circulations, with only partial success.

What does this curious internal disjuncture mean? The answer depends very much on what one understands to be its possible causes and how much stock one puts in each of them. Is it just a matter of technical inadequacy? Did Bulosan's ill health cause him to rush the writing? Was he responding to impatient publishers (E. Kim 1982:56)? Was the affirmative conclusion of the book accidental, subconscious, or shaped by the publishers' desire to increase its marketability during the postwar period (Alquizola 1989:216)?[26] Could a more astute or ruthless editor have healed the disjuncture, tamed the multiplicity of place names, made the work less frustrating to read? I suspect not, unless a total rewriting were undertaken, in which case coerced mobility would have lost its thematic prominence and we would end up with a different book altogether. To me the split is a formal manifestation of Bulosan's impossible self-assignment, which is a legacy of his colonial upbringing. "Taught to regard Americans as [his] equals" while "Western people are brought up to regard Orientals or colored peoples are inferior" (Bulosan 1960:191–92), Bulosan appears reluctant or unable to let go of his old conviction, feeling compelled instead to reconcile the discrepancy by alternating between the two rival stories. The book's lack of directionality, in part a matter of historical veracity, also hints at an uneasy holding-in-suspension of conflicting ideological forces.

Regardless of what really happened, *America Is in the Heart* in its present shapeless shape is already a cultural artifact of long standing, and the more worthwhile question to ask would be why, despite being so problematic, it has kept a place of honor in the Asian American canon.[27] There is, to begin with, the undeniable raw power of many of its sections. The paucity of literary renditions of early Filipino American life, and the book's far-from-subtle indictments of racism (Alquizola 1989: 216), also make the book a favorite choice in Asian American studies and ethnic studies curricula. I venture to submit another speculative reason for the book's enduring status: that it is a prototypical Asian American text, situated clearly in a larger American tradition but also prefiguring certain recurrent Asian American concerns. As an extended mobility narrative, *America Is in the Heart* at once calls upon and subverts mainstream myths, its very artistic imperfections highlighting the acute contradictions at the heart of American cultural clichés. As a concentrated representation of Necessitous motion, it sets forth an important thematic preoccupation and narrative type in Asian American literature. I suspect that its paradigmatic significance must have been keenly felt by many students of Asian American literature, even if they may seek the source of its appeal elsewhere.

UNMAKING HOME: THE JAPANESE AMERICAN AND
JAPANESE CANADIAN MOBILITY NARRATIVE

If *America Is in the Heart* is about the *failure* of home-founding, Japanese American and Canadian narratives on internment are about the *undoing* of home-founding. The series of photographs illustrating Yoshiko Uchida's autobiography, *Desert Exile: The Uprooting of a Japanese-American Family* (1982), is a graphic rendition of this process.[28] Beginning with preimmigration pictures of her parents in Japanese dress (1984:7–9), representing origin, Uchida moves to pictures of her family and community very early on in the book (13, 33, 37–39). The Sunday school group picture—the church members arranged six-deep at the church door, from the toddlers in the front row to the teachers and parents in the back (33)—and the posed portrait of three generations of her family (all seated serenely, the father flanked by mother, wife, daughters; 37) suggest an achieved sense of order, community, stability, and continuity. A front view of the modest but prosperous-looking Berkeley house where the Uchida family lived "until our forced removal" (38) depicts a homebase. It had a comfortable interior for children to grow up in (13) and welcoming front steps for them to linger on (38); from it family members could venture forth on trips to Japan (39), not yet forced to sever their ties with their land of origin. One would have expected such photographs, radiating warmth and security, to add a concluding, crowning touch to a narrative of successful immigrant striving. But for the Japanese Americans, the supposed culmination of their American story was really the beginning of a collective trauma.

The ensuing photographs are striking in their exteriorization and objectification of the Japanese Americans: storefront newspapers headlining "Ouster of All Japs in California Near!" (55), internees lining up in the street with their luggage (65), armed guards checking internees taking the bus to Tanforan Assembly Center (66). These are decidedly not keepsakes taken lovingly by close friends or relatives, but detached, impersonal recordings of a large-scale historical upheaval. The next sequence of five camp photographs form a striking depiction of disintegration: a horse-stall at Tanforan Racetracks converted for family living, with lumber and a broom leaning against a doorway, and a young woman stepping hesitantly onto a plank over the mud (73); internees lining up outside the Tanforan mess hall and sandwiched between a barbed wire enclosure and a tar-papered shack (74); a distant view of Camp Topaz in the Utah deserts, rows of neatly spaced barracks apparently purged of human presence, vulnerable under an open sky (107); clusters of internees waiting for the arrival of their baggage, while the crude, squat buildings, the bright sun, the arid ground, and the vests and hats of the men give the whole scene a transient, almost western flavor (108). The last internment picture would have been more appropriate for the pioneer stage in the group's development, not for more than sixty years into its immigration history on the American mainland: men in boots and hats, taking a break from digging a ditch and posing with their picks and shovels, much like miners in early California mining camps (139). Its air of makeshiftness and exertion contrasts vividly with the polished, composed look of the Berkeley photographs. It is as if we are shown a movie in reverse, with the finished product unraveling bit by bit before our eyes. After the ditch picture, the last two illustrations of the book (which can be read as attempts to affirm regeneration and family togetherness) appear almost pathetically ineffective. In one, father, mother, and the two daughters ("on the day of our departure for the outside world") pose standing on the gravel in front of the anonymous barracks, their formal attire incongruous with the barren setting (143); and (three pages before the end) the four reunited with the grandmother, all standing on a lawn under a tree, obviously doing better now but also visibly older, hinting at opportunities wasted (151). There are no more photographs of houses: home has been undone, and having to salvage from its ruins is not the same as home-founding.

The kind of reversal demonstrated by the pictorial sequence in *Desert Exile* is found in many a Japanese American literary work, such as Monica Sone's autobiography *Nisei Daughter* (1953), Toshio Mori's novelistic tribute to his mother, *Woman from Hiroshima* (1978), and Yoshiko Uchida's novel *Picture Bride* (1987). But it remains for a Japanese Canadian mobility narrative, Joy Kogawa's *Obasan*, to make the fullest exploration of the idea through an Eastward land journey, which also describes a line of literally shrinking domiciles.

KOGAWA'S *OBASAN*: DIRECTIONALITY WITHOUT FREEDOM

Obasan reverberates with *America Is in the Heart* in some ways. It too is about a nation's broken promises, injustices visited on a specific race, and above all, fugitive movements across the land. Sections of *Obasan* are almost as difficult to map as Bulosan's book. The arbitrary and draconian measures issued by the Canadian government, decreeing different destinations for different members of the family both during the wartime relocation (1982:88, 89, 106) and the postwar dispersal to the East (173), are responsible for a profusion of place names in some of the letters written by Aunt Emily during the uncertain first days of the crisis (85–110). The reader, like Naomi, is bombarded with unfamiliar names that have suddenly acquired an ominous ring, all referring to places of potential or actual exile. (Before the evacuation order, all the geography Naomi needs to know is the comfortable interior of her family's Vancouver house [50–53].) The reader is further hindered in the effort to visualize the family's comings and goings by the narrative disruptions discussed earlier in connection with alimentary images. However, after much sorting out, the mobility experienced by Naomi does resolve itself into a one-way traversal from Vancouver to Slocan to Granton (in Alberta), a broadly Eastward banishment from coast to heartland, with secondary dislocations in its wake. In showing greater directionality, then, *Obasan* differs from *America Is in the Heart*.

Nevertheless, for Japanese Canadians and Japanese Americans, directionality of movement, divorced from freedom of movement, is no further removed from Necessity than the Filipinos' incessant circlings and backtrackings. A writer like Monica Sone, intent on rehabilitating her group in accordance with white standards, may try to identify the forced marches of internment with mainstream mobility myths; the concluding chapter titles of *Nisei Daughter*—"Eastward, Nisei" (echoing "Go West, young man!") and "Deeper into the Land"—are meant to endow the Japanese Americans' rebuilding operations with a rosy tint of Extravagant adventure. Kogawa's *Obasan*, however, debunks this kind of facile, if valiant, equation of the spurned with the blessed, the unmaking with the making of home. Through abrupt time shifts and narrative convolutions that belie its relatively manageable geographical foci, the book lays bare the logic-defying outrage of racism and reminds us that the significance of the mobility motif is always fluid and context-dependent; for certain groups, deeper penetration into the land means exclusion from, instead of fuller participation in, the nation's development.

In *Obasan*, Kogawa expresses her obsession with mobility, or more specifically its impairment, in several ways. At times she accents the emblematic aspects of a historical fact: for example, the confiscation of fishing boats (along with automobiles and radios), one of the first anti-Japanese war measures adopted by the Canadian government (*Democracy Betrayed*, 4), acquires a symbolic dimension in the case of a special boat crafted by Uncle (Obasan's husband). Both Grandpa Nakane and Uncle are described as master boat builders (18); the boat seized is a sleek, exquisitely detailed "work of art" designed by Naomi's father and created over many winter evenings—in other words, a labor of love and communal effort comparable to the life the Japanese have built up in Canada.

> "What a beauty," the RCMP officer said in 1941, when he saw it. He shouted as he sliced back through the wake, "What a beauty! What a beauty!"
>
> That was the last Uncle saw of the boat. And shortly thereafter, Uncle too was taken away. (21)

Kogawa also parallels this mass incapacitation, this legalized robbery of means of mobility, with a cluster of images of crippling. As Nakayama-sensei, the minister, puts it in his poetically unidiomatic, provocatively incomplete English, "That there is brokenness" (240). At the beginning of the evacuation, Stephen, Naomi's brother, develops a mysterious limp that persists throughout the many moves made by the fragmented family (89). Of the two children, Stephen is the one more susceptible to racist derisions; in severing his attachment to his Japanese origin, Kogawa implies, he is mutilating a vital part of himself.[29] The young Naomi, too, though more reticent about her racial shame, shares in this process when she takes to hitting her Japanese doll, a gift from her now-absent mother (81). By the time of the train ride to Slocan, the ghost town where Obasan relocates with her two charges, the doll's legs, "though wired in place, [have been] dislocated and she cannot stand on her own" (115). Later in her childhood, Naomi fails to nurse back to wholeness a maimed frog that she associates with her exiled and ailing father, whose death is never announced by the adults. (The frog is named Tad for both Tadpole and Tadashi, the father-prince awaiting miraculous restoration [206].) Well into her adulthood, Naomi still has recurrent nightmares about "flight, terror, and pursuit," which of late end with a horrifying scene of sadistic dismemberment: three Oriental women lie naked in the road, acting seductive in hopes of winning mercy from their armed guards, but the men shoot at their feet anyway. "A few inches from the body, the first woman's right foot lay like a solid wooden boot neatly severed above the ankles" (62). These images of crippling reveals the immobilization that has been masked by the Japanese Canadians' perpetual motion.

But Kogawa's most powerful fusion of "factual" narration with "fictional" imagery is her marking Naomi's Eastward journey of banishment with a deteriorating succession of houses, reminiscent of the entropic photographic series in Uchida's *Desert Exile*.[30] "Not one of us on this journey returns home again" (112). Home for Naomi is the family residence in Marpole, Vancouver, a spacious, flourishing, richly colored, densely textured world sufficient unto itself, where patterns on the rug are "roads," the sofa provides "mountain" and "valley," and war is child's play (50). In this dwelling each room has its function, each person his/her space: a perfect model of pluralistic identity. Private and public, feminine and masculine are compatible and complementary. The darkly paneled, dimly lit, womblike living room where the children hide and play is balanced and harmonized with the music room bright with windows, plants, group activities, and music both Japanese and Western (nobody fusses over that distinction). The bathroom, filled with life-giving moisture, is a place for shared cleansing and renewal (48–49). But this home, like the rest of the Japanese Canadians' property, is liquidated while nominally held in trust by the Canadian government.

Slocan, the first way-station after Naomi's expulsion from Paradise, offers a sagging log hut reflective of their diminished station as social rejects, "just plopped here in the wilderness. Flushed out of Vancouver. Like dung drops. Maggot bait" (118). "A small house for small people" (122). The Slocan house, a temporary retreat into a protective state of near-invisibility, is associated with mud and manure, year-round mist and rain, overgrown greenery. Its partly healing, partly debilitating excessive wateriness[31] is followed by the extreme yin/yang imbalance of an uninsulated shed in the beet fields of Alberta, where Naomi, Stephen, and their surrogate parents next relocate. (Both, of course, represent a falling-off from the moderation of the Vancouver house.) "When we stop finally, it is at the side of a small hut, like a tool shed, smaller even than the one we lived in Slocan" (191). A heat trap in the summer and freezing in the winter, this "chicken-coop 'house' " is juxtaposed against the "real house with a driveway leading into a garage" owned by the white farmer who hires the family for stoop labor (194–95, 192). In the all-purpose shack with paper-thin walls, the family members, once thriving human beings, are reduced by the struggle for survival to a barely differentiated huddle of suffering animal bodies.

When the two children are in their teens, Uncle and Obasan finally get a new house in Granton (209), but this reluctantly adopted resting place is inadequate as home, and both dwelling and residents fall into permanent dryness and stasis. Stephen takes to continual flight—again enforced mobility, now disguised as the voluntary expatriation of the successful cosmopolitan musician—while Naomi settles into a state of suspended animation, "shuffling back and forth between Cecil and Granton, unable either to go or to stay in the world with any semblance of grace or ease" (50). Cecil is where Naomi now lives and works as a teacher, but tellingly her place of residence is never described: she has, as yet, no home—and will not have one until she breaks out of the paralysis of denial.[32]

Obasan is about spiritual rebirth, but not of the rationalizing, self-deluding, flag-waving variety. Unlike in *America Is in the Heart*, where place names are mere points on tangled lines, places in *Obasan* are delineated with an unrelenting physicality. On the other hand, both works are motivated in part by a fear that, despite so much movement and activity, the group may end up leaving no mark whatsoever on a map of someone else's making. Twenty years after the relocation, Aunt Emily and her relatives make a pilgrimage to the interior of British Columbia in search of an answer to the question, "What remains of our time there?"

> We looked for the evidence of our having been in Bayfarm, in Lemon Creek, in Popoff. . . . Where on the map or on the road was there any sign? Not a mark was left. All our huts had been removed long before and the forest had returned to take over the clearings. (117)

The pristineness of the landscape is deceptive. The transient presence of the outcasts must be remembered. Place names vital to a group's history must be rescued from oblivion and registered on a map of one's own making: this is one of the special missions with which the Asian American mobility narrative is charged.

SHAWN WONG'S *HOMEBASE*:
"I MOVE ACROSS AMERICA PICKING UP GHOSTS"

Shawn Wong's autobiographical novel, *Homebase* (1979), which takes this mission to heart with a deep devotion, demonstrates how a master motif like mobility may unify Asian American writers across generations, ethnic subgroups, gender lines, and historical periods in a common tradition. A seamless web of spare, luminous prose weaving together personal memories, evocations of place, reconstructions of family history, and dreams and fantasies, *Homebase* can no doubt be insightfully read without citing any other mobility narratives as intertexts. It is clearly a conscious assertion of the Chinese American's claim to the American land, as Elaine Kim (from gender concerns) and Karin Meissenburg (from historical interests) have both pointed out (E. Kim 1982:194–97; Meissenburg 1987:119–24). Nevertheless, sustained attention to the mobility motif in the book would clarify some of the bases of its America-claiming and reveal its affinities with other Asian American mobility narratives.

Homebase's two epigraphs establish the same tensions that inform the Asian American mobility narratives examined so far in this chapter. The first, a botanical entry on the ailanthus, a hardy tree native to China but now common in California and known for its "ability to create beauty and shade under adverse conditions," pays tribute to the rootedness or at-homeness that the pioneers have achieved in "every type of difficult soil." But the second epigraph, a quotation from an English-Chinese phrase book compiled in 1875, recalls a world as hostile and brutal as that in Bulosan's *America Is in the Heart*: the phrases that the early Chinese immigrant were supposed to learn pertain to death by various means—exposure, suicide, assassination—as well as vigilante violence ("He took the law in his own hand") and being cheated out of one's wages.[33] In this context of bitter Necessity, the concluding English sentences on the page, though technically a lesson on verb conjugation, become an unwitting commentary on the precariousness of the idea of home. "I go home at night. / I have gone home. / I went home. / I abide at home. / I abode at San Francisco. / I have lived in Oakland." Despite the repetition of the word *home*, the shifting list connotes tentativeness rather than certitude, displacement rather than fixity. "I have lived in Oakland"—and where else, one wonders?

The six chapters of the novel go on to develop the tension between at-homeness and mobility, with images of the latter virtually saturating every page. The narrator Rainsford Chan's numerous personal journeys on airplanes, on trains, in fast cars, on skis are symbolically linked with the peregrinations of his immigrant forefathers, builders of California unsung in mainstream annals. On one level *Homebase* is a highly autobiographical work, with uncommon circumstances (losing his father at age seven; being orphaned at age fifteen) setting the narrator apart. Yet because its private grief is interwoven with collective grievances, *Homebase* also belongs with other "public," re-created, usable myths for Asian Americans such as Maxine Hong Kingston's *China Men* (1980). While Rainsford's bereavements fit no representative demographic pattern, they initiate him into the pain of loss and prepare him to identify with his lonely forefathers in their continent-spanning labors. "My great-grandfather had begun a tradition of orphaned men in this country and now I realized I was the direct descendant of that original fatherless and motherless immigrant" (8). Suddenly cast adrift in the adult world, with nothing but the half-controlled, half-surrendering physical sensation of driving to steady him, the narrator begins to connect himself through compulsive movement to his Necessity-driven ancestors. Driving becomes his way of meditating on the meaning of freedom for the Chinese American.

> When I started driving, I used to drive around at night through the hills, through empty streets, just drive around at night to keep from thinking about the pursuit of my own life. To keep from settling down into the dreams of father and mother. But in the end my life was nothing unless I pursued their lives, pursued the life of my grandfather, my great-grandfather. (10)

Driving for Rainsford begins as an anesthetizing escape from the "dreams of departures, people leaving me, of life losing ground" (32), and as an adolescent trial of male mettle ("I want to test myself. I want to feel like I'm being chased on the road at night" [93]). But his solitary night rides soon turn into a quest for origin, continuity, identity, home. "I move across America picking up ghosts" (33).

Toward the end of the book, Rainsford comes to feel that he and these ancestral ghosts are "all the same man" (101). The catalyst for this integration is the realization that America's myths of mobility have failed them all. The narrator is brought up singing "Home on the Range" (2). One of his first memories, fixed in the first sentence of the book, is of driving with his parents from Berkeley to New York and back (1). As a young child he follows his Navy engineer father on his rounds, wearing a "Superman shirt, a white starched sailor's hat, and carrying a replica of a long barrelled Colt" (13), emblems of full participation in American mobility, aerial, maritime, or terrestrial. Rainsford's father is a strong runner and swimmer; he indulges the young boy in his "fantasies and fascinations with planes, cars, cowboys, comic book heroes, and trains" (43)—the key ingredients in the All-American male child's spiritual diet. On Guam the duo love to watch bombers take off and land; in Berkeley they spend hours on end watching trains pull in and out. But when the fifteen-year-old orphan follows his father's lead to become a star athlete, he finds that his taken-for-granted Americanness is hardly apparent to others: he is a credit "to his race" (94), distinguished for being "the first Chinese in the history of this high school to receive [the Most Valuable Player] award in any sport" (93). To his fantasy white bride, an obvious embodiment of mainstream America—"the patronizing, slim, long-legged, fifteen year old high school, whining, teaser of a cheerleader" (82)—Rainsford still has to keep proving he is no less American than her brother (91–92). Mentally she confines him to Chinatown, pestering him to take her there on a private guided tour. "Can we go there today? . . . I'll wear that dress you like so much." Weary of being thus wheedled into self-exoticization, the disgusted narrator snaps back, "Wear pants" (92).

By troping upon the idea of mobility to cover a broad range of American experiences, *Homebase* lifts the growing pains of one young man, such as portrayed in this scene, into a larger context. Without explicitly linking the narrator's social rejection with the large-scale, legislated persecution of early Chinese immigrants (a direct equation would have been unconvincing in any case), Shawn Wong nevertheless shows a continuity between past and present by lyrically interweaving the two. Rainsford laments: "I have no place in America, after four generations there is nothing except what America tells me about the pride of being foreign" (77). This plaint could have been uttered by his forefathers, whose invaluable contributions to developing the continent had not earned them a homestead on American soil. And the forced mobility that is the corollary of imposed homelessness—"We're on the run through America" (76); "I need to keep running" (94)—unites the generations. After working on the transcontinental railroad, the Chinese men were "driven out of the west and chased back to San Francisco" (2), "chased out of the mines" (16), forced to shed their hard-won Chinese American identity and burn "their letters, their diaries, poems, anything with names," along the way (2). As in *Obasan*, the ancestors' repeated and far-flung dislodgments have left no trace: the town of Rainsford, California, in which the narrator's great-grandfather first settled and after which the boy was named, doesn't exist anymore on the American map. "There's no record of it ever having existed" (2).

In meditating upon his forebears' fate, Rainsford's exclusive and unremitting focus is mobility: its various forms, its promises, its elusiveness, its negation. He is drawn to images of immobilization: his great-grandfather feeling "chained to the ground, unable even to cry for help," and tormented by hawks like a Prometheus (14); bodies of railroad workers frozen along the track, not discovered until the spring thaw (18); encampments of Chinese men surviving in snow caves while working on the Donner Summit tunnel (25); the grandfather (a "paper son") detained in the barracks on Angel Island, interrogated on the details of a fictitious home (102–10). Rainsford takes inspiration from the story of his grandfather, who transcended the houseboy role and became a "Chinese *vaquero*" by teaching himself to ride (54–55): a self-

made hero of locomotion. He enters the Chinese American legend of
the Iron Moonhunter, the phantom engine said to take the railroad men
home toward the coast, reversing the direction of their deepening bondage (28–32).[34] He races the night train in his car, mingling in spirit with
the pioneers.[35]

At the end of the book, Rainsford has learned the difference between
his father's innocent way of "claiming America"—a family vacation trip
hitting all the best-known landmarks, just for the sake of being able to
say "we had done it" (43)—and his own, which lovingly traces a route
of places of the heart, creating a "whole vision of my life in America, of
our lives in America" (57). The last chapter of the book is an incantation
of place names. On an imaginary homeward train ride with the spirit of
Great-Grandfather, Rainsford "[says] the names of stations and towns
like prayers, as if they belonged to me": Reno, Verdi, Essex, Bronco,
Boca, Prosser Creek, Proctor's, Truckee, Donner Summit, Cascade,
Tamarack, Cisco, Emigrant Gap, Blue Canyon, China Ranch, Shady
Run, Dutch Flat, Gold Run, Clipper Gap, Auburn, Newcastle, Penrhyn,
Pino, Rocklin, Junction, Antelope, Arcade, Sacramento, Davisville, Tre-
mont, Dixon, Batavia, Elmira, Fairfield, Army Point, Benecia, Port
Costa, Valona, Vallejo Junction, Tormey, Pinole, Sobrante, San Pablo,
Oakland. Each place where Chinese men once lived, toiled, and van-
ished is redeemed by remembrance, put back on the map: the map of
Chinese America. And the American land and the "ethnic" map are now
one. "We are old enough to haunt this land like an Indian who laid
down to rest and his body became the outline of the horizon. This is my
father's canyon. See his head reclining! That peak is his nose, that cliff
his chin, and his folded arms are summits" (114).

This moving ending may make *Homebase* appear to be a fully resolved
work; quoted out of context it may even look pat. Yet Shawn Wong
seems quite aware that it is inherently problematic. The phrase "as if
they belonged to me" signals a knowledge not only of continuing cir-
cumscriptions of the Chinese but also of the limited delivering powers of
word magic. Inventing new mobility myths for Chinese America to
counter mainstream ones entails some amount of romanticization,
which Shawn Wong resists but cannot avoid without invalidating his entire artistic enterprise. Of Donner Summit Rainsford says: "There were
no legends there, only the winters and the deaths. 'My bitterness,'
Great-Grandfather said, 'is not myth or legend' " (112). But of course
we have been presented with just such a legend in which the suffering of
the snowbound workers is transformed into a legacy (25–27). Indeed
the whole book is premised on the demand for relevant legends.
"Today, after 125 years of our life here, I do not want just a home that
time allowed me to have. America must give me legends with spirit. I

take myths to name this country's canyons, dry riverbeds, mountains, after my father, grandfather and great-grandfather" (111).

Moreover, if the conclusion represents a triumph of spiritual patrilineage and a rightful collection of patrimony, it is accomplished by completely bypassing—that is, not redeeming—the feminine principle, which has been suppressed by exclusionary legislation designed "so that the Chinese would gradually die out, leaving no sons or daughters" (16). "Home on the Range" has not been realized; Rainsford's return to his home on the coast, though completing the geographical circuit, also hints at failure to consummate a procreative relationship with the American land. His transcontinental self-assignment "to straighten out America" (80), flaunting his blonde, white bride (known as "The Body" [78]—recall Bulosan's lolling female figure), stems from frustrated desire. Rainsford concedes that she is only a projection (80), and an outdated one at that (he identifies her as "the girl I wanted when I was fifteen" [82]). As for his briefly alluded-to love affair with a Chinese American woman in the heartland of Wisconsin, it has been aborted for some unnamed reason. "She is only the myth of the perfect day until I do get back to her home, she is the summit I must turn to in the end" (79). Such an end, a Chinese American version of the fulfilled pastoral impulse, is still in the future; *Homebase* has only brought Rainsford up to the present.

FRANK CHIN: MAKING AN EXTRAVAGANCE OF NECESSITY

Despite its fascination with fetishes of machismo—the automobile and the train, the highway and the railroad—*Homebase* is a contemplative and contained, even gentle, work. It remains for Frank Chin to bring out the intoxicatingly destructive aspects of mechanized locomotion, the sexual violence implied in the male imagery of continental penetration, and the intense contradictions involved in creating a Chinese American mobility myth around the symbol of the railroad.

Frank Chin begins his explorations of the mobility theme not from a state of homelessness but from too full a sense of home—Chinatown, to him a stagnating enclave of dying men and women, locked up in cramped quarters. Home is the place where he does *not* want to be; his ancestors are to be disowned rather than sought out and claimed. His world is populated by invalids: in "A Chinese Lady Dies," two wheelchair-bound parents, the father a ghostly presence who has to be unfolded and flattened onto his bed every night (1988:116), the mother "enjoying the beautiful symphonic boredom of going dead slowly, of dying minisculely, and wondering aloud at her latest lack of sensation" (114); in "Food for All His Dead," a hobbling, blood-spitting father no longer able to do the lion dance; in "Railroad Standard Time," again a paralyzed father needing his son's time and attention (4). Whereas other Asian American fictional cripples like Stephen in *Obasan*, the amputee Kenji in *No-No Boy*, or the legless young *fan tan* operator in Monfoon Leong's "New Year for Fong Wing" can trace their disability to a specific historical injury to the group (internment; fighting in a national war while allowed only partial national membership) and are thus placed in a historical realm of change and hope, Chin's elderly paralytics appear to exist in a static twilight zone of living death. This state too has its material causes, of course: more ongoing conditions than discrete events, which an informed Asian American reader would be able to fill in (racial persecution, ghettoization, Orientalism, limited employment opportunities, and so forth). But for Frank Chin immobility and mobility are absolute, one might say ahistorical, opposites; the predominant impression one receives of Chin's Chinatown world is that of a timeless (and culpable) immobility, an unalterable *given* of Chinese American existence from which the young must struggle to break free.[36]

To do so, the male protagonists in Frank Chin's short stories and plays[37] perform a move that I call "making an Extravagance of Necessity"—glamorizing (albeit still with a touch of rancorous irony) those aspects of Chinese American tradition that admit of Extravagant interpretations. The speaker of "The Eat and Run Midnight People," describing himself as "outlaw-born and raised to eat and run in your mother country like a virus staying a step ahead of a cure," glorifies the Necessity-driven rovings of his Cantonese peasant forebears: "the badasses of China, the barbarians, far away from the high culture of the North. . . . The dregs, the bandits, the killers, the get out of town eat and run folks, hungry all the time eating after looking for food. Murderers and sailors. Rebel yellers and hardcore cooks" (1988:11).

If one hears echoes of the Old West in this passage, the coincidence is deliberate, for Chin considers western legends as vital a part of his tradition as those of the peasant rebels in the Chinese classic, *Water Margin* (or *Outlaws of the Marsh*),[38] who are compelled by hunger and a natural sense of justice to challenge the emperor's mandate. In Chin's 1972 play, *The Chickencoop Chinaman*, the protagonist Tampax Lum speaks of growing up on Lone Ranger radio plays and believing, from sheer desperation for evidence of Chinese American heroism, that the black-haired cowboy is actually Chinese. In the boy's logic, the Lone Ranger uses the mask to hide his Asian eyes; following Chinese color symbolism, he wears a red shirt for good luck and rides a white horse to bring death. Lum is later disabused of the inspiring delusion that the Lone Ranger represents "Chinaman vengeance on the West" (1981: 32); in a dream sequence, the Lone Ranger shoots Lum in the hand, accuses him of botching a laundry job on his shirt, and announces: "You China Boys don't know what it's like ridin' off into the distance all your life" (35). "Thank me now," he advises, "and I'll let ya get back to Chinatown preservin' your culture" (37). However, awareness of a profound white bias in western tales of fabulous exploits has not prevented Chin from appropriating them for his own purposes. He remains excited by the promise of carefree, footloose roaming held out by the mainstream—the male version, Huck Finn lighting out for the territory, away from the domesticating, emasculating, "sivilising" influences of women. What Chin offers is not so much a critique of existing hegemonic discourse on mobility, with its barely disguised violence and expansionist agenda, as an inversion of it to vindicate hitherto marginalized groups. In "A Chinese Lady Dies," Chin summons up a multicultural vision of havoc-wreaking, order-threatening mobility as *his* "Chinaman vengeance on the West" (the number "108" alludes to the confederation of *haohan* or heroes in *Water Margin*):

> *And El Chino leads an outlaw army of 108 different gangs toward Chinatown Frisco. Motorcycle gangs, Mexican Pachuco gangs in low riders and zoot suits, uneasy Chinatown gangs in jacked-up Detroit iron, Comancheros left over from the Old West, railroad gangs, mercenaries, the black sheep of every religion and philosophy.* (1988:113; italics in original)

Despite this rousing evocation of vast overland armies, converging as one upon the detested home at ocean's edge, the American landscape in Chin's works is remarkably vague. Whereas place names in Shawn Wong's *Homebase* are fleshed out with sensuous details of sun and rain, trees and earth, the American continent for Chin is simply undifferentiated space, a backdrop against which the psychodramas of the hemmed-in Chinese American male are enacted. (A vivid sense of place can only be found in the graphic descriptions of Chinatown's putrefaction.) To the narrator of "Railroad Standard Time," "Home on the Range" brings associations not of prairie vistas but of "high long [notes] up from the navel that [drill] through plaster and steel and skin and meat for bone marrow and electric wires on one long titpopping breath" (1988:6, 7), belted out by the music teacher whose white body is greedily eyed by the boys like a landscape ("in the distance, finally some skin"). As the adult narrator streaks along the highways of the West, listening to country and western music with the same vibrant, open notes, one realizes why Chin's protagonists are addicted to mobility: they want it mainly for the exhilarating rush it provides, a solipsistic sensation of power and domination. Mobility does not situate Chin's male characters in a geographical and historical context, enable them to experience places as accessible and substantial, make them a part of the land through corporeal encounters, fuse private experiences with public presences; instead, mobility insulates them, turning them loose, liberating them from the need to negotiate conflicting cultural claims.

This escapist, self-bracing function of mobility is seen in a revealing metaphor used by Fred Eng, the tour guide protagonist in *The Year of the Dragon*, when he explains to Sis why his humiliating line of work is still satisfying in some perverse way:

> FRED: I talk out loud to myself walking up and down the streets of Chinatown and I'm gone. Outta town. No interruptions. On the Interstate. No arguments. I'm popping the high rhythm six step of a tuned compact car, and I know where everything is. . . . I keep talking, and I feel the whine of the tires echo up my asshole, into my spine, my ribs, into my throat and I have the shoulders of a tiger, the reflexes of an IBM and I am, as long as I'm talking, out of here, running up the road on my hands and feet!
>
> SIS: The Chinatown Cowboy rides again! (1981:119)

Though Fred is caged in Chinatown by his father's expectations and his own weakness, even an ersatz thrill of the kind provided by speeding is enough to make his lot endurable: it is not so much any potential benefit of mobility as the subjective sensation of being on the move and in control that counts. Likewise, Johnny, Fred's younger brother and a "wannabee" juvenile delinquent, gushes about his fugitive adventures with a gang of immigrant youth:

> The only time I ever relaxed in my life I was driving a car full of robbers, man. I didn't know what that Chinese they was talking. But I knew I was doing what they told me, when I drove away from that store. Felt so good. . . . My Chevy was flying down Grant Avenue, man. We musta been doing sixty. And I smoked cigars wit doze dudes. I bashed a language I can't speak. I made friends, man, and didn't give a fuck. (1981:123, 124)

The mobility that Johnny aspires to is reckless abandon, and the male camaraderie-in-mobility that he covets is the faceless strength of mobs on the run.

In this light, the prominence of railroad imagery in Chin's works becomes quite understandable. There is, of course, the historical connection: many of Chin's protagonists belong to a Chinese American "elite" who can trace their genealogy to the original railroad workers. But the railroad provides more than badges of aristocracy like the nineteen-jeweled watch inherited by the narrator of "Railroad Standard Time." (In this case the romance of patrimony may be more fabricated than real: the narrator knows little about his watch-collecting grandfather, who may have been on the "kiss-ass steward service" [1988:5].) The

train—a massive yet delicate piece of machinery whose railbound momentum brooks no resistance—is probably the ultimate source of the
kind of trancelike, visceral excitation craved by Chin's male characters,
and as such it occupies a place of honor in his iconography. The narrator
of "The Eat and Run Midnight People" writes of his work as a brakeman
("the first Chinaman to brake on the Southern Pacific line" [1988:14]):[39]

> We sat down heavily into the gathering density of sound, the rising pitch of
> vibrations and concussive thunders that reached right through the flesh
> and clutched the heart and deeper into the valves of the heart, the lips of
> the valves. Before actual movement I felt the strength of the engine grab
> and in that instant no one spoke. I leaned slightly, poised my body on the
> cresting powerful motionlessness that was beyond my control now, that
> would break into movement carrying me away no matter what. . . . I am
> moving. Being moved. More muscle had to be put into my relaxation. The
> racket of the engines had settled into my flesh, my muscle, all of me and
> become the sound of me being alive. . . . Listen, children. I was riding. I
> would come home to motion, my grandfather. (1988:17)

Balancing with intense concentration on this juggernaut, the brakeman
allies himself with all the power that it embodies, material or symbolic,
and joins in the aggressive subjugation of the American land that is the
nation's manifest destiny. Through the relentless rhythmic pounding of
the engine, indulging in what Kolodny terms a "privatized erotic mas-
tery," he attempts to participate in the white man's "psychosexual
drama of . . . possessing a virgin continent" (1984:xiii).

But such a ride exacts a price in ambivalence, as the paradoxical juxtaposition of "I am moving" and "being moved" implies. For the mobility
myths are not meant for the descendants of the Chinese "coolies" whose
labors made them possible and lent them credence. The narrator of
"The Eat and Run Midnight People" seems at once seduced and repelled
by these myths. Every morning, as he sets out for work, he feels "it is
John Wayne stepping outside and turning a piece of the outdoors into
the goddamned Old West" (1988:15). He walks the railyard knowing
that he—in the sense of a "generic" railroad man, race unspecified—has
been sung about; like his fellow workers, he is "itchy with the rever-
berations of all those songs going off at once" (16). At the same time,
he knows that all this heroic posturing is, in a sense, "nothing but bluff"
(15). When his wife teaches the children to serenade him with "I've
Been Workin' on the Railroad," he finds the song "dumb" and the performance annoying (20). Like Rainsford's Great-Grandfather restrain-
ing the young man from overenthusiastic legend-making, the brakeman
observes: "The sounds of the railyard don't compose music" (22).

Being a brakeman rather than an engineer may provide a small measure of absolution for the heir of the Iron Moonhunter, the wish-fulfilling phantom train of victims of American history, "built by Chinamans who knew they'd never be given passes to ride the rails they laid" (1981:31 [*Chickencoop Chinaman*]). But victim status, if righteous, is neither invigorating nor entrancing. It is undeniably a privilege to be the "intelligence of [the train's] thrusting tons," "at the head end of sixty miles an hour" (1988:21, 22). The brakeman is repeatedly tempted to seize control from the engineer—push him off the train as he fertilizes the land with his "golden urine." But the deed is never carried out. Instead, he vicariously possesses the American landscape: "Between [the engineer's] legs and between his bulk and the wall of the cab, my eyes grabbed up cows, distant farmhouses, far mountains" (21).

The story's intricate maneuvering to maintain a viable ideological stance—somehow balancing "being moved" and "moving"—points up the problematics of creating an appealing mobility myth for Chinese Americans out of obdurate historical material. As we have seen, because of a long-standing history of persecution and discrimination against Asian Americans, horizontal movement across the American landscape cannot easily be dissociated from connotations of Necessity. Chinese American artists, in addition, have to deal with the peculiar irony of the railroad as an emblem of their past. On the one hand, the railroad stands as a visible testament to one of the most vital contributions made by their ancestors to the building of this nation. In the *national* context, the railroad is an incarnation of Extravagant mobility and all attendant opportunities to realize the American Dream. As a mid-nineteenth-century magazine writer phrases it:

> Steam is annihilating space. . . . Travelling is changed from an isolated pilgrimage to a kind of triumphal procession. . . . Caravans of voyagers are now winding as it were, on the wings of the wind, round the habitable globe. Here they glide over cultivated acres on rods of iron, and there they rise and fall on the bosom of the deep, leaving behind them a foaming wheel-track like the chariot-path of a sea-god. (Cited in Marx 1964:196)

(Note how this rhapsodic passage minimizes the physical restrictions of the "rods of iron," substituting a less accurate but more inspirational image of the pathless ocean.) The Chinese American writers' claim to the railroad legacy is a claim to partake of this boundless mobility. On the other hand, in the *Chinese American* context, the railroad is identified with Necessity of the harshest sort. Not only was railroad-building a grueling task for which the Chinese laborers received scant thanks, but the artists cannot forget how the mobility of their pioneer forebears was rigidly prescribed, with a ruthless and predetermined directionality like the railway tracks'. Chinese could go only where they were allowed to go; their admission into American destiny rested on the condition of self-enclosure and self-curtailment. As the Lone Ranger admonishes Tampax Lum, who is listening for the whistle of the Iron Moonhunter, "Hear no evil, ya hear me? China boys, you be legendary obeyers of the law, legendary humble, legendary passive" (1981:37 [*Chickencoop Chinaman*]). There is no way one can conjure up the "evil" oppositional myth of the phantom train without giving the siren songs of the open road at least a reluctant hearing; and vice versa.

When the narrator of "The Eat and Run Midnight People" intones a prayer, asking his grandfather's blessing for his new songs of Chinese America, animal hunger and Bunyanesque heroism are inextricably mixed:

> Ride with me, Grandfather. . . . Ride with me on enginemen's forever longtime hungry stomach home again and again and I will sing of us to your great-grandchildren . . . children, you'll hear laughter like distant dynamite rollicking in our iron lungs. . . . The mountains were bed. Clouds were breath. (1988:8–9)

Is the brakeman a master of balance, or is his mythopoeic venture just a joy ride in a prison on wheels?[40] Is he in danger of being crushed by the conflicting ideological forces he feels obligated to reconcile, like Shannon the switchman "coupled up" between two cars (18)?[41]

The brakeman's way out of this dilemma is to plunge outside history (to borrow Ralph Ellison's well-known description of Tod Clifton in *Invisible Man*). He is haunted and mesmerized by suicidal falling figures: Shannon's naked wife killing herself by doing a swan dive off a trestle (19–20); a girl glimpsed from the train as she dives off the girders, again with arms stretched out "like wings" (12, 21); and a recurrent mental picture of himself crashing: "flying off that Great Northern freight end over end" (15). The vertical motion of the free-fall, in reckless abdication of all control, is to him the only way to break the tyranny of horizontal momentum. Apparently despairing of ever taking the female American land, as the myths of the piercing, conquering railroad promise, he removes himself to "an island without real trains, or great highways" (23): ostensibly a place in Hawaii (10), but really a hallucinatory space of nihilistic, self-immolating solipsism. There on the sand, at the primeval boundary of land and sea, he copulates furiously with an utterly objectified woman, "[a] palpitating beerdrinking sea organism thrown up out of a splash of ocean" (9), and the little death of orgasm, like a spectacular train wreck, obliterates consciousness in a moment of explosive release: "Sand climbed my body like meteors slamming into a molten virgin planet. I felt them all and fucked in a runaway wild engine indifference, digging a hole under us, running from the crash of an idiot

Chinatown brakeman about to come down hard off a running freight" (23). At the end of this moment, which he understands to be temporary (22), he returns from the darkness of unknowing to his inescapable origin:

> I'd been shanghai'd by my monster dong that was rocketing me away with one long hysterical streamline sensation toward parts unknown. I was the great rider, Jonah in the whale, a load of shot in my dad's primed hardon pumping grease out of Ma's little cunt that night in a backyard chicken-coop, in Chinatown, Oakland, California. (23)

The wandering Chinaman's attempted flight from history proves unsuccessful.

Making an Extravagance of Necessity, as a redemptive move, seems doomed by the intrinsic limitations of the unpromising material. When Frank Chin returns to the railroad legend in *Donald Duk* after a long hiatus in creativity, didactic intent has taken over: despite employing a potentially unruly dream mechanism in the narrative, his evocation of the Chinese pioneers' life has become dissociated from gut-churning libidinal forces, sanitized to a point not explainable fully by the juvenility of the central intelligence, Donald, and his eminently edifiable white friend Arnold. It is as if, after struggling for years with raw and impossible contradictions, Chin has decided to settle for a defanged version of Chinese American history and the simple warm glow of ethnic pride.

THE VERTICAL AXIS: FALL AND FLIGHT

In counterpoint to the images of suicidal bodies tumbling into space—the ultimate "trip"—"The Eat and Run Midnight People" presents images that assume the other, affirmative meaning of the word *flight*: birds in exuberant motion. The narrator imagines the Iron Moonhunter's voice, which "rose birds from the bushes, [lifting] eagles from their nests": "They spread their wings on his voice. They rode down the flow of the giant's whisper" (9). In the deserted railyard, the brakeman is spellbound by the lovely sight of pigeons ascending:

> A flight of pigeons flies up out of the mass of boxcars. . . . In this space, this quiet and time of morning, this stillness governed by the internal motion of great engines standing still, the flight of pigeons seems an event. *There's no need to make sense of them and everything here.* (20; my italics)

Obvious sexual overtones aside (13), this Joycean epiphany intimates an autotelic state alternative to the self-sabotaging plunge outside history: one can move up rather than down along the vertical axis. The "event-fulness" of the pigeons' wheeling does not derive from any exertion,

overcoming, imposition of will, combat against clamorous historical demands; the birds simply *are*, sporting "electric colors that make slime
look alive," "the light silent strong feathers of the wings . . . alive with
captured light" (20). The pigeons' flight offer a vision of vitality and
transcendence that the narrator fails to sustain: the engines of the trains
are only dormant, and "it is too late to get out of the way" (21). But the
possibility has been glimpsed.

The motif of ascent attracts many Asian American writers besides
Frank Chin. In a convergence of "archetypal" or "universal" connotations and historically specific meanings, upward movement encodes for
them the impulse toward Extravagance: the urge to exercise one's faculties and experience one's aliveness without interference from extraneous, despotic forces. The imperatives of Extravagance are so strong that
they can be discerned at work even under the grimmest circumstances.
Thus in *Obasan*, for example, the young Naomi, when given a pencil
and paper to keep herself busy at Grandma's funeral, draws a house and
a sky filled with V-shaped seagulls (129), to reflect what the Japanese
Canadians have been systematically deprived of: habitation and unfettered movement. Seemingly dichotomous, these are in fact two congruent forms of fulfillment, victory over coerced mobility. The drawing of
the seagulls is part of an elaborate network of avian images in *Obasan*,
ranging from the abuse of power and privilege exhibited by the authori-
ties (predatory hawks sailing across the chicken yard [188]; the government making "paper airplanes" of Japanese Canadian lives [242]) to the
elusive ideal of the King Bird, godlike dispenser of natural justice and
orchestrator of a pluralistic "great bird choir" (141–42). In each of the
bird images is implied a vertical axis of potential (but in practice invariably frustrated) liberation.

The contrast between Necessity and Extravagance, as defined in the
previously quoted section of *The Woman Warrior* (on Brave Orchid's
habits of thrift versus the no name woman's act of profligacy), is in fact
a contrast between horizontal and vertical motion. Whereas the "river-
bank" of Necessity guiding Brave Orchid suggests linearity, direction,
purposefulness, containment, control, Extravagance involves elevation,
release, expansiveness, nonutility: "[coming] off the ground" (1977:6).
"Whenever we [the children] did frivolous things, we used up energy;
we flew high kites" (6). The contest between Necessity and Extravagance set forth in *The Woman Warrior* is reprised in several works of
Asian American literature. One of them, "Displacement," a short story
by David Wong Louie about a Chinese immigrant couple in the 1950s,
well illustrates the ambiguities inherent in the duality: a dark vision reminiscent of Frank Chin's colors the female protagonist's world as she

gives herself to the call of imaginative self-assertion. The cryptic ending leaves several possibilities open.

Mrs. Chow, emigrating to escape Communism in China and a soul-deadening feudal/colonial education in Hong Kong, ends up immured in the home of a blind, invalid widow as a housekeeper/caregiver, teaming up with her accommodating and unadventurous husband. Their only relief from the routine is to go every Friday night to the beach boardwalk amusement park, whose roller coaster Mr. Chow chooses as the first American object to impress his wife upon her arrival. The roller coaster appeals to him as an abstract idea: America's enviable resources, mobilized for something as inconsequential as play: "All that machinery, brainwork, and labor done for the sake of fun" (1991:21). After the first ride Mr. Chow realizes he prefers to keep his feet "on the ground" (21). But Mrs. Chow is immediately, viscerally attracted by the experience of riding the roller coaster:

> Oh, this speed, this thrust at the sky, this UP! Oh, this raging, clattering, pushy country! So big! And since that first ride she looked forward to Friday nights and the wind whipping through her hair, stinging her eyes, blowing away the top layers of dailiness. On the longest, most dangerous descent her dry mouth would open to a silent O and she would thrust up her arms as if she could fly away. (21)

The roller coaster, for Mrs. Chow, is nothing less than the promise of America, which she intends to make good despite her grim situation.

When Mrs. Chow proposes to move out of the mean-spirited widow's rent-free quarters, Mr. Chow's "very Chinese" and "very peasant" logic of Necessity surfaces. "Why move, he argued, when there were no approaching armies, no floods, no one telling them to go?" (25–26). Mrs. Chow understands this parsimony of the soul but tries to persuade him by reinterpreting (much like Frank Chin) the privation-driven journeys of early Chinese immigrants as acts of Extravagance. If they were all Chows, she teases, "the railroad wouldn't have been constructed, and Ohio would be all we know of California" (26). Mrs. Chow is convinced that, once away from the widow's house, "her imagination would return" (24) (she was once a talented painter in Hong Kong).

At the apartment complex where they house-hunt, the Chows are immediately presented with chores much like the ones they hope to leave behind. The presumptuous manager, a frazzled and neglectful mother innocently spouting racist remarks, thrusts a child each onto husband and wife, taking for granted that the Chinese couple would be grateful for the mere favor of being rented to. (And Mr. Chow, used to his deferential role as the "good" Chinese, does indeed oblige by volunteering to hang up the laundry.) In an ambiguous exchange with her husband (it is not clear whether the Chows have decided to move), Mrs. Chow asks to ride the roller coaster again on the way home, but this time, apparently disillusioned by the house-hunting episode, she can no longer recapture the elation of carefree soaring. Instead, she tastes the kind of free-fall familiar to Frank Chin's brakeman:

> It's gravity that makes the stomach fly, that causes the liver to flutter; it's the body catching up with the speed of falling. . . . Today there was a weightiness at her core, like a hard, concentrated pull inward, as if an incision had been made and a fist-sized magnet imbedded.
>
> Her arms flew up, two weak wings cutting the rush of wind. But it wasn't the old sensation this time, not the familiar embrace of the whole fleeting continent, but a grasp at something once there, now lost. (34)

When she is still buoyed by the prospect of attaining the American Dream, even "down" can be "up," fall can be flight, on the roller coaster. Now the downward pull of "gravity" prevails, back toward the Necessity of poverty, racism, "dailiness," immobilization. The story's title, "Displacement," seems to refer not only to immigration or moving but also to a fitful shifting of experiential reality for Mrs. Chow as she inarticulately struggles against the pressure to "know her place."

The complex ending of "Displacement" introduces another term in the dynamics of displacement and emplacement: human community. A little girl in the roller coaster car, seated next to Mrs. Chow presumably to benefit from the latter's reassuring presence, ends up becoming a source of comfort for the older woman, who feels "anchored by another's being." After she rejoins her husband under a billboard advertising home perms, Mrs. Chow asks him what he would think of her curling her hair. "I won't do it, . . . but what do you say?" (35). As soon as she contemplates this infraction against Mr. Chow's code of austerity, she withdraws it: self-adornment is plainly unnecessary for survival. Yet the author gives a new twist to her impulse toward Extravagance: there is a slight hint that Mrs. Chow, at first unwilling to bear children for her husband, is now receptive to being "womanly" toward him, and that Mr. Chow, unable to "lift his eyes from her," has sensed this shift. At the end of the story she realizes that "the land on the other side [of the Pacific Ocean]" will not "come into view": perhaps this means that America, with all its constraints, is now felt as her true home. This recognition may have prepared Mrs. Chow to accept a more modest and earthbound (but perhaps also more realizable) version of Extravagance leading to the creation of a family: the basis of a stable lateral network of human relationships that constitute at-homeness. This version entails what might be read as a compromise with Necessity, for agreement to bear children is, among other things, a fulfillment of traditional Chinese family values and a further threat to Mrs. Chow's hidden artistic aspirations. On the other hand, to the extent that the Chows are now allies in the new land, starting a family does promise an end to isolation.

The elliptic prose of "Displacement" precludes a more confident reading, yet the interpretation proffered here becomes more plausible if the story is read with Fae Myenne Ng's "A Red Sweater," which explores more explicitly how the contention between Necessity and Extravagance would impact community. The three daughters of the immigrant family represent three possible responses to the demands of Necessity: immobility, fall, and flight. Lisa, the oldest daughter, remains Chinatown-bound and earthbound: she dutifully gives up her studies to stay with her parents, whose own network of horizontal human relationships has been worn down by poverty and the disruptions of immigration. (Though the parents boast of the long-distance discounts from Lisa's job with Pacific Telephone, none of their friends and relatives in China has a telephone.) The second daughter chooses the free-fall of suicide: "Number Two, the in-between, leaped off the 'M' floor three years ago." No reason is given, but the context makes it clear that the exactions of her parents, themselves victims of Necessity, have proved too much for her. Substituting for her stressed-out father, who constantly threatens to jump off the Golden Gate Bridge, the middle daughter joins another Asian American literary suicide, the nameless young woman in Janice Mirikitani's poem "Suicide Note." The less-than-straight-A student plunges from her dormitory window, leaving her body as an apology to her hard-pressing parents (1987:26).

Fall is, in a sense, miscarried or defective flight: the bird imagery recurring in Chin, Louie, and Mirikitani is more than decorative. Both fall and flight could be acts of defiance; both could be means of escape. The third daughter, the narrator of Ng's story, impelled by either greater spunk or greater desperation, elects flight in the dual sense of escape and physical movement in the air: she becomes a Pan Am stewardess. Her act would seem the most Extravagant, yet her airborne voyages are much like the brakeman's rides on the train: confinement to a movable prison. In a mockery of the bird's truly autonomous flight, she moves everywhere but goes nowhere, compulsively and perpetually in passage, severed from the human ties of her ethnic community. "Flying cuts up your life, hits hardest during the holidays. I'm always sensitive then. I feel like I'm missing something, that people are doing something really important while I'm up in the sky, flying through time zones" (33). There is no "gravity" of human commitments to secure her, to give her a "home-base" from which to make truly Extravagant expeditions of discovery and fulfillment.

SPIRITUAL UPWARD MOBILITY AND
SOCIOECONOMIC UPWARD MOBILITY

Images of flight, whether successful or not, point to a crucial and difficult problem in the Asian American artist's effort to negotiate between
the imperatives of Necessity and the imperatives of Extravagance. Flight
removes the individual from the mappable space of terra firma, and a
vexing series of ramifications are uncovered by this observation: no
maps—no earth—no roots—no home. The horizontal plane, as we have
learned, is not only the locus of coercion and stagnation, needfulness
and arrested development; it is also the locus of human habitation, attachment, reciprocity. "Gravity" may impede, but it also sustains. An
image in *The Woman Warrior* sums up this paradox. The narrator, in
search of models of worthwhile feminine lives, imagines her adulterous
aunt to be a courageous practitioner of Extravagance, an escape artist
from the claustrophobic circles of Confucian morality and impoverished
village life. Yet when she pictures the aunt banished to the pigsty, giving
birth alone to her illegitimate child, the dark side of flying becomes apparent:

> The black well of sky and stars went out and out and out forever. . . . She
> was one of the stars, a bright dot in blackness, without home, without a
> companion, in eternal cold and silence. An agoraphobia rose in her, speed-
> ing higher and higher, bigger and bigger, she would not be able to contain
> it; there would be no end to fear. (Kingston 1977:16)

And even after death the aunt is punished by being erased from group
memory, her tale recalled periodically only to illustrate capricious selfishness. How, then, are the promptings of Extravagance to be heeded
without reducing the individual to solipsism and irresponsibility?

This question is addressed in two works: Kingston's *The Woman
Warrior* (especially the "White Tigers" chapter) and David Henry
Hwang's *The Dance and the Railroad*, both of which feature the image
of the mountaintop as a setting for autotelic activity. In the fantasy section of Kingston's work on the childhood of the woman warrior, the
narrator imagines herself called by a bird to the mountains. There, severed from the family's loving support but also exempted from the
drudgery of the peasant's lot, two "immortals" (*shenxian*) immerse her
in intensive martial arts training that seems to lack immediate use.
Hwang's play pits two early railroad workers against each other: one a
supporter of the 1867 strike and a naive spokesman for the American
Dream of overnight fortunes, the other an arrogant and dedicated Peking opera actor who practices his dance steps alone on a mountaintop.
The latter spurns the company of other railroad workers, who seem ob-

sessed with making a living, initially even ridiculing their efforts to improve working conditions.

Since these two works will be discussed in greater detail in the following chapter on play and artistic activity, I will focus here only on the image of the mountaintop and the question of how to read it in the Asian American context. The mountain peak is universally understood as a sacred presence;[42] in the West, Romanticism in particular has made it a symbol for sublimity.[43] Kingston and Hwang also draw upon more specific cultural meanings: in the Taoist esoteric tradition, which informs much of martial arts philosophy, "going up the mountain" (*shangshan*) is virtually synonymous with "seeking a Teacher and learning the Way" (*xunshi xuedao*), or submitting oneself to discipline and discipleship for the sake of perfecting one's practice.[44] Exotic effect is hardly the point of invoking these connotations though. (In fact, the topos of "going up the mountain" is so pervasive in popular martial arts literature and so deeply ingrained in the Chinese language itself that translation inevitably exaggerates its exoticism.) Rather, in the Asian American context, the image of the mountaintop possesses a particular felicity: like flight, ascent to the summit elevates the aspirant to transcendence, distancing her from Necessitous concerns; but unlike flight, it does not remove her entirely from terra firma but facilitates return to community after a period of individual cultivation and expression. The mountaintop thus hints at the *possibility* of reconciling the competing claims of the horizontal and the vertical axis.

As the readings in the next chapter will show, neither *The Woman Warrior* nor *The Dance and the Railroad* presents an unproblematic realization of this possibility. (The parable-like flavor of both mountaintop scenes, played out in geographically unlocatable places, are perhaps not accidental. In Kingston's case, the setting, though vividly depicted in a magical prose, is really a "literary" landscape assembled from the clichés of folklore and legend; in Hwang's, the setting is simply given as "a mountaintop near the transcontinental railroad.") Yet regardless of the indeterminacy of the outcome, and quite apart from questions of authorial intention, the image of the mountaintop retreat speaks to a central issue in Asian American communities: socioeconomic upward mobility. It offers an implicit critique of the preoccupation with socioeconomic upward mobility that has been associated with Asian Americans since the 1960s.

We may not be accustomed to thinking of news magazine articles or sociology papers as intertexts for literary works, but in a sense they are, unless total compartmentalization of reading practices were possible. The upward direction, when encountered in Asian American literature, is naturally reminiscent of the rhetoric of socioeconomic upward mobility so prevalent in the media and certain academic discourses. What is noteworthy about this rhetoric is that it is not the monopoly of the journalistic and social science literature promoting the "model minority," or of successful Asian Americans given to self-congratulation. It also dominates the revisionist writing from the progressive sectors of the community as they work for greater justice and full equality (e.g., Der and Lye 1989). Through their figurations of movement (especially through the image of the mountaintop), creative writers suggest that there is another arena of aspiration, another kind of meaningful upward mobility besides the socioeconomic. In this sense, the narratives that mediate between horizontal and vertical movement, exploring issues of survival, freedom, identity, and community, perform a thought-provoking or even goading function for their readership.

Of course, the two kinds of upward mobility—spiritual and socioeconomic—are hardly mutually exclusive; in the case of Mrs. Chow and the third daughter of "A Red Sweater," for instance, attempt at Extravagant ascent (misguided or not) coincides partially with socioeconomic upward mobility. No doubt greater financial security and social acceptance, the goals of numerous immigrant families, can work to weaken the hold of Necessity and are not to be lightly dismissed. To that extent, spiritual upward mobility is related to socioeconomic upward mobility, often enabled by it. However, the line between engrossment with socioeconomic struggle and materialism is thin. There is also a more fundamental issue: catch phrases like "the broken ladder" or "the glass ceiling," which are often used as rallying cries by community activists, presuppose—and imply acceptance of—a preinstalled, unshakable social structure to which the Asian American is related by the act of scaling and little else. This is an assumption that some Asian American writers are unwilling to leave unexamined.

Distrust of the hierarchial social structure is symbolically communicated in the aforementioned images of suicidal leaps off buildings, which register a protest against the ruthlessness of social demands for performance. Though one cannot destroy the vertical structure that houses the offending institutions, one can at least reject it categorically by physical detachment, accepting self-destruction as the cost of this final dismissive gesture.

We can also discern a critique of socioeconomic upward mobility in the geography of two fictional worlds: Milton Murayama's *All I Asking for Is My Body* (1959) and Bienvenido Santos's *What the Hell for You Left Your Heart in San Francisco* (1987). In the former, the arrangement of housing on the plantation is pyramidal—the *haole* overseer on top, next the Portuguese, Spanish, and Nisei *lunas*, then the Japanese Camp and the more rundown Filipino Camp (1975:28). The colonial system is further reinforced by the Confucian values of the Japanese, who observe a strict order of duties and privileges within the family. At first Kiyo, the narrator, and his fellow Nisei accept the plantation world as natural and immutable; they happily make a windfall from scabbing when the Filipinos go on strike for higher wages. Snooky, the progressive school teacher who is appalled by the "last surviving vestige of feudalism in the United States," attempts to instill some social conscience into his passive pupils, but to little avail. " 'I always thought everybody low on the pecking order hated it. Not so. Not you. You love getting pecked from above, you enjoy pecking those below. Amazing' " (33). Snooky is challenged by Tubby Takeshita, a model "number one son," who defends the pecking order: "It teach everybody to know his place. It make everything run smooth" (34). Snooky concedes that submission to authority is good for efficiency and money-making, but tries to prod the students into thinking about the "primary virtues" in life. " 'What about fresh air and freedom for the individual? What about standing on your own feet? What about thinking for yourself, using your own noodle. Huh? . . . Freedom means not being part of a pecking order. Freedom means being your own boss' " (34).

This is a concept that Kiyo, at the time, can only understand in terms of his much-constricted socioeconomic horizon of expectations: "Freedom means being a plantation boss" (34). Like his older brother Tosh, who gives up a promising career in boxing to help pay off the family debt, Kiyo dutifully stays on the plantation, working his way up from cane cutter and loader to truck driver's helper. But finally, as he contemplates starting his own family, it dawns on him that the game has been rigged from the start:

> The camp, I realized then, was planned and organized around its sewage system. The half dozen rows of underground concrete ditches, two feet wide and three feet deep, ran from the higher slope of camp into the concrete irrigation ditch on the lower perimeter of camp. An outhouse built over the sewage ditch had two pairs of back-to-back toilets and serviced four houses. Shit too was organized according to the plantation pyramid. Mr. Nelson was top shit on the highest slope, then there were the Portuguese, Spanish and *nisei lunas* with their indoor toilets which flushed into the same ditches, then Japanese Camp, and Filipino Camp.
>
> Everything was over-organized. There were sports to keep you busy and happy in your spare time. Even the churches seemed part of the scheme to keep you contented. Mr. Nelson . . . acted like a father, and he looked after you and cared for you provided you didn't disobey. (96)

For the first time, by consciously relating spatial configuration to social hierarchy, Kiyo perceives the "shit" beneath the surface rationality of the paternalistic system. Methodical socioeconomic advancement has lost its allure, and Kiyo begins to understand Snooky's teaching. The image of flight appears: "It was like we were born in a cage and Snooky was coaxing us to fly off, not run away, but be on our own and taste the freedom and danger of the open space" (96). Kiyo's awakening is declared in memorably earthy language: "Freedom was freedom from other people's shit, and shit was shit no matter how lovingly it was dished, how high or how low it came from. Shit was the glue which held a group together, and I was going to have no part of any shit of any group" (96).

Ironically, because the island location of Pepelau allows Kiyo to conflate the effects of disenfranchisement with the effects of geographical isolation from the American mainland, he attaches excessive hope to the physical act of leaving. He volunteers for the army, believing that it provides a chance for escape "on a silver platter" (98); he appears oblivious to the fact that the military is, if anything, an even more rigidly ranked and paternalistic institution than the plantation. The abrupt ending of *All I Asking for Is My Body*, in which Kiyo wins enough money in a crap game to repay the family debt, calls into doubt the logicality of a social system whose promise of ascent through initiative and honest hard work can be undone by a roll of the dice.

Suspicion of socioeconomic upward mobility is not solely the product of an obsolete economic institution, a Confucian upbringing, or island fever. It also informs Santos's novel on Filipino American life set in the Bay Area, *What the Hell for You Left Your Heart in San Francisco.* Though awkwardly written, the book clearly sets out two divergent images of mobility, the horizontal and the vertical, that have become familiar to us by now. The protagonist, David Tolosa, is a young intellectual escaping martial law under Marcos and vaguely searching for his lost father, who used to send money home from San Francisco. He is temporarily taken in by Dr. Sotto, an affluent vasectomy surgeon belonging to the post-1965 wave of professional Filipino immigrants; Sotto and his friends entrust David with their pet project, a slick magazine of Filipino American culture that is also supposed to provide a tax shelter. Horizontal movement is represented by David's restless wanderings in the streets of San Francisco, motivated partly by his reluctance to depend too much on Sotto's charity, partly by a vague hope of finding his father, and partly by the need to gather "human interest" material for the planned (but eventually aborted) magazine. Although the would-be editor is from a much more educated background than Carlos Bulosan's laborers of half a century ago, his encounters with the sorry specimens of humanity that populate the city's mean streets would not be out of place in *America Is in the Heart.* Dr. Sotto's grand tri-level residence on Diamond Heights, on the other hand, embodies the social structure that he and his fellow doctors have successfully climbed and that David is tempted to scale as well. David, installed in an apartment at the lowest level, dreams of ingratiating himself with the influential doctors and being accepted as one of their own.

As David interacts with a broad cross-section of the Filipino American community and learns of the dark secrets of the rich and powerful, he begins to see the illusory nature of his ambitions. The meaninglessness of material success is brought home to him in an incident involving Estela,[45] the Sottos's deformed and retarded daughter, implied to be a victim of her parents' single-minded devotion to "making it." The glittering lights of the city normally have a calming effect on the young girl, but one night, when she looks through a telescope, she throws a violent fit (1987:178), which suggests that the spectacular vistas enjoyed by those who have reached the top really do not bear scrutiny. Paradoxically, it is David's restless walks on the flatlands among the down and out that have given him the most spiritual sustenance. Hence his exclamation: "Thank you, Dr. Sotto, for letting me loose in the city," but also:

> Damn you, Dr. Sotto, for not warning me. Unless you yourself didn't have any idea of what I was bound to see. . . . After a while, Dr. Sotto, this beautiful room you lent me to live in, on top of Diamond Heights, wasn't any good for anything except for writing my heart out, for crying quietly, for God's sake, while I gazed down the hills and valleys of your blazing city and saw old men waiting to die a long, long way from home; and angry young brown boys and girls who cursed their parents and spit on their own images, confused and secretly frightened. (34)

In the end David descends from Diamond Heights; his farewell to Estela speaks of the treachery of the city's contours and the perils of the climb up the power structure. "Look close, Estela, under the stars; see us little brown men and women, walking the streets of the city as they wind and turn and climb upward, without warning about sudden corners and dark alleys on the downward bend" (191).

CONCLUSION

"CELEBRATE AMERICA," urges a postal service message on an aerogram in Mukherjee's *Jasmine*, sent from Flushing, New York, to Jullundhar, India. "TRAVEL . . . THE PERFECT FREEDOM" (83). We have seen from the foregoing analysis of mobility motifs how ironic such a proclamation has been for Asian Americans. From this understanding, it is possible to move on to transethnic comparisons of mobility patterns, in order to further qualify and revise the taken-for-granted national myths tacitly based on a monocultural point of view.

As Janis Stout acknowledges in *The Journey Narrative in American Literature*, in a tantalizing passage that unfortunately remains undeveloped (and omits Asians altogether), westering, though typically connoting "a move from the known to the unknown or from restriction to freedom," "meant different things to different groups" (1983:4).

> American minority cultures have their own directional values. . . . For Chicano literature, the directions of symbolic value, roughly corresponding to the West/East values of Anglo-European Americans, are North and South. For Afro-Americans, too, the original westerly journey could scarcely hold the liberating, hopeful connotations of the founders' tradition, and the return to the home continent is necessarily more fraught with anxiety. Like the Chicano culture, Afro-American culture, through the heritage of the Underground Railway and escape in general, finds the North a locus of freedom and betterment. . . . For the native Indian, deprived of his homeland and forced to migrate to a government reservation, going west could never mean progress but only despair and death. (10–11)

Stout's observations, however sketchy and however bound still to the dominant axis of movement, adumbrate an entire contrastive critical project on American spatial symbols/symbolic spaces. Reservations and the vast spaces separating them for Native Americans;[46] the dreaded "downriver" for African Americans and the river separating bondage from freedom for African Americans;[47] the border and borderlands, often the site of multiple crossings, and the migrant laborer's endlessly looping routes, for Chicanos[48]—these are but some of the examples amenable to study that come most readily to mind.

The prerequisite for valid interethnic contrast is (may we once again remind the "ethnicity school" adherents) a substantial body of meticulous intraethnic scholarship rather than a vaguely patriotic predisposition to detect sameness in one and all. African American investigations of group-specific mobility images provide a good example of how much can be done to push beyond the literal and the self-evident. For instance, Robert B. Stepto, in his *From Behind the Veil: A Study of Afro-American Narrative*, has identified a useful distinction between the northward and the southward journey for blacks (1979:62–91).[49] Though the former plainly refers to escape to freedom, the cultural immersion connoted by the latter would be nonobvious to a casual reader of African American literature; furthermore, in offsetting reactive movement with proactive, the identification of this pattern makes it impossible to subsume black subjectivity under gross generalizations about

American directional meanings. Barbara Christian, in *Black Feminist Criticism*, problematizes the notion of redemptive cultural immersion by pointing out how black women have often had to struggle *against* the sexism of their own communities: for such women, geographical movement back home is not only for learning but also for resistance (1985:178–80). Christian's expertise on black women's literature also enables her to see increased physical mobility for black women characters as a new quality in the fiction of the 1980s, indicative of closer interaction among black women and between them and other women of color. Houston A. Baker, Jr.'s *Blues, Ideology, and Afro-American Literature* builds an African American vernacular aesthetic on the image of the railroad crossing as the site for the cultural productions of the blues singer (1984:7–8); the twist that Baker gives to the promise of the railroad—mobility and freedom—unsettles received views of these American cultural pieties (11–12). Gay Wilentz's study of the Flying African legend, which traces the continuity between the orature of diasporic Africans and modern African American works such as Ishmael Reed's *Flight to Canada* (1975), Toni Morrison's *Song of Solomon* (1977), and Paule Marshall's *Praisesong for the Widow* (1983), is premised on the same dissatisfaction about universalistic reading that motivates my study (1989–90:21) and provides yet another basis for cross-ethnic comparisons of images of transcendence.

In "The Literatures of America: A Comparative Discipline," Paul Lauter, emphasizing as does Stout that mobility means something very different for Yankee men and for women and minorities (1990:15–16), makes a point that can serve as a fitting conclusion to this chapter:

> What is at stake here is not simply a revisionist claim to prior occupation of valued turf—however significant that might be. The stakes emerge if we begin from Toni Morrison's proposition that "narrative is the principal way in which human knowledge is made accessible." The issue is, then, what of human knowledge a particular set of narratives—a canon or a historical construct—encodes, makes accessible—or obscures. (15)

It is to uncovering the obscured that an informed comparativism in ethnic literary scholarship is committed.

Chapter Four

THE ASIAN AMERICAN *HOMO LUDENS*: WORK, PLAY, AND ART

THE ASPIRANTS to transcendence introduced at the end of the last chapter—the Peking opera actor in Hwang's *The Dance and the Railroad* and the young martial artist in Kingston's *The Woman Warrior*—are artist figures. As we have seen, transcendence is suspect in the Asian American context, given the ambiguity of the horizontal axis as the locus of both Necessity and community. Art, by being associated with "high ground," might be expected to be implicated as well. Indeed, if we survey images of artists and their activities in Asian American literature, we do find a large number of works exploring the idea of art as an Extravagant, *playful* act whose raison d'être has to be established. This immediately raises the question of social origin, which has been temporarily suppressed in the foregoing analysis of upward mobility: to what can we attribute such images of art? Are they simply gestures of self-justification on the part of the writers? Is it enough to subsume them under the modern bourgeois concept of the alienated artist (in which case the Asian American artist is no more than a variation on a type)?[1] To what extent has the race of the artist—together with the historical experience it entails—entered into their formulation? What visions of art and its role are offered by Asian American writers, and why at certain historical junctures have they emerged? What is the point, ultimately, of investigating the idea of play in Asian American literature? These questions will guide the inquiry in this, the final chapter of the book.

To say that the raison d'être of art needs to be established is to say that art is perceived as antithetical to self-justifyingly "serious" activities, which, in the Asian American context, we have come to understand as the business of survival. Granting the elasticity of the term *survival*, we still find many of the artist figures in Asian American literature pushing its definition to the breaking point: they play fast and loose with the "common sense" meanings of adequacy and inadequacy, comfort and discomfort, living and perishing, threatening to bring down the communal structure based on a tacit contract of joint struggle. Such figures obviously do not exhaust the representations of artistic activity in Asian American literature, a vast subject that would require a separate book to do it justice;[2] however, the issues they foreground with their proclivities for play are such central ones for Asian American cultural production that they merit some close study.

Hisaye Yamamoto's 1949 short story, "Seventeen Syllables," is in many ways a prototypical tale of the Asian American artist, introducing issues to which later writers on the subject have repeatedly returned. It is a notably interdiscursive text that can be read variously: as a woman's domestic tragedy, as an account of female initiation into adult sexuality and suffering, as a matrilineal story of mother-daughter bonds and secrets, as an immigrant tale of shattered dreams and intergenerational estrangement, as a drama of social class differences erupting after years of dormancy. For the purposes of this chapter, we focus on Mrs. Hayashi, the Issei mother of Rosie (the teenage girl from whose limited point of view the story is narrated), as an artist figure whose haiku-writing triggers a cataclysmic explosion of hitherto barely articulated feelings in herself and in those close to her.

The outline of the story is simple enough: Mrs. Hayashi, the wife of an Issei Japanese American farmer in Southern California, has taken to writing for the weekly poetry page of a Japanese-language newspaper. In time she becomes an "extravagant contributor" (1988:9), and though she takes care to practice her art only after finishing her household chores,[3] she unavoidably begins to slacken in her observance of wifely duties, which for Mr. Hayashi are synonymous with total suppression of individual wishes on her part. Within three months, at what seems to be its peak, Mrs. Hayashi's poetry-writing career is brought to an abrupt end. She wins first prize—a beautiful Japanese print—in a literary contest sponsored by the newspaper. The editor delivers it on a hot day when the tomato harvest has to be sorted without delay; as Mrs. Hayashi lingers in the house to discuss haiku with the handsome, elegantly mannered editor, Mr. Hayashi reaches ignition point. He chases the man out, smashes the picture, pours kerosene on it, and burns it to ashes. It is then that Mrs. Hayashi first reveals her past to Rosie—how she has been hastily married off to Mr. Hayashi in America, in the wake of her thwarted love affair with a social better and an unwanted pregnancy resulting in stillbirth—and extracts from her a reluctant promise never to marry.

In this tale of frustrated aspirations, the central conflict can be understood as Extravagance demanding a hearing in spite of the forces of Necessity, which are amassed in a formidable alliance against the individual woman. Patriarchy is obviously responsible for Mrs. Hayashi's banishment from her family and from Japan, as well as Mr. Hayashi's stringent concept of wifely propriety. More specifically, it is responsible for equating women with Nature, through defining women's creativity solely in terms of (socially sanctioned) biological reproduction. Mrs. Hayano, a neighbor whom the Hayashi family visits at one point in the story, may be read as a personification of mindless Nature—a picture of what Mrs. Hayashi could easily have become. Mrs. Hayano is tied to the natural cycle (her four daughters are named after the four seasons); ever since her first child, she has been afflicted with some unnamed disorder, so that she is now in a retarded, semivegetative state (10). In choosing to discuss haiku with Mr. Hayano, Mrs. Hayashi is asserting a different, forbidden alignment: with the "male" mode of agency, intelligence, articulation. On the other hand, it should be remembered that, given the hardships of Japanese American farm life, even this "male" privilege has had to suffer, and Mr. Hayashi has had to repress his own emotions as well. He is, in this sense, also a victim: men's attempts to control Nature by projecting it as female and subordinate can never be fully successful. When the day grows hot, the tomato crop waits for no one and leaves no room for personal feelings: only the efficiency of a "flawless machine" (16) is allowed, whether from man, woman, or child. Finally, the dictates of the capitalist economic machine do their share of damage: if the tomatoes aren't ready for the produce haulers, they will have to be sold at a lower price to the cannery (15).

Necessity in "Seventeen Syllables" is thus seen to be woven of many strands. Yet patriarchy's role cannot be underestimated, for by permitting only a distorted or displaced expression of women's desires, it lends male demands for compliance a legitimate air of impersonality and "naturalness." Note that Rosie has to use "going to the *benjo*" as an excuse whenever she needs an outlet for her feelings: when she sneaks out for her first sexual encounter in the packing shed, and when she fails to concentrate on the tomato-sorting in her love-struck state. The English word Yamamoto chooses to render *benjo* is *privy*, which shares a common root with *private* and retains traces of its archaic meaning of "hidden, surreptitious, furtive." Rosie's excuse suggests how a woman's desires are tolerated only when couched in terms of the barest bodily needs; because they are "private"—that is, possessing a validity independent of the woman's prescribed social roles—they are perceived to be illicit, as indeed they have been for her mother. In this connection, the apparent shift in the story's focus, from art at the beginning to marriage at the end, is entirely logical, quite apart from questions of narrative art-

istry on Yamamoto's part. An underlying relationship—a Freudian influence, conscious or unconscious, is detectable here—has been posited
between artistic creativity and erotic desire: both are presented as manifestations of an Extravagant spirit, flouting the counsel of a socially defined, rational calculus.

Within the framework of this larger equivalence, certain issues about
the nature of art are foregrounded. At the beginning of the story,
Yamamoto conspicuously presents the technical (not merely expressive)
aspects of Mrs. Hayashi's poetry composition. If the writing of haiku
gives Mrs. Hayashi her first taste of free choice since her disastrous love
affair, this freedom is paradoxically realized only in the presence of *formal* or *structural* rules. As Mrs. Hayashi explains to Rosie, the challenge
of haiku is to "pack all her meaning in seventeen syllables only . . . divided into three lines of five, seven, and five syllables" (8). While Mrs.
Hayashi's explication may have been included to underscore Rosie's distance from her Japanese heritage, it also implies that artistic creativity
derives meaning from being exercised against arbitrary constraints: arbitrary in the sense of "artificial yet voluntarily adopted." (This principle
goes quite unappreciated by Rosie, who admires a silly haiku in English
that sports an extra syllable.)

Yamamoto's focus on the formal, rule-governed nature of art has
some interesting ramifications. Questions on the place of art in Asian
American life are raised by Mrs. Hayashi's absorption in the formal challenges of haiku, which clearly sets her apart from the frustrated Issei
wives in a cluster of thematically similar stories, in particular "Yoneko's
Earthquake" (1951) by Yamamoto herself, and "Songs My Mother
Taught Me" (1976) by Wakako Yamauchi, her literary disciple.[4] All
three female protagonists—Mrs. Hayashi, Mrs. Hosoume in "Yoneko's
Earthquake," and Hatsue Kato in "Songs My Mother Taught Me"—are
unhappily married to men who personify Necessity: hard-working but
austere, taciturn, and distracted Issei farmers, whose emotional side has
been repressed in the struggle to wrest a living from the land. Both Mrs.
Hosoume and Mrs. Kato are romantically involved with younger men—
Marpo and Yamada respectively—who beckon from a more colorful and
refined world of Extravagance. Despite the parallels, however, the three
women differ in their closeness to art. While Mrs. Hayashi is an active
practitioner, Mrs. Kato's involvement is less pronounced or direct; it is
not clear to the narrator of "Songs My Mother Taught Me" whether her
mother is writing letters or poems, and instead of playing music she listens to elegiac Japanese songs on the Victrola. The musician in that
story is male: Yamada, a neatly groomed and elegantly dressed Kibei[5]
who plays a mandolin with "shining pearl frets" (1976:67). Finally, Mrs.
Hosoume's contact with art is mainly vicarious, through her lover

Marpo, who is portrayed as an inadequate though thoroughly likable exemplar of artistic creativity. For him, dabbling in art, like buying fancy athletic shoes or muscle-building sets (1988:48), is a recreational outlet for his youthful vitality. He is described in a deliciously ironic passage as being a musician "(both instrumental and vocal)" and an artist who can paint "larger-than-life" watercolors of movie stars (48). (The daughter is dazzled equally by Marpo's music-making and by the red velvet lining of his violin case, for both of these, like the pearl frets on Yamada's mandolin, signal a surplus over the survival needs that preoccupy the paterfamilias.)

In all three stories, art is again linked to eros. Moreover, whereas the women's yearning for something beyond silent endurance of the daily grind triggers domestic discord in all three cases, the two women without an artistic avocation appear to have created socially more disruptive situations. (Mrs. Hosoume's affair results in an abortion, Mrs. Kato's in an unwanted child who is "accidentally" drowned in a moment of maternal neglect.) Is Toni Morrison's description of the title character of *Sula* (1973)—"Like any artist with no art form, she becomes dangerous" (105; cited by Christian 1985:60)—appropriate for Mrs. Kato and Mrs. Hosoume as well? Can it be said that, having no other outlet for their impulse to Extravagance, the women work with the only material they have, their lives?

THE SITES OF EXTRAVAGANCE

This configuration of characters and activities hints that dedication to the rigorous formal demands of art may have functioned as a sublimating mechanism in the case of Mrs. Hayashi, averting an eruption of energy in the form of sexual liaisons. (Again shades of Freud here.) But there are several indications that there is, perhaps, no such thing as a safe act of Extravagance. Social approval of art is at best limited and contingent, as seen in Mrs. Hayashi's taking of a pseudonym for her haiku-writing. Rosie comments that for a while the family has to live "with two women, her mother and Ume Hanazono." The mother keeps house all day; Ume Hanazono, the poet, comes to life after the dinner dishes are done: "an earnest, muttering stranger who often [neglects] speaking when spoken to and [stays] busily at the parlor table as late as midnight scribbling pencil on scratch paper or carefully copying characters on good paper with her fat, pale green Parker" (9). When Mr. Hayashi burns the prize picture in the climax of the story, the psychological violence is so unnervingly brutal that we understand the blaze to have destroyed Ume Hanazono as well. Mrs. Hayashi's two names then are symptomatic of an inner split, which in turn reflects a larger split within her society: that between "work" and an unnamed entity, which, as I will argue on the basis of intertextual readings, is "play."

Although the word *play* is never uttered in "Seventeen Syllables," Mr. Hayashi's moral leverage over his wife clearly derives from his self-representation as an earnest and responsible *worker*. Of the few phrases he is shown to utter in the course of the story, the majority concern work. When asked to stay longer for a social evening at the Hayanos, he replies: "Work tomorrow" and "We have to get up at five-thirty" (11). On the day of the final crisis, he reminds Rosie there is no time for a break, reprimands her for her careless performance, "only half-joking[ly]" suggests that she relieve herself in the weeds, and orders her to keep sorting the tomatoes as he strides over to the house to confront his wayward wife (15–17). His stance as a necessarily stern taskmaster, toward himself no less than toward his family (a stance that, incidentally, allows his sexual jealousy to be obscured) is meant to contrast with Mrs. Hayashi's selfishness and thoughtlessness. His characterization of Mrs. Hayashi as "crazy" (17) places her outside the bounds of all rationally justifiable behavior.

In "Seventeen Syllables" the opposition between work and play is only implicit; the rest of this chapter will continue to define the opposition, examine how and why it becomes explicit in some cases, and discuss its implications for Asian American literature. For the moment, even if we refrain from labeling Mrs. Hayashi's haiku-writing as "play," we can already see a dichotomy developing:

Work	*X (unnamed)*
Rational, sane	Irrational, crazy
Concerned with survival	Concerned with perfection
Productive	Dissipative
Contributes to common welfare	Contributes only to self
Responsible toward family and others	Irresponsible toward family and others
Realistic, heeding "objective" (physical, economic, etc.) constraints	Unrealistic, blind to "objective" constraints
No room for personal feelings	Indulgent of personal feelings

Given our readings so far on the motifs of alimentation, the double, and mobility, it is evident too that the left-hand column is associated with Necessity, the right with Extravagance.

What is essential to remember about this list is that the epithets in both columns derive not from some impersonal criteria but from the judgment of the "worker," whose authority is "common sense"—that is, the taken-for-granted perceptions of those he considers to constitute respectable society. Thus the site of Extravagance shifts within the cluster of Japanese American stories by Yamamoto and Yamauchi, though the general contours of the contrast are preserved. In "Songs My Mother Taught Me," Kato expresses himself through song only when he is drunk—that is, when he can no longer be held accountable for his weaknesses. As a struggling immigrant tied to an inhospitable land during the Depression, he feels he cannot afford "useless" emotions that divert energy from the business of survival.

> My father was a quiet man. He never revealed that he suspected this was the whole cloth of his life, that he would live and die this way. He never revealed his dream for us, his children, in America, or permitted his own dreams to articulate. Only occasionally when he was in his cups, when the winter rain drowned his hopes for a good harvest, he would sing the saddest and loneliest Japanese songs. (63–64)

When he is sober, he projects onto Yamada and onto women the softer qualities to which the songs give him sporadic access:

> "I could do without that sort. . . . Plucking at that frivolous mandolin every chance he gets, like he was practicing for the pictures or something. The clothes he wears—those two-toned perforated shoes, that downtown haircut, the fancy cigarettes . . . pah! Like a woman! Do you want Tetsuo to get like that? So he works hard. So? Well, he stays only until the harvest is over." (66)

As Kato himself cannot avoid noticing, the antithesis between work and frivolity is not within Yamada (who is, in fact, an excellent farmhand). This inconsistency immediately calls into question Kato's correlating "artsiness" with effeminacy and femininity.

A similar point may be made about Mr. Hosoume's estimation of Marpo in Yamamoto's "Yoneko's Earthquake." At first, Mr. Hosoume considers Marpo, a hard-working and personable Filipino, to be an exception to the "irrefutable fact among Japanese in general" that "Filipinos in general [are] an indolent lot" (47). After the confrontation between the two rivals, Mr. Hosoume replaces Marpo with "an old Japanese man who [wears] his grey hair in a military cut and who, unlike Marpo, [has] no particular interests outside working, eating, sleeping, and playing an occasional game of *goh* with Mr. Hosoume" (54). In other words, not only does Mr. Hosoume connect Marpo's Extravagant inclinations with sexuality (as he has now good cause to do), but he also perceives them to be a *Filipino* weakness, even though the young man has been his "best hired man" (47). For the sake of winning what amounts to a battle of ideology as well as power, he is willing to damage the cause of industry and productivity that he has ostensibly set out to champion. *Filipino* has thus become Mr. Hosoume's code word for Extravagant tendencies; to arrest their invasion of the family, he relies upon a secular asceticism augmented by ethnocentrism. When Mr. Hosoume reproves his prepubescent daughter, Yoneko, for wearing bright fingernail polish, his accusation is: "You look like a Filipino," referring to "another irrefutable fact among Japanese in general that Filipinos in general [are] a gaudy lot" (52). Mrs. Hosoume contradicts him with a fact—that young girls in Japan also go to great lengths to color their fingernails—but of course her observation is irrelevant to the real dispute at hand, which is about power: power to uphold patriarchy and the Necessity that gives it its mandate; power to suppress women's menacing emergent sexuality and related forms of Extravagance.[6]

Whether Extravagance is seen to reside in the feminine or in the ethnic out-group, a process of disowning and projection supported by "public opinion," similar to the one we have seen in the formation of the racial shadow, appears to be operating here. Furthermore, reading the Yamamoto and Yamauchi stories against each other, we discover the boundaries of outsiderhood to be highly fluid. For example, when the ethnicity of the unwanted representative of Extravagance cannot be made into an issue, as in the case of Yamada or the newspaper editor from San Francisco, citified decadence becomes a ready culprit, and Extravagance of spirit, interest in self-cultivation, attention to beauty (of person or of artistic form), come to be located in the city. Though Marpo is Filipino, Yamada is Kibei, and all the women protagonists are Issei, though haiku is Japanese and the mandolin and violin are Western, the same psychological process is found in all three offended husbands. To that extent, we might read the stories as parables on the same fundamental conflict, with certain scapegoats offering themselves as more plausible than others in the situations invented by the authors. In one sense, that the sites of Extravagance shift over so wide a range only testifies to its compelling "universality."

In another sense though, the historical specificity of these sites of Extravagance is of the utmost significance. Even if we believe that the concept of Extravagance speaks to some deep-seated human impulse, the very fact that its manifestations are perceived as alien is a sign that sociohistorical constraints have been at work. In that case, the authors' choices of sites of projection are not fortuitous or incidental; not only do they bear traces of history (e.g., the Japanese Americans' isolation from white society during the pre–World War II period; their relative prosperity compared to Filipinos; demonstrable differences in lifestyle between city and country), but even more importantly, they set the horizons for one's recuperative expectations. For the first-generation parents in "Seventeen Syllables" and "Songs My Mother Taught Me," the possibility of reclaiming Extravagance is situated in Japan, whereas America is perceived as the land of Necessity. The natural hardships of farm life—in "Songs My Mother Taught Me" they are amplified by descriptions of inexorable seasonal cylces, recalling Mrs. Hayano's four daughters—are compounded by legal restrictions: quite literally, the land they cultivate daily is not theirs but "American," because of the alien land laws. Mrs. Kato attempts to seize brief moments of fulfillment with Yamada during the family's vacation in coastal San Pedro—that is, when "ordinary life" and the reality principle are suspended. Situated between land and ocean, America and Japan, mitigating the unrelenting heat and aridity of the Imperial Valley, San Pedro's beaches offer reprieve—but only fragile and illusory reprieve. Given the Necessitous pressures from the American environment, the nostalgic thrust common among immigrants takes on an increasingly romantic cast: art, for those tempted by Extravagance, becomes identified with an idealized Japan. Mrs. Kato's Japan, affirmed by her connection with the Japanese-educated Yamada, is a land of "haunting flutes," "cherry blossoms," "poetry," and "fatalism" (67); Mrs. Hayashi's prize print depicts an idyllic seascape: pink clouds, pale blue sea with sampans, distant pine trees and thatched huts (17).

To the extent that it deflects attention not only from one's American life but also from the Necessitous conditions that first propel most emigrants abroad, this idealization of the land of origin may warrant the pragmatists' charge of irresponsibility. On the other hand, as long as the pursuit of Extravagance is still located within the native culture, its non-realization will continue to be felt, by both the men and the women, as merely a matter of spatial separation and temporal postponement. (In this dualistic view, there is little room for the possibility that pursuit of wealth and status overseas might express an Extravagant yearning, or that interest in the ethereal might itself become an economic activity.) There may be much self-deception in this belief: few immigrants are able to return "rich and triumphant" (Yamauchi 1976:63) to a life of spiritual and material plenitude. Still, when conceptualized this way, Extravagance would entail less disloyalty than if it were assigned to another culture. In the case of "Yoneko's Earthquake," because Extravagance is considered Filipino, to yield to its call (even through as innocuous an act as putting on nail polish) would compound disloyalty toward patriarchy and social class position with disloyalty toward one's ethnic group. The determination and persistence needed to resist the interdictions of Necessity would also be correspondingly greater.

By virtue of their extraordinary thematic affinities as well as Yamauchi's explicit acknowledgments of direct influence by Yamamoto, the short stories on frustrated Issei wives examined here run some risk of being ghettoized as "women's stories" or as highly local "Japanese American stories" from one specific milieu. Yet the issues they raise, about Extravagance in general and art in particular, have continued to resonate with a number of Asian American literary works of widely divergent settings. Unlikely as the juxtaposition may seem, one of the most enlightening intertextual pairings is to read the Yamamoto-Yamauchi stories against Frank Chin's *The Year of the Dragon*, where the implicit antithesis between work and play has come to be articulated with great vehemence, and the perceived possibility of artistic creation has migrated from the ethnic culture to the dominant society.

"T'REE STUPI' PAGE IN A CHEAP BOOK": "WHAT GOOD FOR?"

The Eng family in *The Year of the Dragon* is a family of closet artists. We have already encountered Fred Eng, the embittered writer manqué who now plies his trade as a popular Chinatown tour guide. His younger brother Johnny, a juvenile delinquent in the making, is revealed to be also a nascent photographer. Fred is proud and protective of Johnny's talent ("I let him have the back room of the office for a darkroom. The kid's got an eye, huh?") and attributes the youngster's feistiness to "too much of ma's artistic temperament" (1981:82). The artistic temperament of Ma (not Fred's biological mother; see below) is not much in evidence in the play: she spends much of her time airing her hemorrhoids—the bathroom being, as for Rosie, the only sanctuary available for private gratification—and the crooning of snippets of old songs appears to be her chief artistic activity. Yet in Fred's estimation she could have had a glamorous career as a singer of dangerously sexy songs: "You coulda been a singer, ma. Play Vegas. And I'd write ya spicey songs to slither out of your throat like barracudas" (93; also 137). Of the six blood relatives in the play, half are frustrated artists.

Although Pa Eng, the infirm but still loud-mouthed Chinatown business leader, is a far cry from the laconic husbands in the Japanese American stories, he shares with his younger rural counterparts the role of patriarchal enforcer: he suppresses artistic pursuits in his family because they seem to him so utterly devoid of utilitarian value. Fred is the special target of Pa's policing because, in Chinese tradition, the eldest son is supposed to be the patriarch-in-training. Expectation has been further hardened into command by the fact that Pa, immigrating under Exclusion, has had to create a family and win financial security against great odds.[7] When Pa suddenly presents China Mama, his first wife (previously prohibited by exclusionary laws from entering the United States) and Fred's birth mother, all the latent value differences between father and son erupt. The polarization of Necessity and Extravagance, work and play, business and art is now explicit.

To Pa, the demands he makes on Fred are coherently interlocked in an irreproachable logic. Cultural preservation, filial piety (including toward China Mama, to Fred a stranger), maintenance of the blood line and family name, guardianship of junior family members, attainment of degrees in higher education (preferably medical or legal), upward socioeconomic mobility coupled with undying devotion to a single geographical locale (Chinatown), law-abiding citizenship, commitment to the work ethic, abolition of all unedifying sentiments, prudent expenditure of energy, respectfulness of manner, cleanliness of person—all are Necessary to the patriarch, hence one and the same. Transgression of one injunction means transgression of all, so that, even though Fred has given up college to take over his ailing father's travel business and support Mattie (Sis) through college, he is still judged a failure.

> PA: How you teck care [of the rest of the family], huh? You no self-improvement, no higher education. . . . I sneaking you over Merican what for? Some flop. . . . Goin craze. Too much noises like a wil' annie moo. (109)

In particular, Pa condemns Fred's earlier attempt at literary creation as socially irresponsible—mere child's play, an incomprehensibly absurd waste of time:

> PA: Goot for what? You come home. Who ting you a man? Likee some spoil kit. Dorty ol' clothe. Dorty hair . . . Jus' playing inna college. What good for? You gimme your story. Torty year ol' you come home, what you show for it? T'ree stupi' page in a cheap book? (109)

Furthermore, parallel to the Japanese American men's pitting of in-group against out-group, Pa designates seriousness of purpose and responsible behavior as specifically Chinese virtues; in his memorable phrase: "Jolly time finis! Be Chinese now!" (93). The X of "Seventeen Syllables" has now been named, the battle lines drawn in the open.

While for Fred, as compared to the female protagonists in the Yamamoto and Yamauchi stories (and perhaps Ma as well), artistic creativity is less threateningly tied to sexuality, he is still deprived of his manhood. The emasculation is not, as in the case of Marpo and Yamada, just a matter of negative definition by father figures (although "Who ting you a man?" coming from one's father would certainly have an effect). In his forties Fred remains unmarried; for all his bold dirty talk, one gets the impression that his libido has been rather depleted by the heavy family responsibilities.

DEFINING EXTRAVAGANCE AS WHITE

There is another cause for Fred's emasculation, however—and this leads us to what appears to be the most crucial difference between Frank Chin's understanding of art as Extravagance and that of his Japanese American predecessors. White society has desexed Fred by forcing him into the role of the servile, ingratiating cultural pimp: "You know how the tourists tell I'm Chinese? No first person pronouns. No 'I,' 'Me' or 'We.' I talk like that lovable sissy, Charlie Chan" (114). Such a self-sabotaging role is incompatible with Fred's calling to be a serious writer. The tour guide's spiel, or its literary equivalent, demands suppression or distortion of all individual experiences that do not fit into white society's image of Chinese Americans. Honesty of artistic vision and acceptability by white readers thus become mutually exclusive, which poses a difficulty over and above the dilemma between artistic integrity and commercial success so familiar to the bourgeois writer. To write at all, Fred feels he has to break away completely from the Chinatown world. (That Pa himself has internalized certain demeaning images of the Chinese, even attempting to pass them on to his sons [McDonald 1981:xxiii], only adds to Fred's feeling of beleaguerment.) As Mattie puts it: "Out there [in Boston] we'll be able to forget we're Chinamen, just forget all this and just be people and Fred will write again" (110). In other words, *the potentiality for writing, artistic creation, play, self-actualization, Extravagance, is now placed in white society*, not in the ethnic culture or even, as in the case of "Yoneko's Earthquake," in another (allegedly inferior) Asian culture.

Upon hearing Mattie's statement, Johnny issues a caustic challenge (sounding "low, innocent, and cold," according to the stage directions): "You have to forget you're a Chinatown girl to be just people, Sis?" (110). Johnny's outrage is, of course, directed at the same identification of Asian race with deviance that we have seen in Dale of Hwang's *FOB* and other assimilated Asian Americans haunted by racial shadows. Yet being able to detect a self-handicapping, self-contemptuous assumption is not the same as being free from its hold; Johnny feels no less trapped by his race than Mattie. And Fred, for all the bitingly accurate self-diagnoses of his failure as a writer, fails to disentangle Extravagance from whiteness. On the one hand, he is capable of articulating both the "ethnic" and the "white" impediments to the "great Chinese American novel" (83), which he envisions to be a validation of those authentically Chinese American experiences rejected by the mainstream.

> FRED: I don't wanta be a pioneer. Just a writer. Just see my name in a book by me. About things I like writing about, and fuck the pioneers.

What've the old pioneers done for us, for me? I'm not even fighting nobody. I just have a few words and they come at me. *"Be Chinese, Charlie
Chan or a nobody"* to the whites and a mad dog to the Chinamans ... for
what? To die and be discovered by some punk in the next generation and
published in mimeograph by some college ethnic studies department, forget it. I have to take care of myself now. I have to protect my ... (117; my
italics)

On the other hand, judging from the long-buried concealed fantasy of
self-vindication he reveals to Pa just before their fateful last argument,
Fred can only conceive of literary success in terms of recognition by a
white audience. Trying desperately to communicate with his father,
Fred relates one of the most mortifying and decisive encounters in his
life: having been "caught" as a failed writer by a white high school
friend. Up to that chance meeting in a restaurant, Fred has been secretly
nursing his literary ambitions, writing on napkins for a couple of hours
after his last tour of the day (137). But the probing questions of the
white man, once his fantasized audience ("I remember that guy cuz I
was gonna surprise him") convince Fred of the futility of his dream. "He
asks whatever happened to the Chinese guy, Fred what'shisname, who
was all kinds of student body officer and goin' to bust New York ...?"
(138). In response Fred can only pretend to be someone else, thereby
crushing the artistic or Extravagant part of himself.

This episode suggests that, despite cognitively comprehending the
role of racial oppression in creating his permanent writer's block, Fred's
"default assumption" about success is that it is defined by a white audience, in much the same way that being "just people" and being like the
whites are synonymous in Mattie's vocabulary. Fame within the Chinese
American community, such as his father has achieved, does not count,
since in Fred's scheme of things Extravagance has already been projected and located exclusively in the dominant society. It may be true
that his parents—or limited English-speaking, survival-minded immigrants like them—don't read any of Fred's works (86); this readership
problem is genuine. Nevertheless, another potential audience remains:
fellow Chinese (and Asian) Americans for whom the validity of Fred's
subject matter would not be in question. The fact that he dismisses their
expected appreciation as a meaningful yardstick of success ("some punk
in the next generation," "some college ethnic studies department") is
telling. It signals that the binary distribution of Necessity and Extravagance along racial lines has become naturalized, virtually absolutely: the
process itself has receded into invisibility, leaving the apparently senseless tyranny of Chinese culture in the limelight.

A slippage, in other words, occurs between the comprehensive analysis of artistic silencing presented discursively by the central character and the Chinatown-centered dramatization of this silencing. Of course, Fred Eng's "telling" should not be uncritically interpreted as playwright Frank Chin's "telling" (though a plausible case can be made for regarding Fred as Chin's mouthpiece). But the "showing" does tend to draw attention asymmetrically to the ferocious cult of Necessity embodied by Pa, as well as to the general stunting and deformity of Chinatown inhabitants attributed to that dogma. The Necessity of conforming to white definitions is repeatedly and emphatically alluded to but not woven into the fabric of the plot. In reality, white society should constitute a more formidable foe to the Asian American artist than the dying, ghettoized culture symbolized by Pa; yet in terms of the staged interplay of characters, Pa is the truly worthy opponent and the target of immediate enmity. Compared to his powerful presence, Ross (Mattie's white husband) is an ineffectual clown, and the white tourists addressed by Fred never appear directly in the dramatis personae.

The obscured bifurcation in *The Year of the Dragon*, ceding Extravagance and its expressive channels to white society while designating artistic inhibition as Chinese, ironically replicates the "dual personality" concept denounced by Frank Chin himself in his capacity as a cultural critic. In "Backtalk" (1976), Chin recounts an informal exercise performed on a group of Chinese American college students. After agreeing unanimously that it was possible to separate the "Chinese" and "American" facets of their character, the young people were asked to divide a sheet of paper in half and describe each set of attributes. The finding: "Invariably, everything 'old fashioned, inhibiting, dull, and cowardly' was Chinese. Their interest in 'sex, fun, art, adventure, boldness,' was American" (557). One result of such a hypostasization of the "dual personality" concept is that "Chinatown rejects its writers because writing is an 'American' thing" (557)—which is precisely the view that Fred Eng attempts to defy but that the dramatic action of *The Year of the Dragon* takes as its point of departure. The phenomenon of unconscious replication in Frank Chin's works testifies to the immense power of cultural hegemony: it can insinuate itself into the very fabric of a critique intended to protest its falsehoods and offenses.

So pervasive is the belief in a Chinese/American cultural rift that even a critic as sensitive to sociopolitical context as Dorothy Ritsuko McDonald, in her valuable introduction to *The Year of the Dragon*, can say: "The use of the first person pronouns is for Fred the declaration of his *American individualism and individual rights*" (1981:xxiii; my italics). Such a reading, by tacitly confirming the "tourists' " stereotype of the self-effacing Chinese, veils white appropriation of Extravagant tendencies even further. It must be kept in mind that in *The Year of the Dragon*, the construal of Extravagance as white is partial: it exists in constant tension with another vision of Extravagance that is, in the final analysis, not that different from Yamamoto's or Yamauchi's. Fred, like Mattie, does fall prey to what might be called "the rhetoric of normalcy": "just people" is understood as the deracialized "human" (i.e., white) norm against which Asian Americans appear inherently aberrant, the unconditioned ideal of which they are doomed to fall short. *At the same time*, Fred is also capable of turning around this rhetoric to verbalize an oppositional view, which is that being "just people," without having to submit to an unwritten cultural/political agenda, should be everyone's birthright. In phrases like "just a writer," "just see my name in a book by me," and "I just have a few words" (117), he is claiming entitlement to what comes uncontested to those in power and with choices. Fred's metaphor of emasculation is a metaphor of mutilation, which means the taking away of rightful wholeness. Thus a sense of Extravagance as a natural human desideratum coexists in *The Year of the Dragon* with a definition of Extravagance as white; to me, it is precisely the volatile intermixing between the two—their constant mutual jostling—that makes the play such a central Asian American text.

ACCOUNTING FOR THE MIGRATION OF EXTRAVAGANCE

What accounts for the apparently disparate placements of Extravagance in the Japanese American stories and in *The Year of the Dragon*? Why is it that in the former, the first generation is portrayed as still capable of artistic creativity, however modest, while in the latter art has come to be dramatized as a white activity totally beyond the immigrant's ken?

Since Yamamoto, Yamauchi, and Chin are all American-born, we cannot explain the migration of Extravagance biographically, in terms of the *author's* generational position per se. However, some kind of generational effect is evidently at work in the *characters*, if we assume the intervention ("coming between") of assimilative pressures to be the major cause of alienation between immigrant and American-born generations, hence of the latter's self-alienation and outward projection of Extravagance. (In this sense, *generation* is a convenient shorthand term referring to sensibility or orientation toward America; it is not meant to designate predetermined stages in an inexorable march toward assimilation à la Robert Park.)

As a historical injury toward ethnic minorities, what is commonly known as "Americanization" does not inflict its damage uniformly. In the Yamamoto and Yamauchi stories, the pre–World War II (thus preinternment and prelapsarian) setting, the rural isolation of the Japanese American farming families, and the primitive state of the mass media (Marpo's temperamental radio is the Hosoume children's only window on the American world) make for relatively weak assimilative pressures on the adolescent daughters. The daughters are still capable of empathizing with their parents and noticing their yearning for Extravagance; the experiential differences between the two generations have not yet been mythologized as an unbridgeable chasm. On the other hand, *The Year of the Dragon*, set in an urban Chinatown in 1955 (126) during the xenophobic and repressive McCarthy era, illustrates a world already deeply corrupted by such mythologization—what Fred Eng calls his "movie" (122). (As he confesses, he cannot even "get pissed-off at a white man without [his] voice drifting off into some movie, like a reflex" [122]. He exhorts Johnny to "see another movie for a while," but his alternative script cannot go beyond "Get a white girl while you're young" [123].) As an "Americanized" Asian, Fred may be aware that white society has commandeered Extravagance as its exclusive privilege, but he also perceives the process to be an unalterable given, like a law of physics. As a result, he becomes paralyzed as an artist, unable to write without feeling his work vitiated and himself somehow complicit in cultural hegemony. Moreover, the sense of inevitability deflects Fred's resentment from white arrogation to an easier target: the first-generation Chinese come to be distorted into his nemeses, alien creatures deemed incapable of, or unqualified for, Extravagant activities.

Besides generational differences, there is another fundamental explanation for the bleak vision of Asian American art found in *The Year of the Dragon*. I refer to the institutionalized racism of the publishing (by extension, culture) industry, which has the "gatekeeping" power to regulate access by writers (by extension, artists) of color. This material factor has thus far been overshadowed by our discussion of ideological processes; the two are, in fact, not separable, but for the sake of emphasis a singling out of the material aspect of cultural production is now in order. As much as ideological domination, an economic reality working to express as well as amplify it—that Asian American aspirants to professional artist status can find no secure foothold in the mainstream culture market—has caused art to be construed as *white* Extravagance.

The differential sitings of Extravagance in the works we have been examining are thus also partly a function of how the author envisions Asian American art as an economic activity. (The possible origins of this latter will be discussed later.) In the Yamamoto-Yamauchi stories, artistic activity is largely private. Even when Mrs. Hayashi publishes haiku in the Japanese-language newspaper, she seems to be only seeking affirmation from her Japanese American peers; there is no indication that she is interested in making a career of her writing. Neither Yamamoto nor Yamauchi addresses the question of art's economic status, which is, in contrast, one of Frank Chin's chief preoccupations in *The Year of the Dragon*. Unlike the Japanese American wife, Fred Eng does have *professional* ambitions to make a living from his art—that is, to participate in the American economy as a bourgois artist on the same footing as other bourgeois artists. His frustration is that minority writers who do not reproduce stereotypical images of their group tend to be excluded on the basis of commercial risk, whereas those who do conform to the inherently trivializing popular expectations are made unfit for anything outside the "ethnic niche" of the market.

When Mattie reminds Fred that his writing used to win awards, hs answers: "Still nobody publishes it" (119). In his view, vindication consists of not only critical acclaim but also financial reward, and it is only the latter that can confer professional standing on him as a writer. Fred wants what Pa Eng dismisses as *play* to be recognized as *work*, which cannot happen until the work is *paid*.[8] To some extent, of course, Fred's obsession with breaking into the mainstream market is a matter of placating the materialistic despotism of his father and gaining financial independence. But even more is at stake: the very idea of play is laid open to wholesale reconceptualization when it begins to merge with work. As a rebel against the blinkered, goal-oriented, soul-shrinking survival mode of Necessity, Fred postulates a self-authorizing state of free creativity, a full liberation of hitherto abridged faculties, that can, presumably, be practiced once he gets "out there." This vague hypothetical condition never approaches realizable form within the play; indeed, Fred balks at going to Boston because he does not dare to put the idea to the test. "I'm afraid I'll get out there. Pick up my pen. And it dies. I'll have nothing" (120). But still, the force of his insurgency rests largely upon an effective theoretical demarcation between what Pa wants him to do and what he wants to do. If play and work prove to be unstable and provisional categories, what is the basis of Fred's claim to exemption from Necessity?

DECONSTRUCTING THE WORK/PLAY DICHOTOMY

Thus far, proceeding inductively on close readings of selected texts, we have deferred investigating the theoretical status of the concepts of "play" and "work." Such an investigation is prerequisite to an adequate understanding of certain images of art in Asian American literature; to this task we will now turn.

In articulating the antithesis between work and play in *The Year of the Dragon*, Frank Chin brings his own and other affiliated Asian American representations of art into a vast Western discourse privileging play, which by some accounts spans the centuries from before Plato to Derrida and counts among its major theorists Kant, Schiller, Nietzsche, Arnold, Bakhtin, and Gadamer (Hans 1981; Spariosu 1982:13–52; Kelly 1988). Superficially, many features of the Asian American images of artists and their activities resemble the characteristics of play delineated in this discourse (which has universalistic pretensions to explain the nature of human culture, psychology, art, etc.). For example, when Mrs. Hayashi takes up poetry-writing under the combined pressures of patriarchal prescriptions and natural hardships, she could be searching for what Schiller calls "a happy medium between the realm of law and the sphere of physical exigency," attainable through the contemplation of the beautiful (1971:424 [*Fifteenth Letter*]). When J. Huizinga, author of *Homo Ludens* (1950) and perhaps the most influential modern writer on the significance of play in human culture, states

> First and foremost . . . all play is a voluntary activity. . . . It is free, is in fact freedom. A second characteristic is closely connected with this, namely, that play is not "ordinary" or "real" life. It is rather a stepping out of "real" life into a temporary sphere of activity with a disposition all of its own. (1955:7, 8)

he could be referring to Mrs. Hayashi's haiku composition or Fred Eng's writing on napkins after work, both of which put "ordinary life" on hold and have to be apologized for or defended. Jacques Ehrmann, reviewing the theories of Huizinga, Emile Benveniste, and Roger Caillois, contrasts play and seriousness in a diagram; his chart overlaps remarkably the one I derived earlier from a close reading of "Seventeen Syllables":

seriousness		play
usefulness		gratuitousness
fecundity	which are opposed by	sterility
work		leisure
science		literature
reality		unreality

(Ehrmann 1968:41)

If merely to demonstrate congruence were my aim, any number of decontextualized quotations can be culled from the voluminous Western literature on play—philosophical, aesthetic, anthropological, or psychological—to illuminate this or that playlike facet of art portrayed in Asian American texts.

On the other hand, though the freedom (voluntarism) and gratuitousness (material nonutility) of art are stressed in "Seventeen Syllables" and *The Year of the Dragon*, which would justify a subsumption of these works under a "universal" paradigm of play, certain recurrent themes in Western ludic discourse are noticeably absent or de-emphasized by the Asian American authors, or are otherwise inapplicable to them. The agonistic aspect of play—play as contest, in particular "ruled" group contest, which is often credited with a "civilizing" or social-control function (e.g., Huizinga 1955:46–75; Sutton-Smith and Kelly-Byrne 1984:307)—is absent in our Asian American examples. While many of the recent Western play theorists focus on the aesthetic *response* induced by given works of art (e.g., Kant, Schiller, Arnold, Derrida), the Asian American authors who explore the work/play dichotomy are primarily interested in artistic *activity* or *creation*. Finally, while Western play theorists since Plato have been predictably anxiety-prone regarding the mimetic (hence presumably "depreciative") aspect of play (Spariosu 1982:13–41), in the Asian American works under scrutiny the debate is more about the utility value than the truth value of art.

A convenient point of departure for an inquiry into this issue is provided by neo-Kantian formulations of the play concept, reworkings of "purposiveness without a purpose," in which detachment from practical functions is highlighted. Huizinga asserts: "[Play] is an activity connected with no material interest, and no profit can be gained by it" (1955:13). Benveniste suggests that "play in itself has no practical goal; its essence lies in its gratuitousness" (cited in Ehrmann 1968:35). Huizinga and Benveniste are echoed by Caillois, who maintains that play "creates no wealth of goods": "play is an occasion of pure waste" (1961:5).[9] In a similar vein Eugen Fink maintains that "the *immanent* purpose of play is not subordinate to the ultimate purpose served by all other human activity. Play has only internal purpose, unrelated to anything external to itself" (1968:21). These pronouncements seem to be apt glosses on the artistic activities depicted in "Seventeen Syllables" and *The Year of the Dragon*: they foreground the allure of art to those characters beset by Necessity as well as their vulnerability to utilitarian censure.

Yet according to some other students of the concept, play can never be free from economic contingencies. Jean Baudrillard writes in *The Mirror of Production*:

> Wishing itself beyond labor but *in its continuation*, the sphere of play is always merely the aesthetic sublimation of labor's constraints. . . . Although the concept of non-labor can thus be fantasized as the abolition of political economy, it is bound to fall back into the sphere of political economy as the sign, and only the sign, of its abolition. (1975:40, 41; quoted in Kelly 1988:66; italics in original)

According to Ehrmann, on the level of "conscious social structure" we may observe a play-seriousness dialectic operating, but at a deeper level of analysis play is revealed as unavoidably circulating in an economy. Ehrmann's argument is so compelling that it is worth quoting at length:

> Even if play is understood as a "pure" expenditure, an expenditure *for* nothing, it consumes something nevertheless, if only time and energy, but sometimes also considerable property. It would be appropriate then to account for this expenditure, to learn where it went, what it produced. It was consummated and consumed in play itself, say Caillois and Huizinga. That is why, in their view, play must be accomplished "in an expressly circumscribed time and place." But they fail to see that the interior occupied by play can only be defined by and with the exterior of the world, and inversely that play viewed as an exterior is only comprehensible by and with the interior of the world; that together they participate in the same economy. Play cannot therefore be isolated as an activity without *consequences*. Its integrity, its gratuitousness are only apparent, since the very freedom of the expenditure made in it is part of a circuit which reaches beyond the spatial and temporal limits of play. (1968:42–43; italics in original)

And on Huizinga's statement that play "is situated outside the mechanism of immediate satisfaction of needs and desires," Ehrmann comments: "In play there is no *subtraction* of value (depreciation) but *relocation, redistribution* . . . in pursuit of *immediate* satisfaction of needs and desires. We have seen [in the example of the potlatch] that play consists in giving in order to receive more" (43–44; italics in original).

Ehrmann's deconstructive maneuver radically challenges the work/ play binarism.[10] In proposing in its stead a more capacious and holistic framework for understanding play as an activity embedded in material processes, he speaks to a persistent anxiety expressed by Asian American writers regarding their value to and their place in society—both their immediate ethnic community and the larger world, but especially the former. While artists of color in America do share in the bourgeois artist's general predicament of marginalization and disaffection—a condition that has obtained ever since the early industrialization of Europe and for which the elevation of disinterested play serves as a disguised apologia (Williams 1966:30–48; Sutton-Smith and Kelly-Byrne 1984: 306–308; Kelly 1988, esp. ch. 1)—the reality of racial cleavages daily reminds them of their undeniable implication in the fate of the community. Thus even if, in the face of insistent demands to demonstrate immediate usefulness, they feel compelled to invoke the concept of free play to make room for creativity, they can hardly abandon questions on the moral and political propriety of play.

In Asian American literature, Pa Eng's question, "What good for?" is never far from the consciousness of those writers who endow art with the attributes of play. The artist figures who defy the work ethic and the creed of Necessity are typically shown as grappling (if only implicitly, through discomfiture) with the question of a larger "circuit" in which the *long-term social consequences* of their artistic activity may be taken into account. If they are aware of the larger circuit, they hope to be judged by the projected totality of transactions within it rather than by their seemingly disengaged, self-indulgent expenditure of energy in the present. In other words, in a sense quite apart from the question of remuneration (by which Fred Eng is tormented), play can be work: Extravagance in the short run may be in the service of some Higher Necessity, whose authority derives from a fundamental re-vision of the possibilities of Asian American existence.[11] This would be the "relocation" and "redistribution" of value, the "giving in order to receive more," of which Ehrmann speaks. The project is admittedly "visionary"—in Baudrillard's estimation a mere fantasy. But if play is only the *sign* of "abolition of political economy," it may still serve, I argue, a vital recuperative function, given the many stringencies under which Asian Americans currently labor. An effort to be "just people," we recall, can either consolidate or subvert racial oppression, depending on the convictions that underwrite it and the historical moment in which it is made. The valorization of play in Asian American literature may bear a suspicious resemblance to "art for art's sake," but read in context it points to a "conscientious aestheticism" or "interested disinterestedness" (if such terms may be coined), strategically deployed to counteract the diminishment of being that has historically been assigned the Asian American.

PURPOSELESSNESS WITH A PURPOSE: HWANG'S *THE DANCE AND THE RAILROAD*

The difficulties of arriving at a viable "interested disinterestedness" are explored in David Henry Hwang's 1981 play, *The Dance and the Railroad*, to which we have alluded at the end of the last chapter. The two terms in the title, of course, echo the Extravagance-Necessity division, but they are not neatly mapped onto the two characters in the play, Lone and Ma; rather, the opposition is played out in an ideological tug-of-war with surprising place-switchings and changes of heart. The "railroad"—Necessity in the form of poverty in the home country, financial obligations to the family, natural inclemencies, but especially inhumane treatment by the white man—presses upon both characters, requiring each to take a stand during the Chinese strike for higher wages and shorter hours (the play is set in 1867). The "dance" is represented by Lone, who practices Peking opera steps on the mountaintop after work; however, Ma is also attracted by the "beautiful" movements (1983:64, 73) and asks to be taught. Thus Ma is a spokesman for Necessity only partially, when he is persuading Lone to join the strike; though the newcomer's big dreams are materialistic (making a fortune in America and returning to China in triumph), he is portrayed as having an Extravagant bent, excitable by the epic heroism of railroad building (68) and sufficiently enchanted by Lone's artistry to endure a grueling initiation into apprenticeship. Necessity is embodied more solidly by the unseen workers in camp, or rather the constructed images of them: Ma thinks of them as "men with little dreams . . . [with] little brains to match. They walk with their eyes down, trying to find extra grains of rice on the ground" (69), while Lone contemptuously refers to them as "dead men" (74). Despite his own egotistical ambitions, however, Ma treasures his friendship with the men, whereas Lone dissociates himself from them, fearing the stinting influence of their niggardly mode of existence.

At the beginning of the play, a clash between two concepts of art is presented: one solitary, elitist, and "purposeless," the other communal, populist, and utilitarian. Ma tells Lone that the other Chinamen at camp resent his dance practice and his holier-than-thou attitude: "you never sing songs, you never tell stories" (64). A happy alternative to such self-banishment, Ma takes it upon himself to advise the older man, is to put art to work for a good cause: "That stuff you're doing—it's beautiful. Why don't you do it for the guys at camp? Help us celebrate [the strike]?" (64). Initially, Lone rejects the possibility out of hand, for unlike Ma, he sees his dance practice as different *in kind* from the solidarity-building artistic activities (group singing and storytelling) of the other railroad workers, which to him are too suspiciously close to the mindless recreational huddling of gambling (71). He subscribes to an absolute distinction between the two sets of activities, the key criterion being, for him, freedom of choice. Paradoxically, the choice is to submit himself to another kind of discipline (71)—presumably in pursuit of aesthetic perfection, although the element of aesthetic gratification is almost entirely absent in his account: it seems an irrelevance or at best an incidental charm more apparent to the outside observer than to himself. As he tries to explain to Ma, who voices a marveling admiration for the beauty of his dance steps:

> Are you willing to sweat after you've finished sweating? Are you willing to come up after you've spent the whole day chipping half an inch off a rock, and punish your body some more? . . . It's ugly to practice when the mountain has turned your muscles to ice. When my body hurts too much to come here, I look at the other ChinaMen and think, "They are dead. Their muscles work only because the white man forces them. I live because I can still force my muscles to work for me." (73)

Given the centrality of voluntarism in this declaration, Lone's name is particularly felicitous: although it is obviously based on John Lone, who first played the part in 1981 as well as directed and choreographed the performance (just as Ma's name is based on Tzi Ma, the other actor in the original cast), the connotations of the English word *lone* epitomize one vision of the artist's chosen path.[12] *Lone* simultaneously evokes lofty conviction (rejection *of* society) and friendless isolation (rejection *by* society). Both are deemed inherent to the practice of art, since the artist's self is seen as encapsulated in self-sufficiency, set apart from the docile, unreflecting, and materialistic common man.

To the extent that Lone's dance practice is freely embraced and lacking in utility—indeed, freely embraced because of its lack of utility—it can be read as play; the efforts of the other Chinese in camp are conversely defined as work, namely, involuntary servitude for material returns. (Lone at first interprets the strike as yet another symptom of ever deeper enslavement to Necessity; to assert his independence from it, he expresses disdain for the soulless massses, in haughty terms reminiscent of the aesthete's condemnation of the philistine.) The construal of Lone's practice as play is further supported by a detail in his life story. At the age of ten, Lone is sold by his parents to the opera school for ten years—his first bondage to Necessity; however, after studying arduously for eight years, he is tricked into returning home and put to work yet once more, his promising opera career aborted in order to serve the common good:

> Mother was standing at the door waiting, not sick at all. Her first words to me, the son away for eight years, were, "You've been *playing* while your village has starved. You must go to the Gold Mountain and *work*." (79; my italics)

Given Lone's history, it is only to be expected that dance to him means play, Extravagance, self-fulfillment, whereas railroad-building means work, Necessity, self-denial.

Yet for all its apparent clarity, Lone's manifesto destabilizes the play-work distinction in several ways. If his motto is "I play, therefore I am," it takes the curious form of "I work for myself, therefore I am." Cast in a nonessentialist light, Extravagance is shown to be such only in comparison with the imposed exertions of railroad-building. Like Mrs. Hayashi composing haiku after washing the dishes or Fred writing stories on napkins after guiding tours, Lone practices his art only after paying his debt to society, so to speak; but even more than "Seventeen Syllables" or *The Year of the Dragon*, *The Dance and the Railroad* stresses the interpenetration of work and play, the strenuous discipline required of "true" play (as opposed to, say, the relaxation of gambling). If play involves *forcing* one's muscles to *work* some more after "work," can it still be considered a gesture of Extravagance? Where is the fun or pleasure that everyday usage imputes to play as its distinguishing attribute? Furthermore, Hwang pushes the notion of Extravagance as energy surplus, adumbrated in Yamamoto and Yamauchi's stories, to its very limit until it reaches breaking point. "Weak" artist figures like Marpo and Yamada, whose youthful exuberance captivates others, lend intuitive credibility to the common biological hypothesis that play originates as discharge of surplus energy (Millar 1968:14–16, 35–37). Their expression of Extravagance takes the form of musical or other artistic pastimes, with the term *pastime* assuming the availability of leisure. But in cases where exhaustion from obligatory labors appears more severe than the young men's, the personal investment in Extravagant release more intense, and the concentration and effort called for by art considerably greater, the idea of superabundance begins to be thrown into doubt. Is the energy that Mrs. Hayashi and Fred manage to generate for writing truly excess energy? And what about Lone, whose chosen art, the dance, is as physically taxing as the railroad and does not even allow the respite of exercising an alternate faculty? Do these characters really have a reserve store of energy allocated to play? Or is play cutting into something vital, diverting energy from survival? And if play's imperative is so overpoweringly urgent, may it not be that play too is a need of survival—a Necessity, no less, only differently characterized and designated, and therefore customarily separated from work as if by an unbridgeable gulf?[13]

The meaning of art as Extravagance depends on the postulated existence of a limit: it is by pushing against the supposedly extreme demands of Necessity that writing, for Mrs. Hayashi and Fred, or the dance, for Lone, assumes the redemptive efficacy of Extravagance. Yet if Necessity had been as relentless as the characters perceive it to be, there would have been no energy to spare; to the extent that the aspiring Asian American artists still have some resource left to draw upon, the extremity of Necessity is a fiction—but a fiction indispensable to the integrity and significance of their endeavor.[14] Extravagance needs Necessity to do its work—the baffling collocation of terms here is intended—whereas Necessity, if deprived of the invoked menace of Extravagance, would find it difficult to sustain its mandate. Necessity and Extravagance are invested in each other and constitute each other's condition of possibility; the state of absolute Extravagance, free of all contingencies, is merely an infinitely receding vision. Yet it is also a productive one, in that the quest for it often provides Asian American artists with structure as well as inspiration as they struggle against the tangible constraints of their existence.

One corollary of such an understanding of Necessity and Extravagance is that, as the artist engages in changing sociopolitical circumstances, play and work may undergo continual amendment; for not only are the boundaries between the two porous, the term *boundary* also implies a community with which the individual interacts and against which his/her definitions are tested out. In *The Dance and the Railroad*, Lone moves from a rigid concept of play as the exclusive province of an internally sufficient, asocial (or if needs be, antisocial) self, to one encompassing communal claims and political utility. His change of heart hinges on how the strike is interpreted. Initially he considers the strike, and the group pressure to support it (as Ma urges, "we gotta stick together" [64]), to be a Necessitous encroachment upon his freedom; he is blind to the fact that he exists in symbiosis with those men he professes to despise, relying on his contrived distance from the riffraff to confer "intrinsic" merit on his art. Through arguing with Ma, however, he comes to be persuaded that the strike in fact represents an act of Extravagance, a self-originated decision to take on greater adversity in order to uphold one's dignity; in this sense, it is no different in nature from his own opera practice. Ma contends, in defense of the allegedly myopic and mercenary Chinese workers, "Dead men don't go on strike. . . . Dead men don't complain" (75). After a night of reflection, Lone reverses his stand and agrees to use his art to honor the strike, just as Ma has requested (86–88). What is more, he blends his solitary art—the dance—with a solidarity-building form he has earlier spurned: storytelling, not about established heroes like Gwan Gung (which would merely preserve the culture transported from the old country) but about contemporary people and events (which creates culture—a new Chinese American culture). In collaboration with Ma, he improvises a nontraditional, mock-heroic opera about a Chinaman immigrating, working on the railroad, and going on strike (90–95). His art now partakes of the fluidity and open-endedness of history: the invented opera has no clear-cut ending (95). At the end of Hwang's play, Lone is ready to descend from his protected realm on the mountaintop, to join the other Chinamen in camp. Earlier, it has been the fear of being like the "dead men" that drives Lone to dance. He now respects his fellow workers for their sense of social responsibility ("They're sending money home" [98]), and when he executes one last dance before returning to work, he proclaims: "Today, I am dancing for no reason at all" (99).

Lone's feeling of "purposiveness without a purpose" is the result of having found a purpose for his art: its autotelism consists in having come to terms with a putatively extraneous *telos*. We may in fact invert Kant's dictum and describe Lone's art as "purposelessness with a purpose"; Lone's dance now feels like play, but it functions as work, albeit work of a peculiarly nongainful kind. This paradox illustrates an observation made by Spariosu on the conceptual elusiveness of play: "play seems to have an ontological ambivalence, being both phenomenon and subjectivity. When encountered by those who are not 'in the know,' playing is no different from other human or animal activities; in order to be recognized as play, it has to somehow reveal its *intention*" (1982:13). Because of the mercurial, context-sensitive nature of intentionality as well as the logical unattainability of ultimate Extravagance, Lone's parting insight is more likely a way station than a final resting point in his quest for a "conscientious aestheticism," an art at once engagé and engaging. As if to underline the precarious status of Lone's newfound reconciliation, *The Dance and the Railroad* ends with an unexpected reversal, so that, instead of reaching a consensus and affirming a shared faith, the two men renew the contest, in even more inflexible terms than before. Lone and Ma trade places: as Lone emerges from his solipsism and celebrates the strike as a collective victory, Ma hardens into cynicism, concluding that since the strikers have had to compromise on their demands, their bid for sovereignty of the self is a failure and his own Extravagant bent a worthless liability.

> I've got to change myself. Toughen up. Take no shit. Count my change. Learn to gamble. Learn to win. Learn to stare. Learn to deny. Learn to look at men with opaque eyes. . . . 'Cause I've got the fear. You've given it to me. (98)

In terms of character development, Ma's sudden loss of heart is hardly convincing, but perhaps the schematic tenor of the transformation is revealing: Hwang appears to mistrust too ready a resolution of the work-play conflict. The world of *The Dance and the Railroad* is a homeostatic system in which hypothetical views on art are tested out among contrasting personages, but some unstated "law of conservation" prevents any net gain in freedom.

MARTYRS OF PLAY IN KINGSTON'S *THE WOMAN WARRIOR*

Although here is no explicit indication that *The Dance and the Railroad* is derivative, judging from Hwang's acknowledgments in his prefatory note to *FOB* (which was first produced just two years before *Dance*), it is entirely likely that his handling of the play theme is indebted to Kingston's in *The Woman Warrior*, and Chin's in *Gee, Pop!*, the unpublished precursor of *The Year of the Dragon* (Hwang 1983:3). (On Kingston's part, her foreword to the *Broken Promises* collection praises *Dance* for its ennoblement of not only the pioneer "working man" but also Chinese American artists who "create their own rites": "This play is also about artists who have to support art with hard labor. After work, they practice their art on their own time" [1983:ix].)

Evidence of direct literary filiation would contribute to the argument that play, in the guise of art, is a persistent preoccupation in Asian American literature. However, in an intertextual reading framework, it is perhaps even more encouraging to discover recurrences and resonances in the works of writers free from mentor-protégé relationships, such as Yamamoto and Chin, or else connected through seemingly adversarial practices, such as Chin and Kingston. Having established a network of mutually elucidating images of art, on the basis of both filiation and intertextuality, we are now ready to turn to a close analysis of the play theme in *The Woman Warrior*, the source of the two key terms that have helped order the unfolding of this study, Necessity and Extravagance.

Considering the provenance of the terms, it is hardly surprising to find in *The Woman Warrior* a more sustained exploration of the "art as play" idea than in any other Asian American literary text. Many of the motifs fleetingly addressed elsewhere are here given finely nuanced treatment. In particular, the artist's plea for room to exercise an "interested disinterestedness" is developed through a series of meditations on the fate of women who dare to play and become martyrs to the cause. The last section of this chapter will undertake a detailed reading of *The Woman Warrior* as ludic discourse and proceed to a historicized investigation of the meaning of play for Asian American literature and life.[15]

The idea of Necessity, we recall, is first broached in *The Woman Warrior* when the narrator/protagonist comments on her mother's pragmatic telling of the "no name woman" story. ("My mother has told me once and for all the useful parts. She will add nothing unless powered by Necessity" [1977:5].) The aunt, married to a "Gold Mountain man" and left at home for years as a "widow of the living,"[16] gets pregnant and later commits suicide by leaping into the family well with her newborn baby. While no detail about the circumstances of her pregnancy is forthcoming from Brave Orchid, who considers the wayward woman virtually expunged from family history, the young Maxine refuses to be content with a cautionary tale about the perils of female sexuality and the social burden of womanhood: "Now that you have started to menstruate, what happened to her could happen to you. Don't humiliate us" (5). Instead, what she tries to create from the silence-shrouded incident is a parable of heroic resistance, however modest in scope and fatal in form, to the dictates of Necessity. "Adultery is Extravagance" (7).

Since she cannot even ask about the no name woman's life, Maxine has to invent the circumstances of the pregnancy, which is just as well. In her search for guidance in dealing with the pressures of Chinese

American girlhood, a story of meek submission to rape (8), "rollicking" promiscuity (9), or mere spoiled willfulness (12) would not have served her at all. "Unless I see [the aunt's] life branching into mine, she gives me no ancestral help" (10). Ironically, what Maxine does with the aunt's memory is precisely what the family does with her (the aunt's) life: subject it to the trial of usefulness. But there are also crucial differences: Maxine is free from the moral consequences of attempting to shape an actual life, and even more importantly, the cause she would like the aunt's case to serve is the broader, longer-term one of freedom or voluntarism. Hence the portrait of the aunt as a martyr to the belief in a "private life" (14), a tragic "artist with no art form," cousin to the adulterous wives in Yamamoto's and Yamauchi's stories. Without benefit of clay, paint, pen, or musical instrument, she works in the only medium she has—her life—eventually sacrificing it for the few ephemeral manifestations of sensuous beauty that come her way.

In her imaginative reconstruction of possible versions of sexual misadventure, the one that most appeals to Maxine is that of a woman determined to snatch what "playful" moments of beauty she can from a ruthless routine of physical labor and family service. Maxine sees an obvious parallel between her deprivations as an immigrant's daughter in America and the aunt's as a lowly daughter-in-law in a famine-ravaged Chinese village. The code of Necessity that Brave Orchid enforces on her family, which has been further tempered by the rigors of immigrant life, is of course a legacy from her native land, where scarcity of resources and patriarchal domination have combined to give rise to a rigidly hierarchical, family-centered social structure. Relegated to the bottom of the pecking order, women are expected to toil uncomplainingly and suppress their emotions: "The work of preservation demands that the feelings playing about in one's guts not be turned into action" (9).[17] On one level, the word *play* in this phrase may simply describe light, rapid, and erratic movement, as of sunlight or water. However, in juxtaposition with *work* (the lot of the "heavy, deep-rooted women" [9]), in the context of the no name woman's surmised martyrdom, and especially in intertextual conjunction with other Asian American allegories of female desire, *play* does evoke the entire question of obligations versus options, utility versus gratuitousness. In a by-now-familiar pattern, erotic passion and artistic proclivities are presented as linked, both suppressed by patriarchy as threats to the social order.

In an impoverished environment where a woman's chief function is procreation—and only the useful kind counts: the production of sons to supply extra labor and carry on the family name—the young aunt dares to squander attention on such an insubstantial thing as beauty.

She looked at a man because she liked the way the hair was tucked behind his ears, or she liked the question-mark line of a long torso curving at the shoulder and straight at the hip. For warm eyes or a soft voice or a slow walk—that's her—a few hairs, a line, a brightness, a sound, a pace, she gave up family. She offered us up for a charm that vanished with tiredness, a pigtail that didn't toss when the wind died. (9)

Not only does the no name woman seek beauty in her lover, but she also has the audacity to beautify herself; Maxine imagines her plying her "secret comb" (11), in silent protest of the "no nonsense" hairdos of married women, and in defiance of a climate of public opinion in which "a woman who tended her appearance reaped a reputation for eccentricity" (10). (As Mr. Hosoume has learned to suspect, woman's self-adornment, like her voluntary bestowal of love to a man, can be a dangerous expression of Extravagance.) Maxine would like to believe that, even in a place where women went about their work like "great sea snails," bent under babies, cords of wood, or loads of laundry, "there must have been a marvelous freeing of beauty when a worker laid down her burden and stretched and arched" (11). The inspiration she gives herself through her aunt, her "forerunner" (9), is that such "freeing of beauty" is indeed possible and desirable. The warning she draws is that there is a steep price to pay for violating the authority of Necessity.

Everyone recognizes that a certain amount of concession to Necessity is inevitable, but at what point does the "work of preservation" become tyrannical? What if the "feelings playing about in one's guts" grow too urgent to be ignored? These are questions for which the young narrator, born to survival-obsessed immigrants in Stockton's small, isolated Chinatown, and surrounded by white "ghosts" who expect her to simultaneously assimilate and remain exotic, has no ready-made answers. She must determine for herself what degree of concession to Necessity and what degree of commitment to Extravagance would *feel* right, by meditating on what her kinswoman must have gone through. (Here *meditate* is used the way one speaks of medieval mystics meditating on the Passion of Christ or the martyrdom of saints, referring to a deliberate and painstaking act of immersion in another's experience as a means to self-knowledge and spiritual liberation.) This process of wresting "ancestral help" entails a laborious and active penetration of what hitherto has been forbidden territory in one's mind—like the aunt's crossing of "boundaries not delineated in space" (9). To Brave Orchid, for whom "ancestral help" comes readily in the form of culturally programmed responses, Maxine's way must appear foolish, yet another example of the American-born generation's waste of energy and time. But every time the mother tells a Chinese story, the Chinese American daughter is unavoidably called upon to arrive at a moral applicable to her predicament.

The lesson derived from the no name woman's story is repeated when Maxine is told of the "village crazy lady" stoned to death by the villagers during the anti-Japanese war. Though not a left-at-home "Gold Mountain wife," the village crazy lady is, like the no name aunt, implied to be an "inappropriate woman" who "[longs] after men" (108). Compared to the aunt, who kills herself after the family compound is raided by masked avengers, the crazy lady is more directly the victim of mob violence. Yet the reason why she has to die seems more obscure than ever, and once again it is up to the narrator to piece together a version of the story that would make sense to her. How much detail is actually supplied by the mother is impossible to determine, but what Maxine has chosen to recount constitutes a kind of morality play on the hazards of play, which once again gives her pause in her push toward Extravagance.

The crazy lady is portrayed, like Lone in *The Dance and the Railroad* and Mrs. Oka in Yamauchi's "And the Soul Shall Dance" (another "crazy lady"), as a *dancer*: "[moving] in fanning circles, now flying the sleeves in the air, now trailing them on the grass, dancing in the middle of the light" (10). And like Orpheus, the archetypal artist who charms nature with his music and is eventually torn apart by frenzied Thracian women, she is a music-maker, "singing" in an idyllic setting where the river water "play[s] the pebbles, the rocks, and the hollows" and animals mingle with humans (110). The figure of her flinging droplets of water about from her cup is reminiscent of many other images of divine play and of grace: the goddess Nu-Wa in Chinese mythology who creates human beings by flinging about globs of mud; the heavenly fairy maiden in Chinese folklore who scatters flowers from the air (*tian nu san hua*), the "sweet dew" (*ganlu*) of Buddhist teachings.

But to the villagers conditioned to find a purpose and use in every activity, the crazy lady's frolicking is subversive. (Recall Mr. Hayashi's verdict of "crazy" on his haiku-loving wife.) They cannot remain for long "idle above their fields," "godlike," neither hoeing nor weeding (110).[18] Watching the childlike woman in her bright clothes, they soon start a rumor that she is signaling Japanese bombers with the mirrors in her headdress, and as the rumor gathers momentum they begin to stone her. The crazy lady, unschooled in the creed of Necessity, at first thinks that her persecutors are playing catch with her—"at last, people to play with" (111). But it does not take her long to discover that they are after her life. She becomes yet another martyr to Extravagance.

THE MOON ORCHID STORY:
THE DEVIOUS REVENGE OF EXTRAVAGANCE

Witnessing the stoning, Brave Orchid tries in vain to intervene on behalf of the village crazy lady. This gesture of sympathy might seem surprising in view of her customary pragmatism so prized by the villagers. However, it is only when the desire for play is clearly isolated and readily attributable to insanity that Brave Orchid can afford to recognize it as a spontaneous human need. ("She's only getting drinking water. . . . Crazy people drink water too" [112].) When it is embodied in a form that enters into institutional interactions and affects the social fabric, as in the case of the no name woman, she becomes intolerant, priding herself on being a no-nonsense woman who "[does] not 'long' " (108). Weakness, in both a practical and a moral sense, is to Brave Orchid inseparable from the inclination toward Extravagance.

The tragicomic story of trans-Pacific husband-reclaiming by Moon Orchid, Brave Orchid's sister, which makes up the fourth chapter of *The Woman Warrior*, at first glance appears to be simply a recycled didactic pitting of Necessity against Extravagance, strength against frailty, resourcefulness against ineffectuality, respectively exemplified by the two long-separated sisters. However, deeper analysis reveals Brave Orchid to be an unwitting champion of play, abetting the cause she has declared to be the public enemy. The unfolding of the Moon Orchid story constitutes Kingston's most complex and intriguing statement on the irrepressible nature of Extravagance.

Superficially, the two sisters are diametric opposites. Moon Orchid's very name evokes beauty, evanescence, softness, femininity, poetry, the yin, while Brave Orchid's evokes toughness and militancy. Brave Orchid dismisses her sister as the "lovely, useless type" (148), silly, always "laughing at nothing" (135). Like the village crazy lady, Moon Orchid is small and delicate, with "little fluttering hands" (136), and is fond of ornamenting herself. As with the crazy lady too, "bright colors and movements [distract] her" (142). When she first arrives from Hong Kong, she unpacks beautiful but fragile and impractical gifts for all her relatives (139). In contrast, Brave Orchid wears no jewels, thinking that they get in the way of work (141), and considers Moon Orchid's treasures mere "scraps" transported at needless expense across the ocean. From the hoard of gifts she takes only "what [is] useful and solid into the back bedroom" (141), there to safeguard the family in anticipated times of dearth. When Moon Orchid is put to work in the family laundry, she tangles up thread, "[plays] with the water jets dancing on springs from the ceiling" (158), and giggles at the customers. All of Brave Orchid's children know how to operate the machinery even when they have to stand on crates to reach the controls; and of course Brave Orchid herself is a demon worker, capable of carrying "a hundred pounds of Texas rice up- and downstairs" and working in the laundry "from 6:30 A.M. until midnight" (122).

Moon Orchid's ineptness at work, her lack of serious purpose, her aesthetic bent, her air of distracted innocence, all put her in the rank of the doomed. Indeed Moon Orchid dies an outcast's death, much like the no name woman or the crazy lady. However, it would have been an oversimplification to read her as solely responsible for her tragedy, punished for offending the decrees of Necessity. If that had been the case, the forces in the conflict would have been all neatly lined up, with Brave Orchid grimly defending Necessity while the other artist figures invite self-destruction. If so, Maxine would probably have had an easier time growing up under Brave Orchid's shadow, since simple rebellion would have allowed her to find her path in life. However, in the drama of "At the Western Palace," it turns out to be Brave Orchid who inadvertently indulges in Extravagance, which has been suppressed far too long in herself and now seeks an outlet. Her form of indulgence is to play with her sister's life—perhaps an even more dangerous way of practicing art without an art form than adultery.

Moon Orchid, despite her affinities with the no name woman and the crazy lady, is a loyal follower of the doctrine of Necessity, content to be provided for by her absent husband in the United States. Well-fed and clothed, with a maid to serve her and even a college education for her daughter, she finds little to complain about, although the "feelings playing about in [her] guts," had she allowed herself to listen to them, might have led her to experience no name woman's kind of "longing." Had Brave Orchid not taken matters into her own hands, scheming for years to get her sister into the United States, Moon Orchid would have passed her entire life half-waiting for a definite message from her husband. The energy Brave Orchid expends on the case is considerable, including marrying her niece off to a U.S. citizen to qualify Moon Orchid for immigration, writing daily letters of encouragement, and buying her a plane ticket. Given the fact that Moon Orchid is far from deprived in a material sense (which is the only sense recognized by the code of Necessity), why does Brave Orchid go to such lengths to bring about an "unnecessary" event—an event that need not have happened?

From the way the narrator recounts the story (the episodes taking place at home most likely based on direct observation; those in Los Angeles elaborated from her siblings' brief, casual remarks), it is clear that Brave Orchid, though ostensibly acting as a dutiful, protective older sister, is in fact engineering the reunion for herself. Her excitement at the prospect of a dramatic confrontation is palpable. She is obsessed with the minute details of the scheme. When should Moon Orchid make her grand entrance? Should she do it when only the husband is at home, or when only the "little wife" is at home, or when both are at home? Should she dye her hair to compete with the "little wife," or leave it white to accentuate her suffering through the years? What kind of dialogue would be exchanged between the characters? Would it come to a scuffle? As she tries out various versions, she keeps chuckling and exclaiming to herself, "Yes, coming with you would be exciting" (167), "Oh, this is most dramatic—in broad daylight and in the middle of the city" (169). In short, Brave Orchid is playing—like a movie director fascinated by infinite possibilities, giving vent to her fertile imagination; like the no name woman at her toilet, rearranging this or that detail to hit the "right combination" (10) and make the maximum impact on the intended audience. At times Moon Orchid gets into the spirit of the thing and offers her own scenarios. At times she seems to "listen too readily—as if her sister were only talking-story" (151). When it finally comes down to doing it, Moon Orchid is scared: "I can't do that in front of all those people—like a stage show" (174). Brave Orchid pooh-poohs her apprehensions away as if they merely represented stage fright. The metaphors of artistic activity—drama, storytelling—suggest that Brave Orchid is playing, not with her own life but her hapless sister's. Moon Orchid ends up paying for her sister's bit of Extravagance, with her sanity (she becomes another "crazy lady") and eventually her life as well.

Brave Orchid says, "Oh, how I'd love to be in your place. I could tell him so many things. What scenes I could make" (146). At the actual confrontation, when pressed by Moon Orchid's husband for a valid reason for bringing his wife over, Brave Orchid can only mutter lamely, "You made her live like a widow" (178). Ironically, then, Brave Orchid proves to be a defender of the no name woman, whose sin is to be unable to bear "living like a widow." When the husband argues that, in the practical sense, Moon Orchid has not been living like a widow, he is simply and matter-of-factly giving Brave Orchid a taste of her own medicine. At a loss for a cutting retort, Brave Orchid salvages the situation by resorting to her most characteristic turn of mind—"The least you can do is invite us to lunch" (179)—thereby implicitly admitting defeat. The development of broad farce into a full-blown tragedy is to take a while yet, but Brave Orchid is preserved from a devastating recognition of her responsibility by being thoroughly and obstinately consistent in her conscious maintenance of Chinese values. When Moon Orchid begins voicing paranoid ideas that could be interpreted as cursing her nieces and nephews, Brave Orchid, defining her moral obligations strictly in terms of the concentric circles of relationships that structure traditional Chinese society, stops taking care of Moon Orchid and places her in a mental hospital.

The question posed earlier about Brave Orchid's motives can be rephrased thus: Why does she end up championing the cause of the no name woman, whom she condemns energetically with her conscious mind? In what ways is she like the prodigal, so that she can empathize with her sufferings? Of course, Brave Orchid, typical of the women of the seafaring regions of Guangdong from which many early Chinese Americans originated, has herself been a left-at-home "Gold Mountain wife" for many years. Like Moon Orchid's husband, "year after year," Maxine's father "did not come home or send for her," but "did send money regularly" (71). In the meantime, she has to be the dutiful daughter-in-law and serve her husband's "tyrant mother" (73). For fully two decades she lives as a "widow of the living." These superficial similarities provide some basis for Brave Orchid's unconscious identification with the no name woman. But an adequate explanation must account for the fact that, unlike her sister-in-law, Brave Orchid does join her husband in America, and that by conventional standards she does settle into a satisfactory life with him. An explanation for the urgency of her last fling must be sought in something deeper.

It seems that Brave Orchid's meddling in Moon Orchid's affairs represents an attempt to justify not so much her earlier tenure as abandoned wife as her present life in America. Not only does the latter require of her greater physical stamina, but it also calls for greater sacrifice of her selfhood, for at the time of her immigration Brave Orchid has already had a taste of self-actualization. As a respected lady doctor who is performing a vital function in society but also enjoying her experiences, she appears to have arrived at a resolution of the work-play conflict, a fusion of the useful and the useless. She is intelligent, a shrewd reader of human character, an intrepid traveler, filled with curiosity about her world. In making her rounds as a doctor, she is able to indulge freely in her appetite for experience without incurring the wrath of society.

It would be misleading to credit Brave Orchid with too much deliberateness in deciding to study and practice medicine; product of a transitional period in Chinese history, she has compartmentalized her various and often contradictory beliefs, taking pride at being an independent professional woman as well as a shrewd bargainer who gets herself a slave girl/nurse at a discount (95–96). When she finally makes the move to rejoin her husband in the United States, there is no evidence in the book of any conscious resentment on her part. But there are hints that her life after immigration represents a deplorable falling-off, a drastic and prolonged constriction of being, that silently calls for redress. All of a sudden, she is transformed from a human being enjoying the exercise of all her faculties into a work machine (122). True to her schooling in Necessity, she does not stop to ponder why she has to suffer thus; it is simply axiomatic that a Chinese wife would follow her husband when sent for. But a sense of having lived in vain must have accompanied her resumption of the traditional roles of a woman. She takes the readiest explanation for her disenchantment that comes to hand: things are so much worse because she is living in an alien land. "This is terrible ghost country, where a human being works her life away" (122). When it becomes increasingly plain that she is never going to return "home" to China, she needs another means to assuage this feeling of having been cut off from the fullness of life. A chance to wreak vengeance on Moon Orchid's husband, who dares and manages to find fulfillment in "ghost country" (and as a doctor, no less!), is a chance to vindicate the code by which she has lived but whose desirability and justice she has never bothered to examine. Ironically, the means Brave Orchid has chosen to vindicate Necessity is also an occasion for Extravagance to exact its revenge: in her old age, the no-nonsense "big eater," nemesis of weaklings and aesthetes, experiences "the return of the repressed": a sudden and dangerous eruption of the impulse toward Extravagance.

The meaning that the story of Moon Orchid holds for the narrator is complex and manifold. At the most obvious level, all Brave Orchid's daughters see the aunt as a victim of man's infidelity; their mother tells them vehemently—though totally without rational cause, since their father is already seventy years old—to prevent a "little wife" from entering the family. But an intriguing statement is found after the sentence describing the daughters' reaction: "All [Brave Orchid's] children made up their minds to major in science or mathematics" (186). What do "science and mathematics" have to do with unsuccessful husband-reclaiming? What is the logic binding this apparent non sequitur, which seems significant enough to be the concluding sentence of the chapter, to the rest of "At the Western Palace"? Perhaps, as can be seen in the vast numbers of Asian Americans majoring in scientific and technical fields today (Hsia 1988:127–32), a career in "science and mathematics" represents financial security and upward mobility for immigrant families; a desire to pursue such a career can be interpreted as a desire to defend their mother against the need to be dependent on their father. It also seems to be an affirmation of Brave Orchid's belief in Necessity, in that scientific discipline (or at least the popular perception of it) is "objective" and refuses to have anything to do with the "feelings playing about in one's guts." The children seem to be reacting strongly against the messiness of human involvements in general, preferring the clean and elegant, if sterile, abstactions of the mind. In Moon Orchid's story, the lesson that Maxine derives from the no name woman and the crazy lady is once again confirmed: one invites catastrophe whenever one strays from the prescribed path of Necessity and gives in to the urge to seek fulfillment beyond that provided by creature comforts and a rather unreflecting kind of social approval.

Compelling as this lesson is, it is at the same time seriously undermined by Maxine's imagining of the circumstances of the story. It should not be forgotten that, despite the conventional appearance of "At the Western Palace" as a free-standing, self-contained short story, the narrated events are merely extrapolated, "twisted into designs," from a few remarks made by Maxine's siblings (189–90). In other words, Maxine could have recounted the tale differently; her preferred version bespeaks a deep emotional investment in the disposition of certain details. Her choice is to twist "purposelessness" into the design of an account of tenacious, ocean-spanning "purposiveness." By portraying Brave Orchid as deriving vicarious gratification from manipulating Moon Orchid's life, the narrator is affirming a faith quite contrary to what she is supposed to think. If not even Brave Orchid is exempt from the call of Extravagance, may it not be that Extravagance really should not be gainsaid? Given short shrift by Brave Orchid, that model of efficiency, good sense, and moral strength, Extravagance claims her after years of quiescence, driving her to a single-mindedness normally reserved for the serious business of survival.

Brave Orchid emerges, then, as an imperfect exemplar of the philosophy of Necessity after all. Indeed, she violates her own teaching, thereby proving herself an artist in disguise, not only once but repeatedly, in her Extravagant "talk-stories." In the same way that the heroic feats of the swordswoman in her "talk-stories" negate her endorsement of sexist Chinese maxims, the plenitude of enchanting images called forth by her nightly narratives contradicts the austerity of her explicit instruction. Perhaps the narrator's early characterization of her mother should be revised: in telling stories, Brave Orchid would add nothing *unless she thinks she is powered by Necessity.* She may believe herself to be a custodian of Chinese tradition when she fills her daughter's mind with fantastic legends; in fact, however, Extravagance gets in through the back door, endowing her ostensibly didactic tales with magic. What Brave Orchid does as unwitting wordsmith probably provides the most potent inspiration to her daughter in her quest for a resolution of the work/play conflict.

THE "WHITE TIGERS" FANTASY:
ENVISIONING A LARGER ECONOMY FOR ART

Such a resolution is glimpsed in "White Tigers," the second chapter of
The Woman Warrior, in which the question of the value of art is given
a thorough, if in the end still tentative, treatment. Many of the issues
raised earlier in this chapter concerning Asian American art—woman's
desire, the importance of an art form, the charge of uselessness, account-
ability to the community—are explored in the retold legend of Fa Mu
Lan, the transvestite woman warrior. One of the most significant effects
of Kingston's free adaptations from the traditional tale is to establish a
larger economy in which the "disinterested" and presumably culpable
aspects of art—dedication to perfection of form, nonproductivity, re-
quirement of solitude—are shown to be merely temporary. The artist is
identified with the warrior, the player with the worker, and the question
of "What good for?" dissolves in a vision of successful warfare and tri-
umphal return to the community.

As Kingston's detractors and defenders have both noted, the Fa Mu
Lan legend in "White Tigers" exhibits conspicuous departures from its
best-known ballad version. What motives one imputes to the author
would obviously determine how one reads the liberty-taking. The controversy is too complex to review here;[19] however, if one assumes
"White Tigers" to be a wish-fulfilling fantasy, many apparently egregious deviations fall into place as mirror images of what the Chinese
American narrator finds unwelcome or lacking in her own life. In terms
of the play theme, perhaps the most significant of Kingston's revisions is
the addition of a lengthy martial arts apprenticeship, whose images are
derived from the popular *wuxia xiaoshuo* or martial arts novel.[20] The
apprenticeship, conceived of as a precondition to the adequate execu-
tion of social duties, focuses and promises to reconcile many points of
contention between the aspiring artist, Maxine, and the people to whom
she feels accountable.

The Fa Mu Lan in "White Tigers" is chosen to be a savior of her
people; nevertheless, to be ready for that role, she has to choose as well:
between obedience to an everyday concept of Necessity—in Erhmann's
terms "immediate satisfaction of needs and desires" (1968:44)—and
commitment to what might be called a Higher Necessity. As an ordinary
farmers' daughter, she has her share of chores; these she must now put
aside to train as a warrior, at the risk of feeling guilty for deserting her
needy parents and kinsfolk. The old man, one of her teachers on the
mountaintop retreat, poses the choice thus: "You can go back right now
if you like. You can go pull sweet potatoes, or you can stay with us and
learn how to fight barbarians and bandits" (27). Cultivating sweet pota-

toes serves Necessity: it is obviously productive labor, an immediately visible contribution to the survival of the village. Learning to be a warrior serves a Higher Necessity: it involves the deferment of short-term economic gain for the sake of securing a liberated state of existence for a larger number of people than the family or the clan. What appears to be self-indulgent Extravagance—concentrating on the formal perfection of breathing control, still stances, and fighting techniques while the villagers are suffering from wicked rulers and marauding armies—is demonstrated to be useful in the long run. The martial arts are "arts" (play), but they are also "martial" (work). To quote Ehrmann again: "Far from being a depreciation, the detour of law [rule of the game] as an expression of play constitutes a transfer, a placing in reserve": "since play consists in giving in order to receive . . . later on or . . . in a different form, it fulfills a dual function of expenditure and savings" (44). In the larger economy, when the time for confrontation eventually arrives, the woman warrior is able to draw upon what has been placed in reserve and lead her righteous band to victory. In the meantime, the opportunity to learn to do well one thing at a time, just for the sake of doing it well, constitutes its own delightful reward that more than compensates for the physical rigors of training:

> I worked every day when it rained. I exercised in the downpour, grateful not to be pulling sweet potatoes. I moved like the trees in the wind. I was grateful not to be squishing in chicken mud, which I did not have nightmares about so frequently now. (35)

As we have learned to expect from the examples of Mrs. Hayashi and Fred Eng, what the heroine is opting for is not a softer life but a more arduous one. Nevertheless, "White Tigers" being a fantasy, Fa Mu Lan enjoys several important advantages over her literary forerunners: her sanctuary is far removed from the daily attritions of attention and energy entailed by communal living; her apprenticeship is prolonged and temporally bracketed off (she is gone from her village for fifteen years); she has her biological family's blessing and understanding; and she has a surrogate family of spiritual mentors who encourage her in developing an "interested disinterestedness." When she sees her family's sufferings in the magic gourd and wants to help them right away, the old couple stress the importance of patient training and teach her the art of temporary emotional detachment (38). Trusting her fundamental conscientiousness, the old man and woman do not try to scare Fa Mu Lan into suppressing her sexual desire, as Maxine's "real life" mother does; when she reaches menstruating age, they celebrate her coming of age but ask her to put off having children for a few more years. (She is married off to a loyally waiting mate in a "spirit wedding," which inverts the no

name woman's marriage to an absent husband.) When Fa Mu Lan suggests using her newly acquired skills of control to stop the menstrual
flow, the old woman replies, "No. You don't stop shitting and piss-
ing. . . . Let it run" (37). In other words, the discipline called for by the
warrior's vocation is not just inhibition, which is merely the flip side of
letting go, but a mature recognition of one's full, natural being coupled
with an equal recognition that gratification awaits accomplishment of a
more serious purpose. Unlike the no name woman and other artists with
no art form, who are undone by venting their inclinations in a blindly
instinctive manner, Fa Mu Lan is able to transform her desire into the
controlled exuberance of martial arts movements.

Two illustrations of such controlled exuberance are given in "White
Tigers." By the time Fa Mu Lan is ready for her survival trial in the
mountains, she has mastered the art of running blindfolded so well that
she can virtually fly: "I ran and, not stopping off a cliff at the edge of my
toes and not hitting my forehead against a wall, ran faster. A wind
buoyed me up over the roots, the rocks, the little hills" (29). (Flying, we
remember, is much aspired to in Asian American literature but rarely
accomplished; falling is the usual outcome.) Later, at the physical nadir
of her trial, after a long fast, Fa Mu Lan is granted a vision of enlighten-
ment in which the essence of the cosmos is perceived as a dance.

> I saw two people made of gold dancing the earth's dances. They turned so
> perfectly that together they were the axis of the earth's turning. They were
> light; they were molten, changing gold. . . . And I understand how work-
> ing and hoeing are dancing; how peasant clothes are golden, as king's
> clothes are golden; how one of the dancers is always a man and the other
> a woman. (32)

The dance is a fit metaphor for the ideal of a perfect union of Necessity
and Extravagance. Dance without the necessary constraint of form
would be mere random movement; without the extravagant freedom of
energy, a mechanical abstraction. When the woman warrior is finally
ready to do battle, she goes forth as a dancer, consummately skilled,
whose useful work of vengeance—the "killing and falling" (33)—is a
kind of dance too.

THE ARTIST'S PLEA FOR ROOM

It is easy to detect the parallels between Fa Mu Lan's war on her oppressors and the narrator's—and here she merges into Kingston the author—act of breaking silence about her Chinese American girlhood.
Comparing herself to the legendary heroine, the narrator notes:

What we have in common are the words at our backs. The idioms for *revenge* are "report a crime" and "report to five families." The reporting is the vengeance—not the beheading, not the gutting, but the words. And I have so many words—"chink" words and "gook words" too—that they do not fit on my skin. (63)

But adequate "reporting" has to be preceded by a sustained effort to "make [her] mind large, as the universe is large, so that there is room for paradoxes" (35). The writer's verbal knot-making (190) is contrasted with the artless, impulsive outpouring of personal grievances that Maxine attempts before her mother. The latter is merely personal therapy, "to stop the pain in [her] throat" (229), and even as such it is not truly effective because it is based on a premature fastening of responsibility on one party, when the truth is far more complex and riddled with "paradoxes."

When the narrator states, "The swordswoman and I are not so dissimilar. May my people understand the resemblance soon so that I can return to them" (62), she appears to be speaking for author Kingston as well. The plea is for room: for the practice of "conscientious aestheticism" to be understood as merely a "relocation" or "redistribution" of value (Ehrmann 1968:44) instead of pure wastage. In this light, the story of the theater-loving grandmother and the bandits (240–41), which is usually overlooked in favor of the T'sai Yen story that takes up the final pages of *The Woman Warrior* (241–43), is not merely an inconsequential frame for the latter. If the latter is, among other things, an expression of faith in *inter*cultural communication ("It [T'sai Yen's song] translated well" is the last sentence of the book), the former focuses on the *intra*cultural meaning of art. For once, the reader is given a parable exemplifying the positive consequences of abandoning oneself to art as well as affirming the communality of art. According to Brave Orchid (who tells the story only after learning of her daughter's talk-stories), her own mother once ordered her entire household to attend a play instead of staying home behind locked doors to guard against bandits, as caution would suggest. The bandits did strike—at the theater—but every member of the household somehow made it home safely, "proof to my grandmother that my family was immune to harm as long as they went to plays. They went to many plays after that" (241). The moral drawn by the grandmother borders on superstition, but the story is a corrective to the many other tales of Extravagance punished. At last the narrator's own inclinations are given a stamp of approval by the matriarch (the patriarchal figure is conspicuously absent). Moreover, for once art is valued as a communal, solidarity-building activity beyond short-sighted disputes over its utilitarian value. "I don't want to watch that play by myself," declares the matriarch. "How can I laugh all by myself? You want me to clap alone, is that it? I want everybody there. Babies, everybody" (241). The picture of the family at the theater is reminiscent of a scene in the Fa Mu Lan fantasy: after the woman warrior has tried and executed the oppressors, the villagers tear down the ancestral tablets (symbols of tradition and patriarchal authority). "We'll use this great hall for village meetings," announces the woman warrior. "Here we'll put on operas; we'll sing together and talk-story" (53). This brief episode seems to envision a "postrevolutionary" kind of Chinese American art on which the pressures toward immediate usefulness have eased and in which vengeance is no longer such a burning issue.

All the above ideas about a communal art Kingston goes on to develop in her next major work, *Tripmaster Monkey: His Fake Book*. Wittman Ah Sing, the book's Chinese American trickster hero, is based on Sun Wukong the Monkey King: an Extravagant "player" if there ever is one.[21] Without waiting for the revolution to finish doing its business (the story is set in the turbulent 1960s), and without compromising the pungency of his critical spirit, playwright Wittman Ah Sing puts on a marathon performance that "calls into play" various elements of the Asian American community (269–340). Old or young, foreign-born or American-born, tradition-bound or Westernized, genteel or bohemian, assimilationist or radical—all are given a chance to shine by a determinedly tolerant Wittman. In the generous and elastic form of this "Magic Theater," a virtual encyclopedia of Asian American history and lore is alluded to, acted out, scrambled up, troped upon, celebrated, satirized, and perhaps most importantly, *witnessed* by a laughing, catcalling, riotous audience (something noticeably lacking at the birth of Hwang's prototypical Asian American opera).

> Everyone came—friends, and friends' friends, and family. Not because Wittman had charisma or leadership, and certainly not because of his standing in the community. Nor were they here to feel sorry and give charity. . . . They came because what Boleslavsky said is true: "Acting is the life of the human soul receiving its birth through art." Everyone really does want to get into the act. (Kingston 1989:276)

Framed by chapters entitled "A Pear Garden in the West" (the name of an actual Chinese American opera/drama series in San Francisco) and "One-Man Show" (which concludes the book), the performance fuses the communal and the individual, the political and the personal; the artist is "given heart by a loving community," which in turn blesses his marriage (331).

Roominess cannot get much better than in *Tripmaster Monkey*. But can it not be objected that the enabling condition of such catholicity is potentially its gravest limitation?—that Wittman's all-encompassing show can only exist in language? Like the fantasy status of the "White Tigers" chapter in *The Woman Warrior*, the surrealistic nature of the play in *Tripmaster Monkey* problematizes whatever encouragement its contents offer to the artist: both pieces evince a faith in the performative[22] power of language to talk something into existence—word magic, if you will.

Ehrmann (1968:32–34) has effectively refuted the prevalent Western view that there is a prior, given, more "serious" reality which play imitates in a derivative and "depreciative" manner. He notes: "To pretend that play is mimesis would suppose the problem solved before it had even been formulated" (34). "To define play is *at the same time* and *in the same movement* to define reality and to define culture. As each term is a way to apprehend the two others, they are each elaborated, constructed through and on the basis of the two others" (55). My motive for calling into question Kingston's heartening images is not to devalue fiction or make-believe per se. To be sure, Asian American criticism is not exempt from Platonic anxiety over mimesis; much of the controversy surrounding *The Woman Warrior*'s autobiographical label is generated by the premise that a preconstituted social reality lies outside language, awaiting the artist's faithful reproduction (S. C. Wong 1992). However, the fantastic in both *The Woman Warrior* and *Tripmaster Monkey* is introduced by textual clues, so that the charge of lack of realism is largely beside the point. The key issue, then, is not that Kingston has rendered a community at play where none exists, but that she has called the community to play—urged it to play, lured it to play by vividly rendered visions of freedom—at a particular juncture in Asian American history, which may or may not be able to afford such a move. Much more than the alleged metaphysical parasitism of art on reality, Asian Americans are preoccupied by another question: the artist's alleged economic parasitism on the community.

The mission (whether stated or tacit) of Necessity's adherents is to work it out of existence, to attain Extravagance if not for oneself, then for one's descendants; as we have seen, immigrants in particular are sustained by this dream. Some do, for various reasons, get mired permanently in a survival mode (this mismatch of will and ability is the subject of many a work of Asian American literature). However, in terms of long-range aspirations, the Necessity-driven taskmasters and the practitioners of Extravagance can be said to be in agreement, differing only in their assessment of the current situation. Williams observes: "Art for art's sake is a reasonable maxim for the artist, when creating, and for the spectator when the work is being communicated; at such times, it is no more than a definition of attention" (1966:168). Attention defined is attention diverted from some other concern. Is the Asian American community in a sufficiently forgiving state of existence—comfortably installed in the safety margin, away from the edge of privation—to afford even an "interested distinterestedness"? If the answer is no, then utilitarianism prevails, and the playful artist becomes a superfluity on the Asian American body politic. If the answer is yes, the artist's appeal to a larger economy or "circuit" may be heeded.

This question is, of course, of the kind whose significance lies more in the asking than in the answering. When one attempts to reach a viable stance on the subject, it may be helpful to bear in mind several points. First, Kingston's emphasis on play might have been easier to dismiss as apolitical if it had not resonated so well with other images of art and artists. The understanding that the woman warrior seeks from her community is not that different from, say, the understanding that Fred Eng seeks from his. If even Frank Chin, who in his nonplaywriting capacities is a ruthless advocate of militant instrumentalism in literature,[23] can create a sympathetic character who says "I don't wanta be a pioneer. Just a writer. Just see my name in a book by me. About things I like writing about, and fuck the pioneers" (117), the idea of play cannot be taken lightly. Second, the examples that we have examined in this chapter all come from the writings of American-born authors. Only further study can pinpoint the possible implications of this fact. But even a cursory contrast with Carlos Bulosan's figure of the activist writer in *America Is in the Heart*, whose writing is literally his work and who suffers no qualms regarding his social usefulness, suggests various interacting factors that could affect the treatment of the play theme: besides generational position, we can count overall historical conditions (e.g., the Depression versus the relative affluence of the postwar era); overtness of racist oppression (outright individual persecution versus cultural hegemony and institutionalized discrimination); exposure to American education (a colonial education versus an internal colonial education); social class background (working class or even underclass versus the upwardly mobile); participation in organized politics (joining a revolutionary party versus battling injustice as an individual); and, of course, gender.

It is arguable that those who feel partially enfranchised in American society are more likely to issue a plea for forbearance and invoke the rhetoric of gratuitous play than those who feel almost totally disenfranchised. It is also arguable that today the Asian American community, *on the whole*, has attained a greater measure of security than in Bulosan's period. However, it should also be borne in mind that at any point in time, "the Asian American community" remains a powerful heuristic fiction whose functioning depends on a delicate balancing of unifying and heterogenizing claims. The historical meaning of ludic images in Asian American literature, as well as the meaning of a critical focus on the ludic theme, is also subject to constant shifting.

The Asian American authors' interest in play falls within a period of valorization—some say revalorization—of play in the Western world (Spariosu 1982:32, 41; Sutton-Smith and Kelly-Byrne 1984:306–10). The last few decades, during which Chin, Kingston, and Hwang have been active, have also witnessed a burgeoning fascination among professional literary critics with the idea of play, especially via Derridean deconstruction (Kelly 1988:230–32, 282–311). All the above-cited analysts of the phenomenon—Spariosu, Sutton-Smith and Kelly-Byrne, Kelly—have stressed the supreme importance of placing doctrines of "pure" disinterestedness in their historical contexts and the dangers of taking universalizing claims at face value; to them, the promotion of play is always a *motivated* move. Spariosu observes of the aestheticist attitude that it is "one of the most effective instruments of power at the very moment when it seems most remote from it" (41). The recent voguishness of critical play is especially problematic for students of literature of color. R. Baxter Miller, reviewing poststructuralist trends in African American literary criticism, faults "critical play" for "lay[ing] claim to its own codes of acceptability" and "sever[ing] most ethical ties to the world outside the game itself" (1987:394). Abdul B. JanMohamed and David Lloyd, writing about "minority discourse," warns against the "premature claim to represent a realm of aesthetic freedom and disinterest" in literary studies (1990a:10–11). The weight of all this testimony is sufficient to render suspect any mention of play in a minority context. What then are we to make of the play theme in Asian American literature, and how does the present study of Necessity and Extravagance fit into the picture?

The thrust of this chapter has been to demonstrate that even those Asian American authors most drawn to images of free play have never lost sight of the issues of utility and community: that at heart their "disinterestedness" is always "interested," their "purposelessness" always "purposive." Despite similarities in rhetoric, Asian American literature has never conformed fully to the Euro-American tradition on the treatment of play; rather, as intertextual readings reveal, it has its own set of ludic motifs with its own dynamics of interaction. To the extent the Asian American representations of play constitute an exception to the dominant pattern, it is *partly* exempt from the aforementioned critiques of the privileging of play. The authors are undeniably implicated in the economic system and have their own economic agendas to pursue and justify; herein lies their motivatedness. (As self-awareness on this point varies from individual to individual, some texts will show greater internal contradictions than others.) Moreover, besides the commitment to discipline oneself, to enlarge one's mind in commensuration with the enlarged "circuit" accorded them, the artist can make no guarantee that his/her liberty will not be abused. However, the overall intent of the Asian American artists' self-justification is not to place themselves permanently outside and above the community on an Arnoldian perch of neutrality.

In fact, it can be further argued that, at this juncture in history, the seemingly apolitical advancement of play by Asian American artists serves a political function: it subverts white society's expectations on the Asian American's proper place and stimulates the creation of a heteroglossic Asian American culture. From the "coolies" of the nineteenth century to today's technicians and nonmanagerial professionals, the historical role of Asian Americans has been to serve the interests of the dominant society as "good workers": industrious, focused, dependable, accommodating, serious-minded, eminently *useful*. A general containment of exuberance is no doubt essential to the group's own struggles for survival: it fosters caution, a prudent balancing of gain and loss, conservative husbandry of energy and material. However, a Necessity-driven mentality may backfire when it is typecast as "essentially" Asian American and used to consolidate the existing power structure. By collectively privileging narrow goal-orientation, Asian Americans may end by keeping themselves *subdued* (the dual meanings of the word, "emotional repression" and "conquest," in this case being related). When the development of Asian American culture is thereby slowed, the dominant society is conveniently spared the strain and unsettling that dissident cultural creation brings through its spirited criticisms and self-criticisms, sustained meditations, and Extravagant envisionings of alternative social possibilities.

Stirrings among young Asian Americans to break free from respectable, lucrative but still Necessitous service—by abandoning traditionally "safe" fields like science, engineering, or medicine—have become noticeable of late (Allis 1991). The effort to "[kick] the nerd syndrome" (Allis's phrase) suggests that at least some segments of the community might have become educationally ready (in English),[24] ideologically willing, and materially able to take self-defining culture- and community-building to new levels of intensity. Acts of Extravagance, such as culminate in the flowering of Asian American literature described in the introduction to this study, promise to undo some of the damage inflicted by the pressures against play that have governed Asian American life for so long.

Of course, as soon as this begins to happen, the possibility looms large that another kind of pressing-into-service would take place: Asian American art would become appropriated for mainstream consumption. Certain types of Asian American literature, as we have seen, are already self-prepared for, or susceptible to, this appropriation, and even those works that attempt to break free of constraining expectations are constantly in danger of being read just for their "difference." David Wong Louie has reason to be suspicious of the recent flood of supposedly positive media interest in Asian American writers: he notes that a piece such as *Publishers Weekly*'s "Spring's Five Fictional Encounters of the Chinese American Kind" (Feldman 1991), though well-intentioned, recycles old stereotypes about "alien" Asians ("Introduction," Chin and Louie 1991).

There are, then, limits to a conceptualization of the function of art that depends on an oppositional stance: stereotype-busting is not, in itself, a sufficient raison d'être for artistic creation, though on balance it is no doubt better to have done it than not. Ultimately, the "utility" of Asian American literature consists in what it can do for the broader cultural survival and cultural prosperity of the group from which it springs. Of the function of minority discourse, including its seemingly depoliticized instances, JanMohamed and Lloyd write:

> In the case of minority [cultural] forms even the sublimation of misery requires to be understood as primarily a strategy for survival, for the preservation in some form or other of cultural identity, *and* for political critique. . . . Exactly to the extent that [Third World and minority] peoples are systematically marginalized vis-à-vis the global economy, one might see the resort to cultural modes of struggle as all the more necessary. . . . For many minorities, culture is not a mere superstructure; all too often, in an ironic twist of a Sartrean phenomenology, the physical survival of minority groups depends on the recognition of its culture as viable. (1990a:5–6; italics in original)

What JanMohamed and Lloyd maintain about the survival value of minority cultural production in general can be applied, as well, to the play theme in Asian American literature and the critical attention devoted to its analysis. In the Asian American case, to read interest in play simply as decadent aestheticism is to be misled by inappropriate contexts and intertexts. This assertion is not premised on the belief that art is a protected magic realm in which ideology is erased and sociopolitical forces suspended. Quite the contrary: it is precisely because literature is ideology-infused that even the artist's plea for room to play has important implications for the historical struggles—the political work—of Asian Americans.

NOTES

INTRODUCTION
CONSTRUCTING AN ASIAN AMERICAN TEXTUAL COALITION

1. Since about 1986, tenure-track teaching positions for Asian American literary scholars have been filled or considered at the following institutions: Bowling Green State University; Brown University; Cornell University; George Washington University; Georgetown University; the University of California at Berkeley, Irvine, Los Angeles, Santa Barbara, Santa Cruz, and Riverside; the University of Colorado; the University of Hawaii; the University of Southern California; the University of Michigan; the University of Wisconsin at Madison; Stanford University; and Washington State University.

2. Elaine Kim's *Asian American Literature*, the first book-length study to treat Asian American literature in a comprehensive manner, appeared in 1982; a revised edition is forthcoming. (E. San Juan published *Carlos Bulosan and the Imagination of the Class Struggle* in 1975, but it deals only with one Filipino American writer.) Amy Ling's *Between Worlds* appeared in 1990; Stephen Sumida's *And the View from the Shore*, which contains discussions of Asian American authors in Hawaii, appeared in 1991. Besides single-authored works, there are also anthologies of critical essays, such as S. Lim, ed., *Approaches to Teaching Kingston's "The Woman Warrior"* (1991); Lim and Ling, eds., *Reading the Literatures of Asian America*; and E. Kim, ed., *Writing Self, Writing Nation* (1992). Published proceedings of the Association for Asian American Studies' annual conventions (such as G. Okihiro et al., G. Nomura et al., and S. Hune et al.) contain essays on Asian American literature. Lee C. Lee, ed., *Asian Americans: Collages of Identities* (1992), includes pieces by literary critics. Scholars currently completing book-length studies of Asian American subjects from various American university presses include King-Kok Cheung's study of silence and the narrative strategies of Asian American women writers (Cornell) and David Palumbo-Liu's interdisciplinary study of the representation and ideological function of Asian Americans (Stanford). Also of interest is James S. Moy's *Marginal Sights: Rehearsing Chineseness*, forthcoming from the University of Iowa Press, which contains chapters on Asian American representations in theater and film.

3. The list of recent works to follow is limited to book-length publications. Pieces in magazines and journals, unpublished plays, and children's literature will not be included. No attempt is made to be exhaustive or to screen works by content (e.g., American versus Asian settings or cast of characters), by intended audience, and so on.

4. Obviously this cutoff point is rather arbitrarily chosen. Since the present study does not aim to be bibliographically exhaustive, my "snapshot" of the field must be made manageable. However, 1986 marks the tenth anniversary of the

publication of Maxine Hong Kingston's *The Woman Warrior*, the first major Asian American "crossover hit," and to that extent might be considered a significant date.

5. These include Meena Alexander (*Nampally Road*); Jessica Hagedorn (*Dogeaters*); Cynthia Kadohata (*The Floating World*); Ronyoung Kim (*Clay Walls*); Steven Lo (*The Incorporation of Eric Chung*); Lowry Pei (*Family Resemblances*); Amy Tan (*The Joy Luck Club*); Holly Uyemoto (*Rebel Without a Clue*); and Karen Tei Yamashita (*Through the Arc of the Rain Forest*). Tan's *The Joy Luck Club* became a phenomenal bestseller, and Yamashita won an American Book Award in 1991.

6. Kingston, whose *The Woman Warrior* (1976) won the 1976 National Book Critics Circle Award, published *Tripmaster Monkey: His Fake Book* (1989). Bharati Mukherjee won a National Book Critics Circle Award for *The Middleman and Other Stories* (1988) and went on to publish *Jasmine* in 1989.

7. Hisaye Yamamoto's *Seventeen Syllables and Other Stories* (1988) and Frank Chin's *The Chinaman Pacific and Frisco R.R. Co.* (1989), which make accessible the veteran authors' previous works, both received the American Book Award. Darrell Lum's *Pass On, No Pass Back!* (1990) won the Association for Asian American Studies' 1991 Book Award.

8. For example, Le Ly Hayslip, *When Heaven and Earth Changed Places*; Marlon Hom (recipient of an American Book Award), *Songs of Gold Mountain*; Tooru Kanazawa, *Sushi and Sourdough*; Willyce Kim, *Dead Heat*; Wanwadee Larsen, *Confessions of a Mail Order Bride*; Louise Leung Larson, *Sweet Bamboo*; Mary Paik Lee, *Quiet Odyssey*; Alice Lin, *Grandmother Had No Name*; David Mas Masumoto, *Country Voices*; Margaret Pai, *The Dreams of Two Yi-min*; Ninotchka Rosca, *State of War*; Bienvenido Santos, *What the Hell for You Left Your Heart in San Francisco*; Sara Suleri, *Meatless Days*; Yoshiko Uchida, *Picture Bride*.

9. For example, Asian Women United of California, ed., *Making Waves: An Anthology of Writings by and about Asian American Women*; Misha Berson, ed., *Between Worlds: Contemporary Asian American Plays*; Eric Chock and Darrell H. Y. Lum, eds., *The Best of Bamboo Ridge*; C. Chung, A. Kim, and A. K. Lemeshewsky, eds., *Between the Lines: An Anthology by Pacific/Asian Lesbians of Santa Cruz*; Ketu Katrak and R. Radhakrishnan, eds., *Desh-Videsh: South Asian Expatriate Writing and Art*; Shirley Geok-lin Lim and Mayumi Tsutakawa, eds., *The Forbidden Stitch: An Asian American Women's Anthology*; L. Ling-Chi Wang and Henry Yiheng Zhao, eds., *Chinese American Poetry: An Anthology*; Sylvia Watanabe and Carol Bruchac, eds., *Home to Stay: Asian American Women's Fiction*; Shawn Wong, ed., *Blue Funnel Line*. A shorter version of Wang and Zhao's volume has appeared in translation in China (Wang, Wong, and Zhao, eds.). Lim and Tsutakawa won an American Book Award in 1990.

10. David Henry Hwang's *M. Butterfly* premiered in New York in 1988 (the script was published in 1989). It won the 1988 Tony Award, as well as the Drama Desk, Outer Critics Circle, and John Gassner awards, for Best Play.

11. These include Ai, *Cruelty/Killing Floor*; Meena Alexander, *House of a Thousand Doors*; Marilyn Chin, *Dwarf Bamboo*; Eric Chock, *Last Days Here*; Chitra Banerjee Divakaruni, *The Reason for Nasturtiums*; Kimiko Hahn, *Air*

Pocket; Garrett Hongo, *The River of Heaven*; Lonny Kaneko, *Coming Home from Camp*; Alex Kuo, *Changing the River*; Li-Young Lee, *Rose* and *The City in Which I Love You*; Genny Lim, *Winter Place*; Shirley Geok-lin Lim, *Modern Secrets*; Wing Tek Lum, *Expounding the Doubtful Points*; Linda Watanabe McFerrin, *The Impossibility of Redemption Is Something We Hadn't Figured On*; Janice Mirikitani, *Shedding Silence*; David Mura, *After We Lost Our Way*; Yasuo Sasaki, *Village Scene/Village Heard*; Cathy Song, *Frameless Windows, Squares of Light*; Jeff Tagami, *October Light*; Mitsuye Yamada, *Desert Run*; and John Yau, *Radiant Silhouettes*. Hongo's *River of Heaven* was the 1987 Lamont Poetry Selection of the Academy of American Poets as well as a finalist for the 1989 Pulitzer Prize. Mura's *After We Lost Our Way* was a winner of the National Poetry Prize. Lee's *The City in Which I Love You* was the Lamont Poetry Selection for 1990.

12. First novels published in 1991 include Peter Bacho's *Cebu* (which won a Before Columbus Foundation American Book Award); Fiona Cheong's *Scent of the Gods*; Frank Chin's *Donald Duk*; Gish Jen's; *Typical American*; Gus Lee's *China Boy*; and Gail Tsukiyama's *Woman of the Silk*. *The Kitchen God's Wife* is Amy Tan's second novel.

Debut collections of short stories include David Wong Louie, *Pangs of Love*, which received the 1991 *Los Angeles Times* Art Seidenbaum Award for First Fiction; R. A. Sasaki, *The Loom and Other Stories*; and Marianne Villanueva, *Ginseng and Other Tales from Manila*. Anthologies include J. Chan et al., eds., *The Big Aiiieeeee!*, the long-awaited sequel to the seminal *Aiiieeeee!*; Grace Hong et al., eds., *Burning Cane*; and Marilyn Chin and David Wong Louie, eds., *Dissident Song*.

In other genres, there are Ai's and Chitra Banerjee Divakaruni's volumes of poetry (*Fate* and *Black Candles*, respectively); poet David Mura's account of his sojourn in Japan, *Turning Japanese: Memoirs of a Sansei*; a memoir, *The Lost Garden*, by Laurence Yep, writer of children's books and science fiction; Genny Lim's *Paper Angels and Bitter Cane*, two plays performed some years ago but appearing in print for the first time; Tooru Kanazawa's autobiography, *Sushi and Sourdough*; and Akemi Kikumura's biography of her father, *Promises Kept*.

13. For example, Woon-Ping Chin, *The Naturalization of Camellia Song*; Cynthia Kadohata, *In the Heart of the Valley of Love*; Paul Stephen Lim, *Figures in Clay* and *Mother Tongue*; Lydia Yuri Minatoya, *Talking to High Monks in the Snow*; Gary Pak, *The Watcher of Waipuna*; Sylvia Watanabe, *Talking to the Dead*; and William Wu, *Wong's Lost and Found Emporium and Other Oddities*. N.V.M. Gonzalez, *Bread of Salt and Other Stories*, and Fae Myenne Ng, *Bone*, are forthcoming in 1993.

14. On the *Woman Warrior* controversy, see S. Wong, "Autobiography as Guided Chinatown Tour?" See J. S. Moy for a critique of *M. Butterfly*, A. Pao for an analysis of the play's reception, and M. Alquizola ("The Woman in David Henry Hwang's *M. Butterfly*") for a consideration of the gender and ethnicity issues involved. On *The Joy Luck Club*, see Chin (Letter to the Editor), L. Lowe ("Rethinking Essentialisms"), M. McAlister ("[Mis]reading *The Joy Luck Club*"), and S. Wong (" 'Sugar Sisterhood' ").

15. The most vocal proponent of this approach is W. Sollors ("A Critique of Pure Pluralism"; *Beyond Ethnicity*; "Nine Suggestions"; and "Of Mules and

Mares," among others). Other scholars associated with the approach (and endorsed by Sollors) include M. Dearborn, W. Boelhower, and T. J. Ferraro. E. Fox-Genovese shares many of Sollors's concerns; though she also speaks of the need to "understand the pattern of marginalized cultures in relation to each other" (1990:10), the thrust of her argument is different from that of the "minority discourse" framework, discussed below.

16. The development of the anti-multiculturalist backlash is too complex to trace here. Some key documents in the debate in higher education are collected in P. Berman (1992). Interestingly, even some critics previously known for promoting minority literary studies, such as Gates, have of late been voicing criticisms of multicultural scholarship in terms reminiscent of the "ethnicity school" (Winkler 1990). For refutations of anti-multiculturalist views as represented by William Bennett, E. D. Hirsch, Jr., and Allan Bloom, see P. Lauter's "Looking a Gift Horse in the Mouth," "Whose Culture? Whose Literacy?" and "The Book of Bloom and the Discourse of Difference" (in Lauter 1991:243–86); and Simonson and Walker 1988.

17. For the context and implications of the *Ozawa* case, see Ichioka 1988:210–26 and S. Chan 1991:47.

18. Relevant here is the debate among social scientists on whether Asian Americans constitute a "middleman minority"; for example, E. Bonacich and J. Modell (1980:13–36) are in favor of such a view, E. Wong (1985) against.

19. Space limitations preclude a full account of the changing categories. Some examples will suffice: in addition to Chinese, Japanese, Filipinos, and Hawaiians, Koreans were separately enumerated in 1970 (U.S. Department of Commerce, Bureau of the Census 1979:75); "Asian Indian," "Vietnamese," "Samoan," and "Guamanian" were added to the existing five groups on the 1980 form on the recommendation of Asian and Pacific Americans advisers (Azores 1979:71).

20. See the Introduction (J. Chan et al. 1991:xi–xvi), signed by all four editors, and the lengthy essay, "Come All Ye Asian American Writers of the Real and the Fake" (1–92), signed by Frank Chin alone. As reflected in the subtitle of *The Big Aiiieeeee!*, the editors' interest is now confined to Chinese and Japanese American literature. Except for Sui Sin Far, no Chinese American women writers are represented; among the living male Chinese American writers included, David Wong Louie is the only one not from the 1960s generation and with no record of having been ideologically aligned with the *Aiiieeeee!* group.

21. Here *Asian American* refers to subject matter of study rather than the practitioner's ethnic background.

22. At least not today, when awareness of "Indians" as the first or original Americans has increased considerably. Note that Native Americans did not have United States citizenship until 1924. Tribal citizenship has continued to this day, resulting in dual citizenship (Hoxie 1988:279–80); however, tribal membership cannot reasonably be construed as "foreign." Understanding of the indigenousness of Native American literature parallels that of the Native American's legal status, though recognition of the culture's "prior-ness" is by no means synonymous with respect for it.

23. An interesting recent instance of this tendency is pointed out by Ferraro (1988:183–84; cited in Sollors 1990a:179). Sandra Gilbert and Susan Gubar, in their *Norton Anthology of Literature by Women* (1985), readily accept shared concerns with a fourteenth-century English mystic, Margery Kempe, but describes American-born contemporary Maxine Hong Kingston in distancing terms, as someone from "a culture different from our own" and "another place entirely." Sollors uses this example to castigate women's studies for holding unspoken assumptions about a normative culture, hence to restate the case for a nonpartisan universalism in American studies. To me it proves rather the opposite: that more, not less, particularizing work has to be done to avoid Gilbert and Gubar's kind of bias.

24. *New historicist* is used "generically" here. For some applications as well as critiques of the approach, see Veeser (1989).

25. As Thaïs Morgan notes in her excellent account of intertextuality from T. S. Eliot to Foucault, despite Kristeva's invention of the term, the privileging of the "text/discourse/culture" triangle over the "author/work/tradition" triangle emerges from the cross-fertilization of several major European intellectual movements in the 1960s and 1970s (1989:240).

26. The implications of "play" for students of minority literatures will be discussed in detail in chapter 4.

27. In this study the word *Extravagance* will be capitalized to make it the rhetorical opposite of *Necessity*.

28. According to Chinese Canadian scholar Shelley Wong, the state of Asian Canadian literature is best described as nascent; Asians in Canada did not go through the kind of civil rights struggles that gave birth to the Asian literary movement and sensibility in the United States in the 1960s. It is noteworthy that both *Obasan*, the first Japanese Canadian novel, and Sky Lee's *Disappearing Moon Cafe* (1990), the first Chinese Canadian novel, were marketed and critically received as part of Canadian literature rather than specifically Asian Canadian literature.

29. Asian Canadian writers appear to be increasingly active. Some recent publications include Ivy Huffman and Julie Kwong, *The Dream of Gold Mountain*; Joy Kogawa, *Itsuka*; Evelyn Lau, *Runaway* and *You Are Not Who You Claim*; Sky Lee, *Disappearing Moon Cafe*; Bennett Lee and Jim Wong-Chu, eds., *Many Mouthed Birds: Contemporary Writing by Chinese Canadians*; Rachna Mara, *Of Customs and Excise*; Roy Miki, *Saving Face: Poems Selected 1976–1988*; and Yuen Chung Yip, *The Tears of Chinese Immigrants*.

CHAPTER ONE
BIG EATERS, TREAT LOVERS . . .

1. On the parallels between eating and reading, James W. Brown writes: "*Corpus littéraire, corpus alimentaire*: both are metonymies of the container and the contained. . . . Literature in its dynamic mode encompasses the notion of *écriture* in the same way that food in its dynamic mode entails the act of eating. Seen this way, *nourriture* and *littérature* may be described as transformational and generative processes" ("Littérature et Nourriture," 5).

2. The unusualness of including "raw" historical documents, as well as the demands it places on the reader, are noted by several book reviewers, though opinions on its artistic merits differ. S. Martin praises *Obasan*'s air of "authenticity"; K. Govier admires congruence of form and content: "At times the novel feels like one of the many broken-backed, struggling creatures we encounter in its pages." On the other hand, D. Stanley complains of awkward handling, even implying that Kogawa, in using Kitagawa's papers almost verbatim, has somehow shirked her duties as a novelist.

3. This list is adapted from *Democracy Betrayed*, a brief account of relocation making a case for redress compiled by the National Association of Japanese Canadians.

4. A contrasting treatment is found in Kingston's *China Men*, which contains a catalog of anti-Chinese legislation, "The Laws" (1980:150–58), sandwiched between stories of Chinese American men.

5. See also "If a son shall ask bread of any of you that is a father, will he give him a stone?" (Luke 11:11).

6. T. Ueki (1991) provides an interesting reading of the image of manna.

7. A slightly different version of this story is incorporated into Ng's first novel, *Bone*.

8. But see chapter 4 for my reading of Brave Ochid's subconscious sympathy in her handling of the Moon Orchid affair.

9. Kingston once tried her hand at engineering, in deference to her parents' wishes (M. Chin 1989:17). Tan was expected to be "a neurosurgeon by trade and a concert pianist by hobby" (Kepner 1989:60). Although Frank Chin's generational positioning is different from that of his fictional counterpart, he too experienced serious clashes with his father, who was (like Johnny's) a prominent Chinatown leader and wanted his son to be a credit to the family (Nee and Nee 388–89).

10. There is no single full-length study of the thesis, but Osajima (1988) and Yun (1989), in providing current perspectives on the debate, refer to the evolution of the idea. A list of media articles on the "model minority" is given in Osajima (173 n. 9).

11. Compare the "Balzac paradox" in Marxist literary criticism (Birchall 1977:98).

12. I am indebted to Giulia Fabi and King-Kok Cheung for helping me reach a more nuanced analysis of quasi-cannibalism.

13. Compare Maxine's "Perhaps . . . what I once had was not Chinese-sight at all but child-sight that would have disappeared eventually without such struggle" (239). The term "Chinese" seems to serve the young protagonist as a catch-all for any kind of deviance or perceived deviance from the dominant society's expectations and practices.

14. Frank Chin is preoccupied with the notion of "movies" as cultural conditioning that not only shapes the Chinese American's perceptions but also constrains his vision of possible life choices (e.g., F. Chin 1978:4 and 1970:113, 115, 119, 126).

15. No dates are given, but the temporal setting can be deduced from the fact that the daughters in the story watch *I Love Lucy* while growing up (the comedy series ran from 1951 to 1955).

16. For example, Lu Xun's famous 1918 short story "Diary of a Madman" (1990:29–48, 49–58); and the stories on man-eating ghouls in part III of Nieh Hualing's *Mulberry and Peach* (1981; first published in Chinese in 1976), which are obvious allusions to Lu Xun and an implied critique of the Nationalist regime in Taiwan and the moribund Confucian culture it champions. (These two authors are listed under their family names, Lu and Nieh, in the bibliography.)

17. For example, the Trueblood incident in Ralph Ellison's *Invisible Man*, Pecola's rape by her father Cholly Breedlove in Toni Morrison's *The Bluest Eye*, and Celie's rape by her stepfather in Alice Walker's *The Color Purple*.

18. A similar pattern is found in Louise Erdrich's *Tracks* (1988), but the demarcation between the generations is not immigration but the coming of the white man. Old Man Nanapush and his "family," identified with the dying Indian way of life, are constantly struggling with hunger and privation but accomplished in "big eating" (e.g., 100–105, 145). The Morrisseys and the Lazarres, mixed-blood "treaty Indians" with government connections (and access to food rations), are described as greedy for candy, sugar, and other treats (e.g., 77–78, 179). Whether these cross-cultural parallels exist on a larger scale has to be determined by further investigation.

19. I am indebted to Stephen Sumida for this observation.

20. Chapter 2 provides a full reading of this story.

21. This injunction of "Don't tell" is also one imposed on the narrator in *The Woman Warrior* and on Celie in Walker's *The Color Purple* (Cheung 1988).

22. For this useful piece of cultural information—one that significantly and delightfully complicates my reading of the story—I am indebted to an unidentified Filipino student in UC Berkeley's English Department, who spoke to me after a lecture.

23. The flight of investment capital from certain politically unstable regions of Asia (such as Hong Kong) results in a different sort of Asian immigrant: affluent, cosmopolitan, and likely to find life in the United States a step down rather than a step up.

24. Some of the more problematic and unsavory aspects of "green card marriages" is presented in the first-person account of Larsen (1989), a Thai "mail order bride." I am indebted to Christine So for sharing with me her reading of Larsen's defensive rhetoric.

25. Recent immigration from the Third World is reviewed in Reimers 1985.

26. Fred is Chinese-born but brought to the United States since childhood and raised by a Chinese American mother; in terms of culture he is virtually American-born.

27. Like other Koreans of his time, Han is literate in Chinese and can communicate with the Chinese through writing; as an impoverished new immigrant he frequents Chinatown for its cheap food. Trip's name is, of course, comically apt in view of the outcome of the romance.

28. Lin Yutang, author of such popular books as *My Country and My People* (1937) and *The Importance of Living* (1937) (listed under Lin in the bibliography), built his American reputation on interpreting Chinese culture to Westerners in precisely the way recommended by Chungpa Han's friend.

29. See Zee (1990) for a well-researched and entertaining example of this kind of blend between cultural and gastronomical information.

30. I use the term *right* here to describe an author's vision rather than to express my endorsement of whatever moral prescriptiveness it may connote.

31. Actually the doughnut is European in origin, but in its modern form it is considered a typically American food (Mariani 1983:146–48).

32. Such is the case in Dunn's "No Man's Land," in which the American-born elder son prefers hamburgers to *juk*; or in John Okada's *No-No Boy*, in which a dinner at Kenji's house, complete with a chicken bought from Safeway (123) and a lemon meringue pie (126), is regarded as an affirmation of Americanization.

CHAPTER TWO
ENCOUNTERS WITH THE RACIAL SHADOW

1. For example, in Kingston's *The Woman Warrior*, one finds nightmare images of a "holeless baby" abandoned to die in the outhouse and a child failing to defecate and dying of congestion on top of a modern toilet (1975:101). The narrator feels her parents have been "[funneling]" China into her ears (89) and filling her mind with ideas like "suitcases [jam-packed] with homemade underwear" (102). Her act of telling bottled-up grievances to Brave Orchid is described in terms of the throat bursting (235), so that items keep "pouring out" in random order (236). (See Eakin 1985:265–66.)

In David Henry Hwang's *FOB*, the assimilated Dale and the immigrant Steve engage in a hot-sauce eating contest, each trying to prove himself a tougher "big eater," until both end up coughing and choking (33–34). In Frank Chin's *The Year of the Dragon*, Pa spits blood—a sign of losing control over his defenses against Necessity. His son Fred Eng, the Chinatown tour guide condemned to make a living from self-display, finds his only solace in a kind of controlled puking: beautifully obscene torrents of speech let loose on the tourists, calculated at once to vent his venomous hatred of the Chinatown world and to perpetuate it. Hence his final mock-apocalyptic vision of Chinatown swimming in its own flood of drool, spit out by its corrupt inhabitants (1981:142). Amy Tan's *The Joy Luck Club*, which emphasizes how the desires of Chinese and Chinese American women are suppressed, abounds in images of swallowing, holding back, bursting, and splitting open (e.g., 17, 19, 42–43, 67, 75, 153–54, 215, 217–18).

2. Chin and Chan are evidently influenced by analysts of colonial psychology like O. Mannoni, A. Memmi, and F. Fanon.

3. *Doppelgänger* ("double-goer") was first introduced in Jean Paul's 1796 novel, *Siebenkäs*, with the footnote, "So heissen Leute, die sich selbst sehen" ["So people who see themselves are called"] (Tymms 1949:16). The term also evokes the eerie figure of the death-prefiguring wraith in German folklore (Tymms, 17).

4. The split personality is usually brought up by scholars by way of introducing a more focused discussion of the "true double," however this last is defined. A notable exception is J. Berman 1988; however, the dictionary format may have obliged him to place related subjects under one rubric.

5. Not covered under these are two earlier studies which appear routinely in literature reviews but do not otherwise seem influential for contemporary liter-

ary critics: Lucka 1905, which employs a by-now disfavored moral vocabulary; and Crawley 1908, which is largely anthropological.

6. Miyoshi's 1969 study, organized around several landmark dates to trace the evolution of the Victorian divided sensibility, may also be described as "diachronic"; however, unlike the other works I place in this category, it deals only with British literature.

7. Since we are dealing with English-speaking (in fact, mostly English-monolingual), American-educated Asian writers, an obvious possibility to consider is that they have read classic tales of the doppelgänger and are deliberately using the figure in their own works. I have chosen to suspend judgment on this possibility: the creative process being as complex as it is, even the authors themselves may not be able (or willing) to point to specific antecedents for their works. My concern is not with influence-tracing but with methods of reading and exegesis.

8. The quotations from critics to follow all refer to negative aspects of the self and to that extent leave out the idealized type of double featured in several theories, such as Robert Rogers's "Fair Maid" or C. F. Keppler's "the Beloved." However, even the "good" double results from disowning, taken in its root sense of "not acknowledging as one's own."

9. Ziolkowski reminds us that, before 1800, the double was frequently used in literature for comic effect by exploiting the confusion that arises when a twin or lookalike appears (1977:175). After the obsessive doppelgänger tales of the nineteenth century, the figure has become almost inextricable from phantasmagoric machinery or sinister lighting, making it easy to confuse atmosphere with substance.

10. Keppler, for example, while noting that self-division can be caused by "purely personal problems or by the wider problems of [the protagonist's] culture" (1972:189), does not amplify on the latter. Rogers, as will be seen in a later section of the chapter, touches on race issues (1970:6), but these are of minor importance in his overall scheme.

11. Among the examples most frequently adduced by all three groups of critics are Jean Paul Richter (*Siebenkäs*, 1796–97; *Titan*, 1800–1803), Goethe (*Wilhelm Meister's Apprenticeship*, 1795–96; *Faust*, 1808), Chamisso (*The Wonderful Story of Peter Schlemihl*, 1814), and Hoffmann (*The Story of the Lost Reflection*, 1815; *The Devil's Elixir*, 1815–16); Kafka (*In the Penal Colony*, 1919), Hesse (*Steppenwolf*, 1927), and Mann (*Doctor Faustus*, 1949); Mary Shelley (*Frankenstein*, 1818), Hogg, *Confessions of a Justified Sinner* (1824), Emily Brontë (*Wuthering Heights*, 1847), Dickens (*The Mystery of Edwin Drood*, 1870), Stevenson (*The Strange Case of Dr. Jekyll and Mr. Hyde*, 1886), Wilde (*The Picture of Dorian Gray*, 1891), Conrad (*Lord Jim*, 1900; *Heart of Darkness*, 1902; *The Secret Sharer*, 1912), Woolf (*Mrs. Dalloway*, 1925), and Joyce (*Ulysses*, 1922; *Finnegans Wake*, 1939); Hawthorne ("The Birth-Mark," 1846; "My Kinsman, Major Molineux," 1851), Poe ("William Wilson," 1839), Melville (*Pierre*, 1852; *Bartleby the Scrivener*, 1853), Henry James ("The Jolly Corner," 1908), Faulkner (*Absalom, Absalom!*, 1936), and Nabokov (*Pale Fire*, 1962); Maupassant (*The Horla*, 1887); and Dostoevsky (*The Double*, 1846; *The Brothers Karamazov*, 1880).

12. A case in point is Coates, whose speculations on the emergence of the modern double allude to such material factors as the Industrial Revolution; colonialism; transportation and communications technology; genetic engineering; literacy; even the availability of mirrors in the home (1988:1–6). While such a broad outlook is stimulating, Coates's many astute generalizations will prove useful to the student of ethnic American literature only through judicious borrowing. For example, when Coates observes that "Stories that deal explicitly with the Double seem in the main to be written by authors who are suspended between languages and cultures. . . . The Double is the self when it speaks another language" (2), he is referring to authors like Conrad, Hogg, Stevenson, Henry James, and Wilde, who, relative to an Asian American writer, are not so "suspended." The student of ethnic American literature must generate her own frame of reference.

13. Two among these stand out as offering useful glosses. Gates's *Figures in Black*, especially his controlling idea of blackness as a (reified) trope of difference, is clearly relevant to an Asian American student of the double. Likewise JanMohamed's concept of the "manichean allegory" ("The Economy of Manichean Allegory"), though derived from African colonialist literature, also sheds light on the role Asian Americans play in the white imagination.

14. Kazuko's portrayal of her childhood self as a tomboy actually betrays this same hierarchy of values. In the female context, however, the gender-ethnicity nexus appears more muted; after all, it is more difficult to fault a girl for being "female" than for being "too Asian."

15. Shoyu is a particularly apt symbol of "Japaneseness" because of its rarity in the internment camps and the Issei's attachment to it. In *Nisei Daughter*, Kazuko's mother insists on bringing a can of the prized commodity to Camp Harmony, much to the mortification of her American-born children obsessed with appearing "normal" (Sone 1979:168).

16. Except, perhaps, in the connotation of cowardice in "chicken." However, other instances of chicken imagery in *Obasan* suggest that this connotation is peripheral.

17. The Ancient Mariner analogy is suggested by Hallam, who notes a common tendency for the first self to repeat the story of his symbolic crime against the double as "a (usually) ineffective therapeutic device" (1980:21).

18. This point becomes very clear when we contrast *FOB* with Hwang's *The Dance and the Railroad* (first performed in 1981) and *Family Devotions* (first performed in 1981), both of which also feature pairs of personages with symmetry of movement. In *Dance* Lone and Ma, two early Chinese immigrants, hold conflicting views of America. Even though, like Dale and Steve, they undergo a transformation and emerge with some of the other's traits at the end, there is no "disowning" on either side, hence no racial shadow. They are merely foils to each other (cf. Eder 1978:585–94). In *Family Devotions* we find several pairs of characters—Ama and Popo, their daughters Joanne and Hannah, and the daughters' husbands Wilbur and Robert; members of each pair are as undifferentiated as Tweedledee and Tweedledum. Hwang's intent here is simply to stress the pervasive materialism and resulting soullessness in certain segments of Asian American society. Self-fragmentation is not the issue.

19. For an account of the anti-Japanese movement, see Daniels (1988:100–54). Two earlier pieces of explicitly "alienating" legislation are the 1907–1908 "Gentlemen's Agreement" cutting off the influx of Japanese male laborers, and the California Alien Land Act of 1913 prohibiting land ownership by those ineligible for citizenship—that is, the Issei, whose success in agriculture threatened white farmers.

20. For a discussion of the "Nisei Dilemma," see Modell 1977:127–72, Daniels 1988:172–76, and Takaki 1989:212–29.

21. Here *myth* is used in Barthes's sense of "depoliticized speech," in "Myth Today" (Barthes 1972:142–45).

22. Of course, the trauma of internment does not shape the views of individual writers uniformly. Thus John Okada's *No-No Boy*, a novel first published in 1957 about a Japanese American young man jailed for not enlisting in the army, is much more emphatic in its detection and indictment of racism than Sone's book. Still, Okada seems to agree with Ichiro that his parents' refusal to acculturate is to a great extent responsible for his sorry predicament (Fujita 1986:102, 108). After the 1960s, such a judgment would probably have been rendered more tentatively or more critically.

Okada's renditions of the encounter with the racial shadow—Eto spitting on Ichiro (4); Bull humiliating Ichiro in the bar (74); Taro, Ichiro's younger brother, getting his friends to beat up his renegade kinsman (78–80); Bull hitting Freddie, another No-No Boy (246)—employ bifurcating terms of analysis even as the assimilationism underlying such terms is questioned.

23. In this light, even D. Chang's "The Oriental Contingent," whose brittle upper-class setting seems so remote from the world of political struggles, has been made possible by the Asian American movement. Ethnic has become chic.

24. The family reunification provision of the 1965 Immigration Act makes possible the entry of non-English-speaking, middle-aged immigrants with no immediately transferable skills, like those against whom Stuart rails so bitterly. For an overview of how new immigration patterns changed the social fabric and spirit of the Chinese American community, see Nee and Nee 1972:253–61.

25. Hwang, a relative latecomer, acknowledges a debt to Kingston (*The Woman Warrior*) and Frank Chin (*Gee, Pop!*) (Hwang 1983:3); both Kingston and Chin came of age in the 1960s, and both exert formative influences on younger writers by articulating vital issues in the Asian American experience.

26. The correct spelling of the name is Sui Sin Far.

27. I am grateful to Giulia Fabi, Lisa Lowe, and LaVonne Ruoff for suggesting much of the material in this discussion.

CHAPTER THREE
THE POLITICS OF MOBILITY

1. The term, taken from a 1670 sermon by Samuel Danforth, is the title of Perry Miller's classic study of Puritan thought.

2. Even Thoreau's *Walden*, despite its setting in a fixed locale and its insistence on inner spiritual renewal, can be placed in the frontier tradition (Fussell 1965:191–231).

3. I am indebted to Larry Howe for referring me to some useful titles on the American literature of travel.

4. I said *perception* and not *existence*, for the obvious reason that Native Americans have been conveniently relegated to the subhuman realm to legitimize the conviction of uninhibited freedom. As Boelhower observes: "The Pilgrim voyage was a didactic project with a prefabricated script, and even before setting foot in the new world, they already had an ethical vocabulary for classifying what they would see. . . . For all practical purposes, the white men were going to a place that they considered uninhabited, since the savages, being etymologically 'of the woods,' did not qualify as proprietors or inhabitants" (1987:58–59).

5. The former phrase is a quotation from Bliss Perry cited in Hazard 1927 (without full documentation).

6. Examples of the genre given by Stout include Emerson Hough's *The Covered Wagon* (1922), O. E. Rölvaag's *Giants in the Earth* (1927), Laura Ingalls Wilder's *Little House on the Prairie*, Steinbeck's *The Grapes of Wrath* (1939); and A. B. Guthrie's *The Way West* (1949).

7. In fact, even home-founding narratives are not free from ambiguity, as the endings of *Giants in the Earth* and *The Grapes of Wrath* indicate.

8. Hawaii's island geography, early plantation economy, and differential immigration policy toward Asians call for a separate discussion of mobility images, which will be provided in the section on Murayama's *All I Asking for Is My Body* (below).

9. There appears to be some disagreement amongst historians concerning the dates of the laws. Daniels (1988:138–45) and Takaki (1989:203–208) cite 1913 and 1920 as the dates of enactment of the alien land laws, while Lai and Choy (1973:99) cite 1913 and 1921.

10. I am indebted to Ruthanne Lum McCunn for this information.

11. In 1948, California voters rejected a ballot proposition that would have made the alien land laws harsher. In 1952, in the wake of the passage of the McCarran-Walter Immigration Act, which made Asians eligible for naturalization, the U.S. Supreme Court struck down the alien land laws as being unconstitutional (Daniels 1988:293–99). Finally, in 1956, California voters approved repeal of the laws (Takaki 1989:413).

12. The early chapters of Mary Paik Lee's autobiography, *Quiet Odyssey* (1990), contain some such images, but family issues are their main focus.

13. On how land was registered under corporations or American-born children, or owned through verbal agreement with whites with no legal binding power, see S. Chan (1986:420) and Ichioka (1988:237–40).

14. A number of histories note the many instances of "drivings-out" and massacres, e.g., Tsai (1986:67–72) and Daniels (1988:58–66). On the physical dangers of crossing prescribed boundaries, see Nee and Nee (60).

15. *Paper Angels* won the 1982 Downtown Village Award in New York where it played at the New Federal Theater. Lim adapted the play into a one-hour television drama, directed by John Lone, for American Playhouse in 1985.

16. The internment was later admitted by the government to be unjustified

by military necessity, which was the excuse given at the time; see *Personal Justice Denied*, esp. 18.

17. For a discussion of the phenomenon of picture brides, see Kim and Otani 1983:122–24 and Ichioka 1988:164–75.

18. For example, the mobility patterns of Korean Americans, South Asian Americans, and Southeast Asian Americans are left out of this account.

19. After making the distinction between first-order and second-order map-making in this section, I will assume that the context will make it clear which meaning of the term *map* is intended.

20. I am grateful to Caren Kaplan for allowing me to quote from her unpublished paper.

21. The date of composition of "Be American" is unknown. The story was published twenty-one years after his death.

22. Takaki notes that, on occasion, Filipinos worked for Japanese farmers (1989:321).

23. Because of its first-person point of view, *America Is in the Heart* has often been discussed as an autobiography. For the problematic nature of this designation, see E. Kim (1982:46–49) and especially Alquizola 1989.

24. I am indebted to Frances Loden, whose highly serviceable map of Carlos's wanderings prepared for a course first started me thinking about the mobility theme in Bulosan's book.

25. Alquizola believes that, given the work's contents, "we must conclude that the ideals of America must be 'in the heart' because they are not to be found within the geographical boundaries of this book" (1989:216).

26. In his letters, Bulosan noted the haste that characterized both the writing and the revision of *America Is In the Heart*. Writing to Leopoldo Yabes on 20 August 1946, Bulosan recalls that the writing of the autobiography took twenty-six days, while the revision took five days (1960:34).

27. Among other criteria of canonicity are sales figures over a long period. The University of Washington Press regards *America Is in the Heart* as one of its classic textbook titles. With 30,000 copies printed since 1974 and with sales of 28,000, the Press can safely say that the demand for the book has remained strong and steady over the past fifteen years. (This information was provided to me by a representative of the University of Washington Press in a telephone conversation on 10 September 1990.)

28. My thanks to Betty Bergland, whose paper, "Constructing Subjectivities in the New World: Reading Photographic Spaces in Mary Antin's Autobiography, *The Promised Land*," inspired my readings of Uchida. For a discussion of the significance of visual components in a text, see Genette's notion of the "paratext" (1982:9–10).

29. This point is reinforced by the image of Stephen hitting at butterflies with his crutch while "one butterfly he cannot see"—his soul?—"hover[s] above his head" (Kogawa 1982:123).

30. An analysis of Asian American fictional dwellings would make an interesting addition to Chandler's *Dwelling in the Text: Houses in American Fiction*, which deals mainly with Euro-American works.

31. Naomi is nearly drowned in a lake (148–49) but is rescued by Rough Lock Bill, a Noble Savage figure who offers a vision of natural justice free from concern with skin color (145).

32. I am indebted to Rachel Rodriguez and Saegwon Lee for this observation.

33. J. Chan et al.'s "Resources for Chinese and Japanese American Literary Traditions" (1981:22–24) provides the background information on, and fuller quotations from, the *Phrase Book*. *The Big Aiiieeeee!* reproduces the bilingual booklet in full (1991:93–110).

34. The legend of the Iron Moonhunter is not alluded to in any published source other than Frank Chin's works, Shawn Wong's *Homebase*, and a long out-of-print children's book, Kathy Chang's *Iron Moonhunter* (San Francisco: Children's Books Press, 1977). I am indebted to Laurence Yep, Harriet Rohmer (the editor of Children's Book Press), and Shawn Wong for their help in my efforts to track down the legend. According to Rohmer, *Iron Moonhunter* was written as part of CARP (Combined Asian Resources Project) and was supposedly based on oral history material never made public; Kathy Chang, the author of the story book, is Frank Chin's ex-wife. There seems to be a good possibility that Frank Chin invented the Iron Moonhunter legend.

35. Shawn Wong is a professional race car driver besides being a university professor; as the winner of the National Hot Rod Association 1984 Division Six Championship, Wong can himself lay claim to being a hero of locomotion (Moody 1986:6).

36. The character of Wang Chi-Yang, the father with the chronic cough in C. Y. Lee's *The Flower Drum Song* (1957), is an antecedent of Chin's dying Chinatown immigrants. Despite occupying antithetical ideological positions, Chin and Lee share this perception of "Chineseness" as an incurable chronic condition.

37. E. Kim feels that the central characters of "Food for All His Dead," "Yes, Young Daddy," and "Goong Hai Fot Choy" are "essentially the same" (1982: 181). My readings in this chapter likewise assume that Chin's male protagonists, while not entirely interchangeable, do share a basic affinity.

38. The work previously known to English speakers as *Water Margin* is a classic in Chinese literature based on oral tales; it depicts peasant heroes who form "righteous armies" to defy the corrupt imperial government. The earliest extant written version dates from the sixteenth century. Sidney Shapiro has translated this work under the title of *Outlaws of the Marsh* (1980).

39. Chin himself was the first Chinese brakeman on the South Pacific (Nee and Nee 377), a fact frequently noted in his autobiographical writing and publicity material. The brakeman's job is demanding and often dangerous; the romance of the brakeman's life continues even as the railroad system in the United States declines (e.g., Niemann 1990, writing from a woman's point of view).

40. If memory serves, I am indebted to Andrew Wiget for this formulation when he commented on papers presented at the MELUS-sponsored session, "The New Immigrants in Literature: Asia and Latin America," MLA Convention, 27–30 December, 1988, New Orleans.

41. My reading of "The Eat and Run Midnight People" is influenced by

Cecilia Wang's; she has kindly given me permission to draw on her unpublished paper.

42. Armand Singer cites the Biblical Mount Ararat or Mount Sinai, Grecian Mount Olympus, Navajo Mountain on the Arizona-Utah border, Mount Chomolungma (Mount Everest) of Tibet, and Alaska's Denali-McKinley, among others (1988:877).

43. See, for example, Shelley's "Mont Blanc" and Wordsworth's *The Prelude* (Book 6).

44. What is translated as *dance* in Peking opera is in fact closely related to the martial arts. Peking opera, unlike Western opera which emphasizes singing, is a composite form integrating music, choreographed movement, acrobatics, and spectacular stylized costumes and painted-on face masks.

45. Is the name meant to echo Estella in Dickens's *Great Expectations?* Given Santos's critique of social climbing, this suggestion may not be far-fetched.

46. For example, in James Welch's *Winter in the Blood* (1974), whose drifter-protagonist traverses empty distances physical as well as psychic; or in Leslie Silko's *Ceremony* (1977), where Tayo, the mixed-blood war veteran, returns to Indian land to embark upon a quest for healing (see Kenneth Lincoln's diagram on how Pueblo mythic space is mapped onto local geography [1985: 246–47]).

47. Scholarship on the mobility theme in African American literature will be discussed shortly.

48. For example, in Tomás Rivera's *... y no se lo tragó la tierra* (1971), about the life of migrant farmworkers; in Arturo Islas's *The Rain God* (1984), set in a Southwest bordertown, where inhabitants find cultural and spiritual boundaries more forbidding to cross than legal borders; or in Ana Castillo's *The Mixquiahuala Letters* (1986), in which two female *picaro* figures travel across the United States and throughout Mexico to test the social limits for women of color. Gloria Anzaldúa's *Borderlands/La Frontera: The New Mestiza* (1987) turns the borderlands into a metaphor for a new consciousness characterized by multiple identities and creative contradictions.

49. Giulia Fabi first drew my attention to this passage.

CHAPTER FOUR
THE ASIAN AMERICAN *HOMO LUDENS*

1. For a brief review of some theories on the condition of the modern bourgeois artist, see Schulte-Sasse 1984:vii–xxxix.

2. Carlos Bulosan's labor-organizing writer in *America Is in the Heart* is an obvious exception, as we shall see in the latter part of this chapter.

3. In this she shares a common lot with numerous other aspiring women writers throughout history; see Olsen 1978:6–21.

4. Also related, albeit obliquely in terms of the art theme, are Yamauchi's "And the Soul Shall Dance" (1966; rpt. 1974) and "The Handkerchief" (1961; rpt. 1977). For an account of Yamauchi's relationship with Yamamoto, see the former's statement in F. Chin et al. 1974a:191–92, and McDonald and Newman 1980.

5. The term *Kibei* refers to a Japanese born in America but educated in Japan.

6. In such a framework of understanding, neglect of appearance, as in the case of Mr. Kato or the old Japanese worker, becomes a sign of virtue.

7. Exclusion was in effect from 1882 to 1943; Fred has to be "sneaked in" (F. Chin 1981:109), most likely as a "paper son." In 1922 the Cable Act was passed, according to which any female U.S. citizen marrying a Chinese would lose her citizenship. Hence Ma's remark on the threat of deportation for marrying Pa (99–100). In 1924 alien wives of U.S. citizens of Chinese descent were banned from entry; this restriction was not lifted until after World War II. That is why China Mama joins Pa so late in life. Mattie (or Sis), born in 1938, is referred to as a "very limited edition" (73) because Chinese families were so rare during the pre-1965 period.

8. Jade Snow Wong's vindication at the end of *Fifth Chinese Daughter* is precisely in these terms: she is finally appreciated by the patriarch because she is making money from her pottery—play is now work. Note that while the ceramics studio appears to be a matter of individual enterprise, not subject to institutional gatekeeping as in the publishing industry, and that Jade Snow's art has no overt "ethnic" content, it is still through self-display as a curiosity (her studio is open to public view) and white sponsorship (encouragement of white patrons, customers) that the young woman has been able to succeed. I am indebted to Christine So for pointing out the relevance of *Fifth Chinese Daughter* to this chapter.

9. Note, however, that on this point Caillois makes a distinction between play and art, which may result in products. In play, "nothing has been harvested or manufactured, no masterpiece has been created, no capital has accrued" (1961:5).

10. See Spariosu, however, for a further deconstruction of Ehrmann's deconstruction: "one can argue that in spite of his radical language, he appears, through his concept of play as generator of culture and reality, to be (no doubt "unconsciously") a spokesman for the ideology of advanced capitalism" (1982: 40).

11. Even for Kant, the valorization of play is not final and absolute. Spariosu notes: "Kant distinguishes between 'heuristic' or good fictions and 'mere play' or bad fictions, on the ground that the former serve some kind of 'purpose,' while the latter do not. Then he further distinguishes between truly purposeless (irrational) fictions and fictions which exhibit 'purposiveness without purpose'. . . . The latter category appears as the second term in a binary opposition between work and play . . . [which] seems at first to be privileged, in the form of art, over practical activity or 'work.' However, *art soon turns out to be nothing more than a 'higher' kind of work*, because it serves the 'higher' purpose of (moral) Nature" (1982:23; my italics). What renders this Kantian formulation inappropriate for reading Asian American examples of artistic play is its depoliticization, its cutting adrift of categories like "purpose" or "moral" from their sociopolitical moorings.

12. The characters transliterated as *lone* and *ma*, incidentally, refer to the dragon and the horse, two animals in the "Chinese zodiac" traditionally associated with abundance of vitality.

13. The biological basis for such a view is discussed in Millar 1968:13–58, 243–56.

14. This analysis takes its cue from Derrida's deconstruction of "supplementarity" in Rousseau; see Culler 1982:102–104.

15. Portions of this section have appeared in my "Necessity and Extravagance in Maxine Hong Kingston's *The Woman Warrior*: Art and the Ethnic Experience."

16. For the plight of "Gold Mountain wives," see Hom 1987:43–50, 111–13, 118–47; for the historical causes of lengthy separation between Chinese immigrant men and their wives, see Yung 1986:11, 42.

17. The double meaning of *playing* in this phrase, even if unintended, serves to underscore the thematic opposition between work and play.

18. There seems to be an echo of Western Golden Age myths here, e.g., Hesiod's description of early mortals who "lived as if they were gods"; see Spariosu's explication (1982:16).

19. For a survey of critical opinions on this point, see my "Autobiography as Guided Chinatown Tour?"

20. This influence is briefly discussed in my "Kingston's Handling of Traditional Chinese Sources" (1991a).

21. The Monkey King is the central figure in *The Journey to the West*, the sixteenth-century Chinese novel commonly attributed to Wu Chengen; Anthony Yu provides a complete translation. The recent coincidence of interest in the Monkey King as trickster among non-Anglo writers like Kingston, Timothy Mo, and Gerald Vizenor is interesting and merits investigation.

22. This use of the word *performative* alludes to J. L. Austin's notion of "performative verbs," such as *promise*, utterance of which constitutes accomplishment of the intended act (1962:4ff.).

23. For example, Chin maintains in "This Is Not an Autobiography": "the fighter writer uses literary forms as weapons of war, not the expression of ego alone, and does not fuck around wasting time with dandyish expressions of feeling and psychological attitudinizing. The individual is found in the act of war, of not selling out, not in feelings" (1985:112).

24. Many post-1965 Asian immigrants come in not only highly educated in their native languages but also already proficient in English. However, with a handful of exceptions, artistic creation using English is the province of the American-born. Immigrant literature and art would require a separate study.

WORKS CITED

This list excludes non–Asian American literary works mentioned in the text but not quoted from. The original date refers to first year of publication or performance of the work; subsequent dates are given for reprints or collection volumes (often the source for citations in the main text and notes to this book).

Abrahams, Roger. 1984. "Equal Opportunity Eating: A Structural Excursus on Things of the Mouth." In Brown and Mussell, 19–36.

Ai. 1987. *Cruelty/Killing Floor*. New York: Thunder's Mouth Press.

———. *Fate*. 1991. Boston: Houghton Mifflin.

Alexander, Meena. 1987. *House of a Thousand Doors*. Washington: Three Continents.

———. 1991. *Nampally Road*. San Francisco: Mercury House.

Allen, Walter. 1969. *The Urgent West: The American Dream and Modern Man*. New York: E. P. Dutton.

Allis, Sam. 1991. "Kicking the Nerd Syndrome." *Time*, 25 March: 65–66.

Alquizola, Marilyn. 1989. "The Fictive Narrator of *America is in the Heart*." In Nomura et al., 211–17.

———. 1990. "The Woman in David Henry Hwang's *M. Butterfly*: The Othered of the Stage/Page." Paper presented at the Building Bridges: Race, Class and Gender—Feminisms Across the Disciplines Conference, October, at the University of California, Berkeley.

Asian Women United of California, ed. 1989. *Making Waves: An Anthology of Writings by and about Asian American Women*. Boston: Beacon Press.

Austin, J. L. 1962. *How to Do Things with Words*. Cambridge: Harvard University Press.

Azores, Fortunata M. 1979. "Census Methodology and the Development of Social Indicators for Asian and Pacific Americans." In *Civil Rights Issues of Asian and Pacific Americans: Myths and Realities*, 46–101. A consultation sponsored by the United States Commission on Civil Rights, 8–9 May, Washington, D.C.

Bacho, Peter. 1991. *Cebu*. Seattle: University of Washington Press.

Baker, Houston A., Jr. 1984. *Blues, Ideology, and Afro-American Literature: A Vernacular Theory*. Chicago: University of Chicago Press.

Bakhtin, Mikhail. 1984. *Rabelais and His World*. Translated by Helene Iswolsky. Bloomington: Indiana University Press. Translation of Tvorchestvo Fransua Rable (Moscow: Khudozhestvennia literatura, 1965).

Barthes, Roland. 1957. "Myth Today." In *Mythologies*, 58–64. Translated by Annette Lavers. New York: Noonday, 1972.

Baudrillard, Jean. 1975. *The Mirror of Production*. Translated by Mark Foster. St. Louis: Telos.

Bell, David. 1985. "The Triumph of Asian Americans." *New Republic* (July): 24–31.

Bergland, Betty. 1990. "Constructing Subjectivities in the New World: Reading Photographic Spaces in Mary Antin's Autobiography, *The Promised Land*." Paper presented at the MELUS Convention, Division on Ethnic Literature and the Arts, 21 April, Chicago.

Berman, Jeffery. 1988. "Personality (Double-Split-Multiple)." In Signeuret, 963–70.

Berman, Paul, ed. 1992. *Debating P.C.: The Controversy over Political Correctness on College Campuses*. New York: Laurel.

Berson, Misha, ed. 1990. *Between Worlds: Contemporary Asian American Plays*. New York: Theatre Communications Group.

Bevan, David, ed. 1988. *Literary Gastronomy*. Amsterdam: Rodopi.

Birchall, Ian H. 1977. "Marxism and Literature." In *The Sociology of Literature: Theoretical Approaches*, edited by Jane Routh and Janet Wolff, 92–108. Sociological Review Monograph, no. 25.

Bluefarb, Sam. 1972. *The Escape Motif in the American Novel: Mark Twain to Richard Wright*. Columbus: Ohio State University Press.

Blum, Joanne. 1988. *Transcending Gender: The Male/Female Double in Women's Fiction*. Ann Arbor: University of Michigan Research Press.

Boelhower, William. 1982. *Immigrant Autobiography in the United States*. Verona: Essedue Edizioni.

———. 1984. *Through a Glass Darkly: Ethnic Semiosis in American Literature*. New York: Oxford University Press, 1987.

Bonacich, Edna, and John Modell. 1980. *The Economic Basis of Ethnic Solidarity: Small Business in the Japanese American Community*. Berkeley: University of California Press.

Brown, James W. 1984. *Fictional Meals and Their Function in the French Novel, 1798–1848*. Toronto: University of Toronto Press.

———, ed. N.d. "Littérature et Nourriture." *Dalhousie French Studies* 11: 4–7.

Brown, Linda, and Kay Mussell. 1984. *Ethnic and Regional Foodways in the United States: The Performance of Group Identity*. Knoxville: University of Tennessee Press.

Bulosan, Carlos. 1943. *America Is in the Heart*. Seattle: University of Washington Press, 1973.

———. 1960. *Sound of Falling Light: Letters in Exile*. Quezon City: Dolores S. Feria.

———. 1977. "Be American." *Amerasia Journal* 4, no. 1: 157–63.

Caillois, Roger. 1961. *Man, Play, and Games*. Translated by Meyer Barash. New York: Free Press of Glencoe.

Carby, Hazel V. 1987. *Reconstructing Womanhood: The Emergence of the Afro-American Woman Novelist*. New York: Oxford University Press.

Carter, Dale. 1988. *The Final Frontier: The Rise and Fall of the American Rocket State*. London: Verso.

Cha, Theresa Hak Kyung. 1982. *Dictee*. New York: Tanam.

Chan, Jeffery Paul, Frank Chin, Lawson Inada, and Shawn Wong. 1981. "Resources for Chinese and Japanese American Literary Traditions." *Amerasia Journal* 8, no. 1: 19–31.

———, eds. 1991. *The Big Aiiieeeee! An Anthology of Chinese American and Japanese American Literature*. New York: Meridian.

Chan, Sucheng. 1986. *This Bittersweet Soil: The Chinese in California Agriculture*. Berkeley: University of California Press.

———. 1991. *Asian Americans: An Interpretive History*. Boston: Twayne.

Chandler, Marilyn R. 1991. *Dwelling in the Text: Houses in American Fiction*. Berkeley: University of California Press.

Chang, Diana. 1989. "The Oriental Contingent." In Lim and Tsutakawa, 171–77.

Chang, Kwang-chih, ed. 1977. *Food in Chinese Culture: Anthropological and Historical Perspectives*. New Haven: Yale University Press.

Chang, Williamson B. C. 1989. "*M. Butterfly*: Passivity, Deviousness and the Invisibility of the Asian American Male." Paper presented at the Association for Asian American Studies Conference, 3–4 June, Hunter College, New York.

Chen, Edward, and Wode Henderson. 1987. "The 'English-Only' Movement." *East Wind* (Spring/Summer): 2–5.

Chen, Jack. 1981. *The Chinese of America*. San Francisco: Harper and Row.

Cheong, Fiona. 1991. *Scent of the Gods*. New York: Norton.

Cheung, King-Kok. 1986. "Bienvenido Santos: Filipino Oldtimers in Literature." *Markham Review* 15: 49–53.

———. 1988. "'Don't Tell': Imposed Silences in *The Color Purple* and *The Woman Warrior*." *PMLA* 103, no. 2: 162–74.

Cheung, King-Kok, and Stan Yogi. 1988. *Asian American Literature: An Annotated Bibliography*. New York: Modern Language Association.

Chin, Frank. 1962. "Food for All His Dead." In Hsu and Palubinskas, 48–61.

———. 1970. "A Chinese Lady Dies." In *The Chinaman Pacific*, 109–30.

———. 1976a. "Backtalk." In *Counterpoint: Perspectives on Asian America*, edited by Emma Gee, 556–57. Los Angeles: Asian American Studies Center, University of California.

———. 1976b. "The Eat and Run Midnight People." In *The Chinaman Pacific*, 8–23.

———. 1978. "Railroad Standard Time." In *The Chinaman Pacific*, 1–7.

———. 1981. *"The Chickencoop Chinaman" and "The Year of the Dragon": Two Plays*. Seattle: University of Washington Press.

———. 1985. "This Is Not an Autobiography." *Genre* 18, no. 2: 109–30.

———. 1988. *The Chinaman Pacific and Frisco R.R. Co.* Minneapolis: Coffee House Press.

———. 1989. "Letter to the Editor." *The New Asian Times* 1, no. 5: 9.

———. 1991a. "Come All Ye Asian American Writers of the Real and the Fake." In J. Chan et al. (1991), 1–92.

———. 1991b. *Donald Duk*. Minneapolis: Coffee House Press.

Chin, Frank, and Jeffery Paul Chan. 1972. "Racist Love." In *Seeing through Shuck*, edited by Richard Kostelanetz, 39–52. New York: Ballantine.

Chin, Frank, Jeffery Paul Chan, Lawson Fusao Inada, and Shawn Wong, eds. 1974a. *Aiiieeeee! An Anthology of Asian-American Writers*. Washington, D.C.: Howard University Press, 1983.

———. 1974b. Introduction. In Chin et al., xxi–xlviii.

Chin, Marilyn. 1987. *Dwarf Bamboo*. Greenfield Center, N.Y.: Greenfield Review Press.

Chin, Marilyn. 1989. "Writing the Other: A Conversation with Maxine Hong Kingston" (interview). *Poetry Flash* (September): 1, 4–6, 17–18.

Chin, Marilyn, and David Wong Louie, eds. 1991. *Dissident Song.* A special issue of *Quarry West.* Santa Cruz: Porter College, University of California at Santa Cruz.

Chin, Woon-Ping. 1992. *The Naturalization of Camellia Song* (poems and a performance piece). Singapore: Times Books International.

Chock, Eric. 1990. *Last Days Here.* Honolulu: Bamboo Ridge Press.

Chock, Eric, and Darrell H. Y. Lum, eds. 1986. *The Best of Bamboo Ridge.* Honolulu: Bamboo Ridge Press.

Christian, Barbara. 1985. *Black Feminist Criticism: Perspectives on Black Women Writers.* New York: Pergamon.

Chuang, Hua. 1968. *Crossings.* Boston: Northeastern University Press, 1986.

Chung, C., A. Kim, and A. K. Lemeshewsky, eds. 1987. *Between the Lines: An Anthology by Pacific/Asian Lesbians of Santa Cruz.* Santa Cruz: Dancing Bird Press.

Clough, Wilson O. 1964. *The Necessary Earth: Nature and Solitude in American Literature.* Austin: University of Texas Press.

Coates, Paul. 1988. *The Double and the Other: Identity as Ideology in Post-Romantic Fiction.* Houndsmill and London: MacMillan.

Crawley, A. E. 1908. "Doubles." In *Encyclopedia of Religion and Ethics*, 853–60. New York: Scribner's.

Culler, Jonathan. 1982. *On Deconstruction: Theory and Criticism after Structuralism.* Ithaca, N.Y.: Cornell University Press.

Daniels, Roger. 1988. *Asian America: Chinese and Japanese in the United States since 1850.* Seattle: University of Washington Press.

Davidson, Cathy N., and E. M. Broner, eds. 1980. *The Lost Tradition: Mothers and Daughters in Literature.* New York: Frederick Ungar.

Dearborn, Mary. 1986. *Pocahontas's Daughters: Gender and Ethnicity in American Culture.* New York: Oxford University Press.

Democracy Betrayed: The Case for Redress. 1984. A Submission to the Government of Canada on the Violation of Rights and Freedoms of Japanese Canadians during and after World War II. Canada: National Association of Japanese Canadians, 1985.

Der, Henry, and Colleen Lye, eds. 1989. *The Broken Ladder '89: Asian Americans in City Government.* San Francisco: Chinese for Affirmative Action.

Dirlik, Arif. 1987. "Culturalism as Hegemonic Ideology and Liberating Practice." *Cultural Critique* 6 (Spring): 13–50.

Divakaruni, Chitra Banerjee. 1990. *The Reason for Nasturtiums.* Berkeley, Calif.: Berkeley Poets Workshop and Press.

———. 1991. *Black Candles.* Corvallis, Oreg.: Calyx.

Douglas, Mary. 1972. "Deciphering a Meal." *Daedalus* 101, no. 1: 61–81.

Dunn, Ashley Sheun. 1978. "No Man's Land." *Amerasia Journal* 5, no. 2: 109–33.

Eakin, Paul John. 1985. *Fictions in Autobiography: Studies in the Art of Self-Invention.* Princeton: Princeton University Press.

Eder, Doris L. 1978. "The Idea of the Double." *The Psychoanalytic Review* 65: 579–614.

Ehrmann, Jacques. 1968. "*Homo Ludens* Revisited." *Yale French Studies* 41: 31–57.

Elliott, Emory, et al., eds. 1988. *Columbia Literary History of the United States.* New York: Columbia University Press.

Erdrich, Louise. 1988. *Tracks.* New York: Perennial Library/Harper and Row, 1989.

Evans, Earnestine. 1950. "A Chinese-American Girl's Two Worlds." *New York Herald Tribune Book Review,* 24 September: 4.

Fanon, Franz. 1952. *Black Skin, White Masks.* New York: Grove, 1967.

Feldman, Gayle. 1991. "Spring's Five Fictional Encounters of the Chinese American Kind." *Publishers Weekly* 239, no. 8 (8 February): 25–27.

Ferraro, Thomas Joseph. 1988. "Ethnic Passages: The Mobility Narratives of Yezierska, Miller, Puzo, and Kingston." Ph.D. diss., Yale University.

Fink, Eugen. 1968. "The Oasis of Happiness: Toward an Ontology of Play." *Yale French Studies* 41: 19–30.

Folsom, James K. 1966. *The American Western Novel.* New Haven: College and University Press.

Fox-Genovese, Elizabeth. 1990. "Between Individualism and Fragmentation: American Culture and the New Literary Studies of Race and Gender." *American Quarterly* 42, no. 1: 7–34.

Frazer, Sir James. 1959. *The New Golden Bough.* Edited by Theodore H. Gaster. New York: New American Library, 1964.

Freud, Sigmund. 1919. "The Uncanny." In *Studies in Parapsychology,* 20–28. *The Collected Papers of Sigmund Freud.* New York: Collier, 1971.

Fujita, Gayle Kimi. 1986. "The 'Ceremonial Self' in Japanese American Literature." Ph.D. diss., Brown University.

Fuss, Diana. 1989. *Essentially Speaking: Feminism, Nature and Difference.* New York: Routledge.

Fussell, Edwin. 1965. *Frontier: American Literature and the American West.* Princeton: Princeton University Press.

Gates, Henry Louis, Jr. 1987. *Figures in Black: Words, Signs and the "Racial" Self.* New York: Oxford University Press.

———. 1989. "Color me Zora: Alice Walker's (Re)writing of the Speakerly Text." In O'Donnell and Davis, ix–xxii.

Geertz, Clifford. 1973. *The Interpretation of Cultures.* New York: Basic Books.

Genette, Gerard. 1982. *Palimpsestes: La littérature au second degré.* Paris: Editions du Seuil.

Gilbert, Sandra M., and Susan Gubar, eds. 1985. *The Norton Anthology of Literature by Women: The Tradition in English.* New York: Norton.

Gonzalez, N.V.M. 1993. *Bread of Salt and Other Stories.* Seattle: University of Washington Press.

Govier, Katherine. 1981. *Toronto Star,* 20 June: F11.

Guerard, Albert J., ed. 1967. "Concepts of the Double." In *Stories of the Double,* 1–14. Philadelphia: Lippincott.

Hahn, Kimiko. 1989. *Air Pocket.* Brooklyn, N.Y.: Hanging Loose Press.

Hagedorn, Jessica. 1990. *Dogeaters.* New York: Pantheon.

Hallam, Clifford. 1980. "The Double as Incomplete Self: Toward a Definition of Doppelgänger." In *Fearful Symmetry: Doubles and Doubling in Literature and Film* (Proceedings of the Florida State University Conference on Literature and Film), edited by Eugene J. Crook. Tallahassee: University of Florida Press, 1980.

Hans, James S. 1981. *The Play of the World*. Amherst: University of Massachusetts Press.

Hawthorn, Jeremy. 1983. *Multiple Personality and the Disintegration of Literary Character: From Oliver Goldsmith to Sylvia Plath*. London: Arnold.

Hayslip, Le Ly (with Jay Wurts). 1989. *When Heaven and Earth Changed Places: A Vietnamese Woman's Journey from War to Peace*. New York: Doubleday.

Hazard, Lucy Lockwood. 1927. *The Frontier in American Literature*. New York: Thomas Y. Crowell.

Hirsch, Marianne. 1989. *The Mother/Daughter Plot: Narrative, Psychoanalysis, Feminism*. Bloomington: Indiana University Press.

Hom, Marlon K. 1987. *Songs of Gold Mountain: Cantonese Rhymes from San Francisco Chinatown*. Berkeley: University of California Press.

Hong, Grace, James M. Lee, David H. Maruyama, Jim Soong, and Gary Yee, eds. 1991. *Burning Cane*. A Special Issue of *Amerasia Journal* 17, no. 2.

Hongo, Garrett. 1988. *The River of Heaven*. New York: Knopf.

hooks, bell. 1990. *Yearning: Race, Gender, and Cultural Politics*. Boston: South End Press.

Hoxie, Frederick E., ed. 1988. *Indians in American History: An Introduction*. Arlington Heights, Ill.: Harlan Davidson.

Hsia, Jayjia. 1988. *Asian Americans in Higher Education and Work*. Hillsdale, N.J.: Lawrence Erlbaum.

Hsu, Kai-yu, and Helen Palubinskas, eds. 1972. *Asian-American Authors*. Boston: Houghton Mifflin, 1976.

Huffman, Ivy, and Julia Kwong. 1991. *The Dream of Gold Mountain*. Winnipeg: Hyperion Press.

Huizinga, J. 1950. *Homo Ludens: A Study of the Play Element in Culture*. Boston: Beacon Press, 1955.

Humphrey, Theodore C., and Lin T. Humphrey, eds. 1988. *"We Gather Together": Food and Festival in American Life*. Ann Arbor: University of Michigan Research Press.

Hune, Shirley, Hyung-chan Kim, Stephen S. Fugita, and Amy Ling, eds. 1991. *Asian Americans: Comparative and Global Perspectives*. Pullman: Washington State University Press.

Hwang, David Henry. 1979 (first performed). *FOB*. In *Broken Promises*, 3–57.

———. 1981a (first performed). *The Dance and the Railroad*. In *Broken Promises*, 59–99.

———. 1981b (first performed). *Family Devotions*. In *Broken Promises*, 101–68.

———. 1983. *Broken Promises: Four Plays*. New York: Avon.

———. 1988. (first performed). *M. Butterfly*. New York: NAL-Dutton, 1989.

Ichioka, Yuji. 1988. *The Issei: The World of the First-Generation Japanese Immigrants, 1885–1924*. New York: Free Press; London: Collier Macmillan.

Ignacio. Lemuel F. 1976. *Asian Americans and Pacific Islanders (Is There Such an Ethnic Group?)*. San Jose, Calif.: Pilipino Development Associates.

Inada, Lawson Fusao. 1985. "Standing on Seventh Street: Introduction to the 1985 Edition." *Yokohama, California* (by Toshio Mori). Seattle: University of Washington Press.

Ishikawa, Yoshimi. 1991. *Strawberry Road: A Japanese Immigrant Discovers America"* [Sutoberi rodo]. Translated by Eve Zimmerman. Harrisonburg, Va.: R. R. Donnelly. Originally published by Kodansha International, Tokyo.

Jackson, J. H. 1950. Review of *Fifth Chinese Daughter* by Jade Snow Wong. *San Francisco Chronicle*, 20 September: 20.

JanMohamed, Abdul. 1985. "The Economy of Manichean Allegory: The Function of Racial Difference in Colonialist Literature." *Critical Inquiry* 12, no. 1: 59–87.

JanMohamed, Abdul, and David Lloyd. 1990a. "Introduction: Toward a Theory of Minority Discourse: What Is to Be Done?" In 1990b:1–16.

———, eds. 1990b. *The Nature and Context of Minority Discourse.* New York: Oxford University Press.

Jay, Gregory S. 1988. "American Literature and the New Historicism: The Example of Frederick Douglass." The University of Wisconsin–Milwaukee Center for Twentieth Century Studies Working Papers, no. 10 (Fall).

Jen, Gish. 1991. *Typical American.* Boston: Houghton Mifflin.

Kadohata, Cynthia. 1989. *The Floating World.* New York: Viking.

———. 1992. *In the Heart of the Valley of Love.* New York: Viking.

Kalcik, Susan. 1984. "Ethnic Foodways in America: Symbol and the Performance of Identity." In Brown and Mussell, 37–65.

Kan, Stephen H., and William T. Liu. 1986. "The Educational Status of Asian Americans: An Update from the 1980 Census." *Pacific/Asian American Mental Health Research Center Research Review* 5, nos. 3/4: 21–24.

Kanazawa, Tooru J. 1989. *Sushi and Sourdough.* Seattle: University of Washington Press.

Kaneko, Lonny. 1976. "The Shoyu Kid." *Amerasia Journal* 3, no. 2: 1–9.

———. 1986. *Coming Home from Camp.* Waldron Island, Wash.: Brooding Heron Press.

Kang, Younghill. 1937. *East Goes West: The Making of an Oriental Yankee.* New York: Scribner's.

Kaplan, Caren. 1989. "Remapping or Retelling History? The Politics of Location and the Poetics of Displacement." Paper presented at the Modern Language Association Convention, Division on English Literature Other Than British and American, 29 December, Washington, D.C.

Katrak, Ketu H., and R. Radhakrishnan, eds. 1988–89. *Desh-Videsh: South Asian Expatriate Writing and Art.* A Special Issue of the *Massachusetts Review* 29, no. 4 (Winter).

Kelly, Nancy Webb. 1988. "Homo Ludens, Homo Aestheticus: The Transformation of 'Free Play' in the Rise of Literary Criticism." Ph.D. diss., Stanford University.

Kepner, Susan. 1989. "Imagine This: The Amazing Adventure of Amy Tan." *San Francisco Focus* (May): 58–60, 160–62.

Keppler, C. F. 1972. *The Literature of the Second Self.* Tucson: University of Arizona Press.

Kikumura, Akemi. 1991. *Promises Kept: The Life of an Issei Man*. Novato, Calif.: Chandler and Sharp.

Kim, Elaine H. 1981. "Visions and Fierce Dreams: A Commentary on the Works of Maxine Hong Kingston." *Amerasia Journal* 8, no. 2: 145–61.

———. 1982. *Asian American Literature: An Introduction to the Writings and Their Social Context*. Philadelphia: Temple University Press.

———, ed. 1992. *Writing Self, Writing Nation: A Collection of Essays on Theresa Hak Kyung Cha's "Dictee."* Berkeley: Third Woman Press.

Kim, Elaine H., and Janice Otani, eds. 1983. *With Silk Wings*. Oakland: Asian Women United of California.

Kim, Ronyoung. 1986. *Clay Walls*. New York: Permanent Press.

Kim, Willyce. 1988. *Dead Heat*. Boston: Alyson.

Kingston, Maxine Hong. 1976. *The Woman Warrior: Memoirs of a Girlhood among Ghosts*. New York: Vintage Books, 1977.

———. 1980. *China Men*. New York: Ballantine, 1981.

———. 1989. *Tripmaster Monkey: His Fake Book*. New York: Knopf.

Kitagawa, Muriel. 1985. *This is My Own: Letters to Wes and Other Writings on Japanese Canadians, 1941–48*. Edited by Roy Miki. Vancouver: Talonbooks.

Kogawa, Joy. 1981. *Obasan*. Boston: David Godine, 1982.

———. 1992. *Itsuka*. New York: Viking Penguin.

Kolodny, Annette. 1975. *The Lay of the Land: Metaphor as Experience and History in American Life and Letters*. Chapel Hill: University of North Carolina Press.

———. 1984. *The Land Before Her: Fantasy and Experience of the American Frontiers, 1630–1860*. Chapel Hill: University of North Carolina Press.

Kristeva, Julia. 1980. *Desire in Language: A Semiotic Approach to Literature and Art*. Edited by Leon S. Roudiez. Translated by Alice Jardine Thomas Gora and Leon S. Roudiez. New York: Columbia University Press.

Kuo, Alex. 1986. *Changing the River*. Berkeley, Calif.: Reed and Cannon.

Lai, H. Mark, and Philip Choy. 1972. *Outlines: History of the Chinese in America*. San Francisco: Chinese-American Studies Planning Group, 1973.

Lai, Him Mark, Joe Huang, and Don Wong. 1980. *The Chinese of America, 1785–1980*. San Francisco: Chinese Culture Foundation.

Larsen, Wanwadee. 1989. *Confessions of a Mail Order Bride*. New York: Harper Collins.

Larson, Louise Leung. 1989. *Sweet Bamboo: Saga of a Chinese American Family*. Los Angeles: Chinese Historical Society of Southern California.

Lau, Evelyn. 1989. *Runaway: Diary of a Street Kid*. Toronto: Harper Collins.

———. 1990. *You Are Not Who You Claim*. Victoria, British Columbia: Porcepic Books.

Lau, Joseph S. M. 1980. "Tangrenjie de xiaoshuo shijie [The fictional world of Chinatown]." *Ming Pao Monthly* 173: 63–68.

Lauter, Paul. 1990. "The Literatures of America: A Comparative Discipline." In *Redefining American Literary History*, edited by A. LaVonne Brown Ruoff and Jerry Ward, 9–34. New York: MLA.

———. 1991. *Canons and Contexts*. New York: Oxford University Press.

Lauter, Paul, et al., eds. 1990. *The Heath Anthology of American Literature*. Lexington, Mass.: D.C. Heath.

Law-Yone, Wendy. 1983. *The Coffin Tree*. New York: Knopf.

Lee, Bennett, and Jim Wong-Chu, eds. 1991. *Many Mouthed Birds: Contemporary Writing by Chinese Canadians*. Vancouver: Douglas and McIntyre; Seattle: University of Washington Press.

Lee, Lee C., ed. 1992. *Asian Americans: Collages of Identities*. Cornell Asian American Studies Monograph Series, no. 1. Ithaca, N.Y.: Cornell University Press.

Lee, C. Y. 1957. *The Flower Drum Song*. New York: Farrar.

Lee, Gus. 1991. *China Boy*. New York: Dutton.

Lee, Li-Young. 1986. *Rose*. Brockport, N.Y.: Boa Editions.

———. 1990. *The City in Which I Love You*. Brockport, N.Y.: Boa Editions.

Lee, Mary Paik. 1990. *Quiet Odyssey: A Pioneer Korean American Woman in America*. Edited with an introduction by Sucheng Chan. Seattle: University of Washington Press.

Lee, Sky. 1990. *Disappearing Moon Cafe*. Vancouver: Douglas and McIntyre, 1991.

Lee, Virginia Chin-lan. 1963. *The House That Tai Ming Built*. New York: Macmillan.

Leong, Monfoon. 1975. "New Year for Fong Wing." In *Number One Son*, 3–16. San Francisco: East/West Publishing, 1975.

Lesser, Jeff H. 1985–86. "Always 'Outsiders': Asians, Naturalization, and the Supreme Court." *Amerasia Journal* 12, no. 1: 83–100.

Lévi-Strauss, Claude. 1966. "The Culinary Triangle." *Partisan Review* 7, no. 6: 586–95.

Lewis, R. W. B. 1955. *The American Adam*. Chicago: University of Chicago Press.

Li, David. 1988. "The Naming of a Cross-Cultural 'I': Cross-cultural Sign/ifications in *The Woman Warrior*." *Criticism* 30: 497–515.

Lim, Genny. 1989. *Winter Place*. San Francisco: Kearny Street Workshop.

———. 1991. *Paper Angels and Bitter Cane: Two Plays*. Honolulu: Kalamaku Press.

Lim, Paul Stephen. 1992. *Figures in Clay: A Threnody in Six Scenes and a Coda*. Louisville, Ky.: Aran.

———. 1992. *Mother Tongue: A Play*. Louisville, Ky.: Aran.

Lim, Shirley Geok-lin. 1988. *Modern Secrets*. London: Dangaroo.

———. 1990. "Always Already in Intersection: Feminist and Ethnic Literary Theories in the Quarrel of Asian American Writing." Paper presented at the Fourth Annual MELUS Conference, 20 April, at the University of Illinois, Chicago.

———, ed. 1991. *Approaches to Teaching Kingston's "The Woman Warrior."* New York: Modern Language Association.

Lim, Shirley Geok-lin, and Amy Ling, eds. 1992. *Reading the Literatures of Asian America*. Philadelphia: Temple University Press.

Lim, Shirley Geok-lin, and Mayumi Tsutakawa, eds. 1989. *The Forbidden Stitch: An Asian American Women's Anthology*. Corvallis, Oreg.: Calyx.

Lin, Alice P. 1988. *Grandmother Had No Name*. San Francisco: China Books and Periodicals.

Lin, Yutang. 1937. *The Importance of Living*. New York: John Day.

Lin, Yutang. 1937. *My Country and My People*. New York: Reynal and Hitch-cock.

Lincoln, Kenneth. 1983; 2d ed., 1985. *Native American Renaissance*. Los An-geles: University of California Press.

Ling, Amy. 1990. *Between Worlds: Women Writers of Chinese Ancestry*. New York: Pergamon.

Liu, Melinda. 1991. "Pass a Snake, Hold the Rat: A Guide to Chinese Food You Can't Get in Takeout." *Newsweek*, 29 July: 35.

Lo, Steven C. 1989. *The Incorporation of Eric Chung*. Chapel Hill, N.C.: Algon-quin Books.

Loewen, James W. 1971 (2d ed.). *The Mississippi Chinese: Between Black and White*. Prospect Heights, Ill.: Waveland, 1988.

Loo, Chalsa. 1989. "*M. Butterfly*: A Feminist Perspective." Paper presented at the Association for Asian American Studies Conference, 3–5 June, Hunter College, New York.

Louie, David Wong. 1991. "Displacement." In *Pangs of Love*, 18–35.

———. 1991. *Pangs of Love*. New York: Knopf.

Lowe, Lisa. 1990. "Rethinking Essentialisms: Gender and Ethnicity in Amy Tan's *The Joy Luck Club*." Paper presented at the American Literature Associ-ation Conference on American Literature, 2 June, San Diego.

———. 1991. "Heterogeneity, Hybridity, Multiplicity: Marking Asian Ameri-can Differences." *Diaspora* 1, no. 1 (Spring): 24–44.

Lowe, Pardee. 1943. *Father and Glorious Descendant*. Boston: Little, Brown.

Lowry, Ira S. 1982. "The Science and Politics of Ethnic Enumeration." In *Eth-nicity and Public Policy*, edited by Winston A. Van Horne and Thomas V. Tonnesen, 42–62. Milwaukee, Wis.: University of Wisconsin System Ameri-can Ethnic Studies Coordinating Committee/Urban Corridor Consortium.

Lu, Xun. 1990. *Diary of a Madman and Other Stories*. Translated by William A. Lyell. Honolulu: University of Hawaii Press.

Lucka, Emil. 1905. "Verdoppelung des Ich." *Preussische Jahrbucher*, vol. 115 (Berlin).

Lum, Darrell. 1980. "Yahk Fahn, Auntie." *Echoes from Gold Mountain*. A Spe-cial Issue of *Bamboo Ridge* 8: 38–43.

———. 1990. *Pass On, No Pass Back!* Honolulu: Bamboo Ridge Press.

Lum, Wing Tek. 1987a. "Chinese Hot Pot." In *Expounding the Doubtful Points*, 105.

———. 1987b. *Expounding the Doubtful Points*. Honolulu: Bamboo Ridge Press.

———. 1987c. "Juk." In *Expounding the Doubtful Points*, 91–92.

Lyman, Stanford. 1974. *Chinese American*. New York: Random House.

Lyon, Thomas J. 1989. *This Incomperable Lande: A Book of American Nature Writing*. Boston: Houghton Mifflin.

Mannoni, O. 1950 (2d ed.). *Prospero and Caliban: The Psychology of Coloniza-tion*. New York: Praeger, 1964.

Mara, Rachna. 1991. *Of Customs and Excise*. Toronto: Second Story Press.

Mariani, John F. 1983. *The Dictionary of American Food and Drink*. New Haven: Ticknor and Fields.

Martin, Sandra. 1982. "The Haunting of the Japanese." *The Globe and Mail*, 10 April.

Marx, Leo. 1964. *The Machine in the Garden: Technology and the Pastoral Ideal in America*. New York: Oxford University Press.

Masumoto, David Mas. 1987. *Country Voices: The Oral History of a Japanese American Family Farm Community*. Del Ray, Calif.: Inaka Countryside Publications.

Mazlich, Bruce, ed. 1965. *The Railroad and the Space Program: An Exploration in Historical Analogy*. Cambridge: MIT Press.

McAlister, Melani. 1991. "(Mis)reading *The Joy Luck Club*." Paper presented at the Asian American Cultural Transformations: A Literature of One's Own Conference, 27 April, at the University of California, Santa Barbara.

McCunn, Ruthanne Lum. 1981. *Thousand Pieces of Gold*. San Francisco: Design Enterprises of San Francisco.

McDonald, Dorothy Ritsuko. 1981. "Introduction." In F. Chin, *"The Chickencoop Chinaman" and "The Year of the Dragon,"* ix–xxix.

McDonald, Dorothy Ritsuko, and Katherine Newman. 1980. "Relocation and Dislocation: The Writings of Hisaye Yamamoto and Wakako Yamauchi." *MELUS* 7, no. 3: 21–38.

McFerrin, Linda Watanabe. 1990. *The Impossibility of Redemption Is Something We Hadn't Figured On*. Berkeley, Calif.: Berkeley Poets Workshop and Press.

Meissenburg, Karin. 1987. *The Writing on the Wall*. Frankfurt: Verlag fur Interkulturelle Kommunikation.

Melendy, H. Brett. 1972. *The Oriental American*. New York: Hippocrene.

———. 1977. *Asians in America: Filipinos, Koreans, and East Indians*. New York: Hippocrene, 1981.

Memmi, Albert. 1965. *The Colonizer and the Colonized*. Boston: Beacon Press.

Michaud, Michael A. G. 1986. *Reaching for the High Frontier: The American Pro-space Movement, 1972–84*. New York: Praeger.

Miki, Roy. 1991. *Saving Face: Poems Selected 1976–1988*. Winnipeg, Manitoba: Turnstone Press.

Millar, Susanna. 1968. *The Psychology of Play*. Middlesex, England: Penguin.

Miller, Karl. 1985. *Doubles: Studies in Literary History*. New York: Oxford University Press.

Miller, Perry. 1956. *Errand into the Wilderness*. New York: Harper and Row, 1964.

Miller, R. Baxter. 1987. "Baptized Infidel: Play and Critical Legacy." *Black American Literature Forum* 21, no. 4: 393–414.

Milton, Edith. 1982. Review of *Obasan* by Joy Kogawa. *New York Times Book Review*, 5 September: 8, 17.

Minatoya, Lydia Yuri. 1992. *Talking to High Monks in the Snow: An Asian American Odyssey*. New York: Harper Collins.

Mirikitani, Janice. 1987. *Shedding Silence*. Berkeley, Calif.: Celestial Arts.

Miyoshi, Masao. 1969. *The Divided Self: A Perspective on the Literature of the Victorians*. New York: New York University Press; London: University of London Press.

Mo, Timothy. 1978. *The Monkey King*. London: Abacus, 1984.

Modell, John. 1977. *The Economics and Politics of Racial Accommodation: The Japanese of Los Angeles, 1900–1942.* Urbana: University of Illinois Press.

Moody, Fred. 1986. "Shawn Wong: Seeking a Forgotten Past." *Pacific* (a magazine of the *Seattle Times/Seattle Post-Intelligencer*), 19 January: 4–8.

Morgan, Thaïs. 1989. "The Space of Intertextuality." In O'Donnell and Davis, 239–79.

Mori, Toshio. 1949. *Yokohama, California.* Seattle: University of Washington Press, 1985.

———. 1978. *Woman from Hiroshima.* San Francisco: Isthmus Press.

Morrison, Toni. 1970. *The Bluest Eye.* New York: Holt, Rinehart and Winston.

———. 1973. *Sula.* New York: Bantam.

Mote, Frederick W. 1977. "Yuan and Ming." In K. C. Chang, ed., 125–257.

Moy, James S. 1990. "David Henry Hwang's *M. Butterfly* and Philip Kan Gotanda's *Yankee Dawg You Die*: Repositioning Chinese American Marginality on the American Stage." *Theater Journal* 42, no. 1: 48–56.

Mukherjee, Bharati. 1988. *The Middleman and Other Stories.* New York: Fawcett Crest.

———. 1989. *Jasmine.* New York: Grove Weidenfeld.

Mura, David. 1989. *After We Lost Our Way.* New York: E.P. Dutton.

———. 1991. *Turning Japanese: Memoirs of a Sansei.* New York: Pantheon.

Murayama, Milton. 1959. *All I Asking For Is My Body.* San Francisco: Supa Press, 1975.

Nee, Victor G., and Brett de Bary Nee, eds. 1972. *Longtime Californ': A Documentary Study of an American Chinatown.* New York: Pantheon.

Ng, Fae Myenne. 1986. "A Red Sweater." *The American Voice* 4: 47–58.

———. 1993. *Bone.* New York: Hyperion.

Nieh, Hualing. 1981. *Mulberry and Peach: Two Women of China.* Boston: Beacon Press, 1988.

Niemann, Linda. 1990. *Boomer: Railroad Memoirs.* Berkeley: University of California Press.

Nomura, Gail M., Russell Endo, Stephen H. Sumida, and Russell C. Leong, eds. 1989. *Frontiers of Asian American Studies: Writing, Research, and Commentary.* Pullman: Washington State University Press.

O'Donnell, Patrick, and Robert Con Davis. 1989a. "Introduction: Intertext and Contemporary American Fiction." In 1989b:ix–xxii.

———, eds. 1989b. *Intertextuality and Contemporary American Fiction.* Baltimore: Johns Hopkins University Press.

Okada, John. 1957. *No-No Boy.* Seattle: University of Washington Press, 1976.

Okihiro, Gary Y., Shirley Hune, Arthur A. Hansen, and John M. Liu, eds. 1988. *Reflections on Shattered Windows: Promises and Prospects for Asian American Studies.* Pullman: Washington State University Press.

Olsen, Tillie. 1978. *Silences.* New York: Delacorte Press/Seymour Lawrence.

Omi, Michael, and Howard Winant. 1986. *Racial Formation in the United States from the 1960s to the 1980s.* New York: Routledge and Kegan Paul.

Osajima, Keith. 1988. "Asian Americans as the Model Minority: An Analysis of the Popular Press Image in the 1960s and 1980s." In Okihiro et al., 165–74.

Oxnam, Robert. 1986. "Why Asians Succeed Here." *New York Times Magazine*, 30 November: 74–75.

Pai, Margaret K. 1989. *The Dreams of Two Yi-min*. Honolulu: University of Hawaii Press.

Pak, Gary. 1992. *The Watcher of Waipuna*. Honolulu: Bamboo Ridge Press.

Palumbo-Liu, David. 1988. "Discourse and Dislocation: Rhetorical Strategies of Asian-American Exclusion and Confinement." Paper presented at the Modern Language Association Convention, 27–30 December, New Orleans.

Pao, Angela. 1990. "Contexts and Meanings in David Henry Hwang's *M. Butterfly*." Paper presented at the Association for Asian American Studies Conference, 20–22 May, at the University of California, Santa Barbara.

Pearlman, Mickey, ed. 1989. *Mother Puzzles: Daughters and Mothers in Contemporary American Literature*. Contributions in Women's Studies, no. 110. New York: Greenwood Press.

Pei, Lowry. 1986. *Family Resemblances*. New York: Vintage, 1988.

Personal Justice Denied: Report of the Commission on Wartime Relocation and Internment of Civilians. 1982. Washington, D.C.: Commission on Wartime Relocation and Internment of Civilians.

Petersen, William. 1966. "Success Story, Japanese-American Style." *New York Times Magazine*, 9 January: 20–21, 33, 36, 38, 40–41, 43.

———. 1982. "Concepts of Ethnicity." In *Concepts of Ethnicity*, edited by William Petersen et al., 1–26. Cambridge: Belknap/Harvard University Press. 1982.

Phillips, J. J., Ishmael Reed, Gundars Strads, and Shawn Wong, eds. 1992. *The Before Columbus Foundation Poetry Anthology: Selections from the American Book Awards 1980–1990*. New York: Norton.

Rank, Otto. 1914. *The Double: A Psychoanalytic Study*. Edited and translated by Harry Tucker, Jr. Chapel Hill: University of North Carolina Press, 1971.

———. 1941. "The Double as Immortal Self." In *Beyond Psychology*, 62–101. New York: Dover, 1958.

Reed, Ishmael, Kathryn Trueblood, and Shawn Wong, eds. 1992. *The Before Columbus Foundation Fiction Anthology: Selections from the American Book Awards 1980–1990*. New York: Norton.

Reimers, David M. 1985. *Still the Golden Door: The Third World Comes to America*. New York: Columbia University Press.

Robey, Bryant. 1989. *Two Hundred Years and Counting*. Washington: Population Reference Bureau.

Rogers, Robert. 1970. *The Double in Literature*. Detroit: Wayne State University Press.

Rosca, Ninotchka. 1988. *State of War: A Novel of Life in the Philippines*. New York: Fireside/Simon and Schuster.

Rosenfield, Claire. 1967. "The Shadow Within: The Conscious and Unconscious Use of the Double." In Guerard, 311–51.

Said, Edward. 1989. "Yeats and Decolonization." In *Remaking History*, edited by Barbara Kruger and Phil Mariani. Seattle: Bay Press, 1989.

San Juan, E., Jr. 1972. *Carlos Bulosan and the Imagination of the Class Struggle*. New York: Orion, 1975.

Sanford, Charles L. 1961. *The Quest for Paradise: Europe and the American Moral Imagination*. Urbana: University of Illinois Press.

Santos, Bienvenido N. 1955. "Scent of Apples." In *Scent of Apples*, 21–29.

———. 1967. "The Day the Dancers Came." In *Scent of Apples*, 113–28.

———. 1977. "Immigration Blues." In *Scent of Apples*, 3–20.

———. 1979. *Scent of Apples: A Collection of Stories*. Seattle: University of Washington Press.

———. 1987. *What the Hell for You Left Your Heart in San Francisco*. Quezon City: New Day.

Sasaki, R. A. 1991. *The Loom and Other Stories*. St. Paul, Minn.: Graywolf Press.

Sasaki, Yasuo. 1986. *Village Scene/Village Herd*. Cincinnati: Balconet.

Schiller, Freidrich von. 1971. Excerpts from *Letters on the Aesthetic Education of Man*. In *Critical Theory since Plato*, edited by Hazard Adams, 418–31. New York: Harcourt.

Schulte-Sasse, Jochen. 1984. "Foreword." In *Theory of the Avant-garde*, edited by Peter Burger; translated by Michael Shaw. Minneapolis: University of Minneapolis Press.

Shapiro, Sidney, trans. 1980. *Outlaws of the Marsh*. Beijing: Foreign Language Press.

Signeuret, Jean Claude, ed. 1988. *Dictionary of Literary Themes and Motifs*. New York: Greenwood Press.

Simonson, Harold P. 1963. "Introduction." In *The Significance of the Frontier in American History* by Frederick Jackson Turner, 1–24. New York: Frederick Ungar.

Simonson, Rick, and Scott Walker, eds. 1988. *Multicultural Literacy: Opening the American Mind*. St. Paul, Minn.: Graywolf.

Simpson, Janice C. 1991. "Fresh Voices above the Noisy Din." *Time*, 3 June: 66–67.

Singer, Armand E. 1988. "Mountaineering." In Signeuret, 876–83.

Slotkin, Richard. 1973. *Regeneration through Violence: The Mythology of the American Frontier, 1600–1860*. Middletown: Wesleyan University Press.

Smith, Henry Nash. 1950. *Virgin Land: The American West as Symbol and Myth*. Cambridge: Harvard Unviersity Press, 1970.

Sollors, Werner. 1984. "Nine Suggestions for Historians of American Ethnic Literature." *MELUS* 11, no. 1: 95–96.

———. 1986a. *Beyond Ethnicity: Consent and Descent in American Culture*. New York: Oxford University Press.

———. 1986b. "A Critique of Pure Pluralism." In *Reconstructing American Literary History*, edited by Sacvan Bercovitch, 250–79. Cambridge: Harvard University Press.

———. 1990a. "Of Mules and Mares in a Land of Difference; or, Quadrupeds All?" *American Quarterly* 42, no. 2: 167–90.

———. 1990b. "Plymouth Rock and Ellis Island; or How Ethnic Writers Help to Redefine America." Paper presented at the MELUS Conference, 20 April, Chicago.

Solovitch, Sara. 1991. "Finding a Voice." *West* 30 (June): 18–22.

Sone, Monica. 1953. *Nisei Daughter*. Seattle: University of Washington Press, 1979.

Song, Cathy. 1988. *Frameless Windows, Squares of Light*. New York: Norton.

Spariosu, Mihai. 1982. *Literature, Mimesis and Play: Essays in Literary Theory*. Tubingen: Gunter Narr Verlag.

Stanley, Don. 1982. "B.C.'s Shame and Joy Kogawa's Triumph." *The Province*, 25 July.

Stepto, Robert B. 1979. *From Behind the Veil: A Study of Afro-American Narrative*. Chicago: University of Illinois Press.

Stout, Janis P. 1983. *The Journey Narrative in American Literature: Patterns and Departures*. Westport: Greenwood.

Suleri, Sara. 1989. *Meatless Days*. Chicago: University of Chicago Press.

Sumida, Stephen H. 1991. *And the View from the Shore: Literary Traditions of Hawai'i*. Seattle: University of Washington Press.

Sutton-Smith, Brian, and Diana Kelly-Burne. 1984. "The Idealization of Play." In *Play in Animals and Humans*, edited by Peter K. Smith, 305–21. London: Blackwell.

Suzuki, Bob H. 1977. "Education and the Socialization of Asian Americans: A Revisionist Analysis of the 'Model Minority' Thesis." *Amerasia Journal* 4, no. 2: 23–51.

Tagami, Jeff. 1987. *October Light*. San Francisco: Kearny Street Workshop.

Takaki, Ronald. 1989. *Strangers from a Different Shore*. Boston: Little, Brown.

Takano, Cynthia. 1987. "The Politics of English in Monterey Park." *Rice* (July): 31.

Tan, Amy. 1989. *The Joy Luck Club*. New York: Putnam.

———. 1991. *The Kitchen God's Wife*. New York: Putnam.

Taylor, L. B., Jr. 1974. *For All Mankind: America's Space Programs of the 1970s and Beyond*. New York: E. P. Dutton.

Tsai, Henry Shih-shan. 1986. *The Chinese Experience in America*. Bloomington: Indiana University Press.

Tsukiyama, Gail. 1991. *Woman of the Silk*. New York: St. Martin's.

Tucker, Lindsey. 1984. *Stephen and Bloom at Life's Feast: Alimentary Symbolism and the Creative Process in James Joyce's "Ulysses."* Columbus: Ohio State University Press.

Turner, Frederick Jackson. 1893. "The Significance of the Frontier in American History." In *The Significance of the Frontier in American History*, edited by Harold P. Simpson. New York: Frederick Ungar, 1963.

Tymms, Ralph. 1949. *Doubles in Literary Psychology*. Cambridge: Bowes and Bowes.

Uchida, Yoshiko, 1982. *Desert Exile: The Uprooting of a Japanese-American Family*. 1984. Seattle: University of Washington Press.

———. 1987. *Picture Bride*. Flagstaff, Ariz.: Northland Press.

Ueki, Teruyo. 1991. "The Multicultural Dimensions and Metaphoric Meanings of Joy Kogawa's Imagery in *Obasan*." Paper presented at the Asian American Cultural Transformations: A Literature of One's Own Conference, 27 April, at the University of California, Santa Barbara.

U.S. Department of Commerce, Bureau of the Census. 1979. *Twenty Censuses: Population and Housing Questions 1790–1980*. Washington, D.C.: GPO.

Uyemoto, Holly. 1989. *Rebel Without a Clue*. New York: Crown.

Veeser, H. Aram, ed. 1989. *The New Historicism*. New York: Routledge.

Villapando, Venny. 1989. "The Business of Selling Mail-Order Brides." In Asian Women United of California, ed., 318–26.

Villanueva, Marianne. 1991. *Ginseng and Other Tales from Manila.* Corvallis, Oreg.: Calyx.

Viviano, Frank. 1989. "When Success is a Family Prize." *This World* (a magazine of the *San Francisco Chronicle*), 8 October: 7–9.

Vizenor, Gerald. 1987. *Griever: An American Monkey King in China.* Chicago: University of Illinois Press.

Wald, Alan. 1987. "Theorizing Cultural Differences: A Critique of the 'Ethnicity School.'" *MELUS* 14, no. 2: 21–33.

Wang, L. Ling-Chi, and Henry Yiheng Zhao, eds. 1991. *Chinese American Poetry: An Anthology.* Santa Barbara: Asian American Voices (distributed by Seattle: University of Washington Press).

Wang, L. Ling-Chi, Sau-ling Cynthia Wong, and Yiheng Zhao, eds. 1990. *Liangtiao he de yitu: dangdai meiguo huayi shiren zuopinxuan* [The intention of two rivers: Selected works by contemporary Chinese American poets]. Shanghai: Shanghai Wenyi Chubanshe [Shanghai Literature and Art Publishers].

Watanabe, Sylvia. 1992. *Talking to the Dead.* New York: Doubleday.

Watanabe, Sylvia, and Carol Bruchac, eds. 1990. *Home to Stay: Asian American Women's Fiction.* Greenfield Center, N.Y.: Greenfield Review Press.

Watts, Alan W. 1953. *Myth and Ritual in Christianity.* New York: Vanguard.

Weisstein, Ulrich. 1973. *Comparative Literature and Literary Theory.* Translated by William Riggan. Bloomington: Indiana University Press.

Wilentz, Gay. 1989–90. "If You Surrender to the Air: Folk Legends of Flight and Resistance in African American Literature." *MELUS* 161: 21–32.

Williams, Raymond. 1958. *Culture and Society: 1780–1950.* New York: Harper, 1966.

Winkler, Karen J. 1990. "Proponents of 'Multicultural' Humanities Research Call for a Critical Look at its Achievements." *Chronicle of Higher Education* 28 November 1990: A5+.

Wolfe, Ann F. Review of *Fifth Chinese Daughter* by Jade Snow Wong. *Saturday Review,* 23 December 1950: 37–38.

Wong, Eugene F. 1985. "Asian American Middleman Minority Theory: The Framework of an American Myth." *Journal of Ethnic Studies* 13, no. 1: 51–88.

Wong, Jade Snow. 1945. *Fifth Chinese Daughter.* New York: Harper.

Wong, Paul. 1972. "The Emergence of the Asian American Movement." *Bridge* 2:32–39.

Wong, Sau-ling Cynthia. 1990. "Necessity and Extravagance in Maxine Hong Kingston's *The Woman Warrior:* Art and the Ethnic Experience." *MELUS* 151:3–26.

———. 1991a. "Kingston's Handling of Traditional Chinese Sources." In *Approaches to Teaching Kingston's "The Woman Warrior,"* edited by Shirley Geok-lin Lim, 26–36.

———. 1991b. "'Sugar Sisterhood': Situating the Amy Tan Phenomenon." Paper presented at the Humanities Research Institute Minority Discourse Colloquium, 1 November, at the University of California at Irvine; and at the

After "Orientalism": East Asia in Global Cultural Criticism Conference, 24 April 1992, at the University of California, Berkeley.

———. 1992. "Autobiography as Guided Chinatown Tour? Maxine Hong Kingston's *The Woman Warrior* and the Chinese American Autobiographical Controversy." In *Multicultural Autobiography: American Lives*, edited by James Robert Payne, 248–79. Knoxville: University of Tennessee Press, 1992.

Wong, Shawn. 1979. *Homebase*. New York: I. Reed Books.

———, ed. 1988. *Blue Funnel Line*. A Special Issue of the *Seattle Review* 11, no. 1.

Wong, Shelley. 1990. "The Poetics of a Damaged Life: Joy Kogawa's *Obasan* and David Mura's *A Male Grief: Notes on Pornography and Addiction*." Paper presented at the American Literature Association Conference on American Literature, 2 June, San Diego, Calif.

Wu, William F. 1992. *Wong's Lost and Found Emporium and Other Oddities*. Author's Choice, no. 28. Eugene, Oreg.: Pulphouse Publications.

Wyatt, E.V.R. 1950. Review of *Fifth Chinese Daughter* by Jade Snow Wong. *Commonweal*, 7 November: 182.

Yamada, Mitsuye. 1988. *Desert Run: Poems and Stories*. Latham, N.Y.: Kitchen Table: Women of Color Press.

Yamamoto, Hisaye. 1949. "Seventeen Syllables." In *Seventeen Syllables*, 8–19.

———. 1951. "Yoneko's Earthquake." In *Seventeenth Syllables*, 46–56.

———. 1979. "Life Among the Oil Fields: A Memoir." In *Seventeen Syllables*, 86–95.

———. 1988. *Seventeen Syllables and Other Stories*. Latham, N.Y.: Kitchen Table: Women of Color Press.

Yamashita, Karen Tei. 1990. *Through the Arc of the Rain Forest*. Minneapolis: Coffee House Press.

Yamauchi, Wakako. 1961. "The Handkerchief." *Amerasia Journal* 4, no. 1 (1977): 143–50.

———. 1966. "And the Soul Shall Dance." In *Aiiieeeee!*, edited by Frank Chin et al., 193–200.

———. 1976. "Songs My Mother Taught Me." *Amerasia Journal* 3, no. 2: 63–73.

Yau, John. 1989. *Radiant Silhouettes: New and Selected Poems, 1974–1988*. Santa Rosa, Calif.: Black Sparrow.

Yep, Laurence. 1991. *The Lost Garden*. Englewood Cliffs, N.J.: Julian Messner.

Yip, Yuen Chung. 1990. *The Tears of Chinese Immigrants*. Translated and introduced by Sheng-Tai Chang. Ontario, Can.: Cormorant Books.

Yu, Anthony, trans. and ed. 1977. *The Journey to the West*. Chicago: University of Chicago Press.

Yu, Renqiu. 1987. "Chop Suey: From Chinese Food to Chinese American Food." *East/West News* 21, no. 18: 1, 7–9.

Yun, Grace, ed. 1989. *A Look Beyond the Model Minority Image: Critical Issues in Asian America*. New York: Minority Rights Group.

Yung, Judy. 1986. *Chinese Women of America: A Pictorial History*. Published for the Chinese Culture Foundation of San Francisco. Seattle: University of Washington Press.

Zee, A. 1990. *Swallowing Clouds: Two Millenia of Chinese Tradition, Folklore and History Hidden in the Language of Food.* New York: Touchstone/Simon and Schuster.

Zink, Karl E. 1956. "Flux and the Frozen Moment: The Imagery of Stasis in Faulkner's Prose." *PMLA* 71, no. 3: 285–301.

Ziolkowski, Theodore. 1977. *Disenchanted Images: A Literary Iconology.* Princeton: Princeton University Press.

INDEX

Exclusion period, 56, 125, 228n.7. *See also* Immigration laws and restrictions
Exoticization, 6, 9, 55
Expounding the Doubtful Points (Lum), 75
Extravagance: art and, 175, 189, 191, 192–204, 207, 210; defined, 13–14; historicizing, 173–74; mobility motif expressing, 138, 146–53, 154; race and, 179–80, 181; sexual/erotic link to, 192–94; sites of (play/art), 170–72; treats symbolic of, 44–45, 46, 53. *See also* Art; Necessity/Extravagance binarism
Extravagance/Necessity binarism. *See* Necessity/Extravagance binarism

Falling: images of, 152–53, 156, 157, 204; suicidal, 152–53, 160
Fa Mu Lan, character in *The Woman Warrior*, 30, 202–6
Father and Glorious Descendant (Lowe), 63–65, 66, 70
Fielding, Henry, 63
Fifth Chinese Daughter (Wong), 104; gastronomic tour in, 63–65, 70; generational conflict in, 40
Filipino American literature: mobility motif in, 130–31, 132, 133–36. *See also* Bulosan, Carlos; Santos, Bienvenido N.; Villanueva, Marianne
Filipino Americans, 6, 126–27, 131–33; mobility patterns of, 126–29
First generation. *See* Immigrant generation
First self of Doppelgänger, 79, 88, 100, 109; relation to disowned self, 89, 102, 105; self-reintegration as goal of, 112–14. *See also* Doppelgänger
Fish, Uncle, character. *See* "No Man's Land"
Floating World, The (Kadohata), 120
Flying, images of, 153–54, 157, 158, 165
Flying African legend, 165
FOB (Hwang), racial shadow in, 106–9, 110, 111–12, 177
Food, and eating. *See* Eating motif
"Food for All His Dead" (Chin): expressing sociocultural constraints, 41–42; mobility motif in, 146–47; quasi-cannibalism in, 35–37
Food in Chinese Culture (Chang), 19

Food pornography, 18, 55–58, 61–63; in *East Goes West*, 61–63; gastronomic tours and, 63–65; and Necessity/Extravagance, 59; in *The Year of the Dragon*, 58–61. *See also* Eating motif
Food prostitution, 18, 47–48, 49, 50–52, 53, 54. *See also* Eating motif; Mail order brides; Prostitution
Food-related occupations, 56–57
Forbidden Stitch, The (Lim and Tsutakawa), 8
Fourth Jane, character in *Crossings*, 63
Fred Eng, character in *The Year of the Dragon*, 59–60, 61, 64, 67, 149, 175–78, 189, 203. *See also* Artist figures; *Year of the Dragon, The*
"Fresh-off-the-boat." *See FOB*
Freud, Sigmund, 80, 82, 84, 99
Frontier thesis, 118, 123–24
Fussell, Edwin, 122

Gates, Henry Louis, Jr., 11
Gee, Pop! (Chin), 191. *See also Year of the Dragon, The*
Gender: art and, 168–69; double motif and, 81, 95, 99–101; race and, 165; spatial geography and, 120–21; subordination of women, 30, 32. *See also* Inequality; Necessity; Patriarchy; Psychosexual mapping
Generations: American-born, 40–41, 44–49; conflict and tensions between, 31, 39–42, 41; differences between, 179, 180; immigrant, 28, 50–51, 180, 199–201; unity across, 141. *See also* Necessity; Quasi-cannibalism
Gernet, Jacques, 68
Ginseng and Other Tales from Manila (Villanueva, ed.), 53
Goddess, earth- (American), 74
Gold Mountain wife. *See* No name woman
Govier, Katherine, 19
Guerard, Albert J., 78, 82, 83, 88

Half-Face, character in *Jasmine*, 53, 54
Hallam, Clifford, 78, 79, 80, 89, 99, 105
Hatsui, Mrs. Kato, character in "Songs My Mother Taught Me," 169
Hawaiian literature, 72–73, 224n.8. *See also* Lum, Darrell
Hayashi, Mr., character. *See* "Seventeen Syllables"